About the author:

W A Sumner studied theology at Hull Univeristy and acheieved an M Litt from Oxford University. He has spent many years as a teacher and preacher in schools and churches. He is a reader of the Diocese of Birmingham and is also a hospital chaplain.

MYTH, LEGEND AND SYMBOLISM

W. A. Sumner

The Book Guild Ltd

First published in Great Britain in 2018 by
The Book Guild Ltd
9 Priory Business Park
Wistow Road, Kibworth
Leicestershire, LE8 0RX
Freephone: 0800 999 2982
www.bookguild.co.uk
Email: info@bookguild.co.uk
Twitter: @bookguild

Typeset in Times

Printed and bound in Great Britain by CPI Group (UK) Ltd, Croydon, CR0 4YY

ISBN 978 1912881 277

British Library Cataloguing in Publication Data.
A catalogue record for this book is available from the British Library.

Contents

Acknowledgements

Peter Turner, Peter Kaye, Evelyn Reston, John Cook, Patricia Bates and William Cooper.

The front cover of my first book, The Theology of Paradox; a design by George Sumner, circa 1965.

The front cover of my second book, The Theology of Truth; taken from an idea by George Sumner, circa 1965, and given additional ideas and amendments by Katie Colclough, George's great granddaughter.

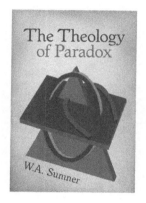 

The front cover of my third book, Myth, Legend and Symbolism was designed by Katie Colclough in 2018.

Preface

Myth, Legend and Symbolism. We all know what legend means; it is something historical which cannot be properly verified. Symbolism is straightforward enough; red means danger and green means safe. But myth? The popular conception of myth means a 'lie' or a 'misconception' or 'wrong idea'. This however is a misuse of the word. What it does mean is some kind of attempt at explaining the origin of the world, its people and by extension, its future. The three matters are closely interrelated and intertwined. The myths of this world, whether ancient or modern, are loaded with symbolisms. Virtually all our myths have some kind of legendary background or anchorage. If one were to imagine that our ancient myths are fading out, one would be sorely mistaken; as ancient ones recede into the background, modern ones spring forth to take their place.

This book begins with a survey of ancient myths which are of great influence on British culture to this day and show no signs of fading out. So, Biblical, Greek, Norse and Celtic myths are described and compared. After that, various other mythologies from different parts of the world, some of which one may never have heard of, are found to have many factors in common with our own more familiar myths. The Chinese, the African, the Cargo Cults, the Huichols of Mexico are examined. It is interesting to see how myths which are essentially Stone Age mentality relate to the coming of Christianity. I have not tried to include those myths which have already been mentioned in my previous books, The Theology of Paradox and The Theology of Truth. If one were still looking for the truth about life and death, these myths in this book may give the reader more cause for thought and evaluation.

The reader may find it strange that some modern mythical material may come as a surprise. But material such a Dracula, Frankenstein, and Star Trek I count as modern myth. This is absolutely fair, since they used traditional mythical metaphors and motifs and simply augment them into something

ix

fantastic and even more frightening. In contrast, there is much scientific and pseudo-scientific material which I include as modern mythology. On this basis, Economics, Psychology, Freemasonry, and yes, Evolution are seen as modern versions of ancient notions, using many of the old symbolisms.

We must forget the idea that mythology means nonsense. It is very much the opposite. Mythology tells us something important about ourselves, the way we think and our conceptions about the future. There are those who imagine that mythology can be dispensed with and we can think 'rationally' about life and its implications. This book will maintain that this cannot be done. Myth is an essential factor in the human psyche, something deeply rooted in our instincts, and that is where psychology comes into the picture. It is inevitable that we ponder the deep matters of Creation and the opposite end, the Apocalypse.

We shall see that eschatology, thoughts about the end of the world are phrased in very much the same metaphors and motifs as Creation. Eschatology is only a futuristic extension of mythology, and is every bit as elaborate and speculative.

I realise that many of the conclusions I reach in this book will be controversial, especially on the matter of Biblical 'mythology' and even more on 'scientific' mythology! But I would suggest you give it some thought and realise that not everything that is pushed at us in the media is free from the other modern meaning of the word 'myth'; wrong idea!

1

Myth as basic to human nature

It has always been a great delight for generations of children to read or
have read to them **Wind in the Willows** by Kenneth Grahame. Strangely,
at first the book did not command much popularity, but due to the efforts
of President Theodore Roosevelt and A.A.Milne, the book came to
prominence and has been an ongoing classic to the present day. The book
is exceedingly well written with excellent use of language and metaphor.
The dominant literary technique is the sustained personification of the five
main animal characters, Mole, Rat, Otter, Badger and Toad. They are so
close to real life and real personalities and as the book proceeds, Toad, with
his manias which land him in so much trouble, augments the humour to the
hilarious level.

But there is one strand which often eludes the reader; that of the way
in which the basic story is interwoven with mythology. This chiefly comes
in chapter 7, The Piper at the Gates of Dawn. Rat and Mole are concerned
because Little Portly, one of Otter's sons, has gone missing, and it is feared
that he might have been killed. Rat and Mole set off in their boat on a
midsummer's evening and row on through the night as far as the weir. The
story becomes increasingly mysterious as they hear a distant piping calling
them. Rat was possessed in all his senses by this new divine thing that caught
up his helpless soul. Eventually, Mole heard it too and was utterly possessed
by it. Then they found an island and landed there. They were struck with
great awe; then they found themselves staring straight into the eyes of Pan,
the piper, the friend and helper, with a smile on his face. Under his feet was
the little Otter, asleep but not dead.

Then the two animals crouched to the earth, bowed their heads and did worship. They were not afraid and yet they were afraid.

It is a most powerful account, possibly a little high-powered for children's reading, and yet it speaks to something deep in human nature.

This is an interesting case of how we move from one level of truth to another. The chapter begins in the same vein as all the others, the account of the animals' adventures and the concern over Little Portly's disappearance. But then it moves away from the literary level to the mythological level. Here we have a Greek god, Pan, playing his pipes in the early dawn. We all know what 'Mother Nature' means and other euphemisms for the Creator God. But here it is done with great sensitivity and understanding of human nature. The reader can hardly fail to engage with the emotions of Rat and Mole; sheer wonder and awe at the beauties of nature. They cannot fail to worship. And the god is kindly, loving , caring for the little otter. We all feel sympathy for a lost baby and the thought that God is caring for him is the completion of the image. The animals would never forget this encounter; neither would any normal person coming up against the divine in such a situation.

As an example of how ancient mythology and modern story-telling are merged together, this is a masterpiece. It is also a lovely example of how a figure from Greek mythology,(1) who is not noted for being kindly and loving (except as erotic love) has been Christianised. Kenneth Grahame has given Pan a human face which exudes caring. This tendency, to Christianise, will be seen when dealing with other myths.

For those who have never had such an encounter with the divine, this may have very little meaning. For those who have had such an experience, there is no doubting the reality of it. There are probably many people in the modern world who have been so blessed; occasionally one will share (or try to share) the experience with others; others may prefer not to discuss it with others for fear of ridicule or persecution. Sometimes we hear of visions of the Virgin Mary , for instance the Portuguese shepherd girls, or of Jesus Christ, for instance Linda Martel.(2) Such Theophanous claims are wide open to false claims, and yet no one can deny that Bernadette Soubiroux was genuinely led to find a spa water spring at Lourdes which has provided healing for generations of people with health problems.

When we consider the Bible, there are various such Theophanous encounters described. There is no need to relate all of them; a selection will be enough. The underlying questions must be, what is the substratum of the account, how much of it is historical or mythological, and what has it contributed to the pattern of religious awareness over the centuries.

We can begin with the encounter between God and Abraham in Genesis; this principally comes in two accounts, Genesis chapter 15 and chapter 18, and both are accredited to the 'J' source, called the Yahwistic source, which is noted for its anthropomorphic approach in speaking of God. A brief resume of the essentials in chapter 15 concerns God's promise that Abraham (called Abram at that stage) would be the father of many nations and the promise of the land we now call Palestine. The essential element from a Theophanous point of view is the passage 15:12ff:

'As the sun was going down, a deep sleep fell on Abram... a dread and great darkness fell on him... behold a smoking fire pot and a flaming torch passed between these pieces (of the sacrificial victims).'

By contrast, the second account starting at Genesis 18:1, occurs at noonday, and his name has been transformed to Abraham;(3)

'... he sat at the door of his tent in the heat of the day... three men stood in front of him... he ran and bowed to meet them...'

The promise of a son to be born is stressed, and Sarah his wife is included in the encounter. This encounter is less frightening but every bit as theologically important as the other one. So much of the future course of events, the theological foundation for three major world religions and the basis of faith is included in these two passages. But the crux of it is that deep dread and awe which Abraham sensed; something that anyone having an encounter with the divine cannot avoid feeling. Naturally, there are those who wish to avoid admitting the historical reality of these encounters, but the evidence for their genuineness must be seen in the way that the Jews, the Christians and the Moslems have turned out to be vast numbers, and also that the Jews have regained their homeland in the Palestine area. But historical reality is not the only vehicle for conveying truth. Relevant to these accounts are the factors of theological and mythological truth. This does not mean that the accounts are wrong, misleading and some sort of deception. On the contrary, historical truth can sometimes, more often than we realise, be some kind of distortion according to the agenda of the historian.

The theological importance of these two passages cannot be underestimated. They are saying in effect that God makes promises to human kind, and moreover he keeps them. It is couched in the metaphor of 'covenant' or 'testament'. The two words mean the same thing and that is what the Bible is in itself, in summary, God's agreement with certain persons. In the Old Testament, it is Noah, Abraham, Moses and David who receive a covenant; in the New Testament, it is Jesus summing up all four of these covenants and giving them to all of humanity in what is called the 'New Testament'. Furthermore, the other implication in it is that the believing soul can and does have an ongoing positive relationship with the Eternal Father, a day-to-day conversation in trust and love. Of course the substratum of all this is actually believing in God. One could say that it was easy enough for Abraham to believe since he had a face-to-face encounter with God. Even then he had to trust in the reliability of his own senses; he might have thought he was hallucinating. But the core of the faith of Abraham can be summed up thus, (Genesis 15:6).

'He believed the Lord, and he reckoned it to him as righteousness.'

We can paraphrase this in this way; 'Abraham trusted in God, and God allowed that to put him in the right relationship with him.'

That sounds a bit sociological but nevertheless that is the basis that all true religion rests upon; not on the trappings, procedures and legalisms, but on that personal, close understanding that there is that divine power that comes into one's life and lifts one above the banalities and absurdities of purely physical existence. This also raises the question of rules and regulations, something which all religions are noted for. That was something which was to come later and did raise the dilemma of whether it was purely belief or adherence to the regulations that gave one salvation. St.Paul devoted much of his epistles to discussing this issue and concluded that faith was the crux of the matter as opposed to good works. This issue re-emerged at the Reformation and is still a matter of theological importance to this day, regardless of whether one is a Jew, a Christian or a Muslim.

Another face-to-face encounter comes with Moses in Exodus 33:17ff. This one is remarkably restrained in its mythological expression. Again it is the 'J' source, but not unduly anthropomorphic in its expression. Moses wants God to show him his glory; this is what many a human soul wants to see, some sort of proof or certainty about God, rather than just having to trust. But God tells him that no one can see God's face and live. Moses is allowed to see God's goodness; that is something that we can all see if we just look at life with our spiritual eyes open. But Moses can only see the back of God, not his face. This is saying, symbolically, that we can see what God has done in the way that our lives, on a personal level and universally, have worked out. In otherwords, with hindsight we can see God's intervention in the course of history. Later, God comes down in a cloud and proclaims his name, YHWH, which is a contraction of 'I am that I am.'(4) This passage is a curious admixture of the mythological with the literal and the personal, as well as the symbolic. It has great depth and for the true believer, it carries its own conviction. Essentially it speaks of the closeness between the Eternal God and the individual believer, but also the assemblage of believing people.

Another crucial account that is clearly connected to the Exodus encounter comes in I Kings 19ff. Here, Elijah has escaped from the wrath of Jezebel and is hiding in a cave on Mount Horeb (which is the same as Mount Sinai). God comes to him to show him how his ministry will continue. Elijah also has a Theophanous experience as there is a strong wind, and an earthquake and a fire, all of which are basically mythological ways of expressing God's power. But essentially God was not in any of them; but he was in the 'still small voice', which Elijah instinctively realised was the true realisation of God. This 'voice' has been equated with one's conscience, but it is more than that. It is that personal knowledge and recognition of God in the human soul. From this encounter, we see that Elijah is understood to be a prophet on the same level as Moses, and that explains why the two of them appeared with Jesus at the Transfiguration. Again, the mythological modes of expression are not overdone in the Elijah account; the personal element, and the overwhelming holiness of God are both very much emphasised.

These four encounters have had a very deep effect on the spirituality of Judaism and also of Christianity. The inclusion of mythological elements serves to augment the mystery and depth in the passages; they are not just trivial encounters and the relationship with God is not easy or commonplace. At the same time, all these accounts are embedded in straightforward narrations of the course of each person's life. This means that there is more to it that just mythology. A personal encounter with God, or a Theophanous experience is in itself not mythology. However, such an experience is very often described in mythological language and metaphors. When God speaks to us, he uses our own language and also our own thought forms which are located in that bunch of instincts which can be called the **id**. This is using the terms coined by Freud and Jung.(5)

Turning to the mythological aspects of these two passages, it would be easy to explain them away as the concoction of someone who was adept at inventing mythology. That would be the simplistic route for one who did not trust the Biblical writers, in this case 'J'. It is important to grasp that in this discussion, 'myth' does not mean 'lie' or even 'misapprehension'. Myth truly means some kind of attempt at explaining the origins of the world and of humanity, and how we relate to the divine, in terms over and above the purely scientific or historical. Myth, in the Bible or in other scriptural writings from around the world, normally uses much the same metaphors or symbolisms. So for instance in Genesis 15:17 'a smoking fire pot and a flaming torch' are seen. Fire, as symbolic, indicates purification, cleansing and the removal of impure elements. Smoke very often indicates the presence of the deity. Also we have the deep dread and awe fall on Abraham, such as we saw with Rat and Mole. We shall see what are the main elements in mythology, its symbolisms and essential thoughts, later in this chapter. But it is a complete mistake to say that mythology is just the invention of clever writers; mythology is an element in the instincts of mankind. It is not a human invention; it is the work of the Creator himself, providing us with a channel by which we can come to know him.

Essential elements in mythological expression

In attempting to see the difference between historical account and mythology, it would now be the right moment to list many of the characteristics which appear in virtually every myth. These may be recorded in literature, but also may appear as folklorist or oral tradition. There are various lesser features which can be discussed later.

We begin with creation from nothing, often a primeval ocean or chaos, and a pre-existent main god brings about the production of lesser gods and the world itself, including humanity. It is very unusual to find that the created world just appears spontaneously with nothing to start it off, although there are a few examples of this. The lesser gods begin to disagree with each other and there is conflict in the heavens. The factor of good and evil, justice and unfairness, soon materialises, and a champion god, usually (but not always) in favour with the top god, takes on the evil influences and defeats them. There are often different versions of humanity, such as giants, elves, animals which are a blending with humanity, and spirits of various levels of good and evil. Sometimes animals speak as if they were humans, and vice versa, humans take on animal traits. The world is divided into three levels; heaven, earth and the underworld. This explains why the number three has such symbolic importance in mythology. In some mythologies, it is more complicated than this, but basically, there are three layers. There are various methods for making a connection between all three levels; the tree, the rainbow, a ladder, a staircase, a cave, a chasm in the ground, and there is a god who is capable of visiting all levels, as a messenger.

The importance of life and death is also stressed. There are various symbolisms connected with this element. The snake, which paradoxically symbolises life and death, and also fecundity, is worked into virtually every mythology. Gold, silver, jewels, crystal, mirrors, translucent stones symbolise eternity, royalty, indestructibility of life, divinity, as well as the ever-present element of snobbery. Every mythology makes an attempt at explaining the question of Theodicy; why do we have to suffer, and more acutely, why do the innocent have to suffer? Even more important is the element of resurrection, which is an instinctive desire in just about everyone.

Normally, there is an awareness of a breakdown in the relationship between the gods and humanity, and the hope that this will be rectified. A sword, a spear or an arrow can indicate the establishment of truth and justice. There are mainly two agents for cleansing, water and fire, for although they are opposites, they are often depicted as working together to restore a cleansed world. The use of blood can also, rarely, indicate cleansing.

There are various minority elements seen in many mythologies, but not all. The aurora, thunder and lightning, rain and drought, innocence, magic, speculation about the stars and planets and how they are thought to condition our lives. Even numbers are believed to hold special significance and symbolism.(6) Some would like to include angels and devils in this list, but that is an issue that will be debated later on; some would argue that they are literally true as opposed to purely symbolic

Worked in with these factors, is the importance of dreams, hallucinations and Theophanous experiences. Another incidental factor is the 'just-so' element, not particularly strong, but reminding us of folklorist explanations for 'why the sea is salty?' or 'why the leopard has spots?' By contrast, however, myth very often has some kind of historical event or legend as its starting point. Sometimes the historical event is almost lost beneath the exaggeration and dramatic augmentation of the myth itself. Almost always, the myth serves some kind of purpose, whether it be religious or political dogma. With this, we can usually see the underlying purpose of it.

Another important aspect of mythology concerns not just the beginning of all things, but the end of all things. This is where eschatology, or the apocalyptic aspect of things comes in. It acts like a book-end in relation to creation; how will it all end? Interestingly, eschatology uses almost all the same imagery and thought-forms as creation. The clearest example of this is in the Bible itself; if we compare the early chapters of Genesis with the book of Revelation, we see that the last book brings the whole thing to completion, and also uses massive augmentation to build up the drama.

These elements are not confined to the beginning and the end of the Bible. There are outcroppings of mythological expression which occur in many places, examples of which have already been cited. Once one has become accustomed to assessing the mythological mode of expression, it is much easier to spot what is happening. That does not mean that the Abraham stories are all myth; what it does mean is that the writer is using mythological modes of expression to appeal to the basic instinctive receptors in human nature. The purpose of that is to provide emphasis to a passage which is theologically or morally important. It is to no purpose to call mythology nonsense. It is a part of our make-up.

There are those who have tried to maintain that most, if not all, of the Bible is myth. There has been a movement in recent time, instigated by Bultmann(7) and others, to demythologise just about everything, especially in the New Testament, and by implication in the Old Testament too. This has remained unconvincing to most rational people. We must recall that the Gospel writers were at pains to point out the reality of Jesus of Nazareth; that he was not some sort of fiction. Opinions will doubtless vary on this matter. There are those of a fundamentalistic view who will insist on the Bible being literally true from start to finish, but if they do, they run the risk of failing to appreciate the richness and value of the mythological parts. Those of a more liberalistic stance will wish to assess each book or portion of book with a view to distinguishing historical fact from metaphor. It is not easy to do this. It is one thing to say that 'common sense' must prevail, but common sense

8

seems to vary from one person to another, and certainly from one culture to another. The essential thing is to admit that the Bible speaks to the soul of all kinds and conditions of mankind.

Since mythology is basic to the human make-up, it would stand to reason that we all need some kind of myth in our lives, otherwise there is some kind of gap in our thinking. This book will examine some of the ancient mythological systems, especially those that have had a major influence on Western culture to this day, and show no signs of diminishing. It is not realistic to recount every world myth; there are masses of material which can be read up from many useful accounts elsewhere. However, just as ancient mythical notions have to some extent faded in people's minds, we notice that modernistic myths have come in to take their place. So, while we cannot believe in a three-tier world any longer (the space rockets have proved it to us!), other more elaborate ideas, which are alleged to be 'scientific' (whatever that might mean!) have taken centre stage. We cannot avoid having a myth. It is not enough to say that one's myth is capable of being 'proved' (whatever that might mean). It is a fact that we need something over and above the purely factual and banal, to offer some explanation for life and death. As one myth dies, another one is invented. Would it be too dangerous to say that we all have to live with some kind of illusion, or even delusion!

This book will also examine some of the modern myths in circulation. It may be that they try to ignore God and the life of the spirit; do they actually succeed in this? Nevertheless, we are still left with those profound questions; why are we here? Is there a life after this one? How do we relate to the rest of creation? How do we relate to the ultimate truth, which is a secularised way of talking about God? Why do we suffer, or why do things go wrong? It will be seen that many, if not all of the ancient symbolisms and metaphors continue to reappear in the myths of the modern world. The chief difference is the influence of technological gadgetry and scientific investigation, but even then, traditional mythological motifs are interwoven with it. Human nature may have changed a little, but not completely.

Footnotes for Chapter 1

1.   See chapter 3 for Pan and Syrinx. The Panes were goat-like half human creatures, always chasing nymphs and nyads.

2. See The Legend of Linda Martel, by Charles Graves. This is anything but legend; more likely historical fact, as Graves did a thorough research into the life of this little healer.

3. 'Abram' means 'exalted father'; 'Abraham' means 'Father of many nations.'

4. Yahweh; a hybrid word which uses the consonants from YHWH and the vowels from Adoni which means 'my Lord'. This is why YHWH is always translated as 'The Lord'.

5. See chapter 19, Mythology and Psychology.

6. See chapter 26 on Numerology.

7. See Amos 5:18ff and also 9:11ff. these are often regarded as apocalyptic and therefore 'late', which implies that Amos could not have produced it. That of course is a circular argument.

8. Bultmann, Kerygma and Myth, 1953 English translation (Fuller).

2

Genesis and mythology

The early chapters of Genesis in the Bible display many features of mythology, which can help us to arrive at a deeper understanding of their importance. Doubtless I shall be dubbed as the worst kind of heretic by those who wish to take these accounts completely literally, but if one does this, it raises all kinds of difficult questions. Just because there are mythological traits in these accounts, does not in itself render them as nonsense. We need to appreciate the symbolisms which are found not just in other parts of the Bible but in other mythologies from around the world.

We begin with the first Creation account in Genesis 1:1-2:4. This is thought to belong to the 'P' source of material in the Pentateuch, dubbed as the 'Priestly' source. This material is noted for being less anthropomorphic and more spiritual or transcendental. But there is no doubt that this passage commands a massive spiritual authority, and still, in this age of scientific cleverness, holds a fascination for us all. What are the salient features of this passage?

Firstly it assumes that there was a beginning of all things; even the scientists today are assuming the same thing, even with Big Bangs to contend with. All things must have had a start somewhere in the remote past. To use the word 'chaos' is to implant a Greek assumption, but it is the same idea as in Greek mythology and many others. There was a primeval ocean before land ever appeared; this is seen in so many myths from around the world.

In the pagan world this passage would have seemed most strange. The idea of one God as opposed to multitudes of them might have seemed to them hilarious, if not impossible. Moreover it goes into details about how creation progressed from basic things to more elaborate things such as plants, then animals then humans. It all happens in an orderly fashion. Now we see the theological agenda behind this scheme. It establishes the six day pattern with the seventh day, the Sabbath as the day of rest, not just for God but for mankind as well. This is heavily stressed in Genesis 2:1-3. Therefore we have the basis for the faith of Israel right from the start, and in a sense the passage is prophetic, because the whole world is now working on a seven-day cycle, even if the 'Sabbath' is timed for a different day of the week according to one's religion.

Another feature is the way in which 'and God saw that it was good' comes round like a chorus. This alerts us to the possibility that the passage was liturgical; it is certainly quasi-poetic. On that basis, we can take it as a kind of song, and if so, it need not be taken totally literally. The repetition of 'and God saw that it was very good' serves to emphasise that Creation is not haphazard, careless or badly thought out. The implication in this is that everything started out as wonderful and faultless; we learn a few verses later that this all slipped and went wrong because of the disobedience of mankind. This means that the question of Theodicy is being raised right at the start of life on this earth; this is an important element in all world mythologies.

One of the crucial elements in this passage is the creation of mankind. 'In the image of God' is also emphasised. At this stage it is not personal; there is no mention of Adam and Eve. In general terms, humanity is devised in two genders, and has authority over all the rest of creation.

Comparing Genesis 1 with Ancient Mesopotamian texts

It is interesting to compare the creation myths of ancient Mesopotamia with the Biblical material. It is almost certain that Abraham, coming from Ur of the Chaldees, would have known these texts; perhaps not all, but enough to know the main thrust of them. In that sense there is a certain amount of historical anchorage for Genesis 1. These ideas would have been in circulation as oral, folklorist material for many generations before being committed to writing. One can view such accounts in Michael Coogan's book, Ancient Near Eastern Texts.

We can start with the myth of **Enuma Elish**,(1) often called the Babylonian Creation Epic; there is no certainty about when it was written, but that is hardly the point; it would have been in the ether for many generations.

Without indulging in too much detail, before the world was created, there was Apsu, the primal god, and Tiamat, a monster of the deep. Marduk, the champion god, comes in to defeat Tiamat, but there are also battles going on in the skies. Apsu regrets producing so many gods who cannot behave themselves, but Tiamat wishes to avoid destroying them. This is reminiscent of God regretting having created mankind (Genesis 6:6). The difference is that this situation occurs before the appearance of mankind. It is interesting that the name Tiamat is phonetically related to the Hebrew word MWTH, meaning 'death'. Marduk, the chief god of Babylon, emerges as the champion as he defeats Tiamat, and becomes the king of the gods. Thus we see the question of Theodicy is answered before the creation of the world itself; evil is defeated by a good god. Marduk then decides to create the human race so that the gods can relax and offload their work on to mankind. There is nothing about humanity being in some kind of spiritual relationship with a god. It was decided that Quingu, one of the original gods, who had incited Tiamat to cause trouble, should be held responsible and his blood was used to create mankind. This episode comes in almost as an afterthought. The whole passage is very different from Genesis. It is confused, heavily repetitious and inconsistent. One is left with the feeling that there is no attempt at an orderly and systematic account as seen in Genesis. There is nothing to suggest a framework for creation relating to the days of the week and the Sabbath; nor is there anything like the story of the Garden of Eden. The main purpose of Enuma Elish was to provide a liturgical basis for the New Year Festival in Babylon;(2) other such mythical material with variant ideas has been found in other cities. Was this type of account taken literally by the people? They almost certainly took it as poetic and figurative.

The Creation myth from **Sippar**,(3) a much shorter account, gives a clearer focus on the appearance of humanity. Again, we begin with a primeval ocean, and Marduk builds a raft on the waters, piling dirt on it, thus producing the land. He created mankind with the purpose of 'settling the gods in the dwelling pleasing to them.' This was done in conjunction with Aruru, a mother goddess. The production of the animals comes after that of mankind; then come the rivers and everything else. This reminds us of Genesis 2 in which the human race appears before the rest of the natural world.

Another myth from **Ashur**,(4) which was found in the library of Tiglath-Pileser 1st (1114-1076 BC) which is contemporaneous with King David, would have been the cultural backdrop for the Assyrian Empire. Even so, it probably went back many centuries before, in oral form. It begins with the heaven and earth being separated. This is a concept seen Genesis 1:6-7, and was a widespread assumption in the ancient world. The Greeks had a giant called Atlas holding up the sky.

After the gods had planned everything, they then decided to slaughter all the pre-existent gods and create mankind from their blood. The purpose, again, would be for mankind to do all the work for the gods, giving them a holiday. Genesis does not go to the anthropomorphism of God using his own blood to create mankind; it is much more spiritual, in that mankind is in the image of God. Again in this account we have the impression that it is liturgical, and hardly any systematic account of creation, still less biological. The way the gods are described makes them seem almost human.

Seeing into the mindset of ancient Mesopotamia, we can say that there were many and varied creation myths in circulation, each relevant to a particular town. They must have known about each other, and probably saw no contradiction between them, just as in Greece there were at least four creation myths in circulation with slightly different ideas. It is hard to see how they could ever have been taken totally at face value. This leads us on to consider the second creation myth in Genesis 2:4 to 3:24. Whoever put Genesis together, possibly Moses, clearly wanted us to see creation from two standpoints; God's activity with creation in general terms, and then God in relation to the coming of humanity when things began to go wrong.

The Garden of Eden

The second creation account in Genesis is clearly from a different hand, the source known as 'J', or the 'Jahwistic' source. This one is far more anthropomorphic, in that God is almost a human being walking about the garden and talking to Adam and Eve as if face to face. Also there are far more mythological features worked into the story. Another important factor is that we have some degree of historical anchorage for the Garden of Eden; we have mention of four rivers; the Pishon, the Gihon,(5) the Tigris and the Euphrates. Also we have the land of Havilah, and Assyria. Two of these rivers and one country are known to us today but locating the Garden of Eden has still been a problem; it must have been, according to this, somewhere in what we now call Iraq or Saudi Arabia. None of this kind of geographical location appears in the Chaldean epics.

As seen with the myth from Sippar, the human race appears before the rest of creation, and also the man appears before the woman. It was God who planted the garden and left the man to tend it. The mythical elements appear very soon; a mist went up from the ground, symbolic of God's presence. There are two trees; the tree of life and the tree of knowledge of good and evil. So the concept of the 'world tree' is there right at the start of the Bible; whether it is meant to be two trees or just one is not entirely clear; this might be an example of Hebrew parallelism.(6)

The creation of woman as secondary to man is clearly a way of justifying marriage and the change in loyalty which takes place. With this we see the 'just-so' element which often occurs in mythology. The fact that they were naked indicates their innocence, just like little children. Again, nakedness is a factor seen with other mythologies, such as the Greek male gods and Odin and Freya. In such examples we may be seeing nakedness as the possession of extra spiritual power; this is something that is seen with shamanism.

The serpent now enters the scene. Virtually every world mythology includes a snake somewhere and often myriads of them. The fact that the snake speaks in human language indicates that this account is parabolic or symbolic. The idea of animals behaving or speaking like humans is also seen in other mythologies;[7] it is almost certainly a way of indicating the unity of creation, that there is not really much difference between animals and humans.

Adam and Eve are tempted by the snake and eat the forbidden fruit, but this was the end of innocence and the beginning of shame. They start blaming each other and the snake, which is typical of human nature. Now we see the explanation for Theodicy; why is life hard and why we have to suffer and die. They are expelled from Eden and the account concludes with a mythological touch; a cherubim with a flaming sword to guard the tree of life. In other words, justice and cleansing will keep humanity away from living for ever.

This is one of the most important passages in the scriptures. It is psychologically penetrating and deals with so many factors in the human experience. The pagan texts which bear some relationship to it are in no way in the same league. Whoever wrote this passage must have been a theological genius, even if we have to disagree with some of his ideas.

The Epic of Gilgamesh in relation to Adam and Eve

This important account stems from the late second millennium, contemporaneous with Israel under Moses, but it must have been in circulation for many centuries before that. Again we have a slight historical anchorage for this tale; Gilgamesh was the legendary king of Uruk (8) and may have been a solid historical character; certainly Uruk was a real city state. We follow the so-called Standard Babylonian Version, but there were various other versions of it in circulation. Gilgamesh has a problem on his mind; why do we have to die? Why can we not live for ever? Even if he is two thirds divine and one third human, it still worries him. He is styled as a great hero, hunter, builder and womaniser.

At this point we have an incidental mention of the creation of mankind. Aruru, the mother goddess, takes a pinch of clay (notice Genesis 2:7 and 3:19) and throws it into the open country. Primitive man, called Enkidu is created, the 'Adam' of Uruk; he was a warrior with shaggy hair. This reminds us of Esau. But he encounters Gilgamesh by a water-hole and he is frightened.

Gilgamesh's father advises him to send a prostitute called Shambat to seduce Enkidu, and we have quite an explicit account of him having a whole week of delight with her. She declares that he has become like a god, having acquired judgement and wisdom. This reminds us of Genesis 3:5 where Adam is likely to become like God, knowing good and evil.

Enkidu encounters Gilgamesh; they have a fight but then become firm friends.(9) Enkidu dies and Gilgamesh mourns his friend. This sharpens that sense of mortality in him; what about immortality? He goes to find Utnapishtim (the equivalent of Noah), whose name actually means 'he found life'. He is known as the only man (and his wife) to whom the gods have given immortality. It is a secret, but unlike Genesis, it is not related to a tree or the eating of forbidden fruit. It is however, related to the survival of the Flood. We shall return to the epic of the Flood later.

After the Flood, Enlil, a god, bestows immortality upon Utnapishtim and his wife. It would seem that there is a plant called 'camel thorn'; if one can win it, one will find rejuvenation. Utnapishtim presents Gilgamesh with the plant, but on the way home, while stopping at a water hole, a snake creeps up and steals the plant. Gilgamesh is torn with grief and despair. So we see that a snake enters the story, and in Genesis 3:1, but this time removes the secret of life, rather than tempting anyone to find it illicitly. Clearly the symbolisms

16

in the Gilgamesh story are as strong as in Genesis, but with a very different thrust. It is all about life and death, and how to sidestep mortality. Here is a young man who cannot face the thought of his waning virility as old age creeps on. It is appropriate that the snake steals the plant; the snake symbolises fecundity as well as life.

The Epic of Atrahasis in relation to the Garden of Eden.

This is another epic from the same part of the world and must have been in circulation about the time of Abraham. It has affinities with Enuma Elish and with Gilgamesh. It briefly mentions, almost in passing, the creation of mankind. There is Nintu, the divine midwife, who mixes clay with his flesh and blood so that a 'god and a man will be mixed together in clay.' The purpose of making mankind is the same as elsewhere, to give the gods a break from toiling on the land. There is very little in the way of mythological symbolism in this account, but it does indicate that humanity is believed to have that element of the divine in it, on the same lines as 'in the image of God.'

Cain and Abel

The first murder comes straight after the Garden of Eden incident. This is no accident; it is meant to show that things having gone wrong between God and mankind, all kinds of other misdemeanours follow on. Again, this story has a slight historical anchorage; Cain went off to live in the land of Nod, east of Eden. We do not know where that was, but the early readers of this book would almost certainly have known. The mythological aspects of this story are hardly there at all. But the story does not really need any supporting evidence. If there is a murder committed, the first people the police will interview are the next of kin; the story is self-evidencing!

Noah's Flood

The next important account with mythological features is the great Flood in Genesis chapter 6 to 9. The space it takes up indicates the importance it has for the faith of Israel and indeed for all of mankind. With this account, we are dealing with two sources, the J and the P, which have been cleverly integrated with each other, but not too tightly since we can discern which is which. The chief discrepancy is the difference of opinion over how many animals of each kind were to be saved. J has it that two of every kind of animal has to be saved; P has it that two of each of the unclean animals should be saved, but of the clean animals, seven pairs should be saved. This all serves to indicate that the Flood incident was widely known in the ancient world, and this is reinforced by the Epic of Gilgamesh and of Atrahasis. This provides us with a certain degree of historical and geographical anchorage, since the archaeologists have found evidence of severe flooding in the Mesopotamian area. Also the mountains of Ararat are still known to us today (Genesis 8:4). It goes further than this, as we shall see when assessing Greek and Chinese mythology and also that of the Huichols.(10) We cannot escape the conclusion that these accounts of the Flood are somehow related to a real disaster in remote prehistory.

The story of Noah also has the element of massive numbers relating to his (and other's) age. Methusaleh is claimed to be 969 years old when he died! No one has really managed to explain this matter successfully. It may be something to do with number symbolism; a separate chapter will be devoted to this enigma.(11)

The Epic of Gilgamesh in relation to the Flood

The story of Noah need not be related here in detail, since it is so well known. The epic from Uruk, recounting Utnapishtim's story is not so well known but is nevertheless most illuminating. The account of the Flood is worked in almost incidentally; here is a man who managed to sidestep death and this is how he did it. It is nothing to do with a tree; it is related to surviving the Flood. A detailed description of the Flood and the construction of the Ark show the similarities and differences. The actual dimensions of the Ark are not mentioned in the Epic, whereas they are in Genesis 6:14-16. Noah has three decks; Utnapishtim has six decks. Both of the boatmen load up with their families and the animals. There is agreement over the storm lasting seven days (Genesis 7:10), but there is disagreement over the length of the inundation and the sequence of the birds being sent out; the raven and the dove are in both accounts. Utnapishtim grounds on Mount Nimbush,(12) whereas Noah lands on the mountains of Ararat. When they emerge from the Ark, both of them perform a sacrifice, which gives a pleasant odour to their respective gods.

It may be a simplistic question to ask, 'which account of the Flood came first?' or 'who copied from whom?' These queries may be unanswerable. We may even be dealing with two separate incidents, since severe flooding in that area was not unusual. It is obvious that Noah's account is far more detailed and focussed. In the epic we see a certain amount of detail but nowhere near as much. One is tempted to say that Noah's account is more original.

The theological thrust of each account is quite different. The Epic is trying to stress the fact that there is no need to despair over death. There are those who survive the Flood and therefore sidestep death. This is a symbolic way of saying that life is eternal and also a gift of the gods. We can compare that with Genesis 6:3 where God says, 'my spirit shall not abide in man for ever, for he is flesh, but his days shall be 120 years.' This means that God is setting a limit on the human lifespan. Noah's account , however, is crucial to the main thrust of the Old Testament. It ends with God making an unconditional promise, a covenant, that seedtime and harvest will never fail as long as the earth exists. The rainbow appears as a symbol of this undertaking; the rainbow appears also in Norse and Japanese thinking, but with a different significance.

The Epic of Atrahasis in relation to the Flood

This is another Epic from Mesopotamia in which the Flood is mentioned. This time the Flood is described in much vaguer terms; in fact the account is quite short. Somebody called Atrahasis survives the Flood by building a boat, but there is no mention of his family or the animals being saved. After this ordeal he made a sacrifice. Enlil, the warrior god, is furious that someone has survived, since the purpose of the Flood was to destroy all of mankind. The gods made an oath beforehand, that no one should be preserved. We can compare this with Genesis 6:13 where God decides that since the whole earth is corrupt and violent, he will make an end of everything. We notice that God makes an oath to mankind after the Flood, that it will not happen again. However, Enki, the chief god, justifies Atrahasis' survival, and says, 'I made sure life was preserved!' That, it would seem, is the theological basis of this Epic, that life is precious and must be preserved.

What is the mythological importance of the Flood? We notice that it involves large volumes of water; that is symbolic of washing, cleansing. We all have that feeling that the earth needs to be cleansed and given a fresh start. That is why the Flood motif resonates with something in human nature. How many children have a Noah's Ark in their nursery? We all know it as a legendary, possibly as a historical reality. But from that legend is developed an exaggerated version which is iconic for us all. We see that the Christians took up the same motif; in I Peter 3:21, it stresses the importance of baptism, which corresponds to the Flood. This gives us a fresh start and a clear conscience. That is the way the ancients managed to emphasise a theological message; through exaggeration and augmentation. This is something that we still do today, in the media, in an attempt to grab people's attention and make some kind of point.

In recent years there have been various attempts at finding remnants of the Ark on Mount Ararat. None of these have been too successful. There are souvenir shops in the area catering for tourist needs. Whatever one may think of this, what it does indicate is the hold that this Flood story has on the human mind.

The Tower of Babel

Another intriguing account from Genesis (chapter 11) concerns the Tower of Babel. The mythological elements in it are sparse but not completely absent. There appears, so far, to be nothing in the ancient Mesopotamian texts comparable with this account; however, the archaeological record is quite fulsome. In the land of Shinar (now Iraq) there were many such towers built and the remains of them can still be seen, made of mud-brick. They are called Ziggurats. They were clearly a precaution against flooding; the Hanging Gardens of Babylon were an elaborate version of the same thing.

The importance of this passage, coming after the Flood, is to show that in spite of the earth being cleansed, the human race is still intent on going wrong. They are trying to probe into the very workings of God; God decides that this is unacceptable. He decides to confuse them, scatter them and they begin to speak different languages. This is the 'just-so' element in the story;

why do we have different languages? It also explains the origin of the name Babylon; we call confused speech 'babble'!

In addition, the story contains a warning to the human race, not to probe too deeply into the workings of God. Now that we are interfering with the very building blocks of life, one must ask, is this entirely wise? How long will it be before it backfires on us? If we can determine the sex of a baby before he is born, how would we cope with masses of Chinese and Arab boys and a severe shortage of girls?!

Psalm 104; another Creation account

It is a mistake to think that the Biblical creation account only occurs at the beginning of Genesis. Psalm 104 is a highly poetic version of creation, and there is no cause to take it literally. When it says that God covers himself with light as with a garment, and rides on the wings of the wind, this is poetry at its most imaginative and beautiful. The whole psalm lifts the soul into ecstasies.

It does not use the pattern of days of the week and there is no mention of the Sabbath. There are certain mythological elements in it, such as fire and flame and there is much mention of water. Also sea monsters are mentioned, such as Leviathan, but this is all part of the poetry.

It is clear what the psalmist is trying to say, his theological agenda. Verse 24 sums it up neatly; 'O Lord, how manifold are thy works. In wisdom hast thou made them all...' It is essentially the same message as in Genesis, that creation is not a chaotic mess; it is all carefully thought out and wonderful. A secondary thrust comes in verse 30, which might remind us of the Flood; 'thou renewest the face of the ground' and verse 35 'let sinners be consumed from the earth.' This is in effect saying that the created world is so marvellous that there is no room for wickedness or moral failure. This is a good example of how a creation myth is adapted to serve a theological agenda.

2 Esdras 6:38ff. Another Creation account

This account is clearly following Genesis chapter 1 more closely, but is less poetic. The scheme of the days of the week is present, but strangely the

Sabbath is not mentioned. Mythological elements are not particularly strong; we have a mention of Leviathan, and of the Firmament. Enoch appears to be equated with a sea monster!

However, the main thrust of the passage is to ask God why the Jewish people are being harassed by the heathen; '... have begun to be lords over us and devour us... and we are given into their hands... If the world be made for our sakes, why do we not possess an inheritance... how long will this endure?' In other words, we the people of God are being dispossessed and persecuted, which is surely a mistake, as the world was made for our benefit, not theirs. Clearly this relates to the Exilic or even post-Exilic situation when the Jews were forced to leave their homeland. This is another clear example of how a creation myth can be adapted to serve a theological agenda.

An Epic tale from Egypt; the Tale of Two Brothers

The relevance of this story to this debate on mythology lies in the relationship between two brothers; one is instantly reminded of the Cain and Abel account in Genesis 4. In fact it begins rather like Genesis, but goes off to include a situation very similar to the Joseph and Potiphar's Wife incident in Genesis 39.

The older brother is called Anubis (which reminds us of the jackal-headed god) and the younger is Bata. Anubis has a house and a wife and Bata lives with them as a son with his parents rather than as brother and sister-in-law. Bata does all the agricultural work, with the cattle and harvests the crops. Anubis appears to share in the work. But one day, Mrs. Anubis, finding herself alone with Bata, tempts him to seduce her, but he refuses. When Anubis comes home she makes out that Bata had tried to seduce her. Anubis is furious and plans to kill Bata. Not just one but two cows warn Bata that Anubis is lying in ambush. In this we see a reminder of Balaam's donkey. Bata runs off and Anubis fails to catch him; this gives Bata a chance to put the record straight. Anubis goes home and kills his wife instead.

Bata then goes hunting and his heart is hung on a pine tree. When the people come from Pharaoh to cut the tree down, Bata dies. Anubis then reappears and finds the heart of Bata and revives it. So Bata comes back to life and the two brothers are reconciled. This reminds us of the reconciliation of Jacob and Esau (Genesis 33). The news of this miracle soon spreads and

Pharaoh is delighted, giving Bata rewards. Later, Bata's wife bears a son and Pharaoh appoints him Royal Son of Kush, and later the Crown Prince. When Pharaoh dies, he becomes the next Pharaoh, and after that his brother takes his place as Pharaoh. In this way, in spite of the differences in the story, the gist of it is that 'the honest lad makes good', just like Joseph. Although much of this is slightly unrealistic, the moral of the tale is quite clear, as with the Joseph saga.

Another interesting feature of this account is the way in which 'the second day' is stated. This comes round rather often, leaving us to wonder what happened to the other days. This is somewhat puzzling. But it does remind us of Genesis 1 in which the days of the week are quoted. The story is not actually a creation myth, but it does contain mythological elements and concentrates on family relationships, something that emerges quite often in Genesis. It would be misleading to attempt to maintain that the one epic copied the other; the differences are too great. Even so, one can see that both accounts probably stem from the same time in the second millennium and roughly the same area. This may suggest that similar ideas were circulating in folklorist circles, just as today, the soap operas circulate much the same ideas in their dramas.

What it does tell us is that the dichotomy between mythology and history is almost certainly an artificial one, as far as the ancients were concerned. The two elements are intertwined. In Genesis we see a gradual slide from mythology into actual history, with elements of both worked in as and when appropriate. The same is true with these epic materials from Mesopotamia and Egypt. The word 'legendary' might well be applied to much of the material in Genesis, but what does that mean in fact? We have so often discovered that legend has turned out to be more substantial than has often been supposed. A prime example of that would be The Iliad and the discovery of ancient Troy. It is a mistake to become too dogmatic about levels of accuracy and truth in these matters.

Essential elements in mythology

One can easily see that many of these elements appear in many contexts in the Bible, not least in early Genesis, but other parts of the Old Testament. This is no surprise, since these documents were produced in a world where mythology was a dominant feature. All the nations surrounding the Hebrews had their own elaborate mythologies, not least the Greeks and the Egyptians. It would be a surprise if the Bible had omitted any of this genre of material. When we look at The Revelation of St.John, we see all of these features augmented to a fantastic level. For that reason we can see that eschatology is just a futuristic version of mythology. This means that an apocalyptic book like Daniel can be seen in much the same light. Of course, the intertestamental literature which offers much on the subject of eschatology can be understood in the same way.

Some have gone further and suggested that much more in the Bible is mythological, including the Gospels themselves. In answer to this, the gospel writers clearly intend us to take their testimonies as historical and literal. Admittedly there are mythological elements included, but their intention is clearly that of showing us that Jesus Christ, the true Son of God, the ultimate champion of good against evil, is the fulfilment and final answer to all these elaborate speculations from the pagan religions.

It would seem that whether we are ancient or modern, there is the need for some kind of mythology. Just because we live in an age of scientific enquiry and questioning, does not mean that mythology has faded out; far from it, the deep questions of life and death, creation and un-creation are still with us and in many ways more searching than before. This book will examine some of the ancient ideas and compare them with the mythology of the present age. That does not mean that we are all as deluded as they were in the past; to be fair we have our own collection of delusions just as they did. What it does mean is that human nature has not changed in that we need to keep on asking those fundamental questions; why are we here and how do we relate to the rest of creation? How do we relate to the ultimate truth, namely God? Interestingly, we shall find that many of the ancient symbolisms and metaphors continue to reappear in today's world. Human nature may have changed a little, but not completely.

Footnotes for chapter 2

1.   Enuma Elish; a city state in Mesopotamia.
2.   The New Year Festival was seen as essential to ensure the harvest for the next year. The King of the city state would go through various rituals in the main temple and there might

be a procession. Parts of the Psalms are thought to relate to the New Year Festival.

3. Sippar; a city state; think of Borsippa.

4. Ashur; this indicates Assyria, the capital being Nineveh.

5. Pishon and Gihon, two rivers not identifiable nowadays, in spite of attempts to find them.

6. Hebrew parallelism; this is a technique found in Hebrew poetry; there was no rhyming. An example would be Psalm 78:54; 'And he brought them to his holy land, to the mountain that his right hand had won.'

7. The technical term for this is 'therianthropism.' This means combining human and animal traits in one person. Much of this is seen in Greek mythology, for instance, the Minotaur, half bull and half man.

8. Uruk; a city state near Babylon.

9. This reminds us of Robin Hood and Little John in their first encounter.

10. The Huichol people of western Mexico, see chapter 14.

11. See chapter 26 for Numerology.

12. Mount Nimbush. The equivalent of Mount Ararat. Nimbush may be mythological.

3

The Book of Daniel

The book of Daniel is the only complete apocalypse in the Old Testament. It is matched by Revelation, coming at the end of the New Testament. There are other fragments of apocalyptic material in both parts of the Bible, but the main outpouring of eschatology comes in the intertestamental period. The book of Enoch, which I have reviewed in the Theology of Truth, came near to being included in the Bible, but many other such works remain apocryphal and pseudepigraphal. The mistake that has been made over the centuries, has been the strong tendency to take these materials totally at face value. Doubtless those of a fundamentalistic frame of mind, will object to this, but I feel that the mythological and symbolic approach is the only way to make sense of these writings.

All this eschatological material exhibits the symptoms of being symbolic, highly-metaphoric and exaggerated. It is a mistake to take them purely at face value; we are dealing here with dream material, pointing to the future. On that basis, we can call it futuristic mythology.

The first clue not to take Daniel purely at face value comes in the first verse;

'In the third year of the reign of JehoiakiM, King of Judah, NebuchadNezzar, King of Babylon came to Jerusalem and besieged it..."

This gives the impression that the defeat and the exile of the Judeans happened in one episode. If we compare this with the account in 2 Kings 23:36ff, the whole matter of the defeat and exile is much more complicated. It involves

JehoiakiM, JehoiakiN, Zedekiah and Gedaliah. Also, if we compare it with Jeremiah 36:1ff, the whole episode is even more complicated. We learn that the King of Babylon's name was NebuchadRezzar, which is more like his actual name.(1)

Clearly there is a problem here. Kings and Jeremiah are clearly much closer to historical realities, given the detail and timings given. Daniel is clearly talking on a different level. It would be unfair to say he is wrong or trying to deceive us. If we assume that this is dream material, and is pointing to the future, then we can see it in a completely different light. We should be looking for symbolisms, and metaphoric expressions, which match up to mythological material and exaggerations found in other parts of the Bible and elsewhere.

One of the noted features of the book, especially towards the end, is this very question of THE END. Does this mean the end of the world, or does it mean the end of the miseries suffered by the Jews, or does it mean the end of waiting for the 'anointed one', which would be the Christ? It is no surprise to find that Daniel makes a certain amount of play concerning the beginning.

Connecting to the early chapters of Genesis.

This is done in a fairly subtle way without it being too obtrusive. At the start (Daniel 1:2) we find that the exiles are taken to the land of Shinar in the area of Babylon, the very district that Abraham came from. Genesis 11:1 actually states that the Tower of Babel was built in the land of Shinar, and that project was to do with confusion of languages. In Daniel we find that the young Jewish men are made to learn Aramaic (2) and we assume that the King of Babylon was trying to unify the language of his kingdom. The book of Daniel slides in Aramaic at 2:4b, in the same way that the book of Enoch does. In the Tower of Babel, the whole earth is involved; in Daniel 2:35 the stone that destroys the great image fills the 'whole earth'. Clearly the great image is just as much an attempt at probing upwards to God as the Tower of Babel was. Another massive image comes in Daniel 3, though perhaps not so tall, but clearly the same motif. The king, Nebuchadnezzar is trying to pose as God, again, in the plain of Dura which is near Babylon. We also have a tree which reaches up to heaven (Chapter 4). This again reminds us of Genesis in which there was a tree of life which was some kind of connection to God. Trees are a very common element in mythology; they appear in virtually every myth, the world over. There is also mention of the Flood in Daniel 9:26, recalling Noah. In Daniel 10:4 he was standing on the banks of the river Tigris. This river is mentioned as near the Garden of Eden (Genesis 2:14). Other rivers are mentioned in both books. Whether the river Ulai is meant to be a real river or just symbolic is an awkward question. But the mention of Susa and Elam involves real locations. Even then, they might be symbolic in the sense of being the centre of a great empire.

In Daniel 8:26 we have a remark that goes 'evenings and mornings' and this reminds us of the first chapter of Genesis in which each day of creation is marked by the same comment. In Daniel 10:12 he is told not to be afraid; this is what God tells Abraham in Genesis 15:1. These various reminders of Genesis are not overdone, but they do hint that as at the beginning so too at the end, God's pattern of salvation will be carried out. But it does raise the question of where the true wisdom is to be found. The book is emphatic that the magi of Babylon have no idea, in spite of their claims, whereas the Jewish boy who knows his Genesis, can answer any difficult question for the king. The other implication in all this is that since the Jewish people are in such difficulties, now is the time to 'go back to basics', in other words, reconnect with the original thoughts with mankind relating to God in the Garden of Eden. All the same, this idea is not given too much emphasis.

Mythological symbolisms in Daniel.

Rather more emphasised in Daniel are various features of mythological symbolism. Most striking is the frequent mention of gold and by association, silver. The great idol in chapter 2 has a head of gold, then its chest and arms are of silver; base metals come further down. In chapter 3 there is a massive idol all of gold. Both of these are symbolic of the Babylonian empire and Nebuchadnezzar himself. In 11:38 and 11:43 we have gold, silver and precious stones. The man dressed in linen in 10:5 has his loins girded with gold of Uphaz and his body is like beryl, and his arms and legs are burnished bronze. We do not know the significance of 'Uphaz'; it may be a real place, or possibly symbolic, as being highly refined, pure gold. We have various mentions of the vessels of the Temple, of gold and silver, being treated with disrespect by the Babylonians; this is symbolic of the way they treated Judaism in general terms. Daniel is offered a gold chain and purple which would indicate royalty or even deity. The tree motif is present, as remarked upon above. A strong emphasis is laid on fire; we have the fiery furnace in chapter 3. In chapter 7, with the vision of God, we have 'his throne was fiery flames and its wheels were burning fire; a stream of fire issued forth from before him...' The motif of fire is an important one, as it indicates cleansing, just as much as water does. The symbol of water is understated in Daniel, unless we see the mention of various rivers such as the Tigris and the Ulai as intended as vehicles of cleansing. But cleansing, in general terms, is a major theme in Daniel; it applies specifically to the Jews, but also to the rest of humanity. This also relates to the motif of innocence as seen in Daniel. Daniel and his three friends keep themselves clear of the decadence of the Babylonian empire. Shadrach, Meshach and Abednego, who are called The Three Holy Children, are not even touched by the fiery furnace, whereas the stokers are slain even coming near the blaze. In other words, the Jews keep their purity despite all the inducements to compromise with the pagans.

We have frequent mention of angels, Michael and Gabriel, but never any mention of devils or Satan. This matches up with the vision of heaven and God in chapter 7, and the Son of Man, but strangely there is no mention of the underworld, or Hell, or even of Sheol. Perhaps Daniel thought that the fiery furnace and the lions' den would be enough to symbolise Hell? An indirect reference to the underworld might be seen in the interpretation of **tekel** (Daniel 5:23) which is explained as 'weighed in the balances'. This idea appears in the Egyptian Book of the Dead, where the judges of the underworld evaluate one's soul and decide on one's fate according to how the balances react.

Number symbolism in Daniel.

This assumes much importance because it is assumed that the END can be calculated. Elsewhere, we have seen that **five, seven, eight, and nine** are all related to the structure of the universe. As far as Daniel is concerned, seven is the important number because it implies the four corners of the earth and the three shelves. This indicates perfection, while three and a half, which is a half of seven, implies trouble, things gone wrong, and evil.

Much of the number symbolism in Daniel is rather obscure. It may have been quite obvious to anyone reading it at the time it was written; the same can be said of Revelation. Some of the symbolisms would have meant a lot to the early Christians in Asia Minor.

The use of three is interesting. There are the three Holy Children who are given three years of education. The whole book begins with the third year of Jehoiakim. There are two attempts at working out the king's dream, but on the third attempt, it is Daniel who solves the problem. We have the third year of Belshazzar. Daniel goes into mourning for three weeks; this was the third year of Cyrus the Persian king.(3) Daniel prays three times a day. In 11:2, there are to be three more Persian kings, plus one more. This motif recalls The Three Holy Children, plus one more which is Daniel. In the fiery furnace one more is seen, the angel, which justifies the courage of the Jewish boys. Is the motif three plus one saying in effect that at the start, things were going right, but at the end of the Persian empire, things were going wrong?

A similar configuration occurs over the number **ten**. In chapter one there are ten days of testing over the issue of diet, and the Jewish boys turn out to be ten times better than the pagan boys. In chapter seven the fourth beast has ten horns, which are explained as ten kings, plus one, which persecutes the Jews. This normally taken to symbolise the succession of the Seleucid kings down to Antiochus 4th Epiphanes. Unfortunately, this is only an approximation. Even so, it gives a general picture of the situation under the Seleucids. Ten reminds us of the Ten Commandments; how to get things right, as indeed the Jewish boys did in chapter one. But by the end, things are going wrong as the Greek empires degenerate.(4)

It is difficult to avoid the idea that these numbers are some sort of code. It may not have been so when Jeremiah prophesied 70 years of exile, but Daniel is now taking it as axiomatic and literal. So in 4:25 when it says that seven times will pass over the king, it is a covert way of saying that the exile will last for 70 years, or to put it another way, the Babylonian empire will only last 70 years (which was approximately true). In 5:20, Darius the Mede receives the kingdom, being about 62 years old. As far as we know, Darius was not a Mede and did not immediately succeed Belshazzar, but the use of 62 is interesting here. Does it mean that the exile is drawing to a close; that those 70 years are nearly over? We see the use of 62 again in chapter 9:26 but its application is not at all obvious. It may be hinting at the post-exilic period down to the appearance of Antiochus 4th Epiphanes. On a literal level, this does not work too well as 62 times 7 gives us 434 years which is too many. But on a figurative level it does work, because the author is saying that the 62 years of exile must be matched by another period of 62 weeks, ie, 434 years during which the Temple will be rebuilt, but in a troubled time.

It is interesting that the image of gold, as in chapter 3 is 60 cubits high and 6 cubits broad. That would be something like 122 feet high and 12 feet in breadth; massive! It is not impossible that such a statue could be constructed (think of the Colossus of Rhodes (5)), but of solid gold? But what is the symbolism in it? 60 is nearly 70; in other words, it is aspiring to be perfect, ie, God, but not succeeding in reaching so high. This may connect with something we see in 8:14, in which 2300 days are quoted for the Temple being defiled and neglected. 2300 works out at just over 6 years, and the golden image was 6 cubits in breadth; in other words, it was a bold attempt but just failed.

There is an apparent contradiction here between 6 years and 3 and a half years quoted for the Abomination of Desolation. Elsewhere in Daniel, half of 7, namely 3 and a half, is the time prophesied for the desolation of the Temple. In 9:27 for half a week the sacrifice will be stopped, in other words, three and a half years. This comes round various times such as in 7:25 ('a time, two times and half a time') and in 12:7. A variant on this comes in 12:11, where it quotes 1290 days which works out at just over 3 and a half years.

There is still a puzzle over 11:12 in which 3335 days are quoted. No one has as yet managed to cast light on this convincingly. This works out at just over 9 years; in other words, nearly ten. We have seen the use of ten earlier in the book; this may be saying that we are nearly there but not quite!

We have to realise that the use of such words as day, week, month and year do not have to be taken literally. They are all interchangeable; this is a feature seen quite often in apocalyptic literature, notably Revelation. We are not seeing precise mathematics here; all these numbers quoted are somewhat approximate and very largely symbolic. A good example of this would be in 9:24, where it says, 'seventy weeks of years are decreed... to bring in everlasting righteousness...' That would be 490 years, assumedly. If we take that from the end of the exile, that brings us almost to the time of Jesus; not a bad estimate!

Exaggeration and augmentation in Daniel

Daniel would not be the first Old Testament writer to use this literary technique, but he almost certainly gave inspiration to Ezekiel and later writers, including Revelation and not forgetting Jesus himself. We can see certain passages in Daniel that can only be seen as hyperbolic; they cannot be taken literally. But it is all done for a purpose.

In chapter 2 the wise men of Babylon are called upon to explain the king's dream, but he does not tell them what it is; they are supposed to guess. When they fail to guess, they are condemned to death. Daniel comes in and describes the dream and gives the interpretation. This is symbolic of saying, with emphasis, that the wisdom of the Jewish boy is a long way ahead of that of the Babylonian magi. In other words, they are all without a clue and Daniel is in line for the king's favour. The image is smashed to pieces by a stone that fills the whole earth; clearly this is exaggeration, but the fulfilment of it was true, that the coming of the kingdom of God, with Jesus, did fill the whole earth and demolished paganism.

The next image completely of gold in chapter 3 is clearly an augmentation of the previous one which was of various metals. This time it is a clumsy attempt at uniting a compound empire; never and easy task. But the Jews refuse to obey the king's command. We notice the rising climax with the instruments which announce the time to fall down and worship, and the tension builds up as the fiery furnace is threatening. Then we see the exaggeration as the Three Holy Children are hurled into the flames, and even the stokers are killed in the attempt. But the three survive with not a mark on them, even if the furnace was seven times hotter than normal. There is another example of augmentation. If we take this literally, it makes no sense; figuratively, it means that nothing will force the Jews into worshipping false gods or compromising with the pagans. This in its own way was a prophecy of what happened in the time of Antiochus 4th Epiphanes.

In chapter 6 we have the famous account of Daniel in the lions' den. Again we have the climactic build-up as the accusers of the Jews raise the emotion over being obliged to worship the king. The phrase 'the law of the Medes and Persians', which is so famous, comes round no less than three times, emphasising the way in which the Jews are being coerced into embarking on paganism. So Daniel is thrown into the lions' den, but it is the king who is ill at ease all night. In the morning, he finds that Daniel is unharmed. But his accusers, when thrown in, are thrashed to pieces even before they land at the bottom of the pit. This is another exaggeration, plus the fact that all their families are condemned as well. So the accusation rebounds on them; this reminds us of what happened to Heman in the book of Esther, and Nicanor in 2 Maccabees, which means that this passage is also prophetic. Incidentally, the Persian emperors did not persecute the Jews, so the passage has to be taken figuratively.

Animal personification in Daniel.

This is a well known technique in apocalyptic literature, and it may be that Daniel provided the initial inspiration for it. It is also seen in many other mythologies, even if it is done in a slightly different way.

It begins in chapter 7 with the four beasts coming out of the sea; the sea, incidentally, is symbolic of evil and the home of monsters such as Leviathan and Behemoth. The lion, the bear, the leopard with four heads and finally a terrible creature with ten horns all appeared. Then came a little horn which uprooted three of the others, and had a big mouth. Clearly this is talking about the successive empires at that time; Babylon, Medo-Persia, Alexander and the Seleucid dynasty. The little horn is taken to be Antiochus 4th Epiphanes, who proclaimed himself as a god. It is hard to say why the lion should symbolise Babylon, and the bear, the Persians. The leopard with four heads could indicate Alexander whose empire split into four kingdoms when he died. The last beast, if it means the Seleucids, with ten kings, would only be an approximation. It is not clear how Antiochus could have supplanted three other kings. Clearly the dream is pointing forwards to the last straw when Antiochus brought matters to a crisis in Judea; Daniel thinks that the kingdom of God will then appear and all these monstrous empires will be destroyed. Much of this is an approximation to the real course of events, but it was accurate enough to cause great excitement for the Jews in the Maccabean age.

The next dream comes in chapter 8 when Daniel is in eastern Persia. He sees a ram with two horns, one bigger than the other. Then a he-goat with a large horn between his eyes, appears in the west and charges at the ram, defeating him. Then the he-goat's horn is split into four; this gives rise to the little horn that grows exceedingly great and makes sacrificing to cease in the glorious land. The interpretation is given later. This time, Babylon is left out of the picture. The ram is the Medo-Persian empire which was an amalgam of Media and Persia under Cyrus. It was so successful that it swept up all of the ancient orient, including Egypt, but it was in contention with Greece. This is the he-goat and Alexander is the big horn. This vision gives a reasonably general impression of the clash between Persia and Greece, which ended with the Greeks dominating vast areas of the known world from Italy to India. But Antiochus becomes the focus of attention as he desecrates the Temple in Jerusalem.

These two animal personifications tie in to a very large extent with the early dreams of Nebuchadnezzar. In 2:31, Daniel describes the dream, in which the mighty image symbolises Nebuchadnezzar. The head is of gold, the breast and arms are of silver, its belly was of bronze, its legs and its feet were a mixture of iron and clay. We can see in this the successive deterioration of one empire after another. The trouble is that if the head indicates Babylon, and the silver the Persians, what was the bronze? The iron is clearly the Greeks, and the mixture of iron and clay could indicate Alexander's policy of intermarriage; but it could also indicate the two Greek kingdoms of the orient. This motif gives a general picture without being too precise.

The next dream concerns the massive tree in 4:13ff. An angel comes and orders the tree to be cut down and the stump bound with iron and bronze. The tree is clearly meant to symbolise Nebuchadnezzar and indicates his defeat by the Medes and Persians. It goes on to depict his humiliation as he has to eat grass and associate with the beasts of the field. Clearly this is symbolic on a more thorough level. The vision is talking about the Babylonian empire in general terms, how it would last about 70 years and be totally routed by Cyrus. This is in fact what did happen, since the Babylonian dynasty after Nebuchadnezzar did quickly deteriorate to the extent that there was not even a battle as Cyrus swept into Babylon.

So we see that with these dreams, we have an impression of the future. None of these prognostications totally agree with each other; indeed, would we expect them to if they are genuine dreams outlining the future? When we come to chapter 11, the dream method fades out and Michael gives a much more detailed synopsis of the future leading up to the kingdom of God coming in. Some of the details match up remarkably well with known events from other sources; other details cannot be verified. So impressive is Daniel's description of history down to the Maccabean age, that 20th century scholars, of an over-critical approach, have dubbed this as vaticinium ex eventu, in other words, describing history as if it were a prophecy; in other words, a late fraud. This, in my opinion, cannot work for several reasons. Firstly, why did not the Jews see it as a fraud and reject Daniel? Secondly, why did not the fraud make a thorough job of it and make all the details fit with known events? Thirdly, why did Ezekiel refer back to Daniel? Fourthly, how could a book such as Daniel accrue enough authority and acceptance into the Old Testament, if it had been written after the Maccabean age?

Symbolisms in names

There is another aspect with regard to Daniel, which concerns personal names. We have seen how number symbolism is important; so too is word or name symbolism. This has more to do with symbolism but there are also implications for mythology.

There is an important difference of opinion over the name of the Babylonian king; NebuchadRezzar. This is the correct spelling which appears in Jeremiah and Ezekiel. It has meaning, as did most people's names in those days. It means 'may Nabu (a god) protect the boundary (or throne)'. But Daniel has it as NebuchadNezzar, which loses the meaning and now appears to mean nothing. Is this just a careless mistake or is it deliberate? If this is genuinely dream material, Daniel may have heard the name or seen it written and got one letter slightly wrong. Another way of seeing it is that Daniel deliberately altered the R to an N in order to destroy the meaning of the word. In other words, to render this great tyrannical king down to nothingness; this is actually what we see in the visions, as the great tree is cut down and Nebuchadnezzar is humiliated.

Daniel's name actually means 'God is my judge'. Changed to Belteshazzar it now appears to mean 'may Balat (Saturn) protect the king'. There is clearly some kind of play on words between this name and Belshazzar who is dubbed as a king, but actually never acceded to the throne. Belshazzar means 'Bel (Baal) protect the king'. The contrast between him and Daniel is quite stark; Belshazzar is terrified, with his knees knocking, but Daniel is supremely confident, wise and able to outline the future.

Hananiah, which was quite a common name in Judaism, and was actually the name of a tower in Jerusalem, means 'God has been gracious'. His name is changed to Shadrach, which means 'the command of Aku (the Moon god).' Mishael means 'a feeling or sensation of God' but this is changed to Meshach, 'who is what Aku is?' Azariah means 'God has helped me' but Abed Nego means 'servant of Nebo (or Nego, another god). We notice the alteration of B to G; is this an attempt at insulting the god Nebo?

All this name alteration ties in with the tenor of the first chapter, in which the king is trying to paganise the Jews. He alters their names and has a policy of introducing them to a new diet, which would have been anathema to the Jewish boys. The policy did not work; Daniel foresaw that the Jews would cling on to their distinctive culture in spite of all inducements to give in. This has been borne out by history.

Consistent with this is the way that the court eunuch, Ashpenaz, appears. We do not know exactly what this name means, but the Hebrew root ASHP means a conjuror or necromancer. As we find later in the book, the king thinks he can rely on such people to interpret his dreams, but it is Daniel who has all the answers. This is like saying, 'the pagan method is a failure; the Hebrew method is the only true way to wisdom.'

Although this symbolism works mainly on meanings of words, there is that substratum of mythology, which assumes we know something about the gods of Babylon. The Jews at that time would almost certainly have known about them.

People have wondered what is meant by 'gold of Uphaz' (10:5) but there is no certainty. My suggestion is that since the root letters of Uphaz (APZ) are very similar to OPR, this may be a corruption of Ophir. We suspect that the gold mines of Ophir were down in the south of Egypt or somewhere in Africa. It is possible that Daniel deliberately altered Ophir to Uphaz. Otherwise he could have heard it or seen it written in a dream and recorded it with a slight mistake.

More obviously, in Daniel 5:25, is a deliberate play on words, which only works in the Aramaic, and is largely lost in an English translation. Mene, mene, tekel, upharsin is the writing on the wall, which Daniel must have 'seen' in his vision. Mene means 'numbered, apportioned' but there is a hint here of a Mina, a very small coin, which uses the same root in Hebrew and Aramaic. Tekel means to weigh in the scales, but the root also implies TOKEL which means a shekel. Then we have Pharsin which means to break in half. It is full of implications. PRS implies half a mina, and also it is the root for Persia (PRS). The U on the start of the word means 'and', but having that makes Upharsin into a pun on gold of Uphaz; the 'in' on the end makes it a plural. So very cleverly, Daniel is saying, 'you are not even worth a halfpenny; your kingdom is doomed to be taken over by Persia.' The symbolism using small change in relation to the Babylonian empire about to collapse, is very apt.

Concluding remarks about Daniel

This book is an amazing document, full of symbolisms and mythological motifs. Clearly it stems from an age when high-powered visionary material was in fashion. It is on the same lines as Ezekiel and Enoch. Daniel is an excellent example of how mythology, with all its strong appeal in metaphors and imagery, can be made to apply to the future, which means it is eschatology. There is no doubting the conviction it has carried with people over the centuries. One person in particular must have read it and applied it to himself; namely Jesus. That verse in Daniel 7:13 is of great importance; 'and behold, with the clouds of heaven there came one like a son of man.' We recall that this crucial statement was the 'last straw' for the High Priests at the trial (Mark 14:61) when Jesus said, 'I am, and you will see the Son of Man sitting at the right hand of Power, and coming with the clouds of heaven.' They took that as Jesus committing blasphemy. In this way, Daniel is one of the great messianic prophets.

Footnotes for chapter 3, Daniel

1. The name Nebuchadrezzar spelt with an R is original. In the Babylonian it is Nabu-kurri-usur, which means Nabu protect the boundary. If we spell it with an N, the meaning is lost.

2. Aramaic became the lingua franca of the Persian empire, and persisted even with the Greek empires. It was the language that Jesus used. Hebrew is closely related to it.

3. Cyrus, the Persian, established his empire in 521 BC. He took a tolerant view of different religions and allowed exiled peoples to return home and rebuild their temples.

4. After the death of Alexander in Babylon, the oriental Greek kingdom split up between his generals. The Ptolemies ruled Egypt up to the Roman empire; the Seleucids ruled what

was left of the Persian empire to the north.

5.   The Colussus of Rhodes, one of the seven wonders of the ancient world, was a gigantic statue standing astride Rhodes harbour. Ships were able to pass underneath between its legs.

4

Greek Mythology

An obvious place to start with non-Biblical Mythology is the rich and extensive culture of Ancient Greece. It is hardly necessary to go into much detail about the gods, heroes and monsters, because there are many worthwhile descriptions already available in libraries and bookshops. With this corpus of material we move away very largely from Biblical thinking, but not entirely. The Hebrews did not approve of Greek culture and made a strong attempt at avoiding its influence; even so, with such a strong and fascinating folklore available it was difficult to exclude elements of it in the long term. The importance of Greek mythology lies in its ongoing influence. It seems possible that there a certain amount of exchange of ideas between Greek and semitic thought. There is no doubt that Roman culture was its main recipient; the Romans took it over lock stock and barrel and simply syncretised the whole thing, just altering a few names of gods. With the end of the Roman Empire, one might have thought that Greek mythology would have faded out too. Not so; with the Renaissance, there was another outburst of this culture superimposed on Biblical and Christian thinking. We have only to look at the iconic artwork of that period, the architectural magnificence, and drama such as Shakespeare to appreciate that Greek thinking was again dominating the scene. Teaching, in the great public schools and the grammar schools was dominated by the classics. Greek influence has continued up to the present day and is a factor in so many aspects of daily life now. It would be tedious to educe an entire list, but a few might be mentioned in passing. Narcissus, a springtime flower, Atlas, a book showing countries, the wedding ring, encircling the 'love vein', Alexander, a boy's name, the Zodiac, the facade of the British Museum, the word 'museum' itself, and one could go on endlessly. This is in contrast to Japanese mythology which has had no influence in Western Culture, at least not until the Second World War, and then only slightly.

This is enough to evidence the hold that Greek mythology has on people's minds to this day. The explanation must surely be that it resonates with something in people's minds. That does not mean that it is true; we do not have to believe in all those gods and giants. But it does connect with something in human nature. Sigmund Freud would probably have called it the **id**, and Jung certainly would. The whole thing forms a fascination for people, even if we know it is all make-believe.(1)

What about the Greeks themselves; did they think it was all imagination? That is a question which is hard to answer, and people have wondered about it. Did they take all those lurid stories literally, or was it assumed to be figurative? Was it on the same level as Aesop's fables? There are indications that some of the Romans took some elements of it completely literally and tried to imitate the gods. Caligula is a case in point; another one is Commodus. (2 &3) As mentioned before, it is quite likely that the Greeks did not really address themselves to this analytical question. They may have assumed that history and mythology were not really any different, in contrast to the way we think nowadays. It is far more instructive to bypass this issue and concentrate on what message the material is trying to tell us. This is why there is no need to relate an entire catalogue of lurid stories about gods and heroes; the approach taken here is to attempt to assess what the ancient poets were trying to say; was it a moral object lesson, or was it a depiction of human nature on a vast canvas, or was it a theological approach to tackle the deep questions of life, such as theodicy, human failure, and the love-hate relationship?

On the question of the literal truth, it is unlikely that the Greeks took everything completely literally in their mythology. We notice that many of the stories have variants, particularly the endings. There is no complete agreement on the process of creation. This may reflect stories coming from different parts of the Hellenic world. They may never have been harmonised since there was very little point in doing so. More likely, they were left with different details so that alternative lessons or morals could be drawn. By the 8th century BC the two poets, Homer and Hesiod had put the material into writing; before that all this material would have been circulated orally, but we all know that when poets take on a theme, they tend to adapt details to suit their agenda, just as much as historians do. On the other hand, there may have been aspects of this mythology which were seen as literally true. We are struck by the fact that many place names and areas of the Mediterranean world are related to the stories. The Pillars of Hercules, the Atlas Mountains, Knossos, Mycene, Athens, just to mention a few, The validation for the importance of Athens is seen in the way that Athena, the goddess of war, became the 'patron saint' of that town. By contrast, there is no attempt at sequencing or dating the stories. This must be because in those times, there was no datum point in history; that was to come with Alexander the Great and the Seleucid Kingdom, followed by the Romans with the founding of Rome. Before that, we have no firm idea of how far back these stories go and in what order. They may have been contemporaneous with the great Epics of Mesopotamia, in which we see a number of similar ideas. This suggests that there may have been some exchange of ideas. Another literal element in all this is the way that sacrifice is endemic in the Hellenic way of life. To omit sacrificing was seriously to invite disaster, and the gods were understood literally to be sustained by the offerings of animals. All the myths have a certain element of sacrifice included in them, and that is probably the most important literal factor in the whole thing.

What does 'myth' actually mean? The Greek word '**mythos**' has a wide range of meaning, but 'lie' or 'misapprehension' is not included in that range. 'A message by word of mouth, a speech, advice, command, order, purpose, a tale, a story, even a fable (such as with Aesop)'. We notice that the element of falsehood does not appear in this list. As far as scholarship is concerned nowadays, there is no precise definition of 'myth', but it seems to be divided into three main types; legends, folktales and so-called 'pure' myths. The prime example of legendary material comes in the Iliad and the Odyssey, both by Homer. It is a mistake to assume that this material is pure fiction. We have managed to identify and excavate places like Troy and Knossos which means there is no reason to doubt the main core of these accounts in historical terms. However, the poet loves to work in theological and mythological strands to enrich and embellish the stories. This helps us to understand how the Greeks understood themselves in relation to their gods and their world. When considering 'pure' myths, it was Hesiod with his **Theogony** who investigated the gods, creation and the coming of mankind down to his own world in the 8th century BC. It is thought this written material was aimed at the rulers in various royal cities and may not have been of much relevance to the villagers working on the land. As far as folk tales are concerned, these tended to be in prose or very easy poems and were aimed at the farm-labouring communities. These might be entertaining stories told round the camp-fire, with a simple moral or caution. It is typical of our thinking nowadays to categorise this material in this way, but the Greeks may never have made any such distinctions. The whole corpus must have had a considerable hold on their souls(4), in the same way that the early written Hebrew material came to be the ruling factor in Judaism. The difference was that Greek mythology never became ' scriptural' in the way that the Old Testament did. The Greeks had to wait for the New Testament to fill the gap and give them what we would call 'a Bible', and this was supported by the Septuagint (5) which was the Greek translation of the Old Testament.

The Greek understanding of God

Although this is not actually stated in the stories, the gods were almost always depicted as stark naked with their pudenda clearly on show. We can see this on the various vases unearthed by the archaeologists and the many statues. The same is true to some extent with the goddesses, except that some of them have a little modesty allowance and some are fully clad. The nymphs and nyads were always completely naked; nowadays this would be classed as erotica; in those days it would almost certainly be seen as symbolic of something. This is in complete contrast to the Hebrew understanding of God, namely YHWH. No depiction of him was ever supposed to be made, and clothing or nakedness was never an issue. What did the Greeks intend by this portrayal? It can be understood as seeing the god as virile, fecund and macho-masculine. Another way of seeing it is to say that the gods felt themselves to be innocent, they knew no shame or embarrassment, like little children. The goddesses, often more modest but not always, often displayed ample breasts which would indicate readiness for motherhood. It might also indicate that they knew a certain degree of embarrassment or shame, or even a degree of inferiority to the men. In the case of Athena with a helmet on her head, this would suggest a woman invading a man's activity, namely warfare; and with Artemis as a huntress. The myths have the gods, especially Zeus, being lecherous, murderous and vindictive.

Does this indicate that the menfolk normally went about naked and behaving like hooligans with the womenfolk? Did the humans model themselves on the gods and goddesses? We know that in the sports arenas, the men did compete completely naked in front of the general public. In that sense, they may have been trying to emulate divinities such as Apollo who were depicted in such terms. But in normal everyday terms, it is more likely that most people behaved modestly and in a civilised manner. So why were the gods seen as misbehaving? To read the stories, there is always the substratum that says that murder, adultery, rape, deception and theft are wrong, in spite of there being nothing analogous to the Ten Commandments. When the gods do misbehave, they usually have to face some sort of revenge or backlash from somewhere or someone. Is this saying, in a figurative way, that if you misbehave, you will have to face the consequences in the long term, very often in the form of poetic justice? Were the humans looking down on the gods as opposed to up to them, assuming them to be a collection of hooligans? Is it saying that there is one law for the human race but no law for the gods? Or is it saying that it is right for the gods but wrong for humans, in other words, a double standard?

None of these imponderables apply if we take the Hebrew theology of God which says that there is only one, possibly accompanied by angels, and since he owns the world – 'the earth is the Lord's and the fullness thereof' (6)– to talk of murder, theft or adultery is meaningless. That solves the problem all in one go. Neither can there be any conflict in heaven, except to say that in later theological thought there was a fallen angel called Satan, but essentially the one God is control of everything. The Greek pattern in which there are swarms of gods emanating from Zeus and other first generation deities, allows for perpetual conflict in the skies with nasty vendettas and cruelties being perpetrated. Was this a reflection of what was happening in the world of men? Or was it an excuse for contentious behaviour? Or was it a sad admission that the world was out of control and a nasty place to live in?

What was the attitude of the gods towards humanity? For most of them it was a matter of indifference; the gods could influence the outcome of anything including a war, but were inclined to swap sides on a whim, as we see in the siege of Troy. Zeus, the king of the gods, did not like the human race at all and did not wish them to receive enlightenment and civilization. Prometheus took pity on the wretched state of mankind, and stole some of the fire from Hephaiston's blacksmith forge and used it to enlighten mankind.

Zeus was furious and had Prometheus crucified on a rock as torture. The play by Aeschylus, Prometheus Bound, (7) goes into poetic elaboration on this theme. In general terms there is nothing of the love of God as shown in the Bible; even more, there is no concept of God making a covenant with certain selected people, on the basis of a deep loving commitment. The gods of Olympus were terrifying, cruel, whimsical and unprincipled. This is an attitude seen in many people today who have not been given a close mystical relationship with the one true God.

Since monotheism was far from their minds, there was, however, some kind of 'pecking order' of the gods, some sort of stratification, which relates to the process of creation. We begin with Chaos, some kind of yawning chasm, or 'the egg of the world'. From this came the 'big four'; Eros, Gaia, Tartarus and Nyx/Erebus. Eros, with his bow and arrow, not only symbolised erotic love, but also the entire reproductive system. Gaia, the Earth, the self-reproducing principle, and she produced Uranus, the sky and Pontus, the waters. Tartarus was not at all productive and was the 'sin-bin' for all those who were too dangerous to live on the earth. Nyx was the night, who with Erebus produced Hemera, the Day. It is interesting to see how much of this ties in with early Genesis, and also differs.

From this point it becomes increasingly complicated, but Zeus, the king of the gods is only a fourth generation god, being a son of Cronos. The whole thing is confused with brothers marrying sisters, gods producing Titans, giants, nymphs, fates and the snake Typhon. One wonders how seriously the Greeks took all this or was it a mild joke to them? Nowadays we see incestuous unions and irregular relationships such as Zeus had with the ladies, as strictly unacceptable. But did the Greeks see it in such terms? Possibly they saw it as inescapable, just as the Judaeo-Christian world had to ask themselves, if Adam and Eve had two sons, how did they manage for wives; did they have to marry their sisters? It is the same old question, if you start with just one source for everything, how does it proliferate without doing a certain amount of cheating?

But the antics of the Greek gods could become really lewd and crude. The 'birth' of Athena is a good example. Zeus was suspicious that his first wife, Metis, would bear a son who would overthrow him one day. So Zeus swallowed Metis, who was pregnant, and forgot about the matter until one day he awoke with a splitting headache. Hephaistos was requested to come and crack his skull and find out the problem. When this was done, out jumped Athena in full armour. Many of the gods and divinities were not born by normally accepted means. Athena was flying towards Athens when Hephaistos attempted to indulge in sexual harassment, but she fended him off with a rock. His semen fell down on to the Acropolis and the future king of Athens, Erichthonius, was born. It is interesting to see how the same process appears in Japanese mythology, in which the Mikado and various local rulers are actually the product of various gods. In this we see the bridge between divinity and humanity; or is it the self-promotion of humanity to semi-divinity, which would give one extra authority in the halls of government?

One really lewd episode concerns Cronos, a third generation god, who caught his father Uranus in bed with his mother, Gaia. He took an adamantine sickle and castrated Uranus. The severed genitals fell into the waters and so seeded Aphrodite (Diana) the sex-goddess. Cronos knew that retribution would come upon him, which meant he had a conscience about the matter, and wanted to prevent the next generation of gods from doing the same to him. He considered forcing the babies back inside their mothers, but a better plan was to swallow every baby as soon as he was born. Rhea, his 'wife' grew tired of losing one baby after another; so one day she wrapped a stone in swaddling clothes and let Cronos swallow that. The real baby, Zeus, was smuggled away by Gaia, his grandmother, and raised in secret. This may sound outrageous to modern ears, but we need to consider the symbolism in it; it is true that Time (Cronos) swallows up everything in due course. But Time, like a machine, can be manipulated and fooled, like an unreliable clock. So Cronos was just as neurotic and suspicious as any earthly ruler in those days (and some now). As for Uranus, demasculated, this serves to remind us that powerful as we may be, it only takes a slight incident at the wrong moment, and everything alters, fundamentally. Powerful figures appear in politics and religion, and then Time sweeps them away.

How do we cope with such anthropomorphic crudities? Can we see in this that humanity is incapable of understanding the divine in anything but human metaphors? Since we have no idea of what the world of the spirit is really like (the Spiritualists may make such claims, but how much of this is mirage and self-deception?), we can only describe the divine in human terms. The same tendency is seen in the Old Testament, where the actions of God are described in much the same terms, but nothing like as lewd as in Greece. Even then, the incident of the Burning Bush in Exodus indicates that God is not to be described in human terms. The phrase **I am that I**

am and the name **YHWH** itself lift the awareness of God above simple human canons of thought. Did the Greeks have the same awareness that the gods were indescribable? We notice that there is another element, not found in Hebrew thinking, that of the heavenly bodies being identified with divinities.

One other element in the theology of ancient Greece, is the way that gods or divinities were promoted to become astral constellations in the night sky. Obviously it could only pertain to the skies about the Mediterranean world. The Southern Cross for example would have been unknown to them; it was known to the Incas, who saw in those configurations the same sort of significance. So for instance, Orion, Bootes, the Corona Borealis, to mention a few, were elements of Greek mythology immortalised in the sky. The planets too, which were known at that time, were all seen as gods, such as Mars, Venus, Mercury (Hermes) Saturn and Jupiter. Uranus, Neptune and Pluto were not known then, having only recently been discovered, and yet mythological names have been given to them. This indicates that Greek mythology, far from being dead, is still very much alive in people's minds and that includes the scientists. It also indicates that the Greeks were not just seeing the activities of their gods as symbolic, but also impinging on people's daily lives. Their gods were not only anthropomorphic but also had that element of transcendence as heavenly bodies.

The Greek understanding of humanity

We have already seen that the dividing line between humanity and divinity is not a particularly crystal clear one. The production of gods seems easily to slide into the appearance of the human race. Interestingly the menfolk seem to appear some time before the ladies. Zeus would only tolerate humans if they were to be kept as nasty, mean and brutish, but it was Prometheus who gave them inspiration and a civilised approach to life, in other words, what we now call the human psyche or consciousness. Zeus was furious and decreed that a thing called 'woman' should be devised, to be a thorn in the side of the men! What a sarcastic view of womanhood: somewhat different from the motive for providing Adam with Eve! However, theologically, what it means is that humans have got that element of the divine in them, that eternal soul which is indestructible.

In general terms, Hesiod saw the life of mankind in terms of a series of ages. First came the Golden Age, populated by men. It is not explained how they managed without wives. Everything was lovely; no problems, all at ease and enjoyment. This came to an end, though there are varying explanations for this (this incidentally is another indication of how the Greeks may not have taken these stories too literally). The main explanation is that Pandora (the equivalent of Eve) was so inquisitive that she could not resist taking a peep inside the urn she had been given; it was 'Pandora's box'. All the evils of the world flew out, leaving just one thing, 'hope' behind.

This ushered in the Age of Silver. Violence, treachery and sacrilege became normal. Zeus decided this age was a failure and removed them from the earth. It does not say quite how he did that, but we can imagine him hurling his thunderbolts around.

This was followed by the Age of Bronze. It was called Bronze because the warriors never removed their bronze armour, since they were perpetually at war. Mars, the god of war, was having a lovely time; he was probably delighted that the humans were intent on destroying themselves. That is a comment that could apply to us in these times. It was then that Zeus arranged the Flood, and Deucalion (the Greek version of Noah) built an ark and survived to see the Age of Iron. He had also survived the end of the Age of Silver. In an account remarkably similar to the Biblical story, the ark landed on a mountain, the identity of which was a matter of dispute. But it was Prometheus who had advised him to build an ark. From Deucalion and his wife came the next instalment of humanity which ushered in the Heroic Age and of the great poets themselves. They felt that the world was complete even if it was characterised by greed and violence. There is the substratum of thought that if everyone put their minds to it, the Golden Age could be restored.

This pattern of thought still influences us today. We are accustomed to thinking that the Stone Age, the Bronze Age and the Iron Age came in a strict series, and now we are in the Nuclear Age. Of course, the reality is, from the anthropological point of view, that these ages did not come in simultaneously all over the world. One example of that is that when the Spaniards (who were firmly into the Iron Age, or Steel Age) landed in the Americas, they found the natives were still in the Stone Age, in spite of having gold and silver. So these ages were not as simple and discrete as one might have imagined.

It is noticeable that the same scheme using metals appears in the Book of

Daniel in the Old Testament. The passage in question is Daniel 2:31-45. In the King's dream described by Daniel, there is a great image; the head was of gold, the breast and arms of silver, its belly and thighs of bronze and its legs of iron. In verse 33 the scheme is slightly altered as the feet become part iron, part clay. This scheme is symbolic of the successive kingdoms down to the divided Greek kingdoms around the time of Judas Maccabeus, an outline that comes over several times in the rest of the book, but using different metaphors.

The question must arise, did Daniel know of Hesiod's scheme of ages? Those who think (8) Daniel was written after the events, as a prophecy after the event, in other words a fraud, will easily conclude that his scheme of metals is some sort of imitation of Hesiod's idea, which was doubtless traditional Greek folklore. On the other hand, if Daniel is to be taken as a genuine prophet seeing the future just before the Exile, that would just allow Hesiod to have taken the idea from Daniel. Even then, if this scheme were assumed to be traditional Greek thought going back many centuries, Daniel could still have taken the idea from that. What could he be saying by using this scheme, with a slight modification? He is saying in effect that all the elaborate ideas of the Hellenic world, stretching back to the alleged Golden Age, are all going to come to nothing. A stone is hurled at the image and it is shattered to pieces; then the stone becomes a great mountain. This means that the Graeco-Roman thought-system will be broken down and God's true mountain (mount Zion) will dominate the picture. In other words, all this mythology will be seen for what it is, a confused mess, and the word of the one true God will be the correction for it.

Another aspect of the Greek view of humanity is the way in which humans and animals are strangely blended together. We have satyrs who were mostly humanoid but had horses' tails and enlarged penises. They were all male as opposed to the nymphs who were all female. Gradually the satyrs lost their equine qualities and became goat-footed and were termed Panes, complete (9)with horns on their heads. They were regarded as lower than humans; even so, some of them could outdo humans in musical skill and also in the consumption of wine. There was also a race of Centaurs, a horse with a human head. They were powerful and passionate and dangerous, unlike the satyrs. Chiron who was a good centaur, had been produced by Cronos seducing a nymph. Centaurs are influential now as the sign of Sagittarius, the archer.

Even more lurid and terrifying is the Minotaur, half man with a bull's head, who was confined to the labyrinth under the palace at Knossos. He was fed by a supply of boys and girls from Athens, every nine years. It was Theseus who posed as one of the boys, entered the labyrinth with a ball of string so that he could not get lost, found the Minotaur and killed him.

Another strange but recognisable creature was the Sphinx; this was a lion's body with a woman's head. It lived near Thebes and would only eat one if one could not find the answer to a riddle; if one did answer the riddle the Sphinx was bound to kill itself. The riddle was; 'It walks on four legs in the morning, two in the day, and three in the evening. What is it?' Oedipus, who had decided to defeat this monster, gave the correct answer; 'a baby crawls on four legs, grows into a man using two legs, and then in old age uses a walking stick, which is three legs.' The Sphinx, in disgust, threw itself off a cliff. Of course, the sphinx is not just a Greek idea; the Egyptians constructed a massive one by the major pyramids. This may indicate that the Greeks borrowed the idea from Egypt.

But what do we make of this half-human-half-beast idea? It can hardly be taken literally. This is of course judging it by 21st century standards of logic; the Greeks may have seen it in quite a different light. For us, what symbolism does it convey? Is it a hint that humanity is actually related to the animals, in which case, the theory of Evolution is not such a modern idea after all. We can see the Minotaur as a man with the augmented virility of a bull? The centaur we can see as a human with horse-like qualities, such as wild and uncontrollable until tamed. The satyrs, being less of a threat, were obsessed with sex and the nymphs and this is another comment on human nature. Perhaps the whole concept is some sort of comment on the worst aspects of humanity.

The symbolism becomes a little more obvious when we consider the so-called 'metamorphoses' in which humans turn into plants or animals. Narcissus is the best example; the handsome boy who was obsessed with his own reflection and so turned into a springtime flower. But he is not the only such case. There is Daphne who was chased by Apollo, and to escape his undue attentions, was changed into a laurel bush; so Apollo made a laurel wreath to go on his head (10) and so it became the winner's crown at the games. Also there was the handsome boy, Adonis, who turned into a red anemone. There is also Syrinx who was chased by Pan; she turned into a reed-bed and so Pan made her into his pipes. There is Echo who was too talkative and so was doomed by Hera to repeat only the last few words of what anyone said. We may be seeing in this that there is a much closer connection between humanity and the natural world.

The myths also play tricks with the human form itself. There were three brothers, the Hecatoncheires, each having 100 hands and fifty heads. This reminds us of elements in Hindu mythology. There is someone called Hermaphrodites, who was two genders at once, a woman with a penis. Such persons do appear nowadays, but rarely; they are called hermaphrodites. The opposite occurs with the god Dionysos, the god of wine, renamed as Bacchus by the Romans; he was a man but with female breasts. His femininity became increasingly accentuated as time went on. Can we see in this a notion in which the unity of mankind is being emphasised? It is also an indication that Greek mythology was not set in stone; it developed gradually.

Another important element is the factor of augmentation or exaggeration. Many of the monsters are made to be deliberately frightening. There are giants, Titans, who are capable of hurling whole mountains at the Hecatoncheires. There is a huge snake called Typhon, having 100 heads which can speak with different voices. Another snake called Ladon with 100 heads is matched by the Hydra with countless heads; when Heracles chopped one off, two more grew in its place. There was Python, killed by Apollo, and Echidna, half woman and half snake. Snakes were not the only terrifying creatures; there was the Nemean Lion, and Cerberus the dog with three heads and a mane of snakes, guarding the entrance to Hades. Also Geryon the herdsman with three heads and his dogs with two heads each of which are defeated by Heracles. What would be the symbolism in these multi-heads? Does it indicate great intelligence or multi-tasking? It might indicate someone who cannot make his mind up, or is in disagreement with himself. At the very least, it reflects the human natural fear of serpents, whether venomous or not, symbolising evil. In many cases, the god or demi-god comes in to slay the monster and relieve the world of overwhelming evil. It also reminds us of the Garden of Eden where the serpent was not exaggerated but was the cause of human downfall. Augmentation is in general a very important feature of mythologies in many parts of the world. It is a technique designed to frighten people and give heavy emphasis to an important message. At the least this is another indication that one need not take these myths too literally; the literal element is the theological message contained in the stories, the defeat of evil. The most graphic example of this is the Revelation of St.John.(11)

Messianism in Greek mythology

One might fairly ask, if the Hebrew tradition had an idea of a Messiah coming to solve all our problems, is such a notion present in Greek thought? It would be fair to say that the answer would be 'yes' in two distinct ways. Firstly, the myths are characterised by three major champions who are partially gods but with a human element. Heracles with his twelve labours is the most obvious, but there was also Perseus and Theseus, whose actions were very similar. There were other less important champions, ridding the human race of one problem after another. We notice that in the case of Heracles, his endeavours awarded him immortality. As his funeral pyre was about to be lit, he was assumed into heaven; was this idea taken from the Hebrew tradition, for instance the assumption of Elijah? (12) As part of his twelfth labour, Heracles has to go to Hades to kidnap Cerberus and also because he killed his wife and children; he needs to be purified and then after 1000 years, begin a new life, like so many others who went wrong in this life. Does this remind us of Karma as in the Hindu theology?

The other element in Greek messianism is the concept of **Theios Aner** which means literally, 'divine man'. This is clearly not a part of mythology. It refers to people like Moses, Abraham, Elijah and other worthies of the Old Testament times; it is clearly not just one person but anyone who could be classed as a man of god. This is, incidentally, evidence that the Greeks knew of the Hebrew tradition and borrowed from it. A good example of this would be how the sacrifice of Isaac appears to be adapted into the story in which Artemis, seeing that Agamemnon was about to sacrifice his daughter Iphigeneia in order to induce a decent wind in order to sail for Troy, the goddess intervened and substituted a deer at the last minute. They did not get as far as including Jesus of Nazareth in their thinking because the main thrust of Hellenism, and its system of thought, was over and the Romans were in the ascendency.

Moral Conscience in Greek thought

With so much behaviour which we would call outrageous, whether of gods or of men, it is worth asking if they had any conscience. In spite of there being no trace of such a thing as an apology or penitence, the answer must be yes. There is a god called Nemesis, who organises retribution on anyone who commits an offence. This ties in with what is called the Neoptolemus principle which means that whatever one does, one can expect the same to be done back to one.(13) This is poetic way of saying, 'love your neighbour as yourself'. We see this idea heavily emphasised in Deuteronomy 28, and again, this may be a case of the Old Testament influencing Greek thought. Also there is a god called Oath, who strikes one when one swears a falsehood; in other words, it will rebound on one. The concept of 'poetic justice' may not be an original Greek notion; it may have originated in the Hebrew tradition, since Moses and his system of thought almost certainly predated Hesiod. The Furies, produced when Uranus' genitals were chopped off, cause one to be haunted by the thought of murdering one's own kith and kin. This kind of conscience applies to men and gods alike. We note that Heracles had to go to Hades to be purified because he had murdered his wife and children.

Theodicy in Greek thought

The question of why there is any evil in the world is not too difficult to cope with in Greek thought. After all with gods like Uranus, who hated their own offspring, and Zeus who had no liking for humanity, the question would be, 'why does anything nice happen in life?' There is a sense in Greek thought that one's good or bad fortune is decided from the skies: the Fates; Clotho, Lachesus and Atropos, apportion one's fate, good or bad and there is not much one can do to alter it. The myth of Pandora's box (actually it was an urn with a lid on) is the Greek explanation for why there are so many evils in the world. This is a poetic way of saying that female curiosity is the basic cause of all our problems. But the one thing that did not escape was hope; this is an indication that in spite of all the negative feeling coming from the skies, mankind can have a glimmering of success or happiness. As far as love is concerned, the myths are only concerned with the eroticism of promiscuity in the skies; there is nothing about **agape** (which approximates to the Hebrew **Hesedh**)(14), that deep committed love that God displays for his chosen people. This was something that the Judaeo-Christian tradition emphasised and which must have seemed very strange to the Greeks before New Testament times.

The Greek world view

The Greeks assumed, as everyone else at that time, that the world was a three-tiered system, heaven, earth, and the underworld. Hades was where almost everyone went when they died and it was like the Hebrew Sheol, a shadowy place where spirits hung about hopelessly.(15) Much depended on whether one's funeral rites were correctly performed; it was seen as particularly harsh on the deceased to omit giving them a proper funeral. Tartarus was even deeper down, a sort of sin-bin for defeated monsters and irredeemably nasty people. If you were very good, you would ascend to the Elysian Fields, which sounds somewhat analogous to the Hindu Nirvana. As one died, one was taken by Hermes to the river Styx and faced with Cerberus the ferocious dog. A couple of coins would ensure that Charon, the ferryman, would take one over into Hades. One might be there for 1000 years, being purified in preparation for one's next life. Escaping from the underworld was seldom done, but not impossible. Orpheus wanted to rescue his wife, Euridice from Hades and she was allowed to follow him back to earth, as long as he did not look back at her; he took a sly peep to see if she was there and that was the end of that attempt. One can see the similarity of this account to that of Lot's wife, only she was turned into a pillar of salt. If one drank from the river Lethe, one would forget all about one's previous life; if one drank from the river Mnemosyne, one would be able to recall something of one's previous life. This is one of the issues that the Hindus have, namely recollecting matters from a previous life. It was never an issue for the Hebrews since they did not have any idea of karma, a theological question that still gives cause for thought in the Christian faith to this day.

Mythology sliding into history

We have already seen how various cities in the Hellenistic world managed to give themselves validation by claiming a certain divinity as its 'patron saint'. Something similar happens at the end of the Trojan War. Although the Iliad, which describes the siege of Troy, has many mythical features, we now know that there is almost certainly a core of historical truth in the account of the Trojan war. As Troy goes up in flames, certain survivors take ship and set off to find somewhere else to start again. After various adventures, Aeneas had a revelation that they should go to Italy. So, after more battles and encounters, the first Romans were actually the rump of the Trojans intermingled with the local Latins. From there, we slide gently into the story of Romulus and Remus and the actual founding of Rome; this is where a datum point appears, namely the AUC dating for the foundation of Rome, 21st April 753 BC. The fall of Troy was calculated to have been 300 years earlier.(16) It is not realistic to think we can disentangle myth, legend and actual history, but we can see the process at work; that attempts at describing one's origins begin with exaggerated and fantastic ideas about gods and a whole array of semi-divine entities. Gradually it slides into everyday realities. But we can see what is going on in people's minds; how do we validate the Roman Empire? Why have they the necessary authority to take over the whole of the Mediterranean world, including Greece and Asia Minor? The reason is, that the Greeks had resorted to underhand methods to destroy Troy, and the Trojans had the high moral ground, and they were the first Romans. This is another subtle example of poetic justice.

We see the same process at work in Genesis, where myth and legend gently slide into historical realities with the actions of Abraham in Genesis 14. The justification for Abraham's authority is done differently; there are lists of ancestors leading back to Noah (the Hebrew version of Deucalion), and before that, back to Enoch and Adam. In addition to that, God promises Abraham's descendants the land of Israel, which is the mythical side of the justification for taking the land.

We notice that the wanderings of the Trojans to find a new location, which is mostly described in the Odyssey by Homer, (taking 300 years), is to some extent mirrored in the Acts of the Apostles by St.Luke. We see Paul in the first missionary journeys going all through Asia Minor (Trojan territory), Northern Greece, Athens, Malta and eventually to Rome. This is not to say that the Acts of the Apostles is legendary, still less mythical, but it is an interesting example of how mytho-legend can come into historical terms, as a sort of fulfilment programme. Is St.Luke, in effect, saying that the ancient stories about the Greeks are finding reality at last as the Gospel is being brought to Rome?

How do we see Greek Mythology in terms of modern social and political motives? We can say that tribal and national identity is very important for a people, just as family cohesion is. The myths have the effect of giving the Greeks a kind of rationale, a sense of purpose, a feeling of being special. The same is true with the myths of early Genesis, in that they give the Jewish faith a firm basis and raison d'etre. Every race or nationality has some kind of myth as its starting point. The Greek one happens to be a lot more elaborate, lurid and extensive than others. This may be an indication that the Greeks thought of themselves as the most important people on earth. In this way, with the Romans taking over their system of myth, including the idea that the first Romans were actually Trojans, we can see how the Roman Empire could imagine itself to be the greatest thing ever; culturally, politically and militarily superior to anything else before or after. In this we see the importance of myth for every version of civilisation. It is interesting that in historical times, every empire that has arisen, has borrowed extensively from the Graeco-Roman material. This would be particularly true for the British ascendency, with its fixation with Britannia, who looks uncannily like Athena with that war helmet! (17)

Greek Mythology and astrology

People's attitudes vary enormously on this subject; horoscopes, birth signs and predictions based on the stars. Some take it very seriously, others are mildly interested and many regard it as ridiculous. There is no doubt, though, that this is a major strand coming from Greek mythology right into the present day. It is thought that this idea goes back to 3000 BC in ancient Babylon. They, it is thought, were the first to work out something which we now call the Zodiac. They had different names for the twelve segments of the year. The Greeks, it would seem, took the idea over and gave the signs of the Zodiac different names. The idea also went eastwards to India and they too had their own list of names and procedures for making predictions. How far this coincided with Hindu thinking would be a good question. But in Greece there is no doubt that the Zodiac was closely related to the astral constellations and gods of their mythological system.

To take a much simplified view of its workings, the sun, as it rises at the vernal equinox, is in conjunction with Aries or Mars. This gives us the start of their year. As the year progresses, other planets or constellations are seen in conjunction with the rising sun, for instance Saggitarius in late Autumn. From this, the year was divided into four seasons, each with three months and each with its own Zodiac sign. These signs were thought to govern one's future and personality; it was one's birth that was significant, as opposed to one's death. The Romans took this system of thought over and took it very seriously; perhaps more seriously than the Greeks did. As time went on, the Jews, who were supposed not to involve themselves in such matters, began to take an interest. Zodiacs began to appear on the mosaics of synagogue floors. A full discussion with technical details is not appropriate at this point, but there are many useful works which do go into the intricacies of astrology if one wished to delve into such matters.

During the so-called Dark Ages, this kind of thinking hardly disappeared. We know that the mediaeval alchemists were deeply involved with the Zodiac. Doctors too, with their blood-letting, would time their treatments in accordance with the Zodiac. To us now, this seems extraordinary, but we must remember that they were living in a different world, where the sciences as we know them now, were in their infancy. Before we start sneering, let us just remember that for all our clever attempts at science, whether it be astronomy or astrology, or medicine, people in ten centuries time may well be laughing at us for our clumsy attempts in these matters.

How much of this conditions our procedures nowadays? Firstly, the financial year runs from 1st April which is approximately the first month of the Zodiac year. New year's day was for a long time related to the vernal equinox. At another stage it went to the autumn equinox and only recently with the Gregorian calendar did it come to be January 1st.

With our investigations into astronomy, it is interesting that very often new discoveries are given a name which is derived from Greek mythology. So the planets Uranus, Neptune and Pluto, for instance, which were unknown in the ancient world and do not fit in with the Zodiac, have been given names derived from Greek and Roman gods. These are not the only such examples. Our nearest star, Alpha Centauri has been given a Greek name.

As an indication of how much hold the Zodiac has on people, there are various popular publications which regularly give people an indication as to what will happen to them in the coming days. There is Foulsham's almanac regularly published which gives an over-view of the year ahead. One wonders how or why these matters persist in an age where scientific and so-called rational thinking is the dominant feature. For astrology to have survived for 5000 years, one would have to say that there must be some element of truth it in somewhere, even if most of it is nonsense.

One might be surprised to learn that astrology was a strong influence on one particular party during World War 2. It is claimed, probably with a lot of truth in it, that Hitler and his entourage allowed Zodiacal factors to condition their most important initiatives. We learn that Himmler was engrossed in that kind of thinking. The Allies realised this and enlisted occultists to work the same method against the Nazis. (18) There will be a chapter on this later (chapter 7).

But what it does demonstrate is the hold that Greek mythology has on our culture to this day. It must have been a very powerful influence, even if it was, by our standards, a lot of nonsense.

One example of a Constellation with Myths

There are many myths in Greek lore, concerning the stars and planets. I have chosen Orion because it is one of the easiest constellations to be seen in the night sky and its shape is quite distinctive. It consists of 17 stars of varying intensity. There are over 50 constellations described by the Greeks, but only 12 of them are included in the Zodiac. Orion is not included.

The myth attached to him is as follows. Orion was the son of Poseidon and Euryale and became renowned as a great hunter and champion not unlike Theseus and Perseus. So he had a skill for removing vicious beasts which were a problem for ordinary humans. He also had little idea of self control and had a habit of raping women, such as Merope. He became involved with Artemis, the huntress, with a certain degree of romance. She killed him in the end and placed him in the night sky. Another idea is that he was killed by a scorpion stinging him, which explains why Scorpio is placed near to him in the sky. Orion is credited with being able to run across the waves.(19)

The same idea comes in the New Testament, when Jesus walks on the water. This is not the only possible link between Christian and Greek mythological thought. We notice that Jesus is not running but walking, and also that he is real flesh as opposed to a mythical person. But in a way, the New Testament passage is saying in effect, that our God, Jesus is not a figure of mythology, but a real person who can really walk on water and prevent someone else from sinking.

Greek Mythology influencing modern science

We are accustomed to using many of the symbols in Mathematics, which have been derived from the Greek alphabet. Also many of the basic processes in Mathematics, such as pi, and phi and much of the geometry we now use, originated with the ancient Greek mathematicians. But this is not mythology. (20)

A good example of Greek mythology invading modern science comes with the concept of 'Gaia'. This is largely to do with the thinking of James Lovelock but is not confined to his books by any manner of means. What do we mean by 'Gaia'? The Greeks began with Chaos, which is strictly speaking a god, but four gods emerged from Chaos; these were, Eros, Tartarus, Gaia and Erebus (Nyx). From these four all the other gods were derived. Why focus on Gaia? She was the earth goddess who needed Eros to fertilise her to produce everything in the natural world. The Greeks focussed more on the later generations of gods, Zeus, Apollo, Athena and Aphrodite, but Lovelock bases his thinking on Gaia. She is seen as the earth with a power and force of her own, a personality who takes badly to being abused. It is almost like talking about 'Mother Nature' but not quite. Lovelock avoids mentioning God until the last few pages of his book, and does not really relate God to Gaia, which is rather strange.

The relevance of all this is the basic concern at present on the subject of global warming. To summarise very briefly, Lovelock is deeply concerned about the emission of carbon dioxide and other greenhouse gases into the atmosphere; this, if not corrected somehow, is thought to increase the earth's temperature and eventually ruin civilisation on this planet. His answer is to leave out fossil fuels and other methods of producing electricity, and embark on nuclear power, specifically the fusion method. This, he claims, will be far more efficient, safe and environmentally friendly. It is easy to get completely carried away by his arguments; in fact, a sense of panic could easily be derived from his thoughts. We have to recall that there are other experts whose views on the matter are not quite so extreme or worrying.

The basic assumption here is that the earth is getting warmer and this is being caused by humanity over-exploiting the world's resources. There is very little consideration given to other possible causes. One such possibility, which Lovelock only touches on slightly, is that the earth may be coming a little nearer to the Sun. No one seems to have any comment to make on this suggestion and indeed it would be difficult to calculate our distance from the Sun in exact terms and also how much it may vary in its orbiting. We are at the stage where we are only just becoming aware of the delicate balancing of gravities between the Sun, the planets in the solar system and their satellites. One could suggest that it would only take a slight variation in the gravitational attractions in the Solar System to produce the effect that we are now seeing; that of variations in climate. The Ice Ages which we know have taken place could all have been caused by an alteration in the Earth's distance from the Sun. If this is true, then there is nothing we can do about it, and to try to interfere with the gravitational delicacy of the Solar System might cause all manner of worse problems.

Lovelock talks in terms of gigantic sunshades erected in space and other weird ideas, but this may be pure science fiction and completely unrealistic. He also talks of amassing carbon dioxide and tucking it away in repositories, but this again may be well beyond us.

Beneath it all is the basic notion that the earth is not just an inert lump of rock but a living Soul which objects to being exploited and will in due course exact revenge. He even draws in the Greek god Nemesis, the element of revenge, to complete the thought. He mentions at times the concept that the Earth is a self-correcting system. This notion is almost certainly a truism; that whatever pollution, imbalance, and misuse of the natural resources has taken place, somehow 'Gaia' manages to correct the balance. This is a concept that ought to be receiving a lot more attention at this time. In theological terms, this concept of Gaia is in effect another version of Pantheism.

Another assumption heavily emphasised in his work, is that mankind is the enemy of Gaia. This was not always the case; in primitive times, he assumes, humanity lived with nature, not against it. Now, it seems we are bringing things to a crisis level with overexploitation of resources. He even goes as far as to say that the world is overpopulated and cannot cope with so many people. How strange that the prognostications of Thomas Malthus should now re-emerge in our own times! What a shame that he does not consider that humanity might still, inadvertently, be carrying out the intentions of Gaia. One such possibility is that all the carbon locked up under the ground, could be coming up to fulfil some kind of purpose, of which we are unaware.

It is interesting that the assumption behind the 'Gaia' theory is very close to Shamanism and also the Japanese concept of 'kami' (which is another mythological assumption). This involves the idea that each physical feature, living or inert, has some kind of spirit living in it. In this sense, the Gaia concept can be seen as a latter day Shamanistic idea that the earth itself has a soul, another version of Pantheism.

The other aspect of these thoughts is that of fear. This too relates to Greek mythology, for all those gods, especially Zeus, used to terrify the humans. They were seen as unpredictable, whimsical and often nasty-minded. How close this is to the Gaia concept as seen in Lovelock's works! It is also further evidence of the hold that Greek mythology has on people's minds to this day, and that includes the scientists.

The Biblical answer to these matters is to some extent mythological but not entirely. If we look at Genesis 8-9 we see that the Covenant of Noah has God categorically promising that seedtime and harvest will never fail and that he will never again curse the ground. God takes into account that mankind is evil, careless and stupid but makes allowances. This is a fundamental element of faith for Christians, Jews and Moslems; that God will maintain the natural processes of the earth regardless. Of course, if one does not believe this, then one will go into a panic over alleged global warming. Another indicator of God's goodwill on the subject of resources comes in Deuteronomy 8:9. There is clearly promised that there will be ironstone and copper ore available in the Promised Land, in addition to all the crops that could be grown. The inference from this is that all those natural resources are deliberately provided by the Almighty, which implies that we do not have to feel guilty about digging out coalmines and drilling for oil. In addition to this, the laws of Moses make provision for the Jubilee year, in which the land will have a rest from producing food. The implication from this is that the ground is there to keep us fed, but must not be over-exploited. Until recently, farmers used to give their fields a three year rotation, so that every bit of land would lie fallow and recover its strength. Nowadays, farmers expect the land to go on producing crops by applying chemicals. The wisdom of this is already being questioned.

So the Bible does have something relevant to say about our present circumstances.

Greek Mythology and modern fim-making

A recent film production by Jonathan Liebesman, The Wrath of the Titans, is almost entirely dependant on Greek mythology. Many of the well known names mentioned before are worked into the story, but the plot appears to be a complete modern invention. Perseus, who is one of the great champions of this system of thought, is renowned for defeating monsters. In the film he slays a two-headed dragon and various other giants. He is half human; half god. When offered the chance to be a god, he declines the offer because he wants to care for his son who is human.

It is interesting that the main gods such as Zeus, Andromeda and Poseidon are portrayed as remarkably human. Zeus looks just like a reasonable old man; this is quite a contrast to the way he is described in the ancient myths. Hades and Hephaistos are much tamer and more like humans than one would expect. Some of the conversations they have with Perseus are quite sensitive, emotional and intense. This forms a complete contrast with the scenes of extreme violence and horror when Perseus fights the monsters. These scenes are enhanced by the virtual reality mode which might frighten many people.

The substratum of the plot is explained by Zeus early in the drama. The humans are not praying to the gods as they used to, and the result of this is that the gods are losing power. The walls of Tartarus are collapsing (although this is not properly explained). We can see in this a thinly-veiled criticism of modern life, in which religious devotion is nowhere near as prominent as it used to be. The inference is that we should begin to take our religion much more seriously. We notice the unspoken Christianising element in this. The ancient Greeks would have said something to the effect that humans are not sacrificing to the gods as much as they used to, and gods need this to sustain them. Now this motif is modified to become that people are not praying to the gods. Also we notice there is the notion of 'the Fall' worked into the film, something which would not have been included by the ancient Greeks. Zeus and his fellow gods appear to be very much Christianised, and Perseus is much more akin to some sort of Messiah, even if he is a violent one. Also, Perseus cares for his son, an idea that would almost certainly have been missing in ancient Greece. The film comes over as a much Christianised version of Greek mythology. The motif of a champion being 'the saviour the world' is very close to a Christian concept.

Footnotes for chapter 4

1. Chapter 19 goes into detail about Freud and Jung in relation to mythology.

2. Caligula (Gaius) had illusions of grandeur and claimed to be a god. (AD 54)

3. Commodus (AD 130) claimed to be Apollo.

4. It is claimed that Alexander the Great kept a copy of the Iliad by his bedside.

5. The Septuagint, the Greek translation of the Old Testament, so called because it took a team of Jewish translators 70 days to complete. It included the book of Enoch. The Christians made much use of the Septuagint.

6. Psalm 24:1

7. Prometheus Bound is given an assessment in my first book, The Theology of Paradox, chapter on Theodicy.

8. This is a feature of 20th century Biblical criticism, called vaticinium ex eventu, in other words, claiming that the 'prophecy' was made after the event and was therefore a fraud.

9. This is good example of how mythical material can mutate.

10. The Olympic Games were the most well-known, but there were the Nemean Games and the Pythian Games at Delphi.

11. Revelation 20:1- 3, in which Satan is bound in a pit for 1000 years.

12. 2 Kings 2:9ff.

13. The same idea comes in The Water Babies, chapter 11, with the fairy Mrs. Doasyouwouldbedoneby.

14. The Greek AGAPE means deep, committed love in contrast to a passing fancy. The Hebrew HESED is translated by agape.

15. Psalm 115:17 'The dead do not praise the Lord, nor do any that go down into silence.'

16. On the assumption that many of the numbers quoted in the ancient world were meant as symbolic rather than literal, this 300 years may have numerological significance. See the chapter on numerology, 26.

17. The war helmet can be seen in many examples of Greek art, whether on vases or statues.

18. See Michael Fitzgerald, Hitler's Occult War.

19. Mark 6:49.

20. **Pi** and **Phi** two mathematical concepts originating in Ancient Greece (Pythagoras). See chapter 26.

5

Gnosticism

Just as Greek mythology is reasonably well known in the modern world, Gnosticism is not at all well known nowadays. What was it? Gnosticism was an abstract philosophical approach to the deep matters of life, such as creation, theodicy and eschatology. It was not all one system of thought, but various attempts at coping with these matters. Each philosopher had his own set of clever ideas, even if much of their vocabulary was the same. It is thought that the main flowering of Gnosticism was in the second century AD in the Roman Empire and by the end of that empire, these ideas were fading out. That is not to say that Gnosticism disappeared for good; very much the contrary. We have seen strange outbursts of it in later times, particularly in the 20th century, often under different labels, but amounting to the same kind of thinking.

Where did it come from? There is no doubt that the Greek philosophers, such as Plato and Aristotle gave much impetus to Gnosticism. This was also combined with much input from the Hermetic literature which stemmed from ancient Egypt. (1) In fact, most of the Gnostic theorists lived in Alexandria and influenced matters in the Orient. It is fairly obvious that at some stage both Greeks and Egyptians grew tired of the fancy mythology of their cultural backgrounds and decided that something more subtle, sophisticated and intellectually acceptable ought to be thought out. Thus we can see that in general terms Gnosticism is a sanitised form of pagan mythology. Instead of gods indulging in all kinds of horrendous behaviour, we have principles and spiritual influences gently interacting with one another in the eternal realms. It was pure speculation and guesswork; nobody actually claimed to have had visions supplying one with this information. At times it does just remind one of the astro-physicists of today with their ideas about heavenly bodies far away. For that reason, it is fair to call Gnosticism yet another kind of mythology.

One of the key words in all this speculation was LOGOS which in Greek means 'word'; but it had much pejorative loading. It implied knowledge, clever information, philosophical insight, secret knowledge about ultimate truths, and much more. This was a word which the Greek philosophers bandied about. It probably began with Heraclitus and went on through Philo, a Jewish philosopher in Alexandria, and then into the Roman world. St.John, in his Prologue for his Gospel, uses it to define Jesus Christ, in terms of being God's essential instrument in Creation.

"In the beginning was the Word, and the Word was with God and the Word was God... all things were made through him... and the word became flesh and dwelt among us...' John 1:1-14.

This must have been quite a daring claim in those days. John has claimed the concept of Logos for the Christian understanding of the incarnation of Jesus Christ. This was a lot further than any philosopher had gone at that time. It is quite clear from John's gospel that Jesus is completely and fully God, but also fully human. He really does die on the cross and is not pretending in some sort of charade. Just because John uses the metaphor of Logos, that does not make him into a Gnostic. Indeed it is just possible that he is using that figure of speech as a counterblast to the Gnostics of his day.

It is quite likely that the earthly ministry of Jesus Christ was the stimulus for what was to follow in the Gnostic circles. It raised the essential question; how could God appear in human form, and having done so, how could he die? Gods are supposed to be immortal, which means there is an inherent contradiction going on here. The Gnostic answer to this was on these lines; that Jesus was some sort of divine appearance on earth, but was not fully human. He did not get crucified, nor did he die; he was some sort of phantom, apparition or charade. They were in denial of the crucifixion and the resurrection; this is a problem which still emerges today, as people simply cannot take on board what the gospels say about the end of his earthly life.

For a long time in the early years of the Church, the Gnostic heresy kept re-emerging under different labels and with slight modifications. The other way round the problem was to admit that Jesus was fully human but to deny that he was fully divine. But that was not Gnosticism; it was the Ebionite influence which was also deemed heretical. By the time we arrive at the formulation of the great Creeds and the Chalcedonian definition, the church fathers had come down firmly in agreement with St.John, that Jesus was fully God and fully human. The only thing they did not say was to term it a paradox of the most stunning kind; if they had, it might have helped people a little to cope with this situation. A full discussion of this issue is found in my first book, The Theology of Paradox.

Who were the Gnostic teachers? One of the earliest was one Simon Magus who was not just a philosopher but also a prestidigitatious trickster. Nowadays we would call him a 'con-artist'. He was active during the later decades of the first century AD, and is claimed to have challenged the people of Rome with the thought 'how could a god suffer?"(2)

An important teacher in Alexandria was Basileides. None of his writings have survived, and we only know anything about him in so much as the Christian apologists quote him as being wrong. Basileides is claimed to have said that Jesus managed to do a substitution on Good Friday, so that Simon of Cyrene was actually crucified in his place. This meant that Jesus dodged out of the problem and did not die at all.

Valentinus was a pupil of Basileides and went to Rome to teach. He nearly became the bishop of Rome but somehow someone with sounder opinions managed to become Pope. Valentinus thought that Jesus was some kind of phantom. He ate in a peculiar manner and never needed to go to the lavatory! This may seem absurd to us nowadays, but it indicates something in human nature. There is the need to think of one's religious leader or 'messiah' as above and beyond earthly degradation. The same trait comes through on the subject of 'virgin birth' and also on the issue of whether Jesus ever married. The same train of thought emerges on the subject of one's local priest or minister; he is assumed to be above and beyond the failings of human nature. That of course, is a very onerous expectation.

Many of the Gnostic writers are not known to us by name and may well have remained shadowy if it had not been for the discovery in 1945 of the Nag Hammadi papyri written in Early Coptic and some in Greek. They give us an insight into the mentality of Gnosticism in general terms. Most of them have no author cited, but claim to be some sort of 'gospel' of the early followers of Jesus. The gospel of Philip, for instance, is thought to be the inspiration of Valentinus. To call these works 'gospels' is misleading because most of them stop short of describing the Passion and Crucifixion of Jesus. This is a clear indication of the Gnostic inability to cope with the Passion. Included in this material is the so-called Gospel of Thomas which contains many sayings of Jesus which do not appear in the New Testament. How authentic they are is difficult to say, but some of them vary only slightly from the canonical gospels and others introduce new ideas which can be understood in the light of the Gnostic influence.

In complete contrast is the book Poimandres (3) (or the power and wisdom of God). This is a portion of the Corpus Hermeticum, which goes back many centuries to ancient Egypt and Greece. However, this work is important because it is clearly a monotheistic work which seems to have no knowledge of Jesus Christ. It may have been produced by or influenced by Jewish thought before 1 AD; otherwise it might be a first century work produced before the ministry of Jesus had become widely known. The influence of Genesis 1:27 is clear from this remark;

"Man was fair, created in the image of God." (page 130 and 135).

Also Greek influence is seen in this remark which could have been derived from the philosophers;

"Thus man is twofold; mortal in body, immortal in essence, subject to fate." (page 132)

There seems to be no difficulty over accepting one God;

"I sing praises to the One God... Holy is God, Father of the All." (page 144).

This raises the question of 'the children of God'. If one uses the metaphor of Father, then sonship clearly follows from this. Indeed we find this in such a remark as 'created man whom he loved like his own son'. (page 130). One might be tempted to see in this an oblique reference to Jesus, and indeed there is a thought very close to Christian thinking;

"The illuminating word that comes from Gnosis is the Son of God.' (page 127).

But this may not be talking in literal terms, such as the incarnation of Jesus. 'Son' here might be intended as something spiritual and theoretical. However, it is easy to see how such a remark could have been useful to the early Christians as a way of understanding the nature of Jesus. After all, they were deeply perplexed about who or what he was, and were searching for some sort of expression that did justice to him. But it would be a mistake to take Poimandres as a Christian work, since it never gets to grips with discussing Jesus of Nazareth and his ministry in any way, shape or form. It is, however, a good example of how Gnosticism as a pattern of thought could be Christian and non-Christian in the early Roman Empire.

So what patterns of thought did they employ? It is useful to have an impression of the vocabulary that the Gnostics employed; it was quite distinctive and also there is a sense of vagueness about trying to define their terms. **Aeon** is an emanation from the First Principle; it can be spatial, or personified, or be a period of time. **Zoe** 'life' is a female aeon. **Archon** means a 'ruler', a celestial being which is not perfect, of which there were seven. One of them was called **Sabaoth. Logos** 'word', an active and beneficial aspect coming from the original one God, also personified, it was a 'buzz-word' in those days. **Monad**, a single divine principle, analogous to God the Father, or Zeus or YHWH, seen in theoretical or philosophical terms. **Ogdoad,** one of eight divine emanations or aeons, also a divine realm. **Pleroma,** meaning 'fulness', but the celestial realms where the aeons live, and can also have a degree of personification. **Sophia** 'wisdom' a divine female influence, the first child of the single divine principle. **Tetrad**, one of the four primary deities, and **Decad**, a collection of ten aeons (Valentinus). **Demiurge** often thought to be a nasty god who actually produced the world of creation, and equated with the 'God of the Old Testament' as in Marcionite thought. (4)

What we notice is that there is a sort of amalgam of Hebrew and Greek thought here; one might almost call it syncretism. It is also fair to say that no single Gnostic theorist had the same system of thought as the others. There are many more strange celestial entities mentioned in Gnostic writings, and doubtless many more will come to light should more papyri be unearthed in the Egyptian desert. One wonders how they managed to invent such imaginative systems! It is obvious that the New Testament does not indulge in such fancy ideas; it just leaves us with the reality of God, as the Father of all, his Son Jesus as a real human person, and the Holy Spirit as active in the world and in the believing soul. That in itself is quite enough to cope with.

In spite of all these elaborate ideas, there is a basis of general agreement between the various Gnostic theorists. We begin with the First Principle, a Monad which is equivalent to the original God the Father. There is a certain degree of personification in this, but the tendency is to make God into some kind of philosophical principle. From this Monad emanate all kinds of other principles, spiritual entities. One in particular is Wisdom who is female; this is clearly derived from the Wisdom literature of the Old Testament, but she is not the only female entity. Sometimes these entities come in a series, like a domino-run; sometimes they seem to spread out directly from the Monad. But at some stage, there is the element of failure working its way in. Some of, or perhaps just one of, these entities is not as perfect as the original principle. There are varying attempts at explaining this but the final result is that when the Creation of the world comes about, it is done by some kind of spiritual entity who introduces a mistake somewhere. It is not the top God who does it wrong; it is one of his offshoots. We can see from this that this provides a rationale for the problem of why a perfect God allows, or causes a world and a humanity which is far from perfect. There are various Creation Myths available in Gnostic thought, none of which is completely in agreement with the others, and none of which is in agreement with Genesis 1-6. Genesis has the One perfect God producing a 'very good' world, and things go wrong because of the disobedience of mankind. So according to the Gnostics, the problems of this world are set to happen before creation actually takes place. This actually agrees with the book of Enoch in which fallen angels are described; the principles, aeons and archons are clearly a philosophised approach to angels. We can see this as an early attempt at demythologisation; but not a fully successful attempt.

In spite of this, the Gnostics nevertheless appear to be somewhat dependant on Genesis. They are also assuming something on the lines of Greek mythology, in which original gods 'give birth' to second and third generation gods, but the crudities and aggression are carefully combed out. But the common thought and thrust is that nagging question in the heart of every person; if there is a good God, why do people have to suffer? And more acutely, why do the innocent have to suffer? How do we apportion blame? Is it God's fault or someone else's? It is the age-old question of Theodicy which goes back to the dawn of civilisation.

The Gnostic writers have various answers to this, all of which originate up in the eternal realms. In the Apocryphon of John, the fault lay with

Wisdom who conceived an idea without consulting her consort; the result was an imperfect birth, someone called Ialtabaoth, a misshapen form, like a snake with a lion's face. No one knows the etymology of Ialtabaoth, but the inference is obvious, that that is how evil came into the world. Now we see how in the Bible Satan is associated with a snake and also (as in St.Peter's epistle), the devil is a roaring lion, seeking whom he may devour.

In the Gospel of Truth (page 190ff) it is nescience and forgetfulness that caused the disparity between the perfect Almighty God and the lower spiritual entities. This lovely paradox sums it up quite succinctly;

"The Father didn't cause this error; although all emanates from Him". (page 191).

This is the paradox that is the substratum of all our attempts at pondering the problem of evil. Once again, this all happens in the eternal realms before the world is created. Forgetfulness is also stressed in the Corpus Hermeticum VII, where it is likened to drunkenness. Conversely, remembering is the key to salvation, finding that secret knowledge, gnosis.

The Gospel of Judas has an even more ingenious answer to the problem. He talks of 'false gods of the lower mind', something sounding like the thoughts of Freud and Jung. Judas also talks of 'those who claim to be like angels... that bring about destruction.' (page 261). There is also someone called 'The King of Anarchy' who seems to impersonate Jesus. There seem to be many such Monarchs, not just of Anarchy but of Obliteration. This is where Judas works in a more Jewish train of thought by mentioning angels. They seem to be ruled by someone called Saklas; there are five angels and they govern Extinction and Anarchy. (page 270). By contrast we have a slight input from Greek thought when he says '... the mistakes inherent in the stars.' (page 272). This raises the age-old assumption that peoples' destinies are decided in advance and that a study of the Zodiac can reveal their futures. It is a miscellany of ideas rather than a systematic scheme to cope with the problem of evil. The main thrust of the Gospel of Judas concerns his role in the betrayal and how it was preordained, which in effect very largely removes the onus of guilt on Judas.

By contrast, the Fable of the Pearl deals with the matter in a much more subtle and poetic way. The usual Gnostic assumptions are cleverly interwoven in the story, in such a way that they can easily be missed. The gist of the story is that a prince of Parthia is given a gorgeous robe, but is told to go to Egypt to appropriate a pearl which is guarded by a snake. In Egypt, he had to assume a humble robe to avoid being identified and seen as suspicious. He finished off serving the Egyptians, but when his royal parents realised this, they recalled him. He managed to take the pearl, threw off the Egyptian robe and took back his royal robe, returning to his kingdom with great joy. The element of being drunk and overfed is worked in, which means that in this life we are in a sort of stupor, not knowing the true knowledge of God. But when one finds the true pearl of gnosis, one can return to the true kingdom and don one's true raiment. This is a gentle but fabulous approach to the problem of evil. It does not actually explain where the serpent comes from or why Egypt, the tyrannical empire is in existence. But it does suggest that this life is an illusion until one finds the deep truths about God. The Fable has a lovely poetic turn of phrase, and gives us so many biblical allusions, including the Pearl of Great Price, the serpent in the Garden of Eden and even the ending of the parable of the Good Samaritan. Although it never actually mentions Jesus Christ, it is clearly a story under Christian influence, even if there is an element of Greek myth or the method of Aesop the fabulist. It has been attributed to Jude Thomas, the apostle.

The Gospel of Mary Magdalene deals with the matter in yet another way. She talks of 'powers' as some sort of spiritual entity. The fourth power assumes seven forms; darkness, desire, ignorance, fear of death, power of the flesh, foolish reason, and self-righteous pedantry. 'These are the powers of anger and doubt.' Now comes the crucial question, 'from where did you come, killer of men; where are you heading, slayer of space?'

But no answer to this question is forthcoming. All Mary knows is that she is free from these powers, 'freed from the world and the chains of forgetfulness.' (page 59).

Here we see the Gnostic notion that it is essentially forgetfulness, bad memory which causes the estrangement between the ultimate Good and the evil of the world. For all their attempts at coping with this problem, they and us today are still grappling with the question. For us in this life, there is no process of logic that can cope with it.

The Apocalypse of the Great Power has yet another approach to the problem, using a subtle blend between pre-existence and creation. It is expressed in allegoro-philosophical terms and never becomes specific about the act of creation. It talks about the Aeon of Creation, and that it was blind (not ignorant this time) (page 149) before it actually constructed the world. A fleshly Aeon entered 'gross bodies', and 'self-corrupted'. Another Aeon mingled with the physical birth and polluted them. The result of this was children of wrath, jealousy, ill will, guile, disdain, strife, mendacity, wicked advice, depression, hedonism, lowliness, corruption, falsity, sickness, bad judgement and depravity. It then goes on to speak of humanity being asleep, in 'the dream of life', and the need to awaken and search for the truth.

Salvation in the Gnostic mode

At this point we begin to see the importance of the Logos of God coming into the world to provide salvation. In the Gnostic scheme, the Monad, the original perfect God, sends his Logos, bypassing all the demiurges and Aeons that have gone wrong, direct into the world to reveal the truth. This is where, for the Christians, the equation between the Logos and Jesus Christ becomes important. The Christian Gnostics could see that Jesus was actually that Logos sent by God. This is clearly spelt out in the Apocalypse of the Great Power. The Saviour is actually the 'Logos of life's Great Power'. (page 154), and this meant the defeat of 'Archonic rule' and that the old Aeons would vanish. However it is as well to note that the name Jesus itself does not appear in this Apocalypse. The whole scheme of Christ's earthly ministry is laid out, not in specific terms, as in the canonical gospels, but in a kind of elevated, indirect fashion, almost as if this world were irrelevant.

This is symptomatic of the Gnostic reluctance to see Jesus as really human. Looking at the titles given to him, he is often called 'the Saviour', 'the blessed One', 'the Living one', and 'Lord', but something which clearly shows him as being fully divine and fully human at the same time, is usually missing. It is noticeable that Jesus' favourite name for himself, 'Son of Man' hardly ever seems to occur. The significance of this term is that it refers to his humanity and his divinity all in one expression. The exception to this is the Gospel of Thomas, where the earthly Jesus and Almighty god are unmistakably equated;

"These are the secret words of Almighty God, which Lord Jesus Christ uttered..." (page 19).

71

Normally Thomas calls him 'Lord Jesus' or just 'Jesus.' But in places, the divinity of Jesus breaks through;

"Then you'll see the son of he who is the living God..." (page 33).

Even more specific;

"I am the Light above them all; I am the All; the All issues from me and reaches me. Cut the wood and I am there; lift the stone, I am there." (page 41). (5)

Clearly this denotes Jesus as eternal, ubiquitous and fully divine. Normally, however, Gnostic works have some difficulty over the Incarnation. In the Fable of the Pearl, there is no actual mention of Jesus Christ, even if there are several allusions to Biblical matters. In the Gospel of Truth, it is clear that Christ is identified with the true knowledge of the Flawless One;

"When Christ came, he became the Gnosis of that secret tome (6) and was crucified. He revealed the tome of his Father by his death on the cross." (page 195).

"And brings forward the intense heat of the godhead that lives in Christ, the Pleroma of Love." (page 213).

What is missing from the Gospel of Truth is the actual name 'Jesus'; this is symptomatic of the Gnostic difficulty over the incarnation. The substratum of it is that they saw Christ and Jesus as two separate entities, which appeared in one person, the historical Jesus of Nazareth. So while the physical Jesus died on the cross, as some will admit, the Christ, the spiritual entity was not put to death. It was later in the Church's history that this was shown to be heretical, that Jesus Christ was one integrated person, both human and divine at the same time.

What we have to remember is that the Gnostic mentality does not necessarily involve an understanding of Jesus Christ. It is a mythological system of thought, plural in nature, which became influenced by the coming of Christianity, but not all its pundits were influenced to the same extent. What is also clear is that Gnosticism, as an array of vocabulary and concepts, had its influence on the Early Church's attempts in coming to grips with the Incarnation. Because there were these people who tried to downplay the human aspect of Jesus of Nazareth, the mainstream Christians were forced to find a way of emphasising the divinity and the humanity of Jesus in such a way as to avoid rendering the Atonement null and void. For the Atonement to have any cogency, Jesus had to have been God and Man in the same person. In that way, he represents mankind to God and vice versa, represents God to mankind; he is the final, ultimate channel of communication between the two entities. If this arrangement is disturbed, then the representation falls apart.

Eschatology in Gnostic thought

We have seen that with Greek mythology, eschatology is hardly ever mentioned. It was almost entirely concerned with Creation and the state of mankind at present. However, there were two important influences that brought eschatology into view; the Jewish hopes of messianism and the end of all things; also the Zoroastrian doctrines about the end of the world. How much the one influenced the other is a moot point, but by the time we arrive in the second century AD, when the full flowering of Gnosticism was thriving, it was not realistic to ignore this element, namely the imminent expectation of the apocalypse. This was something that the Christians were emphasising, and it doubtless stems from the teachings of Jesus himself.

Consequently, there is a certain degree of eschatology in some of the Gnostic material. A good example of this comes in the Apocalypse of the Great Power. It begins with Creation and works its way through the ministry of Jesus Christ. Although Noah is mentioned by name more than once, the name Jesus does not appear. We have mention of 'the Saviour' and 'the Great Logos, the Christ', which is typical of Gnostic thought. The course of history and the ministry of Christ is not at all down-to-earth and realistic as seen in the canonical gospels; it is elevated to a spiritual level and all integrated with Archons and Aeons, which would suggest that the ministry of Christ is way over our heads and in another eternal realm. The apocalyptic portion comes, in which the wicked will be punished and cleansed, souls in torment will be released and everything will return to perfection. Justice and beauty will prevail. However, those who refuse to accept it will not receive salvation; the sons of materialism will die.

It is clear that this kind of apocalypse is very different from that seen in the New Testament. If we compare it with Revelation, St.John is far more real and actual, and also more dramatic. The Gnostic mythology of the end is far more spiritual and less poetic. There is none of the high-flown metaphor and symbolism as seen in pure Judaeo-Christian thinking.

Another Gnostic work called Melchizedek, is dubbed an apocalyptic work but treats the matter in a very different fashion. Again we see the elevated, non-historical method, talking about Aeons, Archons, and spiritual influences in the skies. It centres on Melchizedek, the high priest of Salem, who ministered to Abraham, but the interesting thing is that Melchizedek identifies himself with Jesus Christ, and describes his ministry in terms of a prophecy. He talks of the crucifixion and resurrection in vague, almost theoretical terms, but the gist of it is, that the defeat of evil is accomplished then and there, as opposed to some great dramatic event in the future. On this basis, we could term this book, using modern phraseology, as 'realised eschatology'. In other words, the culmination of the earthly life of Jesus was actually the apocalypse, and those who expect another one to come in the future are under some kind of illusion. In spite of this, there is still that element of the apocalyptic 'secret'. It does not indulge in the unfolding of scrolls, as in Revelation, but we are told to keep the secret, whatever that may be, until we are told to reveal it. Thus, there is still that futuristic element in this kind of eschatology.

It would be fair to say that the Gnostic thinkers did not attach too much importance to eschatology. It was there as an element in the Christian sphere of Gnosticism, but nowhere as prominent and dramatic as in the mainstream orthodox Christian thinking.

Another book called the **First Thought in three Forms,** also has an apocalyptic element, though again, not a particularly prominent one.(7) Most of the book is the words of a female aeon who describes herself in terms of being a voice, and claims to be the channel through which the Word, the Son of God, which we assume to be Jesus Christ, is produced. She claims to be the light that illumines all things. She claims to have revealed herself to the angels and powers in their likeness; then she came among the Sons of Man, looking like a Son of Man 'even though I am the Father of everyone.' This is the nearest we come to speaking about the Incarnation, but she does not go so far as to identify herself with the earthly Jesus Christ. This matter is not clarified; even so, the name Jesus actually appears once at the end. Thus we can claim this work to be a Christian work with heavy Gnostic doctrines worked in.

With regard to the apocalypse, this is again referred to in much the same way as with the others. It would seem that there is an Aeon to come, one that does not change and in which we shall be purified. There will come a time of fulfilment in which the whole of Creation will be shaken. All those spiritual powers and entities will be puzzled as to what is happening. But the challenge now is to listen to what the 'Speech of the Mother of your Mercy', is saying because the secret of the ages is now on offer, and does not have to be lost in ignorant Chaos for ever. One is invited into the exalted, perfect light. Although this is phrased in apocalyptic vocabulary, it is not completely clear whether this simply refers to the life and death of Jesus Christ, or to a future end and recommencement of the world, or universe.

What is missing from this, is any involvement with real people in the physical world. The whole scheme is on a spiritual, eternal level, above the heads of ordinary people. Were it not for the one mention of Jesus at the end, one could suppose that the whole pattern of salvation and the removal of evil, is enacted in the skies. It is interesting that traces of ideas from Greek mythology keep reappearing. Chaos and Fate keep appearing as well as someone who is androgynous; 'I am the Mother and Father since I copulate with myself.' This is an interesting permutation on the paradox of Creation; how does something come out of nothing? But we notice that for all its sophistication, this Gnostic thought has slipped back into the crudities of Greek mythology.

Concluding thoughts on Gnosticism

One wonders how these 'philosophers' managed to think up these elaborate schemes using Archons, Aeons, Powers up in the eternal realms. Clearly it comes across as a sanitised version of Greek mythology with some input from Zoroastrian thinking, Egyptian and Jewish as well. One wonders how literally this material was ever intended to be taken; could it have been intended as purely metaphoric, symbolic and figurative, but rather poor poetically. Clearly there was some attempt at rationalising the Incarnation of Jesus Christ, but not a particularly successful one. When we compare it with the Biblical material, such writers as St.Paul and St.John, for instance, they clearly see Gnosticism as meant to be literally true. This helps to explain why the early church rejected gnostically inspired material. They took it to be the literal truth and never considered it to be figurative. Thus it is easy to condemn the whole thing as nonsense. It is possible that we can see in the words of St.Paul a condemnation of Gnostic cleverness (see I Corinthians 1:20). (8)

How do we see it now? We see it as typical of human nature to speculate on the beginning of all things and also the end. This goes on now, clothed in scientific phraseology and clever gadgets such as radio telescopes. But before we condemn the Gnostics for being stupid, let us remember that what we think we know now may appear stupid in 20 centuries' time.

Another aspect of Gnosticism is its inclusion of angels. This is seen particularly in what is known as the Sethian branch of Gnosticism, which was somewhat different from the Valentinian one. This 'angelic' aspect of theology appears in the Old Testament, notably in the book of Daniel; also in the book of Enoch which goes into much detail about them; also in the New Testament Gospels. Some would see this element as mythological; I personally cannot see why we should not take it as read, that angelic visitations played a crucial role in the pattern of salvation. (9) It would be fair to say that the Gnostics were quite economical on the mention of angels. They might well have said that all those aeons and spiritual powers were a subtle form of angelic activity. In many ways the Gnostic mentality is a precursor of the modern tendency to demythologise everything. This is something that will be discussed later in this book (chapter 24, Bultmann).

Modern and alternative versions of Gnosticism

A system of thought which holds fascination for people is hardly likely to fade out, even if it has been dubbed as heretical. The mere thought that Jesus really suffered during the Passion meets with a negative response from many people. They are in denial of it. We see this with the Jehovah's Witnesses, but it is by no means confined to them. How many people cannot think of Jesus as being fully human, that he might have been married or at least had a girl-friend (Mary Magdalene?). How many people have that instinctive feeling that human flesh is corrupt, disgusting and unworthy of God? This is one of the legacies of Gnosticism.

One of the more noteworthy reinventions of Gnosticism in recent times has been the theorisings of Mary Baker Eddy who was the founder of Christian Science. Whether she realised it or not, in her writings we see the dichotomy between the earthly Jesus and the divine Christ. This is a denial of the unity of Jesus Christ; this is one factor that the Chalcedonian Definition had to clarify. Also the notion that disease is purely a false notion is derived from the assumption that this physical world is non-existent, purely an illusion and that sin too is some kind of self-delusion. Eddy also uses much of the vocabulary of the Gnostics, such as the All, the divine Mother; Whether or not she realised that she was a latter-day Gnostic is a good question.

But of course the main ongoing and historical expression of Gnosticism is the religion known as Buddhism. The essential notion that human desire is wrong and must be overcome is just another permutation on the idea that human flesh or nature is unworthy. Buddhist philosophy embarks on all kinds of elaborate speculations of spiritual entities; it baulks at the notion of gods in the skies and actually has no creational or eschatological mythology as such. This is very unusual with religions. All its speculations, as with the Gnostics, is on the level of philosophical ethereal relationships, which can be investigated by concentrated meditation. There are gods in the Buddhist scheme of things, but they are not celestial beings who create or destroy, as in the western sense. The Buddhist gods are living creatures who have worked their way round the Wheel of Becoming and will go round eternally as if on a fair-ground roundabout, unless they put their minds to attaining Nirvana, which is the permanent escape from the inevitable round of incarnation. It could be possible to see Nirvana as a demythologised version of heaven. We note that some of the Gnostic theorists actually do mention reincarnation, though not in a thoroughgoing way. This was an element in Greek mythology; on the other hand, it is quite possible that Gnosticism was inspired by Buddhist influence coming to the West in the centuries before Christ. (10)

Footnotes for Chapter 5, Gnosticism

1. The Hermetic literature I have reviewed in the Theology of Truth, chapter 25. It now exists in Greek but scholars are trying to reconstruct the original Egyptian.

2. A description of this comes in the Shepherd of Hermas, a work which came close to being included in the New Testament.

3. Poimandres; 'poimen' in Greek means a shepherd.

4. Marcion, a second century Christian, theorised that there were two gods, the God of the Old Testament and the God of the New Testament. This is a notion that still prevails amongst people who cannot see that it is the one and the same God throughout the Bible. Marcion was dubbed as a heretic.

5. One of the more enigmatic verses in the Gospel of St.Thomas. it is just possible that it is a poetic way of referring to the crucifixion and resurrection; the wood equals the cross and the stone is what covered the tomb.

6. Tome is a big book; the apocalyptists had the idea that there were secret scrolls with information to be disclosed at the end of the age.

7. First Thought in Three Forms. Found in Lost Scriptures by Bart D. Ehrmann, page 316.

8. I Corinthians 1:20; "Where is the wise man?... has not God made foolish the wisdom of the world?" This could be a covert reference to the Gnostics.

9. The reality of angels is given consideration in chapter 25, the claims of Emanuel Swedenborg.

10. It is to be noted that Buddhism does not have any mythology, at least in the sense of Creation and the End of the World. If there is any mythology, it is encapsulated in the Wheel of Becoming, which contains gods, devils and all other forms of life. This is why there is no appraisal of Buddhism in this book.

6

Mythology in Paradise Lost by John Milton

It is interesting to find that in a highly poetic work by one of a strongly Protestant stance, that mythology is a prominent feature. John Milton was a Cambridge scholar at the time of the Commonwealth in the 1640's. It goes without saying that he, along with just about everyone else in the Christian world, took the Bible as the literal truth, from cover to cover. It would be anachronistic to call him a 'Bible Fundamentalist', but that is the term used nowadays for those of such an opinion. But it is clear that the Renaissance, with its attachment to Greek mythology, had a profound influence upon him, and this was only just outweighed by his reliance on the Bible. He would hardly have admitted that the Bible contained any mythology; whether he saw the Greek material as mythological or literally true, is an interesting question, which will be addressed in this discussion. He includes many aspects of Greek thought not just as passing remarks but as essential to his argument; he normally assumes that his reader will understand the reference. But that would be a fair assumption, since schools and universities at that time were steeped in Graeco-Roman classical thought. It may never have occurred to them that there was an inherent contradiction involved here. Christian thought is based on monotheism; Greek thought was essentially polytheistic. We see the same situation going on in the works of Shakespeare, and Edmund Spenser, both children of the Renaissance.(1)

Strange as it may seem, the Protestants, with all their emphasis on the Bible being the truth, were (and still are) happy to include all manner of mythological factors which were never included in the scriptures. The chief and highly structural factor was the assumption that evil entered the universe long before the creation of the world or of mankind itself. This idea, taken from the Book of Enoch, gives us the impression that God had created all manner of spiritual entities called 'angels', but one of them, called Satan, disagreed with God and was demoted from Heaven. This is the basic assumption in Paradise Lost; Milton goes to great lengths to elaborate on this plot, decorating it with all kinds of ideas not traceable to any ancient authoritative text. He is dependent on the Book of Revelation, to some extent, but nowhere near as much as one might have expected. The main idea is that Satan, knowing that he cannot overpower God, decides to take revenge by making an assault on the newly-created mankind which is living in idyllic conditions in the Garden of Eden.

The important theological factor here from the point of view of Theodicy (the problem of evil), is that the problem had come into existence before the actual appearance of mankind in the Garden of Eden. None of this is mentioned in the Genesis account. Another mitigating factor is that Satan manages to deceive the angel Uriel, by altering his appearance, and so find the Garden of Eden and the first humans. But the effect it has, is to throw a different light on the Fall of Mankind. In a sense, humanity is slightly less to blame for the first disobedience, and less blameworthy over the first deception, since this kind of thing had already happened in the skies, and Satan was determined to spoil things for the human race. In Genesis, the serpent who tempts Eve is not actually stated to be Satan, or indeed any evil spirit; this equation was to come later. By the time we arrive at Revelation, the serpent is clearly shown as the Devil, and is augmented to be a dragon.

Another important theological factor is that Milton clearly sees the ministry of Jesus Christ, the Son of God as active also before the Creation of the world. Christ's obedience and reverence for God the Father is clearly emphasised, and this stands in contrast to the disobedience of Satan. When we arrive at the New Testament, the disobedience of Adam and Eve is contrasted with the obedience and resistance to temptation as seen in the earthly ministry of Jesus Christ. Also Jesus is not deceived and realises who the Devil is. This is emphasised at Caesarea Philippi when Jesus realises that the Devil is speaking through Simon Peter; 'get thee behind me, Satan.' (Matthew 16:23). The pre-existence of Jesus Christ, the Word of God is discussed in the first chapter of St.John's Gospel, and became an important doctrine in the early church. This is something that the Protestants did not wish to disagree with at the Reformation.

Milton goes into great detail about the battle going on between the good and bad angels. He makes it sound like something out of the Civil War, with armour and spears. All this is poetic and pure imagination. Satan manages to approach Eve while she is asleep and give her a bad dream on the subject of the Tree of Knowledge; again this is pure poetic licence. On the other hand, it is a clever piece of artificial typology; just as Pontius Pilate's wife had a bad dream on the subject of condemning Jesus (Matthew 27:19), so Eve, Adam's wife had a warning about the forbidden fruit. Milton does not hesitate to mention Pandora, the Greek equivalent of Eve, with fine looks, but not a patch on Eve. In a way, both the Greek and the Hebrew versions are agreed that both ladies were endowed with a strong sense of curiosity. Pandora could not resist taking a peep inside the jar, in spite of being warned not to; Eve could not resist the flattery from the serpent. The question now arises; how literally did Milton take Greek mythology, in relation to the Biblical account? The way he mentions the incident, (line 713) gives the impression that he sees the Greek material as just as authoritative as the Genesis material. Can he really be sincere when he says 'more lovely than Pandora, whom the Gods endowed with all their gifts'? Or is this just another example of poetic licence, using Greek mythology as a way of augmenting the emotion? On the subject of the Creation of the world and mankind, Milton is very careful to follow the outline given in Genesis chapter 1. Interestingly, we begin with Chaos, who was a Greek God, the equivalent of the 'Big Bang'. Milton clearly gives Chaos a certain degree of personification, 'for Chaos heard his voice', but one wonders if he really saw Chaos as a kind of god, as the Greeks did. The same could be said about Tartarus, which in Greek thought was a god deep down waiting to receive all monsters and irredeemable creatures; in this case, 'the gulf of Tartarus' is waiting to accept Satan and his host of fallen angels, into his fiery Chaos. The personification is not so strong here, but whether Milton thought of Tartarus as actually a god or just an infernal region, is a good question. But this certainly indicates a subtle blend of Hebrew and Greek mythology.

The pattern of Creation follows the seven days, with the Word of God actually doing the work. When it is finished, the Messiah returns, with the angels, to Heaven. This episode is remarkably economical on Greek mythological references. It is filled out and embellished with mentions of Heavenly Quires, and Golden Harps, and bright Luminaries, and 'the solemn Pipe, and Dulcimer, all Organs of sweet stop... string or golden wire, tempered soft tunings... voice choral or unison'(page 154ff). He includes masses of detail extraneous to the basic Biblical account; this is all very entertaining, but pure imagination, at least as far as we are concerned. Whether Milton himself thought of it that way, is a good question, but a significant remark;

'The stars numerous, and every star perhaps a world of destined habitation.' (page 163).

This is a very modern thought; that there might be life on other far-away planets. In fact, it is the obsession of the age, but as yet there has been no irrefutable evidence of such life on other planets. (2) It is interesting that this idea occurs in the thoughts of Milton in the 17th century. Also Swedenborg entertained the same idea. Even so, the angel tells Adam not to be carried away by such speculation;

'Think only what concerns thee and thy being; dream not of other worlds, what creatures there live, in what state, condition or degree...' (page 169, line 175).

This is probably sound advice to those who are desperate to find evidence of life in other parts of the universe. To concentrate on the problems of this world would be far more constructive.

Related to this thought is the question of where or how humanity managed to appear. Adam wonders where he came from; he asks the animals if they know the answer; 'how came I thus, how here?' but realises that it is because of some 'Great Maker' (page 72). This is the fundamental question at the root of all mythologies from any part of the world. Where did we come from; what does life mean; where are we going? These are questions still at the back of everyone's minds, which explains why mythology has not faded out in modern times; if anything it has increased.

Adam is shown all the animals with a view to naming them. He realises that they come in pairs, as mates, and realises that he has not got a mate; neither does he want an animal as a mate. He sets to work to persuade God to provide him with a mate. He goes into an unconscious state but is aware of what it is happening; God opens up his side and removes a rib in order to form a woman. The way it is phrased, 'wide was the wound' and 'life-blood streaming fresh' reminds us of how Jesus was wounded on the cross (John 19:34). It has all the implications of blood being the essential life in a person. In this way Adam is linked to Jesus right from the start of human history.

It is then that Eve enters the scene, in terms which are almost voluptuous. She is portrayed as a Goddess, with the Graces attending her. Here we see a little Greek mythology slipping into the picture; the inherent contradiction here does not seem to concern Milton, but then this is largely poetry. He takes various liberties with the Genesis account. Another is the general picture of how Satan, as the pre-existing evil influence, is infiltrating Paradise with a view to spoiling it all for humanity. He finds the serpent asleep, and enters into his body; this too is a Greek concept, how a 'god' or spiritual entity can inhabit an animal.

The tension mounts as Adam and Eve discuss working separately from each other. He is afraid that the enemy of which he has been warned, will take advantage of Eve being on her own. Eve has overheard the angel's warning and is aware that something could go wrong. Adam feels confident that the enemy will not succeed in seducing him; but with regard to Eve, that might be another matter. Eve can see that they cannot go through life always on the defensive, a kind of fear that will spoil their marital bliss. On that basis, Eve went off to work alone. It is described in Greek mythological terms, 'like a wood-nymph light, Oread or Dryad, or of Delia's Traine' but yet more like a goddess. It is heavily stressed how innocent Eve was 'with nymphlike step fair virgin pass. Even the serpent was impressed by her beauty and at that point, we see the contrast between degenerate evil and pure innocence heavily underlined. Taking the symbolism in this, these ladies, the Oreads and Dryads wore no clothing, which is a way of emphasising their innocence. (3) Perhaps this is the rationale behind Milton's use of Greek mythology, to augment the poetic and romantic side of the account.

Then the crucial episode of the Temptation comes in. The serpent insinuates himself into Eve's presence, giving her copious flattery, calling her 'a Celestial Beauty'. This, incidentally is an important basis of temptation, the element of flattery, which is seen in the temptations of Jesus. Eve is surprised at the snake talking English (!), and he explains it is because he has eaten the fruit of a certain tree, apples incidentally, and this has given him reason, speech and insight. He leads her to the tree, but she realises it is the forbidden fruit. At this point the snake indulges in more flattery and oratorical skills, just like a Roman or Greek orator. The gist of it is 'I've eaten it, and just look at me!' 'If I can become human, what about you becoming a god; it stands to reason!' 'If everything belongs to God, how can it hurt you?' There is even a little discussion about the theory of evil, if indeed evil really exists. This is of course a very modern thought, that there is no evil and from that it follows there is no Satan. Eve debates within herself; if the snake is still alive, having eaten the fruit, why should I die, as threatened. What is missing is two elements to this piece of reasoning; firstly, what if the snake is telling a lie about eating the fruit; secondly, there is a world of difference between an animal and a human. She eats the fruit and finds it a delight. Then she has the dilemma over whether to tell Adam about it. Will it cause a rift between them? Will it make me superior to him? If I die will he have to have another partner? That thought shakes her considerably; no, he must share the fruit and the results of it. With this we see Milton introducing all kinds of human emotions, filling out the Genesis account.

Eve tells Adam and attempts to persuade him, saying how it has opened her eyes and she is 'growing up to Godhead.' Also the snake has not died and is doing well. Adam is astonished and even petrified that Eve has ignored God's command, but since he does not wish to be left alone if she dies, he cannot face the thought of being solitary again, he decides to share her fate, whatever it turns out to be. He cannot believe that God would destroy the two of them, so he eats some of the 'apple' too. Genesis does not specify the fruit on the tree; it is later tradition that says it was an apple. From this we gain the expression, 'Adam's apple', the bit that got stuck in his throat. Then the earth groans and there is a roll of thunder.

Now, we come to the most contentious element in the story. Carnal desire comes across them, which assumedly had not occurred before. Milton does not actually say they had sexual intercourse, but the hint is there. Innocence was gone and they realised they were naked, destitute and bare. 'Foul concupiscence' and 'guilty shame' are the phrases used. Adam is termed 'the Herculean Samson' and Eve 'the Philistean Delilah', the implication being that she was a prostitute. This a good example of how Milton interweaves Greek and Hebrew thought together. Adam is equated with the Hebrew version of Hercules and Eve the Philistine seductress. None of this sexual element is seen in Genesis; there is no hint that sexual intercourse is sinful. This is something that came in with later thinking, particularly with St.Augustine, and the Protestants laid great emphasis on it. The result has been that the word 'sin' is now a pejorative word with unavoidable sexual connotations. Now they feel the need to make for themselves panties out of fig leaves, 'to hide guilt and dreaded shame' (page 210). One would have thought that the biological difference between them would have been obvious from the start. Genesis has it as 'aprons'.

It is interesting that at that point, Milton seeks to comment on Columbus' discovery, in America, of Indians who wore very little clothing, 'with feathered cincture naked else and wilde.' (page210). He does not actually comment on this, but we know that to this day there are remote tribes in world, who wear very little clothing, if at all. We all know that infants do not seem to worry about nakedness; it is a feature they acquire from socialisation with adults. The nudists will probably tell us that it is a perfectly normal state of affairs, and has nothing to do with sin. Even so, most people understand the emotion of embarrassment at being naked; is this really a hangover from the Garden of Eden?

Adam and Eve now start to blame each other; he thinks she should have stayed close to him; she thinks he could have been seduced by the snake if he had been on his own. It never occurs to them to face the responsibility themselves; this is a very common trait in human nature. One has difficulties is looking oneself in the mirror. The way Milton portrays it, it almost lets Adam out of the responsibility. The passage ends with a very anti-feminist remark from Milton, to the effect that one should never trust a woman, never let her overrule you, and never let her do as she pleases, or you will get the blame when it goes wrong! (page 210).

The news of the Fall reaches heaven via the angels, and God relieves them of blame, knowing how sly Satan can be. God sends his Son, the Word, to issue judgement on the three miscreants. Now a pathway between earth and hell is made, expressed as a Bridge over the Abyss and Night (Nyx). We notice that this is expressed in terms of Graeco-Roman mythology; Nyx and Abyssos are the primal beginnings of life and the Pontiff is the bridge, ie, the Roman Emperor. This means in effect that Satan has easy access to interfere with human affairs, and humans can easily fall into wickedness, failure and death. Satan is quite pleased to announce that he has escaped punishment, since the serpent had to take the blame. But the reply from his supporting team was a gigantic hiss; whereupon Satan fell on his stomach and hissed as well. This is surely a trace of humour in Milton. Satan is now compared with Cerastes, the Hydra, Amphishena, Ellops, the Gorgon, the Python, and Ophion, all of which are some kind of serpent in Greek mythology. Then Satan turns into a dragon, which is an augmented snake, and which anticipates the way he is portrayed in Revelation. The snakes try to eat the fruit of the tree, but it turns to ashes and soot in their mouths, their punishment. So now they are doomed to eat fauna and flora and anything that dies.

There is a preview of Jesus coming to defeat sin, death and the grave (page 229), 'one sling of thy victorious arm, well-pleasing son, both sin and death and yawning grave at last through Chaos hurled, obstruct the mouth of hell for ever... till then the curse pronounced on both precedes.'

We then have a most revealing account of 17th century climatology. It would seem that Milton believes that before the Fall, there were no seasons and the planetary motions were not established. But now, it seems, the Zodiac swings into action, since Cancer, Capricorn, Virgo, Libra, Gemini and the Plaiedes are described; this is a surprise since one would expect strict biblical protestants to ignore such matters. What is intriguing is that Milton seems to know about the axial tilt of the earth, 'the Poles of the earth twice ten degrees and more from the sun's axle...' (page 230); actually we now know it is 23.5 degrees. The implication in all this is that before the Fall, there was no such arrangement, at least in Milton's opinion.

Also we begin to see enmity between animals and mankind. The animals begin to eat each other, and mankind uses animals for food. The suggestion here is that all creatures were vegetarians at one time!

Adam considers that even if his body dies, his spirit will live on and is eternal. He now starts to accept the blame for the curse on humanity, and worries about the problems he has caused for future generations. There is even the suggestion that they ought not to have any children. Eve wonders why God made all the angels masculine but humans as two sexes. We notice the assumption in this that angels are of one gender only. She is distraught and begs forgiveness, and the two of them are reconciled. They decide to have children regardless. Adam reasons that God's punishment is gentler than it might have been; he can see the value of hard work, as opposed to just going through life idling. That can be seen as the Protestant 'work-ethic' showing through. For Eve, the joy of giving birth to a child is compensation for the pangs of labour. They now turn to God to repent and ask for forgiveness.

As we can see, the basic account in Genesis is expanded in all kinds of ways, not just poetically, but geographically, socially, and theologically. It is fascinating to read about the assumptions about angels and devils, and to see how Greek mythology is interwoven with Judaeo-Christian lore. In a way, Milton gives us a window into the 17th century mind-set.

The angels report back to God the Father , and the Son intercedes for mankind. We notice that this anticipates the earthly mission of Jesus Christ in the role of great high priest; at this point the Father actually calls the Son, a 'priest'. But God has decided that mankind will have to leave the Garden of Eden , Paradise, and face the realities of life elsewhere. Michael the archangel has the task of informing them and installing the flaming sword to guard the tree of life. The positive side of this is that in spite of all that has gone wrong, there is still hope available in the long run. This idea, which is not seen in Genesis, ties in with Pandora's box.

Michael arrives in human form to evict them. Eve is distraught about leaving all her plants, and Adam regrets not being able to talk directly to God. But God is still present wherever they go, and the compensation is that they have the whole earth to occupy and exploit. Michael takes him up a high hill to view the whole of the world; this is deliberately done as an anticipation of how the Devil took Jesus up a high mountain in one of the temptations. It is interesting how the 17th century list of countries, with their strange spellings, is elaborated, including places in the New World. Various visions now are shown to Adam.

The first one is the Cain and Abel incident, the first murder, which upsets Adam considerably. He realises that it is essentially his fault that the next generation will go wrong.

The second vision is of the sick and dying, followed by old age, and the question arises as to why this has to happen. Michael explains that if they must misuse life and pervert Nature's healthful rules, what can they expect? To a large extent, it is their own fault, and not entirely Adam's.

The third vision is of a lovely industrious land with good pious men working hard and thriving, but it all goes wrong because in come flirting women who are atheists, and the whole thing degenerates into chaos and immorality. This may be an oblique reference to Genesis 6:1-4, that strange passage where the sons of God take a fancy to the daughters of men. This passage has more than most occasioned much speculation and wild interpretation as to its meaning. But Milton does not attempt to do that. Instead, he seems to be hinting at the Ages of Man as in Greek mythology, and this vision might equate to the Age of Silver. From that we expect the Age of Bronze to emerge, and indeed it does. The Age of Gold might well equate to Eden.

The fourth vision is a scene of towns, forts, armies, battles and violence, which is all blamed on Cain for his murder. Adam is appalled at the bloodshed. But the Age of Bronze was exactly that; nothing but violence. God is now in despair over mankind and decides to cleanse the earth.

This is where the Flood comes in; Milton actually never mentions the name 'Noah', but calls him Deucalion (and Pyrrha his wife) (page 242). Milton recounts the episode quite faithfully, even the contradiction between the animals being two of each or seven of each.(4) The rainbow and the covenant of Noah are described. This scene ends with a hint at the apocalyptic, which never appears in Genesis; '... shall hold their course, till fire purge all things new, both heaven and earth, wherein the just shall dwell.' (page 264). This is another clear example of how Milton combines Greek and Hebrew thought.

The Tower of Babel episode is next to be described. There is reference to a mighty hunter who made himself into a tyrant at that time. This does not appear at all in Genesis, and one might wonder if it refers to someone in Greek thought. Orion the hunter springs to mind, but the tyrant is never actually identified. (5)

We then move on to the Abraham sagas and how he settled in the Promised Land. Israel in Egypt , the ministry of Moses, the ten plagues, the Tabernacle, Joshua, the Temple, the Exile and the return. The coming of the Messiah is seen, with the wise men, and the ministry of Jesus including his death, resurrection, ascension and the coming of the Holy Spirit. This is where the account links back to the beginning, with the promise of a better Paradise provided by Jesus Christ and moreover, a Paradise in one's heart as opposed to a physical one. (page 280). Even the Apocalypse is mentioned, though not in any great detail. With that they leave Eden to face the realities of normal life, husband and wife, hand in hand.

As the book comes to its conclusion with the prophetic element through to the end of time, we see the references to Greek mythology diminish, although not disappear completely. Is this being done deliberately? If so, it may be a way of saying that Hebrew and Greek thought are now being brought to conclusion with the ministry of Jesus Christ. One might say that the Greek element has been brought in to supplement the account from Genesis; however, the way it is done does suggest that Milton was taking Greek mythology just as seriously as the Genesis mythology. When Genesis says, 'the earth was without form and void, and darkness was upon the face of the deep...' (Genesis 1:2) Milton seems to feel he can fill this out with mention of Chaos, Tartarus, the Abyss, Nyx and other Greek proto-gods. It is noticeable that he does not include Eros and Gaia, the sexual and reproductive gods on the same level. Perhaps he felt they were not worthy of inclusion. Another way of seeing it is that he may have intended to 'baptise' these concepts. He must have known that Chaos and the others were seen as gods in Greek thought, and occasionally the personification does show through in the book. But Milton, being a strict Protestant of the Puritan breed, would hardly have taken them to be literally gods. It was probably all figurative and poetic, and that may have been his understanding of Genesis as well. It certainly is for most people today, in the light of what we think we know about Creation and related matters.

Paradise Regained, with respect to mythology, compared with Paradise Lost

This is the sequel to Paradise Lost, and recounts the ministry of Jesus in the early stages, and focussing on the Temptations. Again, Milton embroiders on the Gospel accounts, but not quite to the extent as before. There is no attempt to relate the whole of Christ's life with the miracles, the teachings and the parables. Still less is there any emphasis on the Passion and the culmination of Christ's ministry. What we notice is that the Greek mythological element which was quite widespread in Paradise Lost, is now much diminished. The reason for this is not quite entirely clear, but one might guess that Milton felt that a pagan system of thought might seem inappropriate in relation to the true Messiah of God.

However, taking each reference in context reveals something interesting. On page 296 it says; 'no more with pomp and sacrifice shalt be enquired at Delphos or elsewhere... ' it is saying that the old system of oracle-mongering in the pagan world is now going to be stopped; the true oracle of God is now available, namely Jesus Christ.

On page 302 there is a conversation between Belial (6) and Satan on how to tempt Jesus. Belial has the idea that feminine charms would lure him; after all, Solomon was tempted by his wives, so why not Jesus? But Satan is not convinced. He reels off a whole list of tempting beauties;

'Calisto, Clymene, Daphne, Semele, Antiopa, Amymone, Syrinx...'

But this is in context and Satan is saying that not everyone finds such ladies alluring, the implication being that voluptuousness is a characteristic of paganism as opposed to Christianity. A similar thing happens during the temptation to have a banquet; it is accompanied by nymphs and naiads and fairy damsels, thus emphasising the pagan element in over-indulgence. (page 307).

At this point we see that Milton does not stick strictly to the biblical accounts of the Temptations, whether it be in St.Matthew or St.Luke. There is no mention of Jesus being tempted to turn stones into bread. Instead, the forty days of fasting are linked to Elijah's exile in the Wilderness, where he was fed by angels (according to Milton). Satan tempts Jesus with a table loaded up with delicious food, but Jesus is not deluded. We notice that the Devil does not appear as a snake or a frightening apparition, but as a pleasant, ordinary person, looking really respectable. This is a good example of demythologisation, but is fully consistent with St.Matthew, who simply mentions, 'the tempter'.

The second temptation is all about wealth and glory. How easy it would be if one had vast treasures, to influence, control and outbuy everyone else, but Jesus is not taken in by the spondulics of this world. The glory of this world is not all that it seems. Political power usually results in thieving, slaughtering and enslaving people. At this point, Jesus mentions the son of Jove, and of Mars, but in a negative and critical way, saying that they are found out to be 'rolling in brutish vices, and deformed, violent or shameful death shall be their due reward.'

Satan then shows Jesus the countries of the world with the promise that he could rule them all. The temptation is given extra spice by pointing out that Jesus is to be the Son of David, who had a glorious kingdom; so why cannot Jesus do the same, but on an earthly level? Then Satan takes him to Rome in order to see the glory and power of the empire and the Emperors, but this does not convince Jesus, and rightly so, because he must have known what vices were going on in the imperial household.(7)

Satan then tries to frighten Jesus with thunder and all kinds of overpowering natural phenomena. Again, this is a slight reminder of Elijah's experience in the cave.

The last temptation was to place Jesus on the pinnacle of the Temple and suggest that he should throw himself down in order to induce angels to come to his rescue; but Jesus is not taken in by that. The book ends with angels coming to reward Jesus with a banquet; this again is consistent with Matthew's account which says that 'angels came and ministered to him.' (Matthew 4:11). Milton has Satan completely floored by Jesus' answers, but St.Luke says that Satan departed 'until an opportune time.' (Luke 4:13). This of course is nearer the truth, since the temptations were by no means over and done with, and Jesus had to be on his guard all the time. But as far as Milton is concerned, Paradise is to be regained there and then as the Temptations are resisted, thus reversing the Fall as in the Garden of Eden.

The question is, how literally did Milton take Greek mythology and indeed biblical material? We notice that one of the Temptations is left out and he gives us five temptations altogether. These five are not totally different or contradictory to the Bible; what they do is unpack and embellish the basic accounts in Matthew and Luke. Does this mean that Milton does not take the accounts of the Temptations as literally true? If he can rewrite the New Testament, that is consistent with what he has done with the Fall; the early Genesis story is not taken too literally, but panned out and decorated with poetic devices. One of his main devices is to insert ideas from Greek mythology; there is much of this in Genesis but less in the New Testament account of the Temptations. Does that mean that he does not see Greek mythology as literally true, but just as a poetic device?

If we compare these works with Samson Agonistes, we find that there is no Greek mythology worked in at all. Milton may have felt that it was inappropriate or inconsistent with the subject matter, and this may be a further indication that he saw the Greek ideas as purely poetic and nothing more.

Even so, another context gives us a completely opposite feeling. The lengthy hymn, on the Morning of Christ's Nativity, verse 8 (page 398) we find that the shepherds are sitting in a row:

'Full little thought they than, that the mighty PAN, was kindly come to live with them below.'

Here we see Jesus Christ equated with the Greek god Pan. If we take this at face value, it would mean that Milton was assuming that Greek mythology was worthy of belief and syncretising with biblical thought. Or did he mean it literally? That is the core of the problem, and there is no final answer to it.

Footnotes for Chapter 6

1. Edmund Spenser, The Fairie Queen, reviewed in chapter 10.
2. The idea that there is life on other planets is by no means a modern idea; it is possible that the Greek philosophers thought of it.
3. Innocence is an important element in many world mythologies.
4. In Genesis 7 there is the contradiction between two of each animal and 7 of each of the clean animals. This is explained by the author conflating two sources of information.
5. A description of Orion and his activities are described in chapter 3.
6. Belial is one of the many names applied to Satan, or evil spirits, normally seen in pseudepigraphal literature.
7. The depraved antics of the Imperial household are described in Tacitus and Suetonius. It is more than likely that Milton knew these works; also that Jesus himself would have known about the antics of the Caesars.

7

The Mythology of Atlantis

This is another notion that stems from Ancient Greece, and which holds a fascination for many people, notably in the scientific community. It is estimated that there are about 15,000 different novels on this theme; this must be an indication of the fascination that this notion has on people. It would be more accurate to call 'Atlantis' a legend, as opposed to a myth, but the idea has gone through so many permutations and bouts of wishful thinking, that the term 'myth' could well be claimed as appropriate.

Where or from whom does the idea come? The answer is no less a person than Plato,(1) the famous Greek philosopher; not someone who might be given to fanciful ideas. In two of his books, **Timaeus** and **Critias,** he talks of a continent beyond the Pillars of Hercules, out in the ocean we now call the Atlantic. The Pillars of Hercules are meant to be the straits of Gibraltar, which were known to the Greeks. This would not be the Americas. He describes the island of Atlantis in considerable detail. It had an area of about 600,000 square miles, a flourishing area given to trading, with red, white and black stone buildings. They were given to gentleness and wisdom, a money-less society in which there was sharing. There were ten kings and an army of over a million men. Later, avarice, selfishness and aggression crept in as they embarked on imperialism. All this was happening about 9560 BC (according to Solon)(2). The island sank into the sea, and there is scientific evidence that at about that time there was a sudden and violent period in the earth's history, possibly caused by a meteorite or volcanic activity. Plato explains it as Zeus becoming annoyed at the behaviour of the Atlanteans. Realising that later generations would find this a strain on credulity, Plato insists that this is true. It is thought that

Plato gained this information from the priests of Egypt, during a visit to that country.

Going into more detail on the subject, Plato would almost certainly have maintained that this was historical fact. According to Socrates, Athens was engaged in an all-out struggle with the terrifying and mighty Atlantis, and it was only the Athenean superiority in political and military organisation that allowed them to prevail. The claim is that the Atlantean empire stretched right through Libya up to Egypt and across southern Europe as far as central Italy. Plato goes into so much detail on the matter that Atlantis becomes very real. With so much vivid description, this must indicate that it hardly began as a myth, or indeed a legend. Mythical elements clearly developed later, but that does not cancel out the historical core of the matter, just as the Trojan War is now seen as basically historical, but with mythological additives.

The works **Timaeus** and **Critias**, our source material here, are mainly concerned with discussing ancient Athens as well as Atlantis. The book Critias is left unfinished and tantalisingly leaves us in mid-air as to what Zeus is about to say about the Atlanteans. However, put together with Timaeus, we get a fuller picture, which has all the hallmarks of reality. Plato and his fellow Greeks believed that this massive island sank into the sea during a frightful night of earthquakes and torrential rain. This left the ocean very shallow just beyond Cadiz, and he talks of mudbanks which made the sea unnavigable in places. In fact, to this day there are treacherous sandbanks in that sea-area. There is reference to Gadeira, which is equated with modern Cadiz. Taking this seriously means that any attempt at locating Atlantis anywhere else (such as the North Pole!),(3) is nonsense. In addition, smaller islands in the ocean could be reached, and this must mean the Azores, Cape Verde, and Madeira. Tantalisingly, Plato mentions 'the mainland opposite which surrounds the genuine sea'. We take the 'genuine sea' to mean the Atlantic Ocean, and the 'mainland opposite' means that the Greeks believed that the flat earth was edged by another continent. This may indicate that they were aware of the Americas, but that is not entirely clear. It is possible that the Americas were much nearer to Europe at that time, only to drift further away because of what we call 'continental drift'. Although we normally think of that as a gradual and slow process, dramatic movements are not out of the question, if there are major earthquakes.

The origins of the island called Atlantis is explained by Poseidon, having been allotted this territory by a council of the gods, set to work to establish civilisation on the island. This is how it happened; there was a couple, Evenor and Leucippe, who had a daughter called Cleito. When the girl was old enough, Poseidon took a fancy to her and had her as his concubine. He put defences on the hill where she lived, and created concentric rings alternately of land and water with canals connecting to the sea. Then he organised two springs in the centre, one warm and another cold. He fathered five pairs of twins, divided the land into ten parts, one for each son. The firstborn got the best bit and he was the chief king, called Atlas. All the names of the other kings are quoted; they all worked together without warfare and had an annual conference and sacrifice to clear guilt. These ten dynasties prevailed for a long time and the land prospered. They grew enormously rich and traded abroad. Not only agricultural products were produced, but metal ores from the ground too. They had plenty of gold and something else called 'orichalc' which was second only to gold in value. We now think this was copper. They built palaces and temples which were adorned with precious metals. There is no mention of iron; presumably this was well before the iron age, or even the bronze age.

At this point it is worth commenting that if Poseidon mated with a human woman, what sort of 'god' was he? We can compare this with that enigmatic chapter in Genesis where the 'sons of god' mated with the 'daughters of men'. Are we looking at some kind of genius, hero, or strong man like Hercules, who started out as human but was 'promoted' to a god? Sadly for Von Daniken, this account says nothing about 'gods' appearing in a spaceship from another planet. This theory will be examined in chapter 17. Whatever approach one takes with this passage, it is still difficult to explain it.

Plato goes on to give all kinds of details about palaces, temples and towns. He gives actual dimensions in stades and plethra,(4) and the depth of the canals. Also the building of bridges is mentioned. The people harvested two crops a year. He describes the composition of the Army, with horses and chariots, archers and slingers; but there was no intention of fighting each other. They were intent on colonizing the Mediterranean countries, right up to Greece. After many years of virtuous living it all deteriorated into immoral greed and power. With this we see the decline of a great empire, which is typical of human nature. Zeus could see how things were degenerating and called an assembly of the gods, probably on Mount Olympus. The decision was taken to destroy Atlantis; this explains the night of earthquakes, torrential rain and the sinking of the island into the sea.

It may be safe to say that there is a core of historical reality in the Atlantis idea, but that it seems to have received mythological elements even in Plato's day. These elements have been augmented and transferred to other parts of the world to suit certain political and racist policies. The racist element never receives any comment from Plato. He even remarks that the Atlantean temples did not look like Greek temples; the inference from this could be that he saw these people as Greeks, like himself, but with slightly different ideas on building design. Plato must have realised that later generations would find this a strain on credulity, which is why he insists that all this is true.

Modern evidence for Atlantis

That this, so far, is not out of the question, is supported by the fact that we have found sunken cities in other places.(5) This might have been the result of flooding at the end of the last Ice Age, or of sinkage of the earth's surface. This is actually happening at Baia in the Bay of Naples. Most people assume, following Plato, that Atlantis must have been located out beyond Gibraltar. A minority opinion would be that of Galanopoulos, who believes that the island of Thira-Santorini in the Aegean was the real Atlantis, a volcano which exploded about 1400 BC, scattering its inhabitants to other areas. The weaknesses in this hypothesis are that the date is well within the reach of historical recording in the ancient world; also that the island did not disappear into the sea, but is still there to this day. Admittedly, houses answering the description of red, black and white as in Plato, have been excavated on Thira, but that in itself is not conclusive. It may have been a style common throughout the Greek world. Galanopoulos' investigations are further evidence of the hold this legend has on people's minds.

Actually producing evidence for the existence of Atlantis west of Gibraltar is somewhat more difficult, and yet there are people who are prepared to do searches in the Atlantic for such remains.(6) Already some interesting results have emerged, though not really consistent. In 1968 a dark rectangle on the sea-bed covered by six feet of water, appeared to be an ancient building, possibly a temple. It is located near the north end of Andros Island (Bahamas). In addition, on the Great Bahamas Bank, nine feet deep, were found dozens of pathways with parallel sides, geometric configurations and circular areas. Off the north west coast of north Bimini was found an extensive pavement of rectangular and polygonal flat stones of varying sizes and thicknesses. Some were nearly perfect squares. These were stone blocks of the same size and weight as found in the Pyramids. In addition to this, there is evidence of drastic sinkage of the land about ten to twelve thousand years ago. Off the Island of Andros, an underwater cave contains stalagmites and stalactites 165 feet down in the water. These can only have formed on dry land originally. While this is not direct actual evidence of Atlantis, it does indicate that towns and other structures in the Atlantic basin underwent a sudden and drastic sinkage about the suspected time of the Flood.

Just like the siege of Troy, which was almost certainly a historical event which has been spun into a myth, so too the legend of Atlantis.

Modern mythmongering over Atlantis

All kinds of conjectures have been imagined about Atlantis. The chief one is that Atlantis formed a 'stepping stone' from Europe to the Americas. This would explain such things as the Mayan pyramids being inspired by the Egyptian ones. The weakness in this argument is that the Meso-American pyramids are very different in design and were used for a different purpose. As we have seen, it may be that Plato knew of the 'Americas', but that is not completely clear.

Going on from there, many people conjecture that if Atlantis was such an advanced culture, and they realised there was going to be a deluge, then they would have made sure that their knowledge would be hidden away for future generations to find and benefit from.(7) This is where the whole matter becomes increasingly conjectural and fanciful. There are notions about secret storage chambers under the pyramids and the sphinx and other locations in Egypt. The Andes are imagined to have grottoes full of Atlantean treasures. Even more fantastic, the Himalayas and parts of Tibet are imagined to have underground labyrinths containing artefacts from Atlantis. It gets even more fanciful. The Atlanteans are conjectured to have had all kinds of wonderful ideas, including electricity and airships, and even atom bombs! Even spaceships are in the picture! And now we are only just catching up on them with all our modern developments. And of course, the Atlanteans could not have had these clever ideas all by themselves; the information had to have come from outer space! Much of this information comes from Andrew Tomas and Eric von Daniken.

With this we see the same configuration of thought that goes on over Evolution and the Big Bang nowadays. What happened before, and before that and before that? The problem is, any clever new idea has to have been the inspiration of someone somewhere; why does it have to come from 'gods' from outer space? The substratum of thought in this kind of dilemma, is that ancient people were all stupid, therefore they could not have had any bright ideas. But the evidence is that just as nowadays we have the occasional prodigy, so too did they, and in proportion, their prodigies might have been far more intelligent than ours today. A very simple example comes from the design and construction of the pyramids; there is no need to go into too much detail; they are much cleverer and technologically brilliant than anything we can devise now. Added to which they did not have the resources in gadgetry that we have now. Many examples of the achievements of people in the remote past can be found, many of which defy explanation, but this does not have to involve a source of genius called Atlantis. And why and how the Atlanteans would have decided to drop off their clever ideas into storage areas in wisely dispersed parts of the world, is not really (7)substantiated. There is a lot of guesswork, supposition and wishful thinking going on in this area. Facts are few and far between.

The idea that technological advances had to have been inspired by 'gods' is not a new one. If we look at Greek mythology, we hear of Prometheus, a nice-natured god, who defied Zeus and enlightened mankind with all kinds of ideas. But the same original question crops up again; how literally do we have to take this kind of myth? If we do take it literally, in some sort of fundamentalistic manner, then that will substantiate what people like Tomas and Von Daniken are saying; essentially that 'gods' or spacemen visited the earth in the remote past and put ideas into the heads of primitive mankind. But a non-literalistic approach would be to say that somebody especially gifted (a prodigy) had an inspiration, perhaps in some kind of dream or trance, which would explain technological advances. We must recall that most, if not all scientific discoveries have been made purely by chance or coincidentally. The discovery of the Americas is a case in point; Columbus was not trying to find America; he was trying to find an alternative route to the 'Indies' by going west instead of east. He went to his grave still believing he had landed somewhere in what we now call 'the

East Indies'. He had the idea that the earth was round because he had read some of these things in the ancient Greek philosophers. The idea that the earth was flat was the majority opinion and quite dogmatically enforced up to 1492. How people like Pythagoras deduced that the earth is a sphere and Aristarchus thought that it revolved round the sun is an interesting question, but they must have been regarded as cranks in their day and age. But why people nowadays should imagine that these clever technological ideas must have come from the people of Atlantis is a strange notion.

In addition to this, we must remember that in the ancient world 'gods' were not always what we assume them to be now. For many people there was no clear dividing line between the divine and the human. One could become a god by being a military genius, like Alexander the Great. One could become a Pharaoh, a living god on earth, just by marrying an Egyptian princess; that was the essential qualification, as opposed to being the son of the previous Pharaoh. To think of Prometheus as some kind of divinity who was helpful to mankind is entirely plausible; it does not mean he has to have arrived in a spaceship from another planet. He could very easily have been a very clever person, a genius, who because of his skills, came to be regarded as a 'god'. From there, an entire myth could have been spun about how Zeus punished him, but eventually he was set free and rescued from the underworld.

This brings us to consider that enigmatic passage in Genesis 6:1-4, in which 'the sons of god saw that the daughters of men were fair.' The book of Enoch takes this to mean fallen angels misbehaving with human ladies, but that too is just as mythological, and is biologically rather strange. What it could mean is that the sons of the kings (who were regarded as gods) set out to seduce the ordinary girls. This raises the whole question of Sacral Kingship in the ancient world, but it is a fact that in many countries, the king was regarded as a god, and that was particularly so in Egypt. This passage may have been written at a time before the Israelites had begun to think seriously about the nature of kingship and the fact that God, YHWH, is the only true king.

With regard to technological advances, Genesis also has a comment (4:20-22). Jabal was the father of all nomadic cattle-rearing peoples; Jubal was the father of all musicians; Tubal-Cain was the father of all metal workers, in bronze and iron. There is no mention of divine inspiration for these skills; they all had a father called Lamech, stemming from Cain and going down to Noah. There is nothing extraordinary recorded about these clever people.

Political doctrines derived from Atlantis

Another island which was alleged to have disappeared mysteriously, was the island of Thule, which in time came to be equated with Atlantis. But this one was in the frozen north; there was much disagreement over exactly where it was located, but it was peopled by wonderful, blue-eyed, blond, vegetarian Nordics, in some kind of golden age of the earliest human civilisations. Now we see the racist element coming into the picture. There was a group called the Thule group, founded about 1918, which was aiming at becoming a powerful force in Bavarian politics. The names associated with it were Walter Nauhaus, Von Sebottendorf, Haushofer and Eckart, and later Hitler himself. Their chief obsession was anti-semitism. They had the notion that the German people were the descendants of the Thules, and that they had the right approach to Christianity, and that the Jews were a corrupting influence on the whole picture. The one thing this group lacked was a Messiah, a forceful leader. This is what Hitler came to provide them with; he changed the Thulists into the NASDAP, the German Workers Party, and thus into the Nazi Party.(8) Although Eckart is thought to have heavily influenced Hitler in various ways, not least on the subject of the occult and black magic, there were many disagreements. When the Nazis came to power in 1933, the Thulists were the first to be consigned to the concentration camps.

In 1922 a book called Atlantis; the original home of the Aryans, by Zschaetch appeared, and this completed the equation between Thule and Atlantis. Atlantis was placed at the North Pole; it had been destroyed by a comet colliding with the earth. There were only three survivors; Wotan, who became a god, his pregnant sister and his daughter. They were vegetarians and teetotallers. As they escaped from Atlantis, they sheltered in the roots of an enormous cabbage. Wotan's sister died in childbirth, but her child was fed by a friendly she-wolf. Thus we arrive at Romulus and Remus, which was very convenient for Germano-Italian co-operation. The child, a boy, did not marry his cousin but chose to fornicate with lesser racial breeds. They taught him to eat meat and drink alcohol. It was a Jewish woman called Heid who managed to make a fermentation from the cabbage plant, and that explains how the Jews managed to introduce meat-eating, drunkenness and racial impurity into the pure Aryan breed that had come from Atlantis. Zschaetch also alleged that most of the world mythologies were a distorted recollection of these events. Heid's discovery was Eve offering the apple to Adam; the cabbage was the world tree, Yggdrasil of Norse lore. Now we see how cranky speculative ideas can infiltrate the top echelons of power in government.

It was Himmler, in 1935, someone who was obsessive about racism, who founded the Ahnenerbe, the Nazi occult bureau, and appointed Hermann Wirth as its first director. In addition to Zschaetch's notions, there was a book called Oera Linda published in the 19th century, which 'proved' (!) that all true civilisation had been founded by the Germans. Putting the two together, Wirth arrived at the doctrine that Atlantis was at the North Pole and the Aryans stemmed from there, with their superior civilisation. The Bureau tried hard to research these 'facts' but in spite of spending enormous amounts of money on scientific gadgets, solid proof was found to be somewhat elusive. Wirth indulged in 'intuitive' decipherment of ancient symbols and his wife's ability to commune with the spirit world. This became the solid (!) basis for equating Thule with Atlantis, located in the Arctic, and having a pure Nordic race, worshipping one God, and infiltrating other parts of the world. Sadly they managed to dilute their racial purity by marrying persons of lower racial stock. Thus we see how an augmented myth can be made to support a crackpot political theory.

This was the Nazi version of the Golden Age, a lost paradise in which Nordic supermen ruled the world. The notion of a Golden Age is not confined to Aryan thinking. It occurs in many mythologies the world over, but usually lacks the nasty racialist element. But this explains the motivation behind, not just the urge to reinstate the Holy Roman Empire, but also to recover the purity of Aryan blood with a programme of selective breeding, eugenics and the Final Solution.

Now we see how people like Rosenberg, Hess and Spengler became enmeshed in this kind of thinking. Even the anti-Nazi Steiner had the same sort of ideas but in a different mode. He believed that there was another mythical continent called Lemuria, now lying beneath the Pacific Ocean, and which predated Atlantis. Steiner had all kinds of fancy ideas about the Atlanteans, including the idea that they had airships. It all went wrong because they embarked on black magic. The refugees headed for the Gobi desert and settled in Tibet; more on that subject later.

There was another 'lost land' called Atland which post-dated Atlantis, and was located between Greenland and the Hebrides. Another unexplained catastrophe submerged the country, and the survivors, called Frisians, went abroad founding colonies in Italy, Greece, Germany and even the Inca Empire. Thus we read in the Oera Linda.

We all know that certainty is something to be prized over theorisation. The Nazis sent a mission to the Baltic Sea to find relics of these supposed lost islands. Scientific gadgetry, assumed to find indications of what they wanted to discover, was installed in the Baltic. This was money that could have been spent on defence. Even more hare-brained, were the annual missions to Tibet to link up with the supposed remnants of the Atlanteans. This went on from the mid-1920's until 1942. There was a belief, largely fostered by Roerich, in a place called Shamballah in Tibet. It was a lovely valley but also a system of tunnels where certain people lived and thrived. The Nazis managed to interest some of the Tibetans into coming to Germany and establishing centres and actually fighting on their side. Needless to say, this imaginary place has never been found, in spite of certain elements in Tibet insisting on its existence.

Another theory put forward by Hoerbiger, was the Weltseislehre, or 'the world ice theory', and also known as the 'glacial cosmogony'; this also fascinated Hitler, Himmler and Goebbels. The moon was thought to be made of ice, and the origin of the solar system was blocks of ice colliding with the sun. There had been other earth satellites; all planets spiral towards the sun and then are consumed by it. As they approach the earth, they are captured by earth's gravity and become satellites. Then they fall down and splinter up on the ground. There have been at least six such events before our moon was captured. The biblical flood is one case of a moon-collapse. As the moon comes nearer to the earth, this increases the tidal waves, causing massive flooding. This kind of thinking became popular in Germany, and it seemed to fit well with the Atlantis theory. Even the dinosaurs, as they became extinct, were fitted into this theory.

Someone called Kiss persuaded Himmler to send a mission to Ethiopia in 1936 to find bits of previous moons which were thought to have fallen to earth. Himmler's Occult Bureau set up a meteorological section which would give weather forecasts based on the world ice theory. So convinced were they of its genuineness that the Bureau's weather forecasts became some sort of dogma. It was not until 1941 that doubts about its validity began to emerge; Hitler, on the strength of these forecasts, felt that the German Army did not need winter uniforms as they stormed towards Moscow. In addition to that, Hitler was afraid that shooting rockets into high altitudes would interfere with the 'world ice'. This explains why he actually delayed the commencement of the V2 rockets in 1944. Now we see how too much faith in mythology can backfire on one.

If one were to think that the world ice theory were just about the limit in crazy ideas, one would be wrong. Some of the Nazis preferred something called the 'hollow earth' doctrine. This was speculated by Halley in 1692, who thought that the earth was hollow, with solid outer layers. Although most reasonable scientists dismissed the idea, there was a strand of thinking in America which perpetuated the notion. There were variations on this theme, but a certain Peter Bender, a German fighter pilot in World War I, latched onto the idea and managed to influence Goering. His ideas worked their way into the German Navy; the Luftwaffe too favoured the idea. The relevance of this to the Navy was that it was difficult to detect enemy ships, even with radar at that time. On the assumption that the earth was hollow and we were on the inside of it, it would be easy to bounce radar waves off the opposite shell of the earth; that entailed aiming the equipment up in the air as opposed to parallel to the earth. In spite of much opposition from other Nazis, Bender and his friends managed to persuade the government to finance an experiment on the island of Ruegen, using infra-red rays. Fischer aimed the equipment at 45 degrees at the sky. The experiment proved a failure and Bender and his friends were discredited and sent to concentration camps. Some of them survived the camps and continued their campaign after the war; Fischer went on to help the Americans with their Atom Bomb project.

The Vril society, another Nazi-occultist group sprang on the hollow earth notion. This was because they believed that the 'Secret Chiefs', with whom they had made contact, lived in an underground world, and there were openings at various parts of the world. We can guess which country was a candidate for these openings; Tibet, of course. Hitler, persuaded by Haushofer, believed that the Secret Chiefs lived in Tibet. That was because after the fall of Thule, its survivors went eastwards and settled in Tibet and found underground passages. This explains why the Nazis sent missions into Tibet (1926 to 1942) to make contact with the Thuleans with a view to gaining occult help in the subjugation of the world.

Some of the Vril Society's ideas will seem really bizarre by today's standards. There was the Mesmeric Power which was not exactly hypnosis, but could alter one's personality into a sort of charisma. With this, one could bend an audience to one's opinion; how much of this did Hitler use? With this kind of 'animal magnetism' one could reduce an audience to excitement, hysteria, and convulsions. The Vrils would have said this was because one could harness the 'vril', the energy of life, which was the source of all power in the world, and become master of the earth. This was essentially by making contact with the Secret Chiefs.

The Vrils were dedicated to research into Atlantis, and by implication the Aryan race. It thought that magical powers lay dormant in that Aryan blood. If worked on, one could become possessed of superhuman powers, just like the Secret Chiefs. The earth itself, they believed was a living organism, a vast psychic consciousness. Where have we read of this before; think of James Lovelock! 1909, they believed, was the date at which a new cycle of human evolution would begin; magical powers would usher in a new era in human history. Hitler had joined this society and was deeply influenced by it. He thought that a newly enlightened race of Aryan supermen would be able to travel both backwards and forwards in time. By this they would be able to discover primitive history and also the future destiny of mankind. He also thought that a 'god-man' was the next development in evolution.

With this, we see an important element in mythology; speculation about the origins of all things, and also it swings round to eschatology.

It has already been mentioned that the Nazis were absorbed with the occult, astrology and Satanism, at least, the top echelons of the SS were. Another aspect of it was the mythology of the Teutonic Knights and the Holy Roman Empire. This is where historical reality and legend merge and are plasticined into more mythology. A thousand years ago, the German knights (Ritters) were colonising eastern Europe, in areas that we now know as Poland, Estonia, Latvia and Lithuania. The popular idealistic conception of the knights was that they were very noble; or were they? Hitler had the idea (see Mein Kampf) that Germany would take up and continue this expansion where the Teutonic Knights had left off.(9) It all fitted in with roseate notions about the Holy Roman Empire and Charlemagne; that was one of the main motives for the First World War; to regain parts of France, Belgium, Luxembourg and areas in Eastern Europe. Unfortunately for Germany, the Allies had a different opinion on the matter, and prevailed. The Germans could not understand how this had happened, since they believed they were the best people on earth, with the best army and everybody else was inferior. A reason had to be found. This is where the racist element comes in; it was alleged that the Jews (and the Bolsheviks) had administered the stab in the back. It was not just Hitler who believed this; it was a popular notion, but the Nazis made great play of it. Now we see why the Nazis indulged in mythology about Atlantis and Aryan superiority; they had to justify from supposed history, their claim to be the best people, and to have the right to appropriate territory from other countries. Since the Allies were seen to be capable of matching their arms in battle, it then became necessary to summon up extra strength from the occult and careful timings from the study of astrology.

With this in mind, we can see why Himmler developed Wewelsburg castle into a centre for occult and sinister goings-on for the senior echelons of the SS. No one knows the full extent of what happened at Wewelsburg, but it must have been pretty frightening and disgusting. We can see that the Atlantis element and Aryan superiority are just another type of myth; the Nazis almost certainly took the whole thing literally. This will explain the seriousness with which they sent out missions to various part of the world to find evidence in support of their ideas.

But the weakness with all this occult and astrology is that one's enemies can work the same thing in response. This is exactly what did happen; the British, the Americans and the Russians employed white witches to counteract the Nazi black witches. Also they employed astrologers to discern what moves Hitler was likely to make, assuming that his moves were largely, if not entirely, governed by the stars. The Nazis probably never realised what was happening, which means that their clever methods backfired on them and gave the Allies an advantage.

An important lesson that we can learn from this is to realise that crazy so-called 'scientific' ideas can invade the top echelons of government and result in a lot of wastage of time and money. We ought to be very cautious about the elaborate claims that are made about outer space and other planets; these ideas are claimed to be based on 'evidence' (whatever that might mean). However, our presuppositions on these matters are constantly being found to be wrong or in need of adjustment. We should remember that the dogmatisms that the Nazi's held actually contributed to their downfall. There are many other areas of government policy where this factor could hold true.

Footnotes for chapter 7

1. Strabo and Proclus, two Greek historians.
2. Solon, a Greek philosopher.
3. The Nazi theorists thought Atlantis was at the North Pole (see later in this chapter).
4. Stades were the measurement of the stadium; about 607 feet. Plethron (singular) Greek unit of measurement, about 30 metres.
5. There are other sunken cities in Greek waters.
6. Andrew Tomas is an author who provides this kind of evidence. The Atlantis Legend.
7. It is not clarified how the Atlanteans would have known there was going to be a deluge.
8. NASDAP in full; National Sozialistische Deutsche Arbeiter Partei. German workers' party.
9. See Mein Kampf.

8

Norse Mythology

I have chosen the Norse mythology because, it is the second major influence on modern western thinking after the Greek. It is not quite as important as the Graeco-Roman system, but many countries in northern Europe and North America are very largely under its influence to this day and will continue to be so.

A comparison with the Huichol material, described in chapter 14 is quite striking. Firstly, the Huichols of western Mexico, live in a predominantly warm and dry climate, and in a fairly small area along the Pacific coast. The Norsemen, however, lived in a cold, tempestuous climate, but were spread over a much wider area and came into contact with many other peoples with their own mythologies. It is therefore more difficult to discover the pure unadulterated mythology of the north European races. It is fortunate that there was a historian called Snorri Sturluson who thought to record many of the Norse sagas. It is likely that there were many more myths in circulation but have been lost to history. He was writing just after the Viking age(1), from a Christian point of view, which must inevitably have coloured his accounts to some extent. Later , in the 14th century, there came the Eddas, the Poetic and the Prose ones, which were dependant on Sturluson's work. All these works stem from Iceland, but the Norse system of thought must have dominated all of Scandinavia, Germany, Britain, Northern France, Finland, Russia, Greenland, Newfoundland, and have influenced many other areas. It is no surprise then to find that there are many inconsistencies and contradictions at work, and no clearly connected account.

The Vikings penetrated into the Mediterranean, as far as Constantinople and into the Silk Route to China. They were great traders and adventurers. It would be strange if their mythology had not been influenced by other systems of thought. It might also be maintained that they influenced other systems, since it might appear that their mythology may have stretched further back in time than the others.

There will be no attempt at recounting all the dramatic stories from the Nordic sagas; there are various comprehensive works on this line already. What we need to do is find the essentials of Norse thinking; what were their motives, major assumptions and view of the future. In general terms, their stories are characterised by freezing conditions, bloodshed, revenge, nasty bargaining, and hate. This is in quite a contrast to the Huichol mentality, and somewhat different from Greek thought. We can see how the climate and the topography of the northern countries have conditioned their thinking. We must always remember that the Norse material is being relayed to us through the eyes of Christian writers who unreservedly hated the violence and pillaging of the Vikings.

Some of this material has already appeared in my second book, the Theology of Truth; in an attempt to avoid repeating myself, I am going to focus on material not described so far, and draw from them as many conclusions as is reasonable. It is important to study Norse mythology in relation to Greek material, if only for the sake of assessing together, their continuing influence on modern Western culture. That is in spite of all the attempts made in our times to develop new mythologies, consciously or unconsciously.

Gods and Creation

These remarks are heavily dependent on the description given by Martin Dougherty in his book, Norse Myths. Slightly differing versions may be found in other works, but this is no surprise since Norse mythology was never a completely systematic or unified pattern of thought. It would seem that at the start, there were two lands, separated by an 'abyss'. We notice the Greek word here; the Norsemen called it Ginnungagap; it was empty but charged with magic. On one side was Muspelheim, a land of fire, and on the other side was a land of ice and cold mist. Muspelheim was to the south and ruled over by a fire giant called Surt. There is no explanation for the origin of Surt, but this again brings up the awkward question of 'before that and before that' which still occupies people's minds to this day. Niflheim was to the north and its glaciers poured southwards and encountered the heat, causing it to melt. The droplets formed the primordial Jotunn, called Ymir, another giant. From his sweat came three giants called Jotnar, two male and one female, which were the first of the Frost Giants. We notice that already, before the coming of the human race, thought has to be given to the question of proliferation; there has to be male and female.

The fact that there are two lands of fire and of ice, firstly suggests Iceland. It also is suggestive of the end of the last Ice Age as the glaciers are retreating and human life emerges from the Ice Age. If this is a genuine connection to real history, then here we have another mythology which relates, if even loosely, to geographical realities. From that the bards indulge in augmentation and exaggeration, something that can be seen in so many other myths. The fire giant Surt is clearly related to the volcano Surtsey on Iceland. This may be another indication that Norse mythology is the oldest in the world, and that other mythologies may be derived from it. But that is merely guesswork.

What did Ymir eat? There was a cow called Audhumbla who gave Ymir milk. Then another creature appeared from the ice, Buri, who was the first of the tribe of gods called the Aesir. Buri had a son called Bor and he married a giantess called Bestla, who also had descended from Ymir. In this way, Bor married his cousin (as opposed to his sister!).

Odin was the firstborn of Bor and Bestla; he was half Jotunn and half Aesir. He had two brothers called Vili and Ve. These boys were concerned that Ymir was still producing more Jotnar (giants) so they decided to kill him. With this we have the first murder, which can be compared with the Cain and Abel incident; both are within the family. As Ymir died a torrent of blood drowned all but two of the Jotnar. These were Bergelmir and his wife; they floated away to Niflheim in a boat and so started a new race of Frost Giants. We can compare this with the account of the Flood and Noah. This time the Flood comes before the Creation of the world, and the act of cleansing is applied to the giants as opposed to the human race, which so far has not appeared.

Creation of the world

As Ymir is murdered, his body parts become the physical world as we know it. His skull is the sky, the earth is his flesh and the mountains his bones, and every part of him is used up. He is dead but everything else comes to life from him. In this we see an interesting permutation on Pantheism; that god is equivalent to the creation, but nevertheless dead.

This also reminds us of the Cosmological Argument for the existence of God. This has been discussed in detail in my first book, The Theology of Paradox. To put it briefly, this idea assumes that there has to be a first cause for everything, but after things have been 'kick-started', creation just goes on by itself in some kind of chain reaction. The prime cause is then somehow irrelevant. In this case, Ymir is the basis of everything but is no longer active in whatever developments there may be.

Maggots or worms emanated from Ymir's corpse, so producing the dwarfs. Four of them, Nordi (North), Sundri (East?), Austri (South; think of Austria!) and Vestri (West), had the job of holding up the sky so that it would not collapse on to the earth; the Greeks managed with one Titanic god called Atlas to do this task. Other dwarfs emerged and went to live in an underground world called Nidavellir; does this remind us of the Atlanteans who were to supposed to have occupied tunnels in Tibet!? (See chapter 7 on Atlantis).

In common with every other mythology, the origin of the sun and moon are worked in. Someone (a human?) named his children Sol and Mani because they were so bright and beautiful. The gods were annoyed by this and sentenced the two to go around the sky in chariots, carrying the sun and moon. To keep them moving, two wolves were appointed to chase them; one wolf almost swallows the moon; he manages to take a bite out of the moon, but fails to catch up with him completely. It is unusual that both the sun and the moon are assumed here to be masculine; most other mythologies have the sun as masculine and the moon as feminine (and sinister too).

Odin, the creator and his brothers construct the world around a great ash tree, called Yggdrasil. This is the Norse version of the 'world tree', which appears in virtually every other mythical system. The actual type of tree does not matter; it is according to what would have been growing in that particular territory. The significance of it is that the tree, with its roots, bole and branches form a connection between all three levels of the world, namely, heaven, earth and the underworld. It can be seen as a poetic way of saying that all of life, in whatever form it takes, is basically related and connected with the gods and the demons. The difference here, in Norse lore, is that the three levels are turned into nine compartments, each of which has an offshoot of Yggdrasil's roots integrated with it. We briefly describe each compartment with various comments.

What might be called 'heaven'(?) has three areas; firstly there is **Asgard** where the Aesir gods live, especially Odin and his wife Frigga. It has gold and silver spires. We notice the appearance of precious metals with all their mythical implications. Asgard also has the Hall of Valhol (or Valhalla) where one went if one were slain in battle, in other words, not a coward but a hero. That is a roundabout way of placing a great value on warfare, violence and bloodshed. There was everlasting feasting, drunkenness and battles going on in there; glorious if one is inclined to be of such a mentality! There are some versions that actually equate Asgard with Troy; this again might be an original historical starting point for the myth.

In heaven there is also **Vanaheim** which is the home of the Vanir, another tribe of gods less inclined to violence and more connected with fertility. It was a realm of light and beauty. Not much is known about it, except to say that it is wilder and a dangerous place for those not in harmony with Nature.

Heaven also contains **Alfheim** where the Light Elves live. These were not full-blown gods but more like divinities or spiritual influences. Possibly they were on the same level as the Hindu 'asuras' or 'raksasas' of which there were various grades. It also reminds us of the 'ant people' or the 'bee people' as in Huichol thinking. The ruler of Alfheim was the god Freyr who was a Vanir. He is associated with good harvests and fertility. Later, he joined the Aesir.

Midgard is the world of humans, but the human race cannot see the other worlds. It is surrounded by seas which contain a gigantic serpent called Jormangand, which encircles the earth and bites its own tail. Here again we see the importance of snakes; there is the symbolism of life and death, in paradox. It is not clear whether Jormangand's circle is vertical or horizontal, but that is not of great importance. As well as being connected to Asgard by the tree, there is also a bridge called Bifrost, which can be seen by mortals; it is the rainbow. That is another poetic way of saying that mortals can have access to God and vice versa. In the Bible, the rainbow is a symbol of God's everlasting commitment to caring for this world.

Jotunheim is also on the earth level, but is populated with the Jotnar (giants) who have no respect for law and good behaviour. They are usually at enmity with the gods, but not always.

Muspelheim lies to the south and is a land of fire ruled by the fire giant

Surt. Fire demons live here. Not much information is offered for this area, except to say that it sounds like Iceland.

To the north, and going down below, lies **Niflheim**, as seen at the beginning. All the cold waters of the world come from its well, Hvergelmir. There is a dragon, Nidhogg, that gnaws at the roots of Yggdrasil, and also sucks at dead bodies to get their blood. This is where the Frost Giants live as well as Niflungar (which in German becomes the Nibelungs).

Going down again, we come to **Nidavellir** which might be equated with **Svartalfheim.** This is the cavernous home of the Dwarfs or Dark Elves. They are clever at craftwork but also mischievous and can be nasty-minded. They are thought to cause people to have nightmares. They have to live underground to avoid the sun's rays turning them into stone. One thinks of Jimson-weed man and others in the Huichol sagas. Also Dracula (chapter 22) cannot stand the daylight. Is this symbolic of losing all sense of humanity and empathy?

Finally there is **Helheim (Hel).** This is where our idea of Hell comes from, but it seems not to be fiery. The goddess Hel rules here but in a compartment walled off from the rest of Niflheim. It is a land of cold fog and miserable occupants; those who have been cowards and failed to indulge in warfare.

So with nine compartments in the universe, nine becomes the significant number in Norse thinking. This is in contrast to Judaeo-Christian concept of seven and the Huichol notion of five. The universe is held together by this enormous tree, and there is a well of some kind supplied by Yggradrasil in each area. The well of Urd is in Asgard and Mimir's well is in Jotunheim. It is a way of saying that the whole of life, of whatever quality or form it takes, is basically supplied by one source. The free use of that significant number makes us connect with the essentials of the universe in day to day living.

Like many mythologies, the animal kingdom has an important relationship with the scheme, but somewhat different from what we see with the Huichol scheme. Already we have seen how two wolves are chasing the sun and the moon; also there is Audhumbla the primeval cow, who is swept over into the abyss. There is also a pig, Saehriminir, who supplies the revellers in Vahalla with endless quantities of pork. At Valhalla there is a goat, Heidrun, standing on the roof of the hall, and supplying mead to keep the party permanently intoxicated.

In addition to this, each major god has his animal assistants keeping him company. Odin has two ravens, Hugin and Munin, which seem to personify his thoughts and desires. Odin is noted for his skill in poetry and thirst for wisdom (does this remind us of Solomon?). Also he has an eight-legged horse called Sleipnir, (nine legs would have been a little lopsided!) who went on to father steeds for many of the other gods. With his horse, Odin could ride up and down Yggdrasil in order to visit other compartments in the universe. Odin also has the Valkyries, which are some sort of ghoulish beings; they take people off to Valhalla, but also put curses on people in battle. Odin also possesses the head of Mimir, which having been chopped off in battle, still lives to impart wisdom to the god. Odin also has a magic spear called Gungnir, which the dwarfs crafted from bits from Yggdrasil; it has magical runes inscribed on it.

With the god Tyr, the war god, we see a negative relationship with an animal, the wolf Fenrir. There is some kind of deal made with Fenrir, which involved someone putting his hand in the wolf's mouth. Tyr is the one who gets his hand chopped off to secure the wolf from being a danger to everyone else. Fenrir comes to his end when another son of Odin, Vidar, forces the wolf's mouth open and slays him. This could only be done because Vidar had magical shoes (doubtless supplied by some helpful dwarf).

Thor, the son of Odin, has a chariot pulled by two goats, Tanngrisnir and Tanngnjostr. They could be killed and eaten each night but spring back to life next day, as long as the bones and skin are left intact. Someone broke a bone which rendered one goat permanently lame. Thor does not always use his chariot, as the gods sometimes travel on horseback up and down the Bifrost Bridge. Thor has a massive hammer with which to smash anyone's head in, but he has to have his magical belt on in order to wield it. Thunder and lightning are evidence of Thor on the rampage.

Another negative relationship comes between Loki, the rascal god, and an eagle, who is actually the giant Thjazi in disguise. It seems that tricky Loki meets his match with the eagle, and is forced into a deal to abduct Idun the goddess who has the magic fruit which keeps the gods youthful. Idun, by the way, is associated with a fawn. The end of the story shows Idun with her fruit (apples, as in the Garden of Eden?) restored and the gods reversing the aging process. Here we see the motif of sidestepping death.

Gefjun was an agricultural goddess who had four sons (fathered by a giant; and that was very unusual). She turned her sons into oxen which enabled her to plough the whole island of Zealand in a day, thus winning a big concession out of the king of Sweden.

Njord and Nerthus appear to be a male and female version of the same thing. Nerthus is pictured as being drawn in a chariot pulled by cows. Njord has a son called Freyr; he has a chariot pulled by boars. His association with boars means that many sacrifices of boars are made to him.

Freya, sometimes confused with Frigg, the wife of Odin, has a chariot pulled by two cats, often seen as black or grey. This may be symbolic of cattiness in certain ladies! Also, Freya rode on another boar, Hildisvini. Of more significance is the necklace she obtained from four Dwarfs; it was named Brisingamen; more of that later.

In this way, we can see that the animal kingdom relates to the gods in a different way as compared with the Huichol material. What is missing is the relationship with the world of humans. Norse mythology seldom involves itself with mankind; all the battles and dirty tricks are performed above our heads, or below our feet, but the 'fall-out' still invades historical realities, such as battles and good harvests.

Theodicy; the problem of evil

With Norse mythology, this question could usefully be reversed; the problem of good! So much of the antics of the gods is violence, greed, lustfulness, cruelty and trickery. It would be easy to understand why there is evil in the world; the gods are the main source of it, as well as various giants and elves. One wonders how the human race ever managed to survive. The only god who seems to have been nice-natured is Baldar; this may be a later influence coming from Christianity, since in early sagas he is warlike. He was loved by everyone and very beautiful. We all know the tale of how his mother extracted a promise not to harm him from everything except the mistletoe. Loki then tricked Baldar's brother Hod, into firing an arrow made of mistletoe at the so-called invincible god. The result was his death. This reminds us of Achilles who had just one weak spot. See Matthew Arnold's poem, Baldar's Death. This motif of Baldar's mother forgetting to tackle the mistletoe, ties in with the concept of 'nescience' as seen in Gnosticism (chapter 5).

There is no spiritual figure corresponding to the Devil in Norse thinking. Even Loki, who is up to any filthy trick and vandalism with it, is mischievous rather than totally wicked. There seems to be no god who is well-intentioned towards humanity, except possibly for Freyr, the fertility god who ensures prosperity and good harvests.

The coming of the human race

We have the equivalent of Adam and Eve, the first man, Ask and his wife Embla. They are created from trees after the death of Ymir. Odin, Vili and Ve give them inspiration, intellect and warmth of life, and somewhere to live, namely Midgard. This sounds like Prometheus. The god Hoenir gives them something called Odr which means ecstasy, frenzy and inspiration. Another god called Lodurr gives them good looks and something called La which means 'warmth'. Little is said about the human race until we arrive at the end of the world, Ragnarok. The last two humans, Lif and Lifthrasir managed to survive the apocalypse by sheltering in a tree, possibly Yggddrasil, and so managed to repopulate the world. This again reminds us of Noah and his family.

The Champion mentality

Clearly, Thor is the centre of attention in the Norse sagas. His exploits are dramatic, violent and self-justifying. Whereas the Greeks had various champions, such as Hercules, who were promoted to deity, Thor is a god from the start and is in contention with giants, elves and monsters. This is in contrast to the Huichol idea in which Kauymali is human, even with special spiritual qualities, but never seems to graduate to being a god.

The stories about Thor are not in any coherent sequence. They are just isolated tales which must have been related around the camp fire or hearth at home. Thor was the main focus of worship and was seen as the god most relevant to human activity. We can see the warrior class of Norsemen projected into the skies, even if they did not fight with magical hammers. One wonders if these tales were seen as amusing and hardly to be taken literally. One such example may suffice.

The giant Geirrod manages to capture Loki and makes him promise to hand Thor over to him. Loki talks Thor into visiting Geirrod but leaving his hammer, belt and gloves behind. On the way, Thor and Loki stop at the house of a giantess called Grid. She alerts Thor to the trap awaiting him and loans him a staff, iron gloves and a belt. As they wade up the stream Vimur, they notice Geirrod's daughter, Gjalp, standing astride the stream and urinating into it thus causing a flood. Thor throws a rock at her and the flood ceases.

As they arrive at Geirrod's house, his two daughters, Gjalp and Greip hide under a chair. When Thor sits in it, they push the chair upwards in an attempt to smash him against the ceiling. But Thor uses the staff to push back and breaks both their backs. At this point, Geirrod hurls a chunk of hot iron at Thor, but he catches it with his gloves and flings it so hard that it goes right through a pillar of the house and right through Geirrod's head. Albeit black humour, the Norseman must have chuckled at this tale. We shall encounter a similar story in the Celtic mythology, chapter 9.

A question of scale

We have already noticed that there are different sizes of living beings in the Norse scheme. The gods are pictured in terms of human attributes and dress, and seldom portrayed as naked, as in Greece. In between the gods and the human race are the giants of various kinds, little people such as the elves and dwarfs, and also an assortment of spirits, weird ghoulish entities with magical attributes. There seems to be no systematic definition of these beings and it would be misleading to attempt to categorise them in some kind of modern rational framework. It may be that the Norsemen never really thought about it, and just used the terms freely and for dramatic effect.

To make a list; there are Disir, Fylgja, the Norns, the Valkyries, Einherjar, Berserkers, Landvaettir, Dwarfs, Light Elves and Dark (Black) Elves. Many of these have been mentioned in passing before. The distinction between these entities can often be blurred and imprecise, and it would be unnecessary to go into much detail about their activities. What we need to do is consider the significance of scale going on here(2). Why are there outsized versions of humanity, normal humans and then miniature versions? We shall encounter this matter with the Huichol system, in which a little boy and girl are seen as especially significant; they are the candidates for being shamans. Is this a way of saying that children are nearer to God than adults? Certainly the elves seem to have a close relationship with the gods. With the giants, we are seeing the opposite relationship with the gods; there is a perpetual antagonism going on. Thor goes to some lengths to murder as many as he can; is this a way of saying that adults tend to lose faith and oppose the gods?

From the point of view of historical reality, we must ask the difficult question; were there ever such things as giants? It can be no coincidence that so many mythologies have giants worked into their systems. There are the Titans in Greece, the Bible has giants, called Nephilim, and in China there are larger than life people. Only recently, the archaeologists have unearthed human bones that are much larger than normal, indicating that giants may not be purely the stuff of imagination(3). How we evaluate this has yet to be seen. What we can say is that in the remote past, someone of greater than normal stature has been exaggerated and credited with extraordinary strength both physical and spiritual. This has worked its way into various mythologies. Whether the opposite is true is another question, but of course we know about the pigmies in parts of Africa. The whole question of scale is fascinating and the way to see it is to assess its symbolic value. My suggestion is that there are some who are very close to God, some who are average, and others who are too conceited for their own good and are estranged from God. Another way of seeing it is to say that the dwarfs, the workers, producing helpful artifacts for the gods, are the working class, the humans are the middle class, and the giants are the ruling class or royalty who like to bully everyone else.

Predestination and Free Will

This again is an issue which surfaces in Norse mythology, in quite an original manner. We have already mentioned the Norns; there are three main ones, but all kinds of lesser ones which need not be described, except to say that it meant 'a magic worker'. The three main ones, Urd, Verdandi and Skuld are concerned with Past, Present and Future (but this is a simplification). Urd means,'what was once'; Verdandi means 'what comes to be'; Skuld means 'what shall be in the future'. They are all pictured as female and beautiful; they remind us of the Fates in Greek thought, although one's destiny is not quite so severely marked out as in Greek thinking.

The Norns could be found by Urd's Well, or the Well of Destiny, which watered the tree Yggdrasil. The ladies inscribed each person's destiny on the trunk of Yggdrasil. However this was not immutable; the inscription could be altered according to one's conduct in life. It was like being given a hand of cards; the Norns gave one a range of possibilities and one could work them out according to one's ambitions. One could not go beyond what one was dealt out. This is a fascinating way of exploring the relationship between free will and predestination. On the one hand, God pans out the course of one's life, but on the other hand there is scope for one to modify it in various ways. It is a sort of compromise between total determinism and total freedom. This is theologically very clever, but what it fails to do is to see freedom and fate as both absolute truisms, which forms a stunning paradox. See my chapter on Free Will and Predestination in The Theology of Paradox.

In a way, the tree Yggdrasil also symbolises past, present and future, with the ladies watering it. The roots are what we have done, which cannot be altered even if people do try to rewrite history to suit their preconceived ideas. The bole is the present which we can see and make decisions about. The branches are the possibilities to go in one direction or another, but having chosen a branch, we cannot go back. We have to face up to our decisions whether they turn out to be right or wrong. We might encounter the squirrel, Ratatosk, who is a little trouble-maker, irritating the eagle at the top and the dragon at the bottom, all because he just likes to tell stories and annoy people. Is this symbolic of the tension between good (Odin) at the top and evil at the bottom? In any case, choices made in the branches do have moral implications, and life is a maze of awkward decisions.

To complicate matters, the goddess Freya (or Frigg), Odin's wife, practices a kind of magic called Seidr. This involves divining and manipulating fate. There is not much said on this subject, but the implication in it is that she can foresee the future and also manage to alter it somehow. This is as close as we come to some kind of system of prophecy, but it is nowhere near what we see in the Old Testament or even in Greek lore with the Sybils. Frigg is portrayed as completely naked, which may be an indication of her ability as a shaman.

Law and order in Norse thinking

We are accustomed to thinking that the Norsemen were lawless and unprincipled, but this is only half the story. This is where myth begins to slide into historical realities. It would seem that there was the concept of 'innangard' and 'utgard'; these meant 'within the fence' and 'outside the fence'. This was the normal arrangement in those countries. If one lived within a settlement or enclosure, it was quite civilised with laws being observed. If one ventured forth beyond the fence or defensive wall, laws became nothing and it was outlaw territory; something we might term 'Injun-country'. How did this relate to mythology? The answer is that all those nine worlds were shot through with this contrast. So while Asgard was seen as 'innangard', for instance, while Jutunheim was 'utgard'. This meant that if one went on an expedition for warfare or plunder, the normal rules could be waived; one could steal, murder, take slaves, rape women, all the things one would not do at home. Utgard was not always seen in a negative sense. Humans and gods would see it as a way of gaining spiritual power and wisdom. The primeval chasm, Ginnungagap, was as utgard as it was possible to be and yet, the source of all life.

This helps us to understand the behaviour of the gods, particularly Odin. He was seen as the great lawgiver, and yet, he was capable of all kinds of lawless behaviour. In this lies a strange paradox which applies to the Christian understanding of God just as much. On the one hand, God gives us the Ten Commandments and other precepts, and yet people remark that he appears not to observe them himself.

The best example of this concept sliding into actual history is the 'pale' arrangement in Dublin (and possibly other Irish towns). We can see how this idea of innangard gave the idea of being 'within the pale' and 'beyond the pale', in other words, out in the lawless areas of western Ireland.

The influence of Christianity

We have already seen what is thought to have happened to the concept of Baldar. He is thought to have been a warlike god, but later become civilised and kindly natured. Was this a case of the Norsemen coming up against Jesus and asking themselves, 'have we got anyone as nice as this in our pantheon?' Baldar dies a death, but is not really dead since he goes to Helheim. But everyone knows he will be raised again at Ragnarok, and all will be put to rights. Here again we see the motif of resurrection.

Ragnarok is the Norse concept of the apocalypse. It was to be heralded by Heimdall blowing on his horn, Gjallarhorn, to announce the final battle when the world would come to an end and then make a fresh start. This sounds like 'the trumpet shall sound'(4) and the book of Revelation could have given some inspiration to this myth. Odin retains all the best warriors in Asgard, so that he cannot fail to win against people like Loki and his cronies. One underlying assumption in all these sagas is the indestructibility of life. One may appear to die but one simply reappears in another 'world'. The motif of resurrection is strong everywhere. It may be a Christian influence but not very likely, since virtually every myth has some kind of basic assumption about resurrection, going back well into pre-history. It simply testifies to the feeling that life is precious; it ought not to be destroyed.

One most notable influence of Christianity is possibly the crucifixion of Odin. He decides to hang himself, like a crucifixion victim, from the tree Yggdrasil. He is stark naked and has a spear sticking into him. This goes on for nine days, as one might expect. His motive is not to save the world or help mankind; he is simply trying to gain more power and wisdom for himself. Later he sacrifices one of his eyes with the intention of gaining more knowledge. But we can see the parallels with the passion of Jesus, except that there are some important differences. Whether the Norsemen took this idea from the Christians or not, we will probably never know. It may be a good example of how one system of thought can influence another. The augmentation of three hours on the cross to become nine days, may be a symbolic way of saying 'our god Odin has more endurance than yours!'

We shall see how the coming of Christianity in various parts of the world have made an impact on local mythologies.

Permanent influence on Western Culture

Although the Norse religion and its mythology has almost faded out it would be unfair to say it has disappeared completely. In recent times there have been fresh manifestations of it, albeit in a moderated form. It is possible to find people in Scandinavian countries, who will claim to believe in the old Norse gods.

The chief ongoing influence, which is often forgotten, is the naming of the days of the week. Tuesday is named after Tiw, the god of war; in France this becomes Mardi, after Mars, the Roman god of war. Wednesday takes its title from Odin, or Wotan. Thursday is related to Thor, the champion of the gods; in Germany this becomes Donnerstag, but 'donner' means thunder, which is what Thor used to do with his hammer. Friday is according to Freya or Frigga, the wife of Odin. This scheme was devised by the Christian missionaries as they moved into the northern lands after the end of the Roman Empire. The months of the year are still named after Graeco-Roman gods.

At Christmas time, we are happy to welcome an old gentleman dressed in red with a sack full of toys. This has its origin with the little red goblin who used to appear in northern countries. He had two sacks; one with toys and the other with a stick, and the behaviour of the children was rewarded accordingly. The punishment element is now politically wrong (!) but did persist until quite recent times. Santa Claus is now firmly integrated into Christian values of kindness and joy. People kiss under the mistletoe. As we have seen, the mistletoe was believed to have special spiritual powers in spite of it being flimsy and parasitic. The holly and the ivy are more likely to be related to Druidic mythology. This all goes to show how Christianity has 'baptised' many elements from the ancient pagan mythologies. The resilience of these ideas is exemplified in this way. In Soviet Russia, the Communists tried to rub out Santa Claus. They devised a black and white Santa to supplant the 'real' one. This did not work; the red one survived and is still an influence everywhere.

And what of those dwarfs and elves which are so influential? There is many a child's fairy-story book which thrives on this image. There is the case of the Cottingley Fairies in which fairies (5) were alleged to have been photographed in someone's garden. Much scorn has been apportioned to this incident, and various clever schemes devised to show that the photographs were faked. Be that as it may, it is still evidence of the hold that this kind of thinking has on people. It is one thing to say it is all nonsense, but still we have folklorist ideas about Leprachauns (Ireland) and Tylwyddteg (Wales) and doubtless the Scotsmen have something on the same lines. (6)

Turning to literature, we have most notably the works of J.R.R.Tolkien in such popular publications as The Lord of the Rings and the Hobbit. There are many other such works, perhaps not so well known. These are not just children's reading, but appeal to adults also. This too is evidence of the hold 'the little people' have in people's minds. The explanation is that one can see the symbolism and metaphor behind the characters and situations. It speaks to the human soul; the ancient pagan receptors are still there in human nature in spite of centuries of Christian culture.

We must not ignore the massively influential works of Richard Wagner in his operas, many of which are based on Germanic mythology. Admittedly, this material maybe the German version of Norse mythology, but the essentials of it are still there, in spite of him introducing a few additives such as the swan motif. The Valkyries, the Niebelungen, Goetterdemerung and many other Nordic motifs are used to very good effect, and this makes a most entertaining presentation as long as one does not take it too literally. Unfortunately there was one person, Adolf Hitler, who failed to see the symbolic and metaphoric side of it and took it all far too literally. To this day, the Bayreuth opera house is still as popular as ever, devoted to the interpretation of Wagner's works. His descendants are still in charge of the operation. The Nazi's managed to spin an entire mythology of their own, around a vicious racialist policy, and that has poisoned the whole thing for many people. There will be a critique of one of Wagner's operas later (chapter 9).

How many people recall that St.George, the patron saint of England, had a battle with a dragon and killed it? George is of course a Germanic name; we do not know exactly where St.George originated, but the motif is important for us of a Germanic background. How many battles with dragons take place in the myths? Here is another example of Christianisation of heathen mythology. Norse mythology is deeply embedded in north European culture, and with the English-speaking peoples all over the world.

The classic fairy story of Snow White and the Seven Dwarfs is possibly the apex of Norse mythology interacting with a Christian motif. We have a beautiful princess who has run away to escape her vindictive mother-in-law. She finds the little cottage in the woods and lives with the dwarfs. They are clearly modelled on the Dark Elves who spend their time in tunnels or mines extracting precious metals and gemstones. When Snow White dies, she is entombed in the woods with a ring of dwarfs around her. This is the 'utgard', the wild place, and there is a barricade around her. The handsome prince arrives and kisses her; she comes to life again. This is the element of resurrection which is so common in world mythologies. We can see the arrival of the prince as the Christian influence, namely Jesus coming to the rescue and giving her new life. It is a wonderful story which appeals to everyone who has any imagination at all. It tugs at those basic Nordic instincts in us, and this explains how Walt Disney can produce a cartoon film with so much attraction.

A Narnia story; The Dawn Treader, by C.S.Lewis

It is interesting to go into details about one example of modern mythology using motifs from traditional Norse thinking. It is not possible to know how consciously Lewis worked in mythical ideas, but there is no escaping the reality of the appeal.

The three children are in the bedroom and the picture on the wall suddenly produces a flood which fills the bedroom. They are floating in the sea and a ship, The Dawn Treader, approaches. The prow is unmistakably that of a Viking ship with a dragon on it. We have a mouse that talks and a bull which strongly resembles the minotaur. As they approach the island, there is a massive golden treasure. Then there is a fight, firstly with the islanders and secondly with the sea serpent which coils around the ship. Fortunately, a dragon, who is very fierce and fire-breathing, comes to their rescue and fights the serpent. Someone has a magic sword which finishes off the serpent. No one ever dies in this story, but always there is the awareness of another world. So much of this is reliant on Norse mythological images.

The Christian influence comes at the end, when Aslan the lion comes to reassure them. He tells them that he will always be with them. How much does that remind us of what Jesus said to his disciples in his last moments on earth? (7) In this we see the same process as noted in so many other cultural factors which rely on Norse (and other) mythologies; that of Christianity 'baptising' the story and giving a promise for the future.

The Weirdstone of Brisingamen, a children's novel by Alan Garner.

This high-powered adventure story which appeals to adults as well as children, relies heavily on images from Norse mythology; it also works in elements from Celtic mythology (Welsh). There is no need to recount the story in detail, but the gist of it can be related very briefly.

A farmer was off to market to sell his white horse. A strange apparitional figure appeared in the road and offered to buy it. In the end, the farmer and his horse were taken down a tunnel to where there were 140 knights, all with white horses except for one. The farmer was told to fill his pockets with gold and jewels in payment for his horse. Inadvertently, he picked up the weirdstone of Brisingamen and not realising its significance, it stayed in the family until it came to Susan. It was no surprise that when Colin and Susan came to stay at the farm, the people of the next world, realised that the jewel was in the area and went all out to retrieve it. The whole story revolves around the attempts to take the jewel, but in the end, that strange figure, Cadellin, manages to take possession of it, since it was his in the first place. He needed the weirdstone in order to activate those 140 knights.

Like all good mythological accounts, the story is based on a real part of Cheshire, around Alderley Edge where there were ancient copper mines and folklorist tales concerning the occupants of the tunnels. Whether the author realised it or not, many of the personal names and images are taken directly from Norse mythology. This all adds to the mystique and appeal of the story. This simply goes to show how much ancient pagan motifs have not faded from people's instincts; it all resonates with something in the nature of the British people.

We can begin with the weirdstone itself. It is an ancient spell stone; another name for it is Firefrost. This instantly reminds us of the beginnings of creation, where there were two lands, one frozen and the other fiery with an abyss in between. We recall that Freya (or Frigg) had a magic necklace given to her by the Dark Elves, who demanded her sexual favours. That element, of course, has to be left out of a children's adventure story! The necklace was called Brisingamen but there is no mention of one stone in particular being especially magic. The Dark Elves the **svart** (meaning black) have to live in tunnels since they cannot stand the daylight. They are pictured as evil, and will stop at nothing to steal the weirdstone. The Light Elves also are mentioned, the Lios-Alfar, and they are helpful and friendly.

We also have mention of Grimnir who also wishes to possess the stone. Grimnir is an alternative name for Odin. It turns out that Cadellin, the rightful owner of the stone, is the brother of Grimnir. Both of them are giants. Also there is the ice giant Rimthur, and the giantesses, called Mara. They are dubbed as stupid, trollwomen, one of which turned to stone. There is even mention of Ymir, the primal giant, who, when he died, had maggots crawling out of his body, namely the elves. There are black and white Svarts, some of them man-sized.

It is possible that the author did not know the exact meaning of some of the Norse material. Nastrond, far from being a person, is a part of Hel, one of the nastiest parts of it as well. Ragnarok is a good Norse word but it is not a person; it is the day of doom, the Apocalypse when the world will be destroyed and start again. Some of the words may be pure invention, such as Fenodyree, Orgelmir, Earldelving, Valham, Stromkarl and Gondamar. Even then, they add to the fascination in the story.

The use of animals and birds is also in keeping with Norse culture. Selina Place, the witch, has two bull terriers. There is a kestrel called Windhover. There are flocks of crows or rooks that are constantly spying on the fugitives; the farmer's barn is crowded with owls. There are magic weapons such as Dyrnwyn the two handed and two bladed sword, with golden serpents on the blade, belonging to Fenodyree, the dwarf who is dressed as a miniature Viking. There is Durathror, another dwarf, the son of Gondamar, and he has a magic cloak called Valham. Does that remind us of Valhol (Valhalla)?. There is a Stromkarl who plays a magic harp with silver strings. Also these spiritual powers are able to change themselves into something else as a disguise, such as the 'day trippers', or the friendly woodcutter in the clearing, or a bird.

One thing missing from this material is the Norse gods themselves, even if Ymir and Odin are indirectly included. This may be an example of the process of Christianisation. Also we see that in spite of there being plenty of violence, hardly anybody actually gets killed. Also Cadellin, who in theory might by Vili or Ve, the brothers of Odin, is nice-natured and protective towards the children. That would hardly figure in genuine Norse tradition. Another thing missing is the concept of the World Tree, which should have been Yggdrasil in Norse thought. The nearest thing we have to this is a sheet of fire, which comes up from the floor to form a column against the ceiling of the cave.

This brings us to the Welsh (Celtic) elements in the story. We begin with 140 knights who are waiting in readiness to spring to the defence of this country; this reminds us immediately of the Knights of the Round Table of whom there were actually as many as 150. The wizard, Cadellin is clearly the equivalent of Merlin (Merddyn). Cadellin is obviously a Welsh word rather than Norse. We have Llyn Dhu (black lake) over which Grimnir hovers in a fog. With another lake we have Angharad Goldenhand, the Lady of the Lake and the Island of Logris. Dyfed is mentioned as also a stone circle which takes us back to ancient Druidic thought. Although King Arthur himself is not actually mentioned, we have two names that are very close; Arthog, who is a very nasty elf, and also Durarthror (a dwarf). We do not quite get as far as including the Holy Grail, but Fenodyree's sword is clearly modelled on the idea of Excalibur.

At the very beginning of the novel , we have a horse that can see an apparition but not the farmer. The horse does not actually start talking English, but this does remind us of that strange story in Numbers.(8)

In general terms, the Weirdstone of Brisingamen is a good example of how ancient mythological ideas from different sources, can be worked into an exciting adventure story. The main tenor of the whole thing is the struggle between good and evil; although the 'goodies' appear to be at a disadvantage and likely to be defeated, there is always that crucial intervention from someone who is sympathetic and cannot afford to allow evil to prevail. Taking the whole thing as symbolic, as Alan Garner almost certainly intends us to do, indicates that the human race and some of the spirit world can and should work together to combat wickedness. Eternal justice and fair play is also a strong element in the story. Susan has to part with the weirdstone, but she is given a silver bracelet in compensation for her loss. In this way, the story has the traditional happy ending.

The Hobbit, a series of novels by J.R.R.Tolkien

This material pre-dates C.S.Lewis by a decade or so. The first book came out in 1937 and has had a fascination for many people. It is clearly another element in modern mythology, but uses many ideas from not just Norse traditions but also Celtic. Greek influence is very small but there nevertheless.

The Norse element is clearly the leading thought. The book begins with a depiction of runes, the ancient Viking script which even now we are not completely certain about how to translate. The whole account concerns Bilbo Baggins, a little chap who is 'innocent', even if he is an accomplished burglar. He comes up against all kinds of 'little people', elves, dwarves, goblins and also trolls which are much bigger. All this is Norse lore and is compounded by their having tunnels in mountains and performing all kinds of craftwork, especially jewellery. This reminds us of the dark and light elves. Many of the personal names remind us of Norse gods, such as Thror or Thorin (Thor) and Kili and Fili (Vili and Vi). Baggins finds an invisibility ring, not that invisibility is confined to Norse traditions, but the ring, which symbolises eternity, works its way into Wagnerian thought in those operas. In addition we have the Archenstone of Thrain, which is clearly another version of the Weirdstone of Brinsingamen, or the philosopher's stone. The aim of the story is to reclaim the vast treasure, in gold and silver, that the dragon Smaug has stolen.

This is where the Celtic influence comes in. Aggressive dragons are a strong element in Welsh thought. Also there is a wizard called Gandalf who is kindly disposed to Baggins, and could be seen as the equivalent of Merlin. Also we have the elfish sword Orcrist which could be seen as Excalibur.

There is a river running through the forest. If one falls in it one loses one's memory. Whether this idea occurs in Norse or Celtic thought would be difficult to say, but it does come in Greek thought. It is the River Lethe, but that is in the underworld and the memory loss is permanent.

It is interesting that although the story comes to the climactic battle between good and evil, none of the groups of people are dubbed as totally good or bad. Even Baggins himself, the hero, is not totally one thing or the other; he is mixture, and also somewhat unsure of himself. This is a very modern trait, but also much nearer to reality.

Tolkien does manage to include some new mythological ideas. No one has even heard of a 'hobbit' before, and the dragon was also puzzled since he could not define a 'hobbit' smell. But now, a race of prehistoric people, short in stature, has been named after Bilbo.

We even have the motif of resurrection included, though this is never a strong motif;

'I am he that buries his friends alive and drowns them and draws them alive again from the Water.' (Bilbo Baggins).

In common with Edmund Spenser, there are bursts of antique wording using obsolete words. This is done to enhance the antique tone of the book. We can contrast this with the occasional burst of modernistic 'chatty' prose as the author explains things to the reader. In general terms, this is a very good example of modern mythology. Its starting point may have been ideas from the Water Babies, or Peter Pan, or indeed The Wind in the Willows with that little innocent living in a hole in the ground. Even so, there is much originality in The Hobbit.

Siegfried, an opera by Wagner

It is well known that Wagner was steeped in Norse or North Germanic mythology; we shall see later that there is a certain input from Celtic lore.

Taking one opera as an example, Siegfried, we see many images derived from Norse traditions. Siegfried himself is the young, fearless champion who is not afraid to tackle the dragon, Fafner. We see the preparation of a special sword, as Siegfried uses the remains of his father's sword, which was broken, and produces a weapon worthy of the battle. It is never actually called Excalibur, but the inference is there. Siegfried is probably intended to be an image of Thor, although this is never stated openly in the opera. He has a belt and gloves like Thor, but not a hammer. The sword is called Nothung. Siegfried has a horn which he blows, reminding us of Heimdall. He also has a 'tarn-cap' which can confer invisibility, and a golden ring, which he takes from the dragon. This symbolises eternity.

Siegfried is an orphan, but has been raised by a nasty dwarf called Mime. The dwarf is quite happy to frighten Siegfried with tales of how dreadful the dragon is, but is happy to let the lad make an attempt at killing Fafner and then taking the treasure off Siegfried. For this purpose, Mime produces a poisonous drink and tries to persuade Siegfried to drink it; the lad is too wise to be persuaded into it. He takes his sword and kills Mime. We also have mention of light elves as well as black ones that live in caverns with the Niebelungen.

Wotan, the Wanderer, is an important element in the plot. This is clearly Odin, who wears a blue cloak and a broad-brimmed hat, but even then his one eye becomes obvious towards the end of the opera. Wotan talks a lot about gaining wisdom from the Norns. His spear is broken by Siegfried.

Yggdrasil, the ash tree appears in the plot, though the name itself is not quoted. Siegfried uses ash from it to stoke the fire of his forge when producing his sword. Giants are mentioned but none actually appear in the drama.

The climax of the plot comes when Siegfried comes across Brunhilde. She is an exceedingly beautiful lady. The two of them fall desperately in love and that brings the drama to a close.

Wagner uses many images from Norse mythology but is not above making a few innovations for the sake of the drama. The operas are still a major feature of German culture to this day and the descendants of Wagner are still in charge of the original theatre in Bayreuth. A certain Austrian corporal and his entourage also found much encouragement from Wagner's operas, although it is worth adding that there is absolutely no anti-Semitic sentiment in this and the other Wagnerian operas cited in relation to mythology.

Footnotes for chapter 8

1. Snorri Sturluson, an Icelandic historian, dated about 12th century.

2. The issue of scale will be discussed in the chapter on Evolution, chapter 21.

3. Giants have been regarded as imaginary, but recently, large human bones have been found on Sardinia. Also the local people have traditions about them.

4. The trumpet sounding is the traditional signal for the apocalypse. See I Thessalonians 4:16 and also Revelation chapters 8 and 9.

5. The Cottingley (West Yorkshire) Fairies caused a stir many years ago. Children playing with a camera managed to capture pictures of fairies in their garden. Attempts at showing how they were faked have been tried, but not totally successfully.

6. The Celtic peoples have a fascination for the little people. Leprachauns in Ireland and Tylwyddteg in Wales. The Scotsmen have got Brownies and Boomans for instance.

7. The last words of Jesus to his disciples in Matthew 28:20.

8. A horse that spoke is recorded in Numbers 23. This is a minority element in mythology.

9

Celtic Mythology

This mythological system of thought is the third most important influence on the Britain of today. Unfortunately, we do not have much information to go on, since the Christian missionaries made a thorough attempt at blotting out native Welsh mythology. It is thought that many of the details of the Welsh system were grafted into features of Christianity, such as saints. With regard to Irish mythology, we are more fully informed since certain persons recorded much of Irish thought; the texts are the Books of Leinster, the Dun Cow, Ballymote, and the Yellow Book of Lecan. All of these were produced well before anything of the Welsh material was recorded. The chief source for Welsh mythology now is the Mabinogion which was produced in the 14th century, well after Welsh mythology had more or less faded out. This explains why our knowledge of it is to say the least, sketchy. However, on the assumption that the Welsh were every bit as Celtic as the Irish, we can tentatively reconstruct various aspects of thought by reference to the Irish material. Another source is to study the descriptions made by the Romans as they pushed back the Celts; the problem with this is that people like Tacitus and Suetonius(1) are happy to describe the antics of the Druids, from the Roman point of view, but this was decidedly negative. Sadly, there was no one like Snorri Sturluson to give us a full picture of Welsh mythology, and as far as we can assess, reasonably unbiased. The result of this is that assessing the influence of Welsh mythology on modern Britain is not easy. We can say that the name London, our capital city is based on Celtic gods, but that is about all, at least from the cultural point of view.

However, there is one very important element coming from Welsh mythology, on the political and religious level. It is the Arthurian legends and myths. This material has had a very decisive influence on politics in the Middle Ages and down to the present. Also, the religious climate in this country has some kind of grounding in those legends. The influence of King Arthur and his Knights is not confined to Britain; it had its influence in France and Germany. More of that later. Our knowledge of Arthur is much more extensive, even if seen through the eyes of mediaeval writers. Geoffrey of Monmouth (1138) was the first to produce a literary text about Arthur, followed by Marie de France, Chretien de Troyes, Wace and Layamon; each writer has his own interpretation and bias to bring to the legends. By the end of the Middle Ages, we see two masterpieces by Sir Thomas Malory, Sir Gawain and the Green Knight, and Le Morte D'Arthur, and in addition, Edmund Spenser's Fairie Queen (1596)(2). Coming up to the present day, there have been many renditions and variations on the theme of Arthur, in poetry, literature, films, artwork and drama. This all goes to show the hold that this motif has on the British mentality. It is a good example of how a sketchy legend stemming from the early 'Dark Ages' has been spun into all kinds of mythological possibilities, often with a political or religious agenda.

Arthur is of course excellent material for children's story-telling, as long as we omit such factors as Lancelot and Guinevere cheating on Arthur. Possibly the latest such work as been the Weirdstone of Brisingamen by Alan Garner. As seen in the chapter on Norse mythology, there are many elements grafted in from Welsh mythology. (The same is true for Harry Potter, reviewed in chapter 23.) There are some Welsh names slipped in, such as Llyn Dhu (Black Lake). Essential to the story is a wizard called Cadellin, who is clearly modelled on Merlin (Merddyn), and the sword Excalibur appears under the name Dyrnwyn. The 140 knights awaiting the call to defend the country is clearly based on the Knights of the Round Table.

Celtic Deities. The gods

It is easier to study the Irish gods, since we know much more about them, and they would appear to be the same as the Welsh ones were. They seem to be somewhat different from those of other pantheons. Moreover, the sculptural renditions of them are much cruder and less graphic than those found in say Greece or Egypt.

The Dagda. He is dubbed as the 'father of all' or the 'lord of perfect knowledge'. This does not mean that he produced all the other gods, but that he was omnicompetent. He was pictured as gross and ugly, pot-bellied and coarse, like a typical agricultural labourer, wearing a tunic that was slightly too short to cover his buttocks! He had a club which was so heavy that it had to be mounted on wheels. With one end he could kill nine men at a time and with the other end restore them to life. Again we see the motif of resurrection. He was therefore the lord of life and death. Also he had a cauldron which never went empty and no one ever went away hungry from it. The Gundestrup Cauldron made in silver gilt and belonging to the 2nd century BC was found in Denmark, and is a good example of Celtic metalwork. In one sense he was a fertility god. He was also a builder of fortresses. As a harpist he called forth the seasons of the year, in the Celtic calendar. Here we see the connection between the god's abilities and the rituals which took place four times a year, and especially on November 1st, Samain(3). One task at Samain was for The Dagda to be faced with a hole in the ground filled with porridge, and he had to eat it all; which he did. After that he made love to Boanna at the River Boyne. She became pregnant but since she was already married, they had to conceal the matter. The Dagda made the sun stand still so that the baby was conceived and born on the same day.

Angus. He was the illegitimate son of The Dagda, dubbed as the god of love, who could help people with entanglements in their love-life. Angus had a dream in which he saw his lover, Caer Ibormeith. She could take the form of a swan, but did not have any regard for him in any other form. On 1st November, Angus turned himself into a swan and she accepted him. They flew three times round a lake and then they went off to his palace, which is now located at Newgrange, or Brug na Boinne. Here we see a slight historical grounding for this myth. Also it helps to explain the importance of swans in European myth, a motif taken up by many composers and artists in the 19th century. We think of Neuschwanstein castle, the royal palace in Bavaria.

Lug. He again was a multi-tasking god, not unlike The Dagda. However, he had a sling and a spear. He turned himself into a hero by slinging a stone into the one eye of Balor, the champion of the Fomorians. He was pictured as a handsome young man who managed to displace The Dagda but not violently. One wonders if this saga has borrowed something from I Samuel(4), in which David hit Goliath with a stone in his face. Also, a one-eyed god appears in Norse thought, namely Odin.

Other gods, of which we know a very little were **Nuada**. He lost a hand in battle (like Tyr). He had a sword which was invincible, not unlike Excalibur. There was **Ogma** the champion, **Gobniu,** the backsmith and brewer and **Dian Cecht.**

The goddesses

These are more related to fertility, **Danu, Anu and Brigit.** Not much is known about them except to say that Brigit was associated with learning, culture and skills. This explains why she was grafted into Christianity as a saint.

Macha was also a fertility goddess, concerned with not just the soil, but man's fertility. She was a warrior queen associated with **The Badb** and **the Morrigan.** We notice that Selina Place in the Weirdstone of Brisingamen is dubbed as a Morrigan. Macha died giving birth to twins; the reason for this was because she was forced to race against the horses of Conchobar. Having won she was in no condition to give birth.

Deidre of the Sorrows

This lady is not so much a goddess but rather a royal princess. Before she was born they heard her crying inside the womb. It was prophesied that she would bring ruin on Ulster. People wanted to put her to death, but she was very beautiful. The king, Conchobar, wanted to marry her when she was of age. He sent her away to be raised by foster parents. She met one of the king's knights, Naoise; they fell in love and eloped to Scotland.

Conchobar enticed them back to Ireland. When they came, a man called Eoghan was ordered to kill Naoise. She declared that she hated the king. So he decided that she would live six months of the year with him and the other six months with Eoghan. Deidre rejected this idea, and threw herself from a chariot, preferring death to that arrangement.

In this saga we see a motif similar to Persephone and also Inanna(5), which is a 'just-so' motif for explaining the seasons of the year.

Oisin and Tir Na N'og

Oisin was the son of Finn MacCumhail, a great warrior. Oisin married Niamb of the golden hair, and they went to the Land of the Young. They could have lived there for ever; it was a way of avoiding death.

Oisin grew homesick and wanted to see his family in Ireland again. Niamb agreed but warned him not to dismount from his horse. As he arrived in Ireland he realised he had been away for hundreds of years; all his family were dead. As he rode along, some men asked him to help lift a slab of marble. Instead of dismounting, he leaned over and then fell out of the saddle. As soon as his body touched the ground, he began to age and go blind. He could not return to Tir Na N'og.

It is interesting that this myth ties in with Utnapishtim and other attempts at sidestepping death. The lesson is that death will catch up on us at some stage.

It is fair to say that such folklorist sagas may have been circulating in Wales as well as Ireland.

Bran the Blessed. Taken from the second Branch of the Mabinogion

We can cite a couple of sagas from the Welsh tradition, taken from the Mabinogion. There is nothing specifically stated about the Welsh gods, which is understandable since this work was written eight or nine centuries after the area had been Christianised. Bran may well have been a god once upon a time, but is now styled as a great giant champion, king of mainland Britain with his capital in London. The name Bran actually means a raven or a crow; this reminds us of Odin with his ravens. There is no mention of Arthur in this saga, and the impression given is that this story relates to a time before the Roman invasion, when the Celts ruled all of Britain and Ireland. His title was Bendigeidfran. Fran is just a variant on Bran. He married his sister Branwen, to Matholwch, kind of Ireland. In this we see that there was much interchange between Wales and Ireland which did not cease when the Roman and the Christian eras dawned. Matholwch insulted and humiliated Branwen and this precipitated a war. The Welsh came over in ships with a massive armada, but the Irish prevailed. This was because they had a cauldron that could revive the dead; ironically, the cauldron had been given to them by

Bran; even then, the cauldron had been purloined from Ireland. How often do we see the motif of resurrection in mythologies all over the world? The battle was more like a stalemate and only a few of the Welsh managed to escape back to Wales. Bran was wounded and knew he was going to die. He ordered his men to cut off his head and take it back to London. There is a tradition that the head miraculously kept on talking, although this is not stated clearly in the Mabinogion; might this idea have been taken from Norse tradition, in which the Giant Mimir's head was able to talk and give wisdom to Odin? Bran's head was buried in Gwynfryn, the white mound, on which the Tower of London now stands. The head was intended to be a defence against invaders. Not only does this link up with the ravens at the Tower, but also the Knights of the Round Table who are expected to spring to the defence of Britain in the event of an attack.

The story is characterised by people taking offence at the slightest thing and revenge being exacted. This serves to give the impression of a pre-Christian tradition. There are many remarks which are Christian orientated, such as 'May God prosper you...' but this may be anachronistic along with many other features. The writer would hardly have quoted pagan gods who were more or less forgotten by the 14th century.

The story is interesting because it in effect links the fortunes of Great Britain back to the Ancient Britons. The motif of a protecting influence which will repel foreign invaders is a strong one, running through the sagas of Arthur and the Knights who are expected to rise up again to defeat Britain's enemies. The British are to this day proud to proclaim that no foreign power has managed to invade them since 1066. Another tradition says that if the ravens desert the Tower of London, then Britain will fall. Now we can see how an ancient Celtic tradition is at the root of a modern myth. Bran's skull is assumedly still there, facing eastwards, under the White Tower!

Gwydion the magician; taken from the fourth branch of the Mabinogion

This saga could well be entitled 'the Adventures of Gwydion'. The Lord of Gwynedd was a ruler called Math, and he had a nephew called Gwydion. The interest in this tale is that it portrays many of the cultural assumptions of ancient Celtic life, not least the importance of magic. Also, symbolism, which is not at all obvious to us, plays a very large role.

To manage life at all, Math has to have his feet in the lap of a virgin all the time. He has a girl called Goewin for this purpose, but Gwydion's brother, called Gilfaethwy takes a fancy to her. Perhaps to take his mind off her, Gwydion proposes a visit to Pryderi's realm in Ceredigion to try to obtain a herd of pigs which appear to be new to Wales. On arrival, Gwydion magics twelve horses with hounds and saddles, made out of toadstools, to exchange for the pigs. Pryderi is deceived, but not for long, as the magic soon wears off(6). Conveying the pigs northwards, various places receive a name connected with pigs; Mochdref, Mochnant, another Mochdref and a pig pen at Creuwrion(7). Pryderi's army meets them and there is a massive slaughter. Rather belatedly, Gwydion and Pryderi agree to single combat to settle the matter and save lives; Pryderi is killed and the men of the south go back home lamenting.

At this point Gilfaethwy coerces Goewin to sleep with him, much against her will. She is honest enough to inform Math of this, but he marries her all the same.

Math has a punishment waiting for Gwydion and Gilfaethwy, which they accept. For a year they must be turned into a stag and a hind. When they come back, they have a fawn, who is changed into a boy called Hyddwn, who is baptised. For the second year they must be a boar and a sow; on returning they have a piglet who is turned into a boy called Hychddwyn. For the third year they must be a wolf and a she-wolf; their cub is turned into a boy called Bleiddwn. With their punishment completed, Math now wants a real virgin; he is offered Gwydion's sister, Aranrhod. But Math wishes to test her; he makes her step over his magic wand to be assured of her virginity. To his amazement, out drops a baby, who comes to be called Dylan. He goes off to the sea and likes to swim like the fish(8). Then there is a second baby; this one is doomed to have no name, no weapons and no wife. This boy is a beauty; he takes a fancy to Gwydion and follows him around. He develops the skill of shoe-making; thence he gets the name Lleu Llaw Guffes, which means 'the fair haired one with skilful hands.' Gwydion takes him to Aranrhod's castle. By a magic trick he deceives Aranrhod into thinking they are under attack, so, not realising that this is her son, she gives both of them plenty of weapons.

Still, Lleu Llaw Guffes has no wife. Math and Gwydion decide to create a woman for him, by putting oak, broom and meadowsweet together; her name is Blodeuedd. They rule a cantref in Ardudwy (which is still identifiable today). While Lleu is away one day, Blodeuedd takes a fancy to a huntsman called Gronw Pebr and sleeps with him three nights running. They decide on a plot to kill Lleu Llaw Guffes. Gronw spends a year making a spear on Sunday mornings. Then they trick him into having a bath by the river, with a goat in attendance. As the spear hits him, he turns into an eagle and flies away.

Saddened by this trick, Gwydion goes in search of this eagle and finds him up a tree. He is shedding maggots and rotten flesh, which is scooped up by a massive sow. Gwydion entices the eagle to come and land on his hand and then magics him back to being a human, namely Lleu Llaw Guffes.

To settle accounts with the adulterers, Gwydion turns Blodeuedd into an owl, a bird that can only operate by night and is shunned by all the other birds. Her name is changed to Blodeuwedd, which is the Welsh word for an owl. With regard to Gronw Pebr, he is challenged to have a spear hurled at him, to even things up. He persuades Lleu Llaw Guffes to let him hide behind a big stone, on the assumption that the spear will not hit him. But Lleu Llaw Guffes hurls the spear so hard that it goes right through the stone and into Gronw Pebr's back, killing him. To this day, we are told, there is a stone called Llech Gronw, situated by the river Cynfael in Ardudwy, with a hole right through it. So Lleu Llaw Guffes ruled his cantref prosperously and eventually became the lord of Gwynedd.

This is obviously a moral tale, that adultery is wrong. The Welsh regarded the sanctity of the marriage bed very seriously, as well as young ladies being virgins until they were married. There is never any mention of any kind of wedding ceremony; they just slide into bed with each other, but that binds them together.

It is interesting that the spear that killed Lleu Llaw Guffes had to be made on Sunday mornings at the time when Mass was being said. How strange that a holy time like that could be used for such an evil purpose! Does this indicate a time when Christianity was only just gaining a foothold in Wales, and the pagans were still superstitious about various matters?

We notice the usage of three in various modes in this account. Three is a significant number in many variations of myth.

As with the ravens, we also see another possible accretion from Norse mythology. Thor is claimed to have hurled a spear so hard that it went through a stone pillar and killed a giant who was hiding on the other side. It is the same motif; 'you think you can hide from eternal justice, but it will catch up with you no matter how you try to avoid it.'

We are struck by the frequent use of magic in this story; both Math and Gwydion have magic wands and use them to interesting purposes. This must have been a land of shamans, wizards and witches, which indicates a pre-Christian setting. There seems to be little conscience over the slaughter of masses of men, just because a herd of pigs has been stolen; even so, the unfairness of it does occur to Math, whereupon he suggests a single combat to settle the matter. When Pryderi is killed, it is in effect saying that the magician is right and the man who was swindled was an idiot. Nowadays, we would not see it in quite the same way!

There is the fascination and envy over a new animal in Wales, the pig. The fact that it eats nasty things like maggots and rotting flesh is surely a comment in itself. Possibly, the Celtic welsh saw the pig in the same light as the Jews, namely, an unclean animal. They may have derived this idea from the Bible.

This saga gives us a fascinating insight into Celtic lore at the start of the Christian era.

We can see possible Christian accretions in these sagas, with the spear being thrown at Lleu Llaw Guffes; this is what happened to Jesus. Moreover, Jesus did die and eventually he ascended, not unlike an eagle. Also Lleu Llaw Guffes is unmarried, as we suppose Jesus was. Blodeuwedd is turned into an owl; in Christian tradition an owl symbolises wisdom, which is what Jesus had. Is this symbolic of the Welsh pagans being converted to Christianity?

King Arthur

The whole question of the historical reality of Arthur is confused by the fact that there was a Welsh god called **Artor**, a ploughman and a boar god. It is possible that Arthur was named after Artor. However, there seems little doubt that there was such a person, active in the century after the Roman occupation had ceased, and as the Saxon invaders tried to take over England. The name Ambrosias Aurelianus has been offered as the real Arthur. Other names have been offered. But since that person has been confused and equated with many mythical elements from Wales, it is not easy to separate fact from imagination. Every depiction of Arthur and his knights has been done with the assumptions of late mediaeval chivalry; the shining armour, ladies waving handkerchiefs from castle battlements and many other sentimental accompaniments. It is useful to know that in spite of all the mythological augmentation that has raised Arthur's profile over the centuries, there is nevertheless a certain amount of historical and geographical grounding as a basis for it all.

From the geographical angle, it is thought that Tintagel Castle was Arthur's birthplace. Maiden Castle in Dorset is believed to have been a part of the kingdom of Logres. Near Salisbury is Stonehenge and Badon Hill nearby is possibly the site of the battle of Badon which held up the Saxons for fifty years. Cadbury Castle might be Camelot. Wales has numerous places associated with Arthur, for instance Caerleon; Carmarthen (Caer Myrddin; the town of Merlin), indicates that Merlin was from south Wales. There are a few bits of evidence that Arthur was active in Southern Scotland; Arthur's Seat at Edinburgh is an example.The most intriguing tie-up comes with Glastonbury. The monks of the abbey managed to unearth a grave with a man and a woman (with golden hair), which they took to be Arthur and Guinevere. Avalon fits well with the Somerset levels which in those days were mostly lakes and marshes.

From the historical angle, there are various literary works stemming from the early Saxon times which give us some indication of Arthur's activities. The earliest mention of Arthur is in the Latin manuscript, the Life of St. Columbanus. It is a 7th century document which means it can only stem from about a century after the supposed time of Arthur. There is Gildas(9) who wrote The Ruin and Conquest of Britain. Sadly we do not know much about Gildas, except that he probably wrote about the mid 6th century, which would be not long after the assumed time of King Arthur. Although the book mentions the Battle of Badon, he does not actually cite the name 'Arthur' itself, which seems rather strange. When we come to the Annals of Wales, which are thought to be after 956 AD, we have two clear mentions of Arthur, one with the Battle of Badon and the other with the Battle of Camlann, at which he was mortally wounded. He won twelve battles, and this was due to his profound Christian faith. The History of the Britons by 'Nennius' dated about 801 AD or earlier, goes into much more detail about Arthur and his battles, with especial interest in the last battle, at Camlann. Arthur seems not to have been mentioned in the Anglo-Saxon Chronicle nor in Bede's Ecclesiastical History of the English People, but this is understandable since both works were concentrating on the arrival and conversion of the Saxons, which would be mostly after Arthur's time.

When talking about the historical Arthur and his court, it is as well to remember that the evidence for his existence is not particularly firm. We are dealing with a time in British history which was turbulent, disorganised and violent, and with no one who set to work to record all the events. The fact that Arthur is not mentioned in some early documents does not have to mean that he never existed. Vice versa, the fact that he is mentioned in some documents not far off the period in question, does not have to mean that he really existed. A lot depends on how one interprets the literary material; some are highly sceptical and critical; others are prepared to accept such references at face value. Personally, I think there was a warrior chieftain or king, who was based in South Wales and whose exploits did involve many parts of the British Isles; he successfully held back the Saxons as they expanded into England and interfered with Wales. It is also clear that Arthur had some influence abroad, by which we mean France, and in particular Brittany.

By the time we arrive at the Norman period and Geoffrey of Monmouth, we see the traditions about Arthur strung together and romanticised, exaggerated and mythologised. The reality may have been somewhat different. There is no need to relate in detail all the legends and possible inventions about Arthur and his knights; these can be read up in any romantic novel. But the key to understanding Geoffrey of Monmouth is that he was living at a time when the Normans had just taken the crown of England by force, and the legitimacy of their regime was very much in question, even if it was a slightly better claim than King Harold had had.

It was Henry 2nd, crowned in 1154, who realised that Merlin's prophecies and Arthur's heroic leadership, could be used to legitimise the Norman regime. Henry was coping with a French monarchy which claimed direct descent from Charlemagne, the great Holy Roman Emperor; this gave them immense political prestige. Henry's answer was to relate himself to King Arthur, another great Christian monarch of the sub-Roman era. He was related to Wales, which meant that the Celts in Wales could see Henry as their natural leader; also Arthur was believed to have campaigned widely in England, even as far as Scotland, which meant that he could be seen as a great Christian emperor on the same level as Charlemagne. Geoffrey's masterstroke was to collect the scattered references and legends about Arthur and construct a coherent account, with any amount of mythical and fanciful additions. We cannot really assess how much invention went on, but clearly Geoffrey was seeing the Arthurian traditions through the eyes of a mediaeval courtier. He could hardly have avoided this. But the political ploy, as the substratum of this account, is very clear. Arthur was being used to justify the Norman monarchy, with overtones of national unity. After all, if Arthur could induce all his knights to eat with him at a round table, why could not Henry's barons do the same thing and co-operate with their monarch? In this we see the importance of myth as underlining and justifying a political agenda.(10)

The importance of this surfaces again at the end of the mediaeval period. During the 15th century, there was an ongoing civil war, now called the Wars of the Roses. It was all about the genuine claim on the throne. It was no accident that Henry Tudor (who happened to be Welsh anyway), came from Brittany (which had Arthurian connections), and took the throne by force from Richard 3rd. Henry's claim on the throne was vestigial to say the least, but his ploy was to claim that he was descended from the wonderful King Arthur, who was waiting in readiness to come to England's aid in dire adversity (so the tradition goes). It was no accident that Henry 7th named his son and heir, Arthur (!), and a national tragedy when the lad died on his honeymoon. The same notion prevails to this day; we note that one of Prince Charles' names is Arthur.

What of Edmund Spenser with his Fairy Queen? Clearly this is referring to Elizabeth 1st, who used to dress up in elaborate costumes, not unlike a fairy. We shall see that Spenser used the motifs from Arthurian legend and myth, and also produced various royal lineages to indicate the legitimacy of his rule, and that of the Tudors as well. The amazing thing from our point of view was to make Arthur out to have been a fairy, and not just him, but Henry 8th too. This was another attempt at justifying Elizabeth's claim to the throne, after all the disputes that had preceded her accession(11). Spenser even embarks on proving that a woman could be an effective monarch, which many at that time would have doubted.

We can see in the stories about Arthur the motif of the unlikely claimant on the throne. Even if Arthur was the son of Uther Pendragon, he was not known to the barons as such until it came to a dispute over the succession. There was the sword set in a stone, which no one could pull out. It was Arthur who casually pulled it out whereupon people came to the realisation that he was the rightful heir to the throne. Does this incident remind us of Alexander and the incident of the Gordian Knot?! The long term effect of this feat is that an unlikely 'upstart' snatching the throne might actually be the right person at the right time. So it was with Henry 2nd and Henry 7th. How convenient that Arthurian interest should surface just at the right time to justify their accessions!

During the next three centuries, the fascination with Arthur seems to have gone quiet. However, in Victorian times we see another outburst of interest in these matters. One wonders whether Victoria herself, whose claim on the throne was just a little 'last gasp', could have been related to the Arthurian motif. Was it any coincidence that Disraeli called her 'the Fairy'? By the mid-Victorian era we see various artists using wonderful imagination in portraying aspects of Arthurian legend. Rosetti, James Archer and Edward Burne-Jones in particular produced lavish artworks, riddled with sentimentality, but very far from basic realities.(12) It was Tennyson, who produced the poem The Idylls of the King, and The Lady of Shalott, which appear to have started the craze which has built up into the 20th century. This seems to coincide with the rapid growth of the British Empire; to link one's country's fortunes with what was assumed to be the first native born emperor, Arthur, would be a wonderful way of seeing the British ascendency as legitimate.

The 20th century sees the full flowering of decoration, exaggeration and invention over the legends concerning Arthur. Now we have giants, goblins, fairies, wizards, beautiful princesses and handsome princes; all these are ingredients which make for superb children's bedtime reading. It goes further than that; films, drama, novels, all kinds of artistic outpourings have made Arthur into something fantastic, but probably very far from the historical truth.

This is where we can say that mythology has really taken over. If we study a children's story book of about 1950, entitled King Arthur and his Knights, by Harry Theaker published by Ward, Lock & Co., we see just about every element of mythology worked in, making a superb account but clearly miles away from reality. There is Gold, silver, snakes, little people and big people, magic, even a special tree (!), jewels, a magic sword, the champion element, mist, everlasting justice and fair play, resurrection, the underworld and a separate world for the fairies. Whether the author ever realised what he was doing, is a good question, but what it does indicate, is that these mythological elements are endemic in human instinct. That explains why they have such a hold on people's imaginations. We can also see why Arthur and the legends surrounding him have had such an appeal not just in Britain but in France and

Germany, and even further afield. The USA has not been slow in indulging in 'Arthurology'.

The Holy Grail

So far we have not commented on another aspect of Arthurian lore; that of The Holy Grail. This is another obsession which is still teasing minds even now. The tradition is that Joseph of Arimathea, who was at the Crucifixion, managed to save the cup that Jesus used at the Last Supper, brought it to England, landing probably at Weston-super-Mare, and arriving at Glastonbury. He stuck his staff into the ground and it struck root and continued to blossom on Christmas Day. Somehow, this motif came to be worked in with Arthur. Sir Percival, having learnt about the Grail from Merlin, went in search of it, but in vain. The Grail has never been found but the search for it is still a mania with people in the Western world. There are various artefacts which are claimed to be the Grail. A recent TV programme about the Holy Grail, allegedly traced it to a family home in mid-Wales, the Powells, and we were shown a glass artefact, admittedly damaged, but still recognisable as a piece of Roman glass. There is also the so-called Nanteos cup, kept in North wales, but made of wood. One of the springs at the bottom of Glastonbury Tor once yielded a blue glass artefact which some concluded was the Grail. If the Grail ever were to be found, it would be a problem to be certain of its authenticity(13).

The connection between Joseph and Glastonbury has persisted over the years. Even if the thorn bush there now is not the original,(14) people still come to see it in the hopes that it will flower on Christmas Day. Consequently, Glastonbury has been a mecca for pilgrims, even if the abbey was wrecked at the Reformation. It is fair to say that Glastonbury with Walsingham in Norfolk, can claim to be at the spiritual heart of the nation, a well-spring of spirituality for all Christians in these islands.(15)

What do we make of the Grail legend? It is claimed by some, for instance Giles Morgan, that the Grail motif has a mythical, pre-Christian significance. The cup or cauldron motif is seen in Greek and Norse mythology, and speaks of healing and holding the blood of a god. This might help us to understand that the Grail of the Last Supper was not only used for drinking the wine, but also (it is alleged) was used to catch some of the blood of Jesus at the

Crucifixion. If there is any substance to this pre-Christian idea, it would simply show that this is another example of how the early Christians adapted a pagan motif to underscore their teachings. The same could be said for the rest of the Arthurology as it came to substantiate early Celtic Christianity.

`It is certainly true that elements of early Christianity came direct from Jerusalem early in the Christian era. They worked their way into Celtic Britain, particularly Wales and Ireland and had different procedures from the Roman Christians. The Romans sent a missionary, St.Augustine to Canterbury at the same time as the Celtic church, with such figures as St. Columba, St. Aidan and St. Chad were working their way down towards the south. The two contingents met in the Midlands, and there was a problem over different procedures, notably the method for calculating the date of Easter. At the Synod of Whitby, these matters were settled. However, at the Reformation, when the question arose as to why the English should take any notice of the Pope, there was an appeal to the idea of the original Church of England, namely, the Celtic influence. Needless to say, the Celtic influence is still with us today; one might call it the 'Iona influence'. The most noticeable Celtic influence is that many ancient churches have square-end chancels, as opposed to apsidal ones.

We can see in the Grail legend the symbolism of 'the true Christianity' coming to Britain independently of Rome. This is important for a country that (at the Reformation) broke away from the main source of authority, the Pope, and needed to substantiate or legitimise its claim to be a proper sort of Christianity. Joseph and the Grail tells us, symbolically, that the real Christianity came direct from Jerusalem and the Last Supper. This is an interesting example of how mythology, based on a sketchy legend, can be used to justify a religious settlement.

We note that the motif of the Round Table also came over with Joseph of Arimathea.(16) He had a silver round table, whereas Merlin made a bigger one out of oak, for Arthur to use. The small silver table was hidden away with the Grail. We can see in this, symbolically that there is equality between believers, or should be, just as there was equality and unity of purpose amongst the knights, even if Arthur was the king. It goes further; the knights took a vow of chivalry which meant that they rescued maidens in distress, helped the poor, defended the weak and many more noble things. All of these are Christian virtues as emphasised in the Gospels, especially Luke. What it is saying is that the British people have as their foundation, fair play, kindness and a sense of justice. Also there is the tendency to go into the attack when evil looms.

With this, we see the importance of mythology as underpinning a whole nation's morality and spirituality, not to mention its political arrangements. In addition to this, there is the fascination over the Holy Grail; the main theme of The Da Vinci Code (discussed in Chapter 26) is the hysteria over tracing the Grail on the assumption that it is hidden somewhere in Rosslyn Chapel in Scotland. When it is pointed out that the Grail is not there after all, this may be an indirect way of saying that this quest is rather like trying to locate the end of the rainbow; in other words, a self-induced hoax!

The fascination with the Holy Grail has hardly diminished with the twentieth century; in fact it has received more augmentation. Such writers as T.S.Eliot, J.R.R.Tolkien, T.H.White and Joseph Campbell have all allowed the influence of the Grail to be a substratum of their stories. Most significantly, Karl Jung, the great psychologist came to grips with the Grail motif. He thought that the quest for the Grail symbolises the process of 'individuation' and also is symbolic of our efforts to achieve the ultimate goal of perfection. See chapter 19 for a detailed treatment of Jung.

Arthur in The Mabinogion

This most significant corpus of Welsh literature stemming from the 14th century throws much light on Arthur as a Welsh King. Its relevance here is that it harks back to many centuries earlier, at a time when the Roman Empire was receding from Britain and the Saxons were only just beginning to infiltrate from Germany. It must have been a time of uncertainty, chaos and political violence, with petty kingdoms struggling with one another. Arthur is styled as an 'emperor'; he has numerous sub-kings at his court, which is mostly at Caerllion on the river Wysg (what we would now call the River Whisk). But his influence is clearly to be found all over Wales, Cornwall, Ireland, 'England' and even parts of 'France', especially Brittany. What really helps us to pin the timing down, is the Dream of the Emperor Maxen; he was Maxen Wledig, Magnus Maximus (circa 383 AD), who was proclaimed Emperor in Britain, invaded France and was eventually defeated by Theodosius. The Celts had much respect for him, even if he denuded

Britain of troops for its defence. This is a very good historical anchorage for the Celtic myths which follow.

For most of these accounts, Arthur is not in the forefront of the action; he is the strong influence which relies on a reputation already earned, as his minions go out to seek adventure and defeat evil. We also have mention of Guinevere (Gwenhwyfur), but other than that, he seems to have an entourage of knights with different names. So we hear of Peredur; is this Pellinore or Percival? Also there is Owain; is this Sir Gawaine? More certain is Tringad, or Sir Tristan. Excalibur is not actually cited as such, but a sword used by Arthur is described; there is no mention of hurling it back into a lake. The long list of names and geographical locations, many of which can be located today, makes the whole account very real. There is no reason to doubt that these traditions are based on real events and personalities in the mid-6th century, as the Celts attempt to reassert themselves after the fall of the Roman Empire. This was somewhat belated as the Germanic peoples are encroaching and the Battle of Badon is mentioned. Arthur is usually somewhere in the background; in the Dream of Rhonabwy, he is playing a board game rather like chess,(17) and allowing the battles to continue in the middle distance. Clearly he was resting on his laurels!

What is missing, strangely, is any mention of Merlin. It is fair to say that wizards are mentioned in the stories. There is no mention of Joseph of Arimathea, or of the Grail or of a round table of silver or of oak.

As accurate history, we must be aware that much of this material is symbolic. When it talks of ravens fighting, it is really talking about Arthur's men. When Owain goes in quest for a tree and a well, this is hinting at the Tree of Knowledge and the well is the water of life. In fact there are quite a few indirect Biblical allusions which indicate a strong Christian influence on Celtic culture. There is the mention of Judgement Day and 'the uplands of Hell'. Also there is mention of 'a spear' which has much significance; is this referring to the Spear of Destiny as seen in the museum in Vienna?(18) Owain has a lion as his helper; is this symbolic of Jesus Christ helping him on his quest?

As another aspect of symbolism, we must assess the mythology which is blatant in all of the Mabinogion. It would be fair to say that virtually every element of world mythology can be evidenced from these stories. There are various occasions in which a knight kills a snake, usually an enormous one. Clearly, Wales never had such creatures, even if there were adders and grass snakes. This must be symbolic of the champion defeating evil. The same is seen in Greek mythology, and one wonders whether Celtic mythology has been influenced from the Graeco-Roman world. There are places where the hero defeats other monsters and giants; is this recalling the Seven Labours of Hercules?

There is much mention of Gold and silver, with jewels. This is the normal symbolism for deity, royalty and eternity. This element is not overdone, as in works like the Iliad, but still we have helmets made of gold (!) which would have been quite ridiculous. The motif of resurrection is also included, though not quite so overdone. We have two people who have died or almost died and yet rise up again to fight another fight. Geraint is an example of this.

Also we have dwarfs and giants and misshapen creatures, not unlike Norse mythology. Also we have what appears to be a unicorn; a 'stag' with a single horn which is aggressive. Peredur kills him. Quite often we have a grey-haired man. This is not explained, but it might be symbolic of a sage or a wise man, or even a wizard. We have a case, in the saga of Culhwch, of someone who can talk to the birds, notably blackbirds. This ties in with the ability of St.Francis and also of St. Beuno,(19) both of whom were reputed to converse with the animals.

Number symbolism is present, though not very prominent. Nine is the significant number in Celtic thinking, though this is not explained. Since Norse mythology also saw nine as important, there may have been some exchange of ideas over that. In addition, there is a significant colour, yellow, which appears very often. This too is not explained, but it may relate to the colour of gold. Red and black are also worked in, though not as significant.

In general terms, the element of exaggeration is present, but it has to be said that it is nowhere near as emphatic as in other mythologies. One could see the whole Mabinogion as an augmentation of the reign of Arthur, but it is difficult to know where to draw the line between literal historical truth and fanciful ideas.

The motif of the tree is also present, and there are various trees described. One of them has a horn hanging on it, which when blown, disperses the mist, which is symbolic of God's presence. The horn may be a substitute for a trumpet, which as such reminds us of the 'last trump' as in St.Paul's epistle. Also we recall Heimdall's horn, Gjallerhorn.

The main thrust of the stories, is the champion (a well-established feature of mythology), the 'tough-guy' knight who goes in search of adventure, usually to find a beautiful young lady that he has come to hear about. Usually the young maiden obliges by agreeing to the match, but her opinion on the matter is normally of no consequence. The whole tone of the work is of knights picking a fight with each other, often for no particular reason at all. Violence and bloodshed is described in a matter-of-fact manner, whereas nowadays we would regard it as infantile and immoral. Since the whole work is saturated with Christian tone, this seems rather strange. We notice that the original Celtic gods are never mentioned; this indicates that the Christian missionaries made a thorough job of wiping out paganism. And yet, we still have the aggression on almost every page. Is it possible to see this as symbolic rather than literally true? Is this pattern of thought derived from Revelation; the final battle between good and evil, and the eradication of evil?

The Mabinogion is rich in many such possibilities, but sadly it does not actually prove or disprove the actual existence of Arthur, Merlin, the Grail and the Round Table.

Tristan und Isolde, an opera by Wagner

This opera, which does not involve Germany at all, concerns a love situation on the Celtic fringe of Britain. It has been arranged for Isolde to marry King Mark of Cornwall. Tristan, who is a knight somehow associated with the Round Table, has already killed Mordred who was Isolde's fiancé. Tristan and Isolde are on a boat trip from Ireland to Cornwall, when they both drink a love potion and fall desperately in love. King Mark is anxiously looking out for the ship, but Melot, one of his courtiers informs him of what has happened. Tristan and Melot have a sword fight, and Tristan is mortally wounded. He dies and so does Isolde; it is rather like the plot of Romeo and Juliet. King Mark seems to take it all very calmly; perhaps he is wise enough to understand that people cannot help falling in love.

The whole opera is highly emotional and the underlying lesson is that love is supreme to anything like a political alliance. There is no mention of King Arthur or the Round Table or the Holy Grail. However, with the implication that Tristan is a Knight of the Round Table, the inference is there nevertheless. What it indicates is that Arthurian legend has its influence further than one might think; right across Europe and into Germany, and gave the Nazis a lot of mythical encouragement.

Parsifal, an opera by Wagner

This opera too is strongly under the influence of Celtic mythology, even if King Arthur is not involved. Instead it is centred on the Holy Grail and the Spear of Destiny (an artefact which fascinated Adolf Hitler). It would seem that Hitler found the opera Parsifal deeply moving, but strangely it was banned during the Third Reich! In short, there is a castle with the knights of the Grail guarding it and the Spear as well. The king, Amfortas, has been injured by the spear. A prophecy has said that it can only be healed by a 'pure fool, enlightened by compassion', an innocent youth. A swan is shot down by an arrow, and a young archer is dragged in, clearly not knowing what he is doing. The knights think this youth may be the fulfilment of the prophecy.

The youth now goes to the magic garden of Klingsor, a sorcerer, and flower maidens try to seduce him. It is Kundry, a mysterious, ageless woman, who is the Grail's messenger, who identifies the youth as Parsifal. Now he realises his mission, that of saving the brotherhood of the Grail. The magician hurls the spear at Parsifal, but he catches it in midair, and that destroys Klingsor's realm.

Parsifal now brings the spear and touches Amfortas' side, thus healing him. This saves the brotherhood of the Grail. Parsifal is accepted as the redeemer and king of the community.

Quite clearly, there is a lot of additional mythological material as compared with the traditions seen in Geoffrey of Monmouth and Mallory. We can see that as augmentation, and also that Germany has claimed Arthurian legend for itself. The Grail, being covered up, is now revealed and glows around the hall. This is an interesting exaggeration intended to emphasise the wonder and fascination of the Grail. In the original stories the Grail and the Spear are not associated with each other.

In Arthurian lore, Sir Percival (Parsifal) spends much effort in his quest to find the Grail, but never actually finds it. Wagner has given the whole motif a much stronger and climactic conclusion.

There is no denying the Christian substratum to the whole plot, and some of the motifs in it remind us of Edmund Spenser's method. He had beautiful women who were seductresses but underneath were evil and ugly.

Clearly, there is much symbolism in this opera. Parsifal mostly symbolises Jesus Christ as the healer and redeemer. The sorcerer, Klingsor, who is trying to destroy the knights of the Grail, stands for evil, and actually tries to kill Parsifal. The whole opera is probably deeply symbolic, even if it is quite fanciful and mythologically exaggerated.

Footnotes for chapter 9

1. Tacitus and Suetonius, Roman historians who described the Britons.
2. Edmund Spenser, an Elizabethan poet, wrote the Fairie Queen, reviewed in chapter 10.
3. Celtic Festivals; Imbolc (Feb 1st); Beltane (May 1st); Lugnasad (Aug 1st); Samain (Nov 1st).
4. I Samuel 17.
5. The myth of Inanna, from Mesopotamia concerns the passing of the seasons, see The Theology of Paradox. Persephone is the Greek version of this.
6. The concept of magic 'wearing off' appears in Harry Potter, chapter 23.
7. Mochyn is the Welsh for a pig. Many places reflect this legend.
8. This is reflected in Tom, in the Water Babies, chapter 11.
9. The Mabinogion comments that Gildas was Arthur's priest.
10. Edward 1st may have had Arthurian mythology in mind when he instituted the Knights of the Garter.
11. The idea of a female monarch was difficult for many people. Queen Matilda was always doubted. This was because the French had the Salic Law which meant that there could be no female monarch in France. This mentality influenced thinking in England.
12. Pre-Raphaelite artists of that era are; Dante Gabriel Rosetti, John Everet Millet, William Holman Hunt, William Morris, Edward Burne-Jones, Aubrey Beardsley. They epitomise the mentality of that age, extreme sentimentality about the Mediaeval age.
13. A recent TV programme about the Holy Grail, allegedly traced it to a family home in Wales, the Powells, and we were shown a glass artefact, damaged but recognisable as a piece of Roman glass.
14. The thorn tree at Glastonbury seems to be a Middle Eastern type; this would tend to support the claim that it was originally Joseph's staff.
15. The Spiritual centres in the British Isles are Glastonbury, Walsingham, Lindisfarne, Iona, and Bardsey.
16. Wace appears to be the one who introduced the idea of the Round Table.
17. The game, like chess, was Gwyddbwll, meaning 'wood sense'. The king tries to break out from the centre of the board but is surrounded by a ring of pawns who are trying to stop him. The Irish version of this is Fidceall.

18. The bejewelled spear in the museum at Vienna is claimed to be the spear that was used at the crucifixion. Hitler and the Nazi's were fascinated by this artefact.

19. St. Beuno, the northern version of St. David, established a centre at Clynnog Fawr, Gwynedd. He is reputed to have been able to talk to the animals.

10

The Fairie Queen by Edmund Spenser

This monumental work by Edmund Spenser appears in an Everyman edition edited by Douglas Brooks-Davies. I have concentrated on the first three 'books', but the work was more extensive and Spenser had intended to produce even more. It is of an influential genre of material which can be termed 'Christian fantasy'; another such example would be the Water Babies which will appear in the next chapter. In this type of literature, we see the lavish use of fairies and mythology for the purpose of furthering a political issue. In Charles Kingsley's case it was Socialism and educational policy; with Spenser it was the legitimacy of the rule of Queen Elizabeth 1st, and by implication the whole of the Tudor dynasty. It also included a polemic about the underdog and female rights, and also against unmerited violence. As with the Water Babies, there is a strong awareness of another world, that of the fairies, and the dividing line between the two worlds is not particularly clear. Whether or not one believes in fairies is of no importance, in fact it is irrelevant. The essential issue here is that life is working on two levels; the physical world that we can all see, and the world of the spirit. With Spenser, there is very little that can involve the physical world. The whole account is about fairy knights and their deeds of derring-do. Nowadays we would see a book based on fairies as something for children's bedtime reading, and indeed, the Water Babies would almost fit that bill. Spenser's Fairie Queen, however, is in no way children's bedtime reading. It is very hard-going. For us, to call King Arthur a fairy would seem absurd, even if he is only legendary. For Spenser, however, and the readership of his day, calling Arthur and his knights fairies would almost certainly have seemed massively promotional. It would raise them to a level above this mundane world and give them an extra authority.

The Fairie Queen is written entirely in poetry and in a stringent form of stanzas, which have come to be termed Spenserian Stanzas. It is nine lines of iambic pentameters, the last line being a hexameter. The rhyming scheme is ABABCDCDD.(1) This prevails throughout the entire work and must have taken an enormous amount of skill to accomplish. The way it is done strongly reminds us of Chaucer's methods. He used 'Ottava rima' and 'Rime royal'. While Chaucer used the English of his day, now termed Middle English, Spenser seems to imitate Chaucer's English, making it sound almost certainly antiquated for an Elizabethan readership. He uses antique phrasing and semi- obsolete words. A good example of this would be Deheubarth, which appears in Holinshead,(2) and means South Wales. What is his purpose in doing this? It would have given the Elizabethan public an impression of antiquity and the nobility that goes with it. It is not for nothing that the ancestral connections of the British monarchy are somehow connected to the fairies (as he sees it). We would now see this as rather silly, but in his day and age, it would have given the reigning dynasty more spiritual authority and legitimacy.

We need to see this work against its background in the late 16th century when Queen Elizabeth was on the throne. It was a time of great religious and political turmoil as the Reformation stirred up all kinds of problems in Western Europe. The essential issue here was Elizabeth's claim on the throne. Even though Henry 8th had named her as his successor after Edward and Mary, there were many of the Roman Catholic persuasion who could not accept Elizabeth's claim. This was because although Mary was the daughter of Catherine of Aragon, and Edward was the son of Jane Seymour, both marriages being regular, Anne Bolynne's marriage to Henry was seen as invalid by the Pope. This meant that Rome dubbed Elizabeth as a bastard and therefore unable to qualify as a monarch. The result of this was the saga of Mary Queen of Scots with her counter-claim on the(3) English throne, and also the Spanish Armada, both of which came close to removing Elizabeth from office. She was never really comfortably ensconced on the throne. Nevertheless, the majority of Englishmen were delighted to have her as queen and were prepared to go to any lengths to support her, after the horrors of Queen Mary's reign. All this is the substratum of Spenser's work.

To understand the work, we have to realise that it is saturated with allusions to Greek mythology. Douglas Brook-Davies has helpfully provided an explanation of the Greek terms used, otherwise many a modern reader would find the work unintelligible. A good example would be that Spenser seldom mentions the Sun; he talks about Phoebus, which means the same thing. He mentions Zeus quite often. Also 'bloudy Mars' occurs quite often, which means 'war'. 'Bloudy' here is not meant as a swearword; it means what it says, bloodshed, or blood red. Sometimes we have latinised myth, such as Neptune instead of Poseidon, and Ceres, the Roman god of plenty, but that does not alter the heavily mythologised thrust of the book. Just about every element of mythology is to be found in Spenser's work; snakes, giants, elves, swords, blood, trees. Most importantly is the chasm between good and evil, seen in virtually every myth the world over. The characters are either very good indeed, marvellous, virtuous, beautiful, magnificent, or by contrast, very bad indeed, vicious, filthy, morally corrupt, dishonest, evil. There seems never to be anyone somewhere in between as a mixture of good and bad. This ties in with the element of exaggeration which dominates the stories. It has the effect of heavily dramatising the whole work. There is nothing ordinary, commonplace or neutral in it. In places he is clearly imitating the style of the Iliad. Those iambic pentameters, which are found so often in Shakespeare, indicate that that was the mentality of the age, namely the Renaissance.

The other mythological element which is just as important, is the allusion to Arthurian lore, which is an aspect of Celtic mythology, as seen in chapter 9. Arthur himself keeps appearing in the sagas, although he never seems to be the centre of the story. Often he is referred to obliquely. He is at this time dubbed as a Prince, but the importance of him as underpinning the British monarchy is an essential substratum of the whole work. The knights in shining armour with the same code of chivalry, are the main structure of the stories, and this must remind us of the Round Table. The Holy Grail is mentioned once, and magician Merlin receives various mentions. Sometimes he is the subject of an oath, 'By Merlin!' Norse mythology is hardly involved. It is an interesting amalgam of Greek and Celtic imagery, but the whole intention is to support the rule of Elizabeth 1st. Christian values, of the most puritanical kind are being recommended in the sagas; this helps us to see The Fairie Queen as an important ethical work as well as political. The whole work is allegorical; there is no way in which it can be taken literally; one has to adjust one's mind to the figurative level for the whole thing, with the exception of the genealogical lists of royal figures that are supposed to be Elizabeth's forbears.

The First Book

This book concerns the Redcross Knight and his fair lady Una. Having a red cross on his chest would indicate that he was a crusader, and this in itself is a kind of throwback to Mediaeval times. The theme is of 'holiness' and we see Redcross making strenuous efforts to avoid sliding into sin or corruption. One of the recurring features of the book is violence and bloodshed. Every time two knights encounter one another, they immediately assume there has to be a fight to the death. Sometimes this results in a stalemate and a peace conference, which is followed by them deciding to combine their efforts. How literally do we take this? Is Spenser advocating violence? That would not appear to work too well with Christian love and peace. However, we can see it as slightly satirical, as he is hinting at how ridiculous the aggressive attitude of the knights was, and how it need never have happened. Indeed, in Book 2, canto 2, number 27ff, Medina manages to persuade two knights to stop being foolish.

> '... their deadly cruell discord to forbeare and to her just conditions
> of faire peace to heare.'

The basis of their aggression is that they all have short tempers, and easily fly into a rage, especially if their lady-love is threatened. Indeed the second book is entitled Temperaunce; this does not mean abstention from alcohol; it means keeping one's temper, being moderate rather than flying to extremes. Again, the mention of 'wrath' in many places, may be intended as symbolic. The main intention is probably to show that the Christian knights were, or should be, highly motivated to pursue their causes.

Redcross' main purpose is to embark on adventures and win battles for the sake of Gloriana, the Queen of Fairies. This is an allusion to Elizabeth 1st. She is never directly mentioned in the work, but there are many indirect remarks about her in differing phrases. This simply underlines the respect, if not awe that Spenser had for his Queen. Redcross fights various monsters, dragons and giants. We notice that he encounters a Saracen who is equated with 'sans-foy'(4) which means faithlessness. Also there is a 'sans-loy' (5) which means lawlessness, which may amount to the same thing. Redcross defeats the Saracen. This is only partially realistic since the Crusades were only ever a partial success and eventually ended in a debacle.(6) But this is not meant to be taken literally; it is about the Christian coping with lack of faith and law and winning through. The other important strand in the book is the role of Fidessa (Duessa), and this is all about deceit and false appearances. Duessa is seen to wear a triple crown (!) which would be a reference to the Papacy as being deceptive and false. At one stage Fidessa takes Redcross to a Christian house and he is schooled in righteousness by Charissa. Thus he realises his sins and comes to repentance and recovery of his strength.

Duessa may appear to be a kindly, helpful lady, but in fact that is all deception. She takes Redcross to a very elaborate castle which is symbolic of pride. It has a maiden queen with a dragon under her feet, but she is the queen of hell. She has six wizards as her advisers; idleness, gluttony, lechery, wrath, sloth, and envy, but Redcross is not taken in by any of these. The latter end of Duessa can only be a touch of humour. She has been taken captive by Redcross' squire, but they decide not to kill her. They strip her off completely, only to find that beneath all that beauty, she is only a filthy old hag and revoltingly ugly; then they let her run away.

At one point, Redcross has been taken prisoner, and is held in a dungeon. This is where Arthur comes to the rescue by forcing his way into the castle, defeating a giant, and then releasing Redcross. We are then treated to an account of Arthur's origins, of how, when he was born, he was given to a Fairy Knight and raised in chivalry, in Rauran (the antique name for Merionethshire which has associations with the Tudors) by the River Dee. Merlin was his tutor and advised him of his royal background. He fell in love with the Queen of the Fairies and has been seeking her ever since. We may see in this that Arthur symbolises Jesus, in that he rescues the Christian soul from prison. This motif of seeking is a recurring theme in the book. There is always someone seeking someone, whether it be a knight longing for his lady or vice versa a lovely lady trying to find her hero. This too is symbolic of the Christian life; we do not have the image of the pilgrimage of life, but we do have the endless quest for the truth and salvation.

The final scene in book one is so appropriate; the wedding of Redcross and Una. The Queen wants Redcross to come back to the castle and marry the princess who is actually Una, and thus receive the kingdom. A messenger appears with the message that Redcross is already engaged to Fidessa (Duessa), but everyone sees that this is a fraud. In other words, the forces of evil never stop trying to disrupt one's commitment to the basic love between them. Again, this might appear to be a touch of humour. The marriage goes ahead between Redcross and Una, but sadly, he still has that urge to find the Fairy Queen, so he has to go off on his travels again.

Important politically is the way in which an aged holy man who lives in a chapel on a hill by a half-dead oak, gives him a vision of Jerusalem as his final goal. Redcross is then identified with St.George, but first he must come to the end of all his battles and be cleansed from all his guilt. Then he will be able to join with all the chosen of God in his New Jerusalem. At this point, Arthur, who is not really aware of his origins, is now claimed to have sprung from the Saxon kings. (There is a slight disturbance in time sequence here!) Taken from his cradle and raised in Wales, this implies that Arthur is the heir not just of the Ancient British kings, but also of the Saxon ones. This gives further strength to his right of sovereignty and by extension, that of Queen Elizabeth.

Theologically significant is the occasional comment about life and death. There is a Well of Life, which Redcross, walking backwards, near to death, falls into it and is restored. 'For unto life the dead it could restore.' A similar situation occurs when Redcross is fighting a dragon and has to retreat. He backs into the Tree of Life, which God had planted, and that revives him in order to kill the dragon. This takes us back to the Garden of Eden and the implication is that Redcross has managed to reverse the mistake made by Adam. Is this an indirect way of saying that Redcross is some sort of Jesus figure? However we may see it, it has the implications of resurrection and Redcross is more than just a virtuous fairy knight; he is associated with Jesus Christ.

In this way, the Fairie Queen is full of richness and symbolism which are pointers to the Christian life and the path of salvation.

The Second Book

This work is concerned with Sir Guyon, another knight who comes to be allied with Arthur. The theme is Temperaunce, but the saga continues from the first book, almost seamlessly. The disgrace of Duessa has annoyed the Archimago (who has appeared before). He is some kind of wizard who supports Duessa and is bent on wreaking revenge on Redcross. It is thought that the name Guyon is derived from Gihon, a river in the Garden of Eden, but the name also reminds us of Guy of Warwick, and it is also a Norman French name. He is the essence of temperance and makes friends with Redcross. Guyon also has a Palmer with him, which would not have been a feature of Elizabethan England. A Palmer was one who had effected a pilgrimage to the land of Israel and (7)come back with a palm frond. This was a feature of Mediaeval times as opposed to Reformation times, and has the effect of giving Guyon the same air of antiquity as Redcross has. The Palmer has the task of giving Guyon wise advice and cooling his ardour.

A very strange scene occurs when Guyon finds a woman by a stream. She has been stabbed, but he manages to save her life. She has a baby, and her knight, Sir Mordant, is lying dead. The lady also dies and Guyon buries the two of them. As for the baby, Guyon adopts him and tries to wash the blood off his tiny hands, but with no result. This could be symbolic of saying that one could be innocent and yet guilty, paradoxically. The little red fingers become a reminder to seek revenge; he is named Ruddymane.(8) Later, someone called Trompart tricks Guyon into thinking that it was Redcross who killed Sir Mordant, but this deception does not work. It goes to show that sin is not something superficial; it works its way into the very fabric of one's heart and soul.

An interesting juxtaposition between two brothers comes in canto 5 and following. Pyrocles and Cymocles appear as knights who contend with Guyon. Pyrocles symbolises 'fire'(9) and Cymocles symbolises 'water'. (10) We notice that both of these in mythology are indicative of cleansing. Cymocles, as one might expect, finds a river with a boat waiting by the Idle Lake and a beautiful lady called Phaedria (joyful) waiting for him. They row out to an island and she lulls him off to sleep and leaves him there. The lady fetches Guyon across too, but he is rather more careful with her. When Cymocles wakes up, he picks a fight with Guyon, but Phaedria intervenes, and here we have another polemic for peace.

'Debateful strife, and cruell enmitie the famous name of knighthood fowly shend; but lovely peace, and gentle amitie, and in amours the passing hours to spend...'

In other words, 'wouldn't you rather make peace and be friendly?'

Strangely, the two brothers did not learn their lesson, and later on they find themselves fighting with Arthur, who overcomes them. He offers them release but they refuse it and so are killed.

Another interesting scene is where Guyon encounters Mammon,(11) someone we know from the sayings of Jesus. Mammon is dubbed as the god of this world and is all about materialism; riches, renown, honour, estate, and consumer goods. He takes Guyon to see his treasures and stacks of money. Guyon is not tempted because he knows that money causes problems and greed is the thing that ruins the world. He is shown the underground vaults, which remind us of the elfin bankers in Harry Potter (chapter 23), except that they contain all the evils; revenge, despight, treason, hate, jealously, fear, sorrow and shame. Guyon is not impressed, so Mammon shows him more; the giant Disdayne, then the room of royalty in which is Ambition, and then the golden chain which is the daughter of Mammon, and so offers her to be his wife. Honest Guyon says he is already engaged. Mammon grows angry and shows him a fruit tree in the garden; is this another link to the Garden of Eden? But the Greek element is worked in nevertheless, because we see Tantalus trying to snatch the fruit, but never quite managing to reach far enough. Is this another slight inclusion of humour? Eventually Guyon goes into a trance, but the Palmer finds him and stirs him up from being 'dead'.

Predictably, we are treated to another justification of the Tudor monarchy. Arthur and Guyon arrive at Alma's castle. She is a very beautiful virgin and is clearly another image of Elizabeth. They are shown into an antique library in her castle and one of the books is a history of Britain and is in praise of the Queen who is descended from Arthur. This time we are taken back to remote prehistory when, it would seem, Britain was not an island, but connected to Europe and was peopled by the Celts throughout. One wonders how or why Spenser knew about that. It was peopled with giants and beastly men who were defeated by Brutus,(12) the great grandson of Aenias. He had three sons; Loctrine who ruled Brittany, Albanact who ruled the northern parts, and Camber who took the west, and this explains the names Cambria and Cumbria. Now the kingdom of Logris is mentioned and the River Severn, a name derived from Sabrina, a princess of this time. She had a son, Madan, who was too young to rule. The Brutus who killed Caesar is now mentioned, but the line of celtic kings goes on down to King Lear and his daughters. The founding of Cairleill (Carlisle) and Cairleon (Caerleon), and Cairbadon

(Bath) are mentioned as well as Glamorgan. The fairy element in the royal list comes with Guitheline and his wife Mertia, who was thought to have been a fairy.

The line of Celtic kings comes down to Roman times with Julius Caesar's attempted invasions and then Claudius who succeeded. This was the time of Kimberline (Cymbeline), and the revolt by Bodicea is mentioned. Also the coming of Joseph of Arimathea bringing the Holy Grail to the West country is recorded, although Glastonbury is not mentioned. Hengist and Horsa are also mentioned. Towards the end of the Roman era, Constantine is alleged to have had two sons, Ambrose and Uther Pendragon, who was the father of Arthur.

Much of this may have been taken from Geoffrey of Monmouth's history, but some is thought to be Spenser's own invention. It is clear what he is trying to say; that Arthur was not just an ordinary adventurer; he was connected to the Ancient British line of kings and also the Roman Emperors. Another aspect of it is that sometimes, the female element in the line of monarchs is instrumental and influential. This is a hint that there is no reason to question the legitimacy of a female monarch in the Tudor dynasty. This is a bit more polemic.

It now goes further, for this ancient book that Guyon is reading, goes back to Prometheus who created and animated the first humans. The first man was called ELFE,(13) which means 'quick', and he found a woman called FAY (14)who was the mother of all the fairies. This means that all the kings of old were actually Elfin, and their line came right down to Oberon and Tanaquill, and then to Gloriana. We all know what that name symbolises! Incidentally, Oberon is equated with Henry 8th and Tanaquill was a Roman Queen, but is another image of Elizabeth 1st. This brings us to the third book.

The Third Book

The third book also contains another attempt at justifying the authority of Arthur and the British line of monarchy. This book has Britomart as the main character. This is another knight, but a female in armour this time; we can all guess who this symbolises! She dresses up to look like a common person and goes to visit Merlin in Cairmardin (Caermarthen). Merlin is the great wizard and soothsayer the like of which has never been seen before or since. He is alleged to have not been normally begotten, but the progeny of Maltida of the royal house of Montgomery and of a spirit, which explains his extraordinary spiritual powers. Merlin is not deceived, and recognises Britomart for what she is, and bursts out laughing; she is most embarrassed. Merlin proceeds to tell the future, starting with Britomart being espoused to Arthurgall, who is the equal of Arthur.

We now receive an admission that Arthur is not a fairy, even though people think he is. He is the son of Gorlois, the brother of the Cornish king Cador; this would support the claim that Arthur was born in Tintagel Castle. This also starts the notion that Arthur is always ready to spring to the defence of Britain against all invaders. It goes on to describe Arthur's resistance to the Saxon invasion. It gives details of Vortipore and Malgo, Careticus and Gormond, Cadwallin and Edwin. From this we see that the Celtic royal line is somehow interwoven with the Saxon monarchy. This would have to be done if the Tudors were to be able to claim descent from the Saxons and the Normans as well as the Celts. We can see that this justification for the Tudor dynasty is important, since Henry 7th's claim on the throne was vestigial to say the least.

The importance of Britomart cannot be underestimated. The name Britomartis seems to be an amalgam of 'Brit' plus 'Artemis' the Greek goddess of hunting. Indeed, a character called Belphoebe,(15) a huntress, appears providentially just in time to save Timeas, a squire, from dying. She is dubbed as a pure virgin and moreover virgin born. She has no original sin, as we would expect. This reminds us of St.Mary but also of St.Anne, and she is also an image of Britomart.

The third book is subtitled Chastity as well as The Legende of Britomartis. It contains many scenes which advertise the decency of chastity, some of them mildly humorous. One such is when Florimell is out in a boat with a fisherman, and he tries to seduce her. She refuses him! Whereupon Proteus appears and consoles her. She is faithful to her fairy knight Marinell. Proteus takes her to his cave and tries to seduce her, using all kinds of disguises. He even makes himself look like a Fairy Knight, but nothing would persuade her. In the end, he throws her into his dungeon, but endless captivity was preferable to losing her chastity or betraying her love.

At Castle Joyeous there is a Lady of Delight. The whole was a bastion of luxury, full of knights and damsels excersising their sensual desires with

Cupid having a wonderful time. The Lady manages to persuade Redcross to take his armour off, but Britomart refuses to disarm and only let her face peer out at them. The Lady assumed that Britomart was a man, and was attracted to her. Waiting until dead of night, she stole down into the bedroom and crept into bed with Britomart. It took some time for Britomart to realise she had company, but then jumped out of bed and screamed blue murder. The rest of the house was roused and came running, some armed. They found the two women on the floor, Britomart waving her sword about. Someone, Sir Gardante, let fly an arrow at Britomart, injuring her slightly, but she flew at them with her sword and Redcross joined in with her. They took their journey at once, even if it was the small hours. This account, being slightly humorous like a Whitehall farce, underlines the importance of adhering to one's commitments, rather than being enticed into superficial relationships. Here we see that the suit of armour is not meant to be taken literally; it is symbolic of being on the defensive against easy temptation. Britomart's remark about love is very apt;

'That truth is strong, and trew love most of might, that for his trusty servants doth so strongly fight.'

Britomart is also chased by the evil Magus and a lascivious forester. She is firmly set on being faithful to her Arthurgall. Another scene concerns Florimell again. She finds a cottage where a witch lives, who has an idle son. The boy takes a fancy to Florimell, but she escapes. The witch conjures up a beast like a hyena to catch Florimell. She intends to drown herself in the sea rather than be caught by the beast, but providentially she finds a boat on the shore. Sadly, her palfrey is eaten by the hyena but a knight, Sir Satyrane, appears just at the right moment, having followed the trail of her golden girdle and knowing it was his lady love who was in difficulties. Always, Florimell's virginity and constancy is emphasised and it is rewarded in the end.

Another scene in which Britomart is in temptation, is when Paridell takes a fancy to her. He must have been a flighty character since he sees another (married) woman, Hellenore in a castle. Her husband, Melbecco, is a miser and uncouth, and keeps Hellenore in confinement. Paridell manages to elope with her, but Malbecco is furious and gives chase. He finds Braggadocchio and Trompart. Braggadocchio promises to kill Paridell and recover

Hellenore. Paridell appears to have forsaken Hellenore, but the satyrs have found her, and they are far more lecherous, dancing and kissing in the forest. The knights persuade Malbecco to bury his treasure rather than cart it all round the forest. Malbecco finds the satyrs and decides to impersonate them so that he can get near to Hellenore and recover her. She prefers the satyrs and refuses to come away. Malbecco goes back to dig up his treasure, only to find that someone (Trompart?) has stolen it. In despair, Malbecco jumps off a cliff but fails to kill himself. He lives a miserable existence in a cave, appropriate for someone who did not know how to love his wife and centred his life on worldly wealth.

> 'Yet can he never dye, but dying lives, and doth himself with sorrow new sustaine, that death and life attonce unto him gives, and painful pleasures turns to pleasing paine.'

This sums Malbecco up very neatly, and indeed all those who fail to put love as the main centre of one's life. It is a lovely turn of paradox, but also brings out a factor seen in many mythologies, that of the tension between life and death. We see that particularly with the Dracula stories, the concept of being 'undead', the sort of state in between living and complete death. It tells of the importance in people's minds, of the value of life and the significance of death.

The virtue of purity is heavily emphasised in this book. How often do we have virgins mentioned and the colour white or ivory, which are symbolic of chastity? The book ends with what could be seen as the contrast to purity, a masque in which Cupid is the leading role. This reminds us of some of the masques that appear in some of Shakespeare's plays. It begins with Ease and goes on to Fancy, Desyre, Doubt, Daunger, Feare, Hope, Dissemblance, Suspect, Griefe, Fury, Displeasure, Pleasaunce, Despight, Cruelty, Reproch, Repentance, Shame, Strife, Anger, Care, Unthriftihead, Losse of Time, Sorrow, Chaunge, Disloyaltie, Riotise, Dread, Infirmitie, Vile Povertie and lastly Death with Infirmitie. All these prance around the room three times and then disappear into an inner room as the door closes. Britomart tries to follow them and eventually gains entry, only to find she is fighting with an enchanter and nearly kills him. She spares his life on the understanding that he will free Amoret. The chain with which the enchanter had tied Amoret up, is now applied to him and Britomart fetches her out, to find Sir Scudamore who is in despair. The couple embrace and are happy in their love.

It is interesting that in book three there is yet another attempt at relating the knights to ancient Troy. Sir Paridell, the one who abducts Hellenore, recites his lineage. He relates how Paris abducts Helene away to Troy, which instigates the Trojan War. The destruction of Troy sees the rump of the Trojans wandering around until they land in Italy and found Rome, and so Julius Caesar comes to Britain. Thus Paridell maintains that the Britons are really the Trojans, and that he himself is a Trojan, and that London is actually Troynovant (meaning 'new Troy'). This is not quite the same as substantiating the importance of Arthur, but it is the same sort of mentality. If one can relate oneself to something ancient, that gives one a great deal of influence, if not authority.

Thus we see that The Fairie Queen is heavily dependent on Greek mythology and what is claimed to be actual Greek and Roman history. How accurate all this is, is not the point. It is all a matter of justifying the rule of Queen Elizabeth. Quite obviously, there are many examples of women being in a leading role or some kind of champion. Britomart is a prime example of this, but there are several others. Here we see myth in its important role of supporting a political regime; the Tudor dynasty itself, with all its awkward counter claims and in particular the 'bastard' Elizabeth, who could easily have been displaced by Mary Queen of Scots, or overwhelmed by the Spanish Armada.

Footnotes for chapter 10

1. This was the normal poetic method in Greek literature, the iambic pentameter;
2. Holinshed was a Mediaeval historian, much used by Shakespeare.
3. Mary Queen of Scots was descended from Henry 7th and her son became James 1st in due course.
4. 'Sans-foy' means 'without faith'.
5. 'Sans-loy' means 'without law'.
6. Spenser might not have realised what really happened on the Crusades. He might not have wished to admit that they were a failure.
7. The Palmer. A mediaeval pilgrim to the Holy Land who brought back a palm branch and relics, which he might sell. This explains the modern phrase 'to be palmed off with...'

8. Ruddymane means 'red hand'.

9. The Greek 'pyros' means 'fire'.

10. The Greek 'cyma' means a 'wave'.

11. Mammon as seen in the teachings of Jesus. See Matthew 6:24.

12. Not the Brutus who stabbed Julius Caesar.

13. Compare this with Alf, the first man in Norse mythology.

14. Fay means 'a fairy'.

15. Belphoebe means 'joy'.

11

The Water Babies

This children's novel by Charles Kingsley, published in 1863, has had a very wide influence on British culture. Kingsley was born into a comfortable, 'well-heeled' society which meant that he could go to Oxford. He was ordained into the ministry of the Church of England, but took up parishes in poor areas and devoted himself to helping the poor. One could say that he was one of those at that time, with a strong social conscience, along with Lord Shaftesbury and Dr.Barnardo. He can be termed a Christian Socialist, which at that time would have rendered him quite unpopular with certain elements in society. The Water Babies underlines the plight of children, orphans, who are shamelessly exploited and maltreated, something which was all too often assumed to be the normal thing. It is an all too obvious socialist propaganda cleverly wrapped up in a fairy story, and using various elements of mythology. It is an engaging tale and has captured the imagination of millions. The fact that it is a fairy story is irrelevant; the true message is all too important. As an example of the adaptation of mythology in mid-19th century thinking, this book stands out as exemplary. It would seem that each day and age has to have its social, scientific and political issues emphasised in some kind of mythological presentation.

The outlines of the story are well known , that a little boy called Tom is forced to go up chimneys to sweep them for a chimneysweep, called Mr.Grimes. He escapes one day and goes into a stream with the fairies and becomes a water baby. Putting aside the incredible aspect of this, that he managed to grow gills and breathe under water, we must appreciate the symbolic aspects of this plot. Here is a little boy who has never known any proper parents who cared for him, nor any home life. He associates with other such boys and has no idea of moral conduct or religious faith. In effect he is innocent; how often do we see this element in world mythologies? However, he is covered with soot and the only wash he ever has is when he cries and his face is streaked. That is quite often since Grimes beats him regularly. Tom comes to realise that there are people who are completely white and clean. He is fascinated by the girl Ellie in her bed, as he inadvertently comes down her chimney into her bedroom. This is his moment of escape. He is not just evading Grimes and the household chasing him on the assumption that he has stolen something. He is also seeking cleansing, washing, and this is compounded by his desperate thirst and hunger. At last he comes to a stream in the hills, takes off all his filthy rags, goes to sleep, and enters into the water. This is symbolic of cleansing, an element seen so often in world mythologies. The ordinary people conclude that he is dead, but paradoxically, he has entered into a new life in a new world under the water, and this is another important mythological element, that of resurrection.

It would be wrong to assume that everyone in the normal world was against Tom. All he has ever known has been brutality , hunger and filth. But there is an enigmatic Irish woman who seems to have his best interests at heart and follows him over the moor. Is this his guardian angel? Also the teacher at the dame school realises what his state is and tries to help him. But most people see him as an object of shock and horror and immediately assume that he is a criminal. Only the squire, Sir John, seems to realise the true situation and offers a reward for Tom's rescue. This is symbolic of those who know there is something wrong going on but rather belatedly try to correct the matter.

We may assume that the fairies, who never actually show themselves to Tom in the early parts of the story, symbolise the world of the spirit, possibly God himself. This is exemplified by Tom seeing a picture of Jesus caring for the children and also as crucified, in Ellie's bedroom. Once in the river, Tom is able to talk to all the creatures, including the otter, the salmon, the caddis fly and others. There is the interesting contrast between Tom who has descended into the water, and those creatures that as larvae develop under the water and then emerge to fly around in the air, such as the dragon fly. This too is a clever way of symbolising the relationship between this world and the next, the divine. To emphasise the element of cleansing, Tom comes to realise that some creatures actually shed their skins and emerge as clean and their real selves. He wants to do that too. The fact that he is naked in the water is also an indication of his innocence, and reminds us of Adam and Eve.

Living in an age which regarded itself as 'rational', the question of whether such things as fairies exist does emerge. The answer, in effect, is that just because you have never seen a fairy, does not mean they do not exist. This dilemma is accentuated by the Professor's attitude when he fishes Tom out of the water. Ellie cries out, 'it's a water-baby!' We notice the faith of a little child. But the professor snorts, 'Water-fiddlesticks, my dear!' and turns away sharply. In other words, he is refusing to accept the evidence in front of his eyes. Tom was given two fancy names, Holothurian and Cephalopod, but the professor was not really facing realities. In essence, the existence of fairies is irrelevant to the main thrust of the book. We can all see that it is symbolic; that the fairies represent the unseen world of the spirit, perhaps of God himself. That is something that far more people are aware of, and some have actually seen evidence of it for themselves. However, the use of mythological ideas, coming from Norse and Celtic culture (just a little comes from Greek culture (p.127), is a poetic way of lifting the argument above the banal level of a political tract. It captures our imagination far more thoroughly than just a plain prosaic statement.

The same strand of thought comes with the two 'old lady' fairies that Tom comes to be confronted with; Mrs. Bedonebyasyoudid (p.129) and her sister Mrs. Doasyouwouldbedoneby (p.153). This is where Tom begins to learn his moral lessons; that he cannot behave like a hooligan and expect to get away with it. It is the Old Testament configuration in poetic narrative. If you do good, you will be rewarded and if you do bad you will be punished. Looking at it positively, it amounts to 'Love thy neighbour as thyself.' He has to learn the hard way what guilt is. In a scene which is clearly modelled on the Garden of Eden, Tom wants to find where all those sweeties are coming from, that the fairy hands out. He traces it to a treasure chest with the lid wide open, unlike Pandora's box. He feels really bad about taking one sweetie, then another and he cannot stop himself before he has eaten the lot. He does not realise that the fairy is watching all the time. When it comes to handing out the sweets next day, he cannot look her in the eye. When he tries to eat his handout, it makes him sick. Then he grows spines all over himself. This is symbolic of guilt, stealing the forbidden fruit. In the end, he confesses it all to the fairy and she forgives him. But he has to live with the spines for much longer; this indicates that though there is forgiveness, we also have to live with the consequences of our misbehaviour. Tom has to learn not to play cruel pranks on the sea creatures. But it goes further than that. The fairy shows him what happens if you sit back and never do any work. He is shown the famous nation of the Doasyoulikes in the land of Readymade at the foot of Happygolucky Mountain. These people did nothing but enjoy themselves; life was never a struggle. Tom thought that was ideal, but the fairy showed him that through successive disasters, these people degenerated until they actually turned into monkeys, clearly a debased form of humanity.(1) In this we can see a thinly veiled propaganda on the subject of the Protestant Work Ethic. The conclusion is that Tom cannot go on playing about like a baby forever; he must face up to life and become a mature man.

So Tom sets out over the ocean, in search of the Shiny Wall, or Peacepool. After many adventures in the North Atlantic (?), he learns a lot about life. His main quest is to find out what happened to Mr. Grimes and eventually he is taken to a prison where the sweep is being held. On the roof, which is covered with hot cinders and ashes, which do not stick to Tom's feet, he finds Grimes stuck, head and shoulders, in a chimney. He cannot light his pipe, is denied any beer, but continues to emit foul language as before. Tom wants to release him, but he cannot. On hearing about his old mother, who turns out to be the kind dame in Vendale, Grimes bursts into tears and shows genuine remorse. He fears it is too late to mend the situation. The fairy then releases him from the chimney, but he is then committed to sweeping the crater of Mount Etna. We can see that as partial forgiveness, but not a complete release from our wickednesses. A most telling remark is 'save us from the consequences of our own actions.' (page 231). It is poetic justice; you get what you ask for, or what you imposed on others will be imposed on you. Poetic justice is a strand in Greek mythology and is also an important motif in Deuteronomy 28. Eternal justice is an important strand in most mythologies. The other lesson is that we should not leave it too late to put things right.

There are many other elements in The Water Babies which are taken from various mythologies. We already know about the fairies, specifically sea fairies as seen with the Nereids, such as Eunice, Polynoe, Phyllodoce and Psamathe, all from ancient Greece. But there are also unicorns, fire-drakes, manticoras, basillisks, amphisboenas, griffins, phoenixes, rocs, orcs, dogheaded men, three-headed dogs (Cerberus) and three-bodied geryons, some of which appear in Harry Potter. Prometheus, Epimetheus and Pandora, as well as Mount Erebus are mentioned too. With regard to Norse culture, there are giants, one of fire and one of steam, and a very old giant who is 'collecting new species'. Does this remind us of Darwin? There is a sea serpent which reminds us of Jormangand and a deep chasm in the sea which reminds us of Ginnungagap. There is a one-eyed bogey which can be taken as Odin. He is concerned that Tom will be trying to steal the precious metals that shoot up from the chasm. This is where gold and silver are mentioned as well as other metals which are found in ores. In general terms, Kingsley is economic on the precious metal factor and even more so on the motif of the world tree, which never seems to appear. There is just the occasional mention of jewels, but there are substitutes such as the beautiful colours of the dragonfly.

In case one were thinking that Kingsley is totally naive about the state of contemporary scientific knowledge, there are various passages in the book that show he has much awareness of the Theory of Evolution and other matters related to it. We notice that the Professor is a naturalist but Kingsley is quite sarcastic about such people. This is a telling remark; 'I believe that naturalists get dozens of them (water babies) when they are out dredging, but they say nothing about them and throw them overboard again for fear of spoiling their theories.' How often do we find that a scientist tailors the evidence to fit some pre-conceived notion?! In 1863, The Theory of Evolution would have been 'hot off the press'. This gives an extra relevance to that idea, seen above, that humans could have debased themselves into monkeys, as opposed to the other way round.

The professor, failing to take in the evidence of his own eyes, is then driven out of his mind by a terrible old fairy. Now he is demented to the puzzlement of the doctors. Now comes the sarcasm about the medical profession. 'Of course every one of them (the doctors) flatly contradicted the other; else what use is there in being men of science.' (page 106) Kingsley gives us a massive list of possible conditions with methods of dealing with them. Here is a sample of the crazy ideas considered; bullyings, coaxings, good advice, mild tobacco, oil of wormwood, starvation, opium, strait-waistcoats, and boring a hole in his head! (page 108). It is interesting how some of these are still in vogue and others are definitely out of fashion. 'Good advice' might now be rephrased as 'counselling'! At times, it sounds like Mary Baker Eddy who denounced all these strange medical methods but did agree with the placebo.(2)

Kingsley is also sarcastic about book-learning and education. In Waste

Paper Land we have the vision of children cramming for their exams. Examination is dubbed as a great idol, in other words, an obsession which distracts us from the true purpose of education. The examiners are shown as some kind of tyrants. Has it all come full circle with the tyranny of Ofsted and an excess of intelligence tests in our own times? We notice that Tom's education is a series of visionary experiences going up to the Polar Ice Sheet, different encounters with real life, as opposed to mugging up material from books. The book ends with Tom becoming a great inventor, and man of science, who knows all about everything. This is because he has real experience of the world. We notice that the old lady in Vendale, with a clutch of children doing 'the three R's' in the dame school, is not criticised, in fact she is shown up as caring and with a natural rapport with children.

The book ends with a lovely romantic conclusion as Tom is reunited with Ellie, his sweetheart. We would all expect them to be married and live happily ever after. This is where a subtle anticlimax comes in; fairies are not supposed to get married, it is claimed, though we would all say, 'why not?' After all, they are in some kind of Heaven, and angels do not marry like mortals, so Jesus assures us.(3)

Apart from being a very successful and caring parish priest, Kingsley was also a naturalist and wrote various books on marine biology and geology. He had a deep faith that everything that the scientist investigated was simply the wonderful workings of God. The physical world, for him, was far more filled with miracles than any fantasy story.

One might ask whether there could be some sort of confusion here between the antics of the fairies and the mission of Jesus who did so many miracles. We could say that the message of the Bible has through Kingsley's book, received even more mythologisation than there is in it now. Bultmann would doubtless object. But we must recall the importance of mythology. It appeals to so many of the basic instincts in human nature. Poetic justice, cleansing, repentance and forgiveness are just some of the strands in this story. To portray these matters in mythological terms has the effect of emphasising the social message and stirring the imagination. There is that emotion raised, 'do not leave it too late.' This goes a long way to explaining why the book had such an impact on thinking in the late 19th century. Tom, the downtrodden orphan turns out to be an expert, knowing all about everything. He is the little hero, a motif seen in so many myths; this reminds us of Kauymali (chapter 14), and of little David who prevailed over the giant.(4)

With regard to eschatology, there is hardly anything said on this level. There is that strange word Cocqcigrues which is not explained. It seems to be some time in the future when things will turn out right. This might be Kingsley's intimation of the apocalypse, that there is a time of promise waiting in the future.

A fairy story like this stands in stark contrast to the rational, scientific, industrial age of the mid-19th century. Are we seeing the same configuration with the appearance of Harry Potter?

The concept of the apocalypse is cleverly worked in with the motif of St. Brandan's Isle. St. Brandan is, of course, a real Irish missionary saint of the early years in the Christian era in the Celtic regions.(5) He is credited with exploratory voyages going west over the Atlantic in a boat made of cowhides. If we are looking for historical realism or some kind of legend as the starting point for Kingsley's saga, this could be it. Kingsley even links it in with the legends about Atlantis which disappeared beneath the waves.(6) Not only does this raise up a romantic notion about a blessed island which seems to indicate Heaven, but St. Brandan is expected to awake once more and resume teaching the water babies, but some think he will sleep on, for better or worse 'till the coming of Cocqcigrues'. The whole concept of a magical fairy island, which only some can see, gives a lovely poetic touch to the whole story; this is the home of the water babies.

One thing that is heavily emphasised in the story is Tom's loneliness. For a long time, he has no one to play with. This is augmented by his longing for Ellie, but also, he spends a lot of time asking various fish where the water babies are. None of them seem willing or able to tell him. Eventually, he meets one of them and he becomes the centre of attention; they are all delighted to have a new recruit. Loneliness is a factor seen in several myths. Adam was all alone in the garden, while all the animals had partners. This is played through in the Temptations of Jesus, where he is all alone with the wild beasts (Mark 1:13). Loneliness is not something that we enjoy and it engenders sympathy.

Another factor emphasised is the wonders of Nature beneath the sea. There are hard remarks made about humans dumping rubbish in the sea, and the water babies do not like having to clear it up. This sounds like 21st century environmentalism. Tom is constantly amazed at the beautiful things like sea anemones on the sea bed. This is emphasised by the fact that he is a complete ingénue, and finds all these things a total novelty. Kingsley displays a full knowledge of what goes on beneath the waves, and this underscores his skill as a marine biologist.

On the face of it, the Water Babies is plainly a fairy story couched in the sentimental tones of mid-19th century children's literature. There are various social and political issues concealed in the story, some of them highly relevant to today's world. If it were the accepted thing that little boys could be exploited like Tom, being sent up the chimney, this must cause us to consider in what way our children nowadays are being overtaxed, frightened and not given a fair chance in life. All the high-pressure approach to education, for instance, which is regarded as the normal thing nowadays, ought to be reconsidered and modified. One has the feeling that Kingsley would have been a valued asset to educational thinking today. One can encourage children to think for themselves, rather than just be indoctrinated or programmed. This is a telling remark which makes Kingsley a very modern thinker; 'It is not good for little boys to be told everything, and never be forced to use their own wits.' In other words, train people to think for themselves, as opposed to being brain washed all the time.

Moanna by Walt Disney

Another 'children's' production which works in much the same way is the recent Walt Disney feature film, Moanna. It uses the cartoon mode of production but also the virtual reality method which makes this CD very effective and entertaining.

Briefly, the story concerns a south sea island near Tahiti, where the people are very happy with their life and self-sufficient. The chief has a daughter called Moanna and she is expected to inherit the 'throne' in due course, as the chief has no sons. There is a strong family feeling as mother and grandmother are influential in the ruling dynasty. However, a problem is creeping up on this community; the fish in the lagoon have disappeared and the coconuts have developed a disease. Moanna is sure that she should venture out beyond the lagoon in search of new food supplies or possibly a new island to inhabit. The story is mainly about her adventures away from home and her return as the old island home is re-created and the problem is solved.

This production is notable for its inclusion of just about every element of mythology that could be worked in. I understand that this has been done deliberately; it is also to very great effect. It would be easier to mention the mythological elements not included. These would be gold and silver, and snakes and possibly trees. The substitute for trees is that distinctively shaped mountain which has a pile of stones on the top, for each successive chief. That mountain looks suspiciously like Mount Meru, the holy mountain of Hindu mythology.

Highly significant is the use of jewels. Moanna has a pendant with a green opal round her neck, which she regards as her lucky charm. She goes to all kinds of lengths to retain it, even when the giant throws it into the sea, or the cockerel swallows it. Otherwise we have a giant crab covered with diamonds.

We have two significant giants in the story. The first one, who begins by disliking Moanna, is in the sea and can turn himself into a giant fish or a bird. As the story progresses he comes to like her and support her. The other giant is a volcano fire giant, not unlike Surt in Norse mythology,(7) but he is defeated by the sea giant; the volcano is tamed.

As Moanna returns to her island, which has been stripped bare with no life remaining, the goddess of the island appears. This goddess has a strong resemblance to Moanna and is clearly about to bless the land. As the goddess sinks down and melts into the landscape, all the greenery comes back and the island regains its productivity. This is a highly effective rendering of the concept of Pantheism, how the land, which is being recreated, is actually the goddess; it is done in typical Disney poetic and sentimental terms.

Just as the Water Babies has various topical messages to impart, so too has this production. We notice that Moanna, a girl, is in line to inherit the chiefdom. She is actually termed a 'princess'; this must jar on the susceptibilities of our American friends. (They cannot cope with the idea of a woman president or indeed monarchy!) So it is egalitarianism but on a different level. The other strand is about environmentalism. Moanna goes to find new territories or food supplies but eventually returns to a renewed homeland and her family are delighted. How does this compare with our attempts at colonising other planets on the assumption that this world is insufficient for our needs? The message is that the world ought to, and can, be renewed and sustain us all. The 'stay-at-home' policy is a strong one in this story. Another strand in this saga is the role of Moanna's grandmother, who dies, but comes back as a ghost. Here we have the awareness of the world of the spirit and the ghost assures Moanna that she will never be alone; grandmother will always be near her in whatever dangers threaten.

One thing very much in common with the Water Babies is the fact that Moanna can dive down into the ocean and not drown. She goes into underwater caves and encounters crabs and other creatures, but the sea giant comes too and sometimes leads the way. We are fascinated by this underwater world. Also she can fly up into the sky, which Tom did not seem capable of doing. She does not seem to have a boyfriend, except to say that she has a cockerel as a familiar who accompanies her in all her adventures.

One novel element in this saga is the fact that the sea-giant's tattoos can actually move and give him advice. This reminds us of something in Harry Potter, where the pictures on the wall move and talk. This is an example of modern augmentative mythology and is done quite dramatically and effectively.

It is unfortunate that the whole production is somewhat spoilt by the free reign of sloppy indistinct speech full of America colloquial slang. This renders the conversation difficult to follow. It is a feature in common with Star Trek and Star Wars. What a shame they seem incapable of speaking clearly!

Do you believe in fairies?

Since Spenser and Kingsley make much use of fairies in their story-telling, this raises the question of whether there are such things as fairies. Solid evidence for their existence might be on hand, but this is a matter of dispute to this day. In 1917 two girls, Frances Griffiths and Elsie Wright borrowed a camera and claimed that they had taken pictures of fairies. This took place in Cottingley, near Bradford. Naturally, arguments have raged over the genuineness of these images. They seem real in the photographs, but then as we all know, photographs can be faked.

Conan Doyle, the famous creator of Sherlock Holmes, investigated the matter and came to the conclusion that the pictures were genuine. Others could not believe it.

In later life, Elsie admitted that the fairies were a fake. She claimed that they were cut-outs from a book and then mounted on hatpins. The image of the girl in the background was done by double exposure (something that we cannot do now with our digital cameras). Frances admitted that while some of the pictures were fakes, other were not. I have to say, on watching the TV programme on the subject, that the later pictures could be faked, but the first ones are of a different texture and could be genuine. As one would expect, some people ignore what the girls have said and form their own opinion on the matter. If indeed the pictures were fakes, the children would have to have been very clever!

The Cottingley faires is an intriguing matter, but it does not really prove or disprove the existence of fairies. It is worth mentioning that the Celtic peoples have their own collection of 'little people'. The Welsh have the Tylwydd Teg, the Irish have the Leprachaun and the Scots have Boomans and Brownies and a few other funny people. These things are almost certainly based on real life experiences in rural areas.

It is a mistake to become too dogmatic about the existence or non-existence of fairies.

Footnotes for Chapter 11

1. This may be another side-swipe at the Theory of Evolution, which had become famous at this time. Kingsley sees monkeys as a degenerate form of humanity rather than the other way round. We note that some African tribal mythologies agree with that; see chapter on African mythology.
2. For a treatment of Mary Baker Eddy's thoughts on Christian Science, see chapter 9 in The Theology of Truth.
3. Matthew 22:30.
4. I Samuel 17:41.
5. See The Brendan Voyage, by Tim Severin.
6. See the chapter on Atlantis, number 7.
7. See chapter 22 in The Theology of Truth, and also chapter 8 in this book.

12

Chinese mythology

I have chosen Chinese mythology as a complete contrast to anything in the western world. Whether we realise it or not, Greek mythology has and still does exert a massive influence on thought in the western world. That includes all areas of culture, not least the scientific community. But Chinese mythology has had no influence at all in the West, at least not until very recent times. This is because China has been an isolated culture for thousands of years, in spite of trade links which have been in action many hundreds of years through the Silk Route. We have only really become aware of Chinese thinking when the great explorers succeeded in discovering alternative routes to the Far East. Even then the Chinese were not eager to disclose their secrets concerning such things as the production of silk and porcelain.

The situation over religion also forms a complete contrast with the West. We are accustomed to thinking in terms of Judaism interacting with Egyptian, Canaanite and Greek theology. None of these had any influence in China. It was Confucianism blended with Taoism and later Buddhism which entered the scene from India. At first, Buddhism was not particularly welcome as it was not at all positive about family values; however, later it managed to merge with the native religions. There was never any real clash of thinking between these three; they co-existed quite happily into modern times, and one wonders how or where to draw the line between one religion or another. The Communist upsurge may have dented religion in China but there is still much residual religious impulse in the population. The latest development has been the coming of Christianity in recent times. It is difficult to assess what is really going on since the government does not really want to admit to the existence of religion at all.

It would be a massive task to recount every aspect of Chinese mythology, folklore and legend, as indeed with the Greek material. Much of this can be discovered from several well-produced books on the subject, listed in the bibliography. But the main essentials ought to be explored, and their symbolisms discussed. We begin with the Jade Emperor, the supreme god in the Taoist pantheon. He wears a piece of white jade on his forehead as a symbol of purity; otherwise a Tai Chi symbol. Jade is like onyx or alabaster; semi-translucent, carvable and inscribable. It is highly prized in China and some superb artworks have been produced in jade. It may be that onyx and alabaster were not known in China; vice versa jade only recently became known in the West. We notice that the Jade Emperor is depicted fully clothed in ceremonial robes; he is never stark naked (as with the Greek gods). We could say that he is roughly analogous to YHWH, but only very approximately. Even though he is the chief of the pantheon, he is also in some sort of Trinitarian relationship. There are Three Emperors of Heaven; past, present and future. The Emperor of the present is also known as the August Personage of Jade, the supreme **yang** principle. He has a wife, the Queen Mother of the West, Hsi Wang Mu,(1) the ultimate **yin** principle. The other two components in the trinity are the **Tao,** which is strictly speaking not a god but a philosophical principle and **Lao Tzu** who was an earthly philosopher who graduated to divinity. While the God of the Hebrews, YHWH, is active and communicative, and eager to make an arrangement with humans, the Jade Emperor is distant, passive and will only converse with the human Emperor who lives in Peking. He has an entire court, and a wife called Xi Wangmu,(1) just like Zeus with Hera. The court in Peking is a mirror image of the heavenly court; it is all about bureaucracy and good order and a meritocratic system. One's conduct is noted by the household god, Zao Yun, and the information sent to the Jade Emperor who will decide on one's fate after one's death. There are various heavens and hells (18 in number) to which one might be consigned. This again is a system of court cases as one's bad conduct is assessed, but there is also the reality of starting a new life as someone else. Zao Yun can be seen as the equivalent of Hermes, the messenger god. The theology of reincarnation may not be original to China; it may have arrived with Buddhism, but the Taoist idea of hell is much more severe and threatening than in Hindu-Buddhism. Heaven , or paradise, is at K'un-lun mountain and is presided over by The Queen Mother of the West, and also there are the Isles of the Blessed.

Another important factor is to realise that the rich traditions of Chinese mythology never became any sort of scriptural basis for any of their religions. The real basis of their religions has been the writings of Lao Tzu, the **Tao Teh Ching** and of Confucius, the **Analects** and various Buddhist holy writings. Much of this is on a philosophical line and does not really touch on Chinese mythological thinking. The opposite approach is seen with the Judaeo-Christian approach, in which we see mythological material forming a starting point in the early chapters of Genesis and reappearing in various places further on in the scriptures. When one says 'mythological' ones does not imply that it is untrue or pure fiction. What it does say is that the Hebrew tradition knows how to work in the deepest and most basic impulses in human nature into the general theology of its system. This method is not seen in Chinese thought. There is never any mention of the Jade Emperor or the Yellow Emperor or of dragons in Chinese scriptures.

Who was the Yellow Emperor (often called Yao or Huang-Ti)? He is often confused or equated with the Jade Emperor. However, this is one of those figures going back into the mists of primeval time. He must have had a massive reputation since his burial mound is surrounded by the Terracotta Army,(2) which is still being excavated. The colour yellow is important as symbolic of deity, royal power and nationality. Yao is pictured as bringing the dynasty of human emperors into existence, probably about 2600 BC. He was the one that brought order, unity and stability to China, when there were numerous small states in contention with each other. He was not 'God Almighty' in the western sense, but a very powerful force as a substratum of life in China. It is he, some say, that is believed to have caused the great Flood, for the same reason as in the West; the wickedness of humanity that should be punished. We notice that the 'folk-memory' of the Flood is present in China as well as everywhere in the West. We have to conclude that the Flood is not just a myth but some kind of legend with a historical anchorage somewhere. An attempt was made to stop the flood in China by the Yellow Emperor's grandson, Gun, who stole magic soil from heaven to soak up the water. Unfortunately the fire god, Chu Yung noticed the theft, chased after him and slew him. Some say that his grandfather, Yao, was furious and caused more flooding and ordered Gun to be killed. But when he was stabbed, it was not blood that came out, but a young dragon, named Yu, and he finally stopped the flood. Yu had the sense to ask permission to take some magic soil from heaven. He was capable of assuming the form of a dragon, or a bear. He succeeded in stopping the floods. Now we see why dragons are connected with the supply of water; either a downpour or a drought. With the Yellow Emperor, this may be the nearest we come to some sort of Devil or Satan; otherwise there seems to be no such figure in Chinese thought.

It would be a mistake to equate the dragon with the Devil. Chinese dragons are an essential element in folklore and mythology. Even if the Yellow Emperor is depicted with dragons on his vestments, this does not imply that they are evil. They are powerful but also kind and wise; they rule nature and bring water and rain. They symbolise good luck, wealth and justice. They also symbolise the Chinese emperor and royal power. This explains why the emperors' robes and the palaces are decorated with dragons. There is also a Dragon King who lives beneath a lake; he is helpful and powerful enough to defeat a nasty god. There is also a story of how a boy, in a drought, managed to find a pearl which had the effect of augmenting the contents of the rice jar and also the money in their savings pot. When he swallowed the pearl, he turned into a dragon and jumped into the river; but it was the end of the drought. To this day, festivals in China will include people dressed up as dragons, not unlike a pantomime horse. They appear as comical, jocular and great fun, although there may be a substratum of seriousness in the playacting. By contrast with western thought, in which dragons are seen as terrifying and evil, and perhaps an augmentation of a snake, the Chinese dragon is a positive symbol, life-enhancing and helpful. It is an important part of their background culture. Whether there ever were, historically, such creatures as dragons, is an interesting question. The Kommodo dragon,(3) which still exists in some parts of the world, it is hardly a convincing explanation; it is a massive lizard, slow and non-aggressive. But it is indicative of something, that widely separated parts of the world have some kind of folklorist memory of a dragon, even if the symbolism it conveys is rather different.

There are many Dragon Kings, Lung-Wang, and they receive their authority direct from the Jade Emperor; their purpose is to make sure the rain is apportioned to each region.(3) There are four main Dragon Kings, one for each of the four seas which surround the mainland of China. They are brothers, each living in a palace, and having ministers and an army of fish, crabs, crayfish, which patrol the sea-bottom. More relevant to the people are the local Dragon Kings; every well or stream has its own Dragon King which must be sacrificed to. They are represented in their temples as a mandarin in ceremonial costume. It is the Dragon King that brings the rain. If there is a drought, the dragon might be fetched out for a procession in the town, or his effigy placed by the roadside to induce rain. If there is too much rain, again the local Dragon King will be asked to solve the problem. They are the ones who contact the Jade Emperor , rather than the people themselves. Here we see the element of intercession or an intermediary, the assumption being that God is too remote or holy for humans to make the approach.

The symbolism in the dragon may be difficult for us in the West to appreciate. My suggestion is on these lines. The dragon is an exaggerated or augmented version of the snake. The snake is a paradoxical creature in that it symbolises death but also life; this notion is seen in so many cultures across the world. With the Chinese climate being what it is, drought, alternating with an excess of water, we have the juxtaposition of life and death, a finely balanced situation which one hopes is controlled by God. The dragon is directly in touch with God to keep things in balance. Wealth and good fortune are heavily dependent on the good offices of the Dragon King. It is tempting for us in the West to see the Dragon as threatening, cruel and evil. But in Chinese thought, the emphasis is different. Evil, Satan and the Devil are not at all a strong element. It would be true that there are evil spirits, but the powerful spirits, namely the gods, are almost all well-intentioned towards humanity. This ties in with the thoughts of Confucius. He does not have any kind of idea of what we would call 'original sin' or wickedness in human nature. He has an entirely optimistic view of human nature, which reminds one of modern Humanism.

Feng-huang

As the female counterpart to the Dragon motif, there is the tradition of a mythical bird, somewhat analogous to the Phoenix, except that she does not jump in the fire. The Feng-huang puts in a very rare appearance, when something auspicious is taking place. This might be a great event, or related to an important ruler. When the Yellow Emperor (Huang-ti, or Yao) came to die, there was an appearance. She has a beautiful song, and likes human music. A description of her can be most perplexing; she has the breast of a goose, the hindquarters of a stag, the tail of a fish, the neck of a snake, the forehead of a fowl, the down of a duck, the marks of a dragon, the back of a tortoise, the face of a swallow and the beak of a cock, and is nine feet tall.

Can all this be included in one creature? Hardly! Clearly there is the element of exaggeration involved here, and also different parts of China might well have some of these ideas but not all. The symbolism in it is fairly obvious in places. If it is nine feet tall, that matches the nine layers of heaven, earth and hell, as in Chinese thought. The breast of a goose might suggest good meat to eat. The hindquarters of a stag might indicate speed. The tail of a fish would suggest association with the main Dragon-Kings who patrol the seas. The neck of a snake means life and death paradoxically intertwined. The forehead of a fowl, such as a chicken, might mean always feeding. The down of a duck means softness or tenderness. The marks of a dragon associates her with the dragons. The back of a tortoise is most significant since the Chinese see the world as planted on the back of a black tortoise. The face of a swallow might indicate speed. The beak of a cock might suggest always prying into things. To us in the West, this bird might seem most strange, but to the Chinese, it is probably loaded with significance and subtle meaning.

The Ch'i-lin

This is another elusive mythological creature, related to the dragons. Like the Feng-huang, this beast only appears when someone like a sage or an illustrious ruler is about to be born or die. It can be seen as the Chinese version of the unicorn. It has a single horn on its forehead, a yellow belly, and a multi-coloured back. It has the hooves of a horse, the body of a deer and the tail of an ox. It is gentle by nature and is the ultimate vegan; it will not eat living vegetation. The first Ch'i-lin is said to have appeared in the garden of the Yellow Emperor (Huang-ti), and two were seen in the capital of Emperor Yao. This was an indication of the benevolent rule of both emperors. With regard to Confucius, a Ch'i-lin appeared to his mother during her pregnancy. She coughed up a tablet of jade with an inscription foretelling the greatness of her son. Confucius' death was presaged by a Ch'i-lin being injured by a charioteer.

This idea is not purely a Chinese idea. The 'unicorn' can be traced to ancient Mesopotamia. The idea spread westwards into Greece and the Roman Empire and also eastwards into India and thence to China. The idea may be based on a real animal, possibly an aurochs, but exaggeration and symbolism appear to have elaborated the idea. The western unicorn is pure white with a purple head, flashing eyes and a red dot on the end of his horn. He is much more aggressive and also difficult to catch, moving very fast. As with the phoenix, the unicorn came to be symbolic of Jesus Christ in later art.

Again, the symbolism of the Ch'i-lin can be seen as important, but perhaps more obscure. The yellow belly clearly means the Chinese have claimed him for their own, and he is related to the Yellow Emperor and the Yellow River. The hooves of a horse suggest speed, which would be true. The body of a deer suggests strength and timidity, along with the dappled back. The tail of an ox might also indicate strength. This combination of animal features goes somewhat further than in Greek thought. The horn without a red spot would suggest the animal is not as aggressive as the western unicorn. This is yet another example of how a literal, historical feature has become something mythological, every bit as much as the Yellow Emperor. How literally such a thing can be taken is again a good question; do the Chinese think of the Ch'i-lin in literal terms, or purely in symbolic terms? Opinions on this may vary in China, just they do in the West. It is alleged that the Bible contains references to a **re'em** which has been translated as a unicorn, but also as a rhinoceros. A lot depends on how one sees these things. In every context in the Bible, of which there are about half a dozen, the word **re'em** appears in a poetical setting, and it would be senseless to take 'unicorn' in a literal interpretation.

Chinese Creation mythology

We have to notice that it is not the Jade Emperor who creates the world. This is done by Pan Gu, a primal god who was in a deep sleep as he built up strength to create the world. As he awoke he found chaos and darkness. In anger he lashed out with his fist, making a massive booming sound. Does this remind us of the 'Big Bang'? Heavy things settled downwards and lighter things floated up to form the sky. Pan Gu feared that they would close in again so he stood between them to keep earth and heaven apart; as he pushed harder and harder, earth and heaven moved further apart until he felt the heavens would not collapse back. So he let go and went back to his sleep. As he slept his body turned into the rest of the universe.(4) The mountains, soil, plants, trees, the rivers all were derived from his body, even the morning dew which was his sweat. As he slept, he died.

We notice that Pan Gu reminds us of Atlas, the Greek god who held up the sky, only Pan Gu was not tricked into holding up the heavens. Strangely, he is a sleepy god, not particularly active and at the end very passive, in fact the opposite of YHWH. There is poetic sensitivity in this account, and also a generous degree of pantheism in the sense that the god is actually the physical world.

The formation of the human race was not done by Pan Gu; (4) it was a female deity called Nu Wa. She admired Pan Gu's world but felt there was something missing. She took clay and formed a man; as she placed him on the ground, he came to life. Nu Wa was thrilled with him as he danced around, so she made more and more little figures. She realised that as they grew older, they would die, so she devised procreation so that babies could be born and perpetuate the human race. Everyone was happy; it was a kind of golden age. But a problem arose; someone (the Jade Emperor) left the clay figures out in the rain and so they were deformed. In other words, the human race is a deformity of what it should have been. This is an interesting and mild approach to explaining the problem of evil. We notice that in common with Genesis, mankind is created from clay.(5) Also in this we see the urge to overcome the finality of death; man's immortality is ensured by the production of children.

Nu Wa is the goddess of creation and of marriage. She has a husband called Fu Xi. He invented fishing, having watched a spider making a web. He also invented fire and China's first system of writing. How much of this reminds us of Hephaistos? Both Nu Wa and Fu Xi had a human head but a snake's or a dragon's body. With a human head, this symbolises sympathy with humanity and the snake's body suggests fertility, life, but also paradoxically, death. We already know what a dragon symbolises. It is interesting that Nu Wa is sometimes understood to be Fu Xi's wife; at other times his sister. An inconsistency like this is a strong indication that no one ever took these myths literally. It is always metaphoric and symbolic.

Also we notice that human skills and inventions are credited to the intervention of a god. Again, is this to be taken literally? Can we see in this that inspiration and useful discoveries are found and then attributed to the help of a certain god? In attributing it to the intervention of a god, this is a roundabout way of giving the invention authority and a degree of holiness. This can almost certainly be one of the motives in creating a mythology. An example of this would be that getting married and having children is encouraged by the god; something that we see in Genesis.

The eight immortals, Pa-hsien

Characteristic of many mythologies, is the element of promotion, as seen with Heracles and others in Greek thought. In China we have eight legendary persons who were devout in their Taoist faith and practice through which they were given immortality and the right to attend the banquets given by the Jade Emperor's wife. Here again is something that must have begun as historical figures who have been augmented into divinities; even so they are not full-blown gods. They are depicted as standing on little octagonal incense altars. They are all wearing ceremonial robes and headdresses. A description of them follows; the details tend to vary, possibly through regional differences of ideas: (6)

Han Chung-li (Zhongli Quan); He began life as an officer at court, but in later life gave it up to become a hermit. He is credited with the ability to turn base metals into silver, and would give to the poor. A tale about him has him meditating in a cave, when the rocks cracked open and revealed a new chamber within, from which came a strange light. In there was a casket of finest jade in which were the secrets of immortality. The cave was filled with heavenly music and colours. A stork flew in and carried him off to the Isles of P'eng-lai. He is known as the True Active Principle and is associated with the army. He has two emblems, the Peach of Immortality and a fan made of feathers. He is pictured as an old man with a large stomach and a carefree air. He is regarded as the leader of the immortals.

Chang Kuo Lao (Zhang Guo Lao). He is seen as an old man and so represents the elderly; paradoxically he gives fertility to young couples. He also has magical powers. He was invited to court, but fell down dead at the temple gate. As he lay dead and decomposing, he miraculously came back to life, and acquired greater magical powers . The emperor asked Fa-shan, a Taoist sage about Chang Kuo Lao. Fa-shan's answer was that if one spoke about him, one would drop dead. Ignoring his own advice, Fa-shan whispered that Chang was really a white bat; he fell down dead at once. Chang was summoned , sprinkled water on his face, and Fa-shan revived. Chang went back to his hermitage and died; later his tomb was opened to reveal no sign of his body. Chang had a magical white donkey (or mule) with which he could travel thousands of miles in a day. This animal could be folded up like a piece of paper but unfolded again when Chang blew water on it. His symbol is a peacock feather or a peach of Immortality, or a paper horse. He is shown riding back to front on it. We notice the element of resurrection twice in this tradition, and also, with his tomb being empty, the element of 'assumption' not unlike what happened to Moses, Elijah and Enoch.

Lu Tung-Pin (Lu Dongbin); There are many stories about this Immortal, the most famous is the 'Rice Wine Dream'. He became a pupil of Han Chung-Li. They met at an inn and Chung-Li realised that not only was Lu politically ambitious but also a scholar and deeply thoughtful person. Lu fell asleep and dreamed of his success at court and then his fall from grace and ruination. When he awoke, Chung-Li was there to advise him. He renounced court life and followed Chung-Li to study and meditate. He would travel as an oil salesman, giving immortality to anyone not greedy. For one old woman he threw magical rice into her well; it yielded only wine, and made her fortune. He was also a skilled swordsman; his sword was used to punish the wicked and do good. This sword can make him invisible, only to reappear like an 'avatar'. He is shown holding a male child; this infers that one's descendants will become aristocrats. He also represents students. His title is Pure Active Principle. The sword or a fly-whisk are his symbols.

`**Ts'ao Kuo-Chiu (Cao Guojiu);** This is another one who was important at court, being the brother of the Empress Ts'ao, but gave it all up to be a hermit. He represents the nobility. The story goes that a scholar and his wife were invited into the palace by Ching-chih, the younger brother of Ts'ao. He got them drunk, slew the scholar and tried to rape the wife. She resisted him but he had her thrown into the dungeons. But the ghost of the scholar appeared to the Imperial Censor, begging for justice. Ts'ao had advised Ching-chih to have the woman executed, so she was thrown down a well. The spirit of planet Venus came to her rescue and she escaped the city. Noticing a procession, she tried to appeal to what she thought was the Censor, but it was not; it was Ts'ao. He had her beaten with iron rods until she was all but dead. However, she revived and managed to contact the Censor who was furious. Both princes were arrested and Ching-chih was executed for murder. The Emperor declared an amnesty for all prisoners. It dawned on Ts'ao Kuo-Chiu that his life had been meaningless, so he gave up everything and went off to be a hermit. He kept one keepsake of his life in the palace, a tablet of gold. It came to crossing a river and he wanted to pay the ferryman, showing him the tablet. The ferryman took offence at this, so Ts'ao threw the tablet into the river; this impressed the ferryman, who was actually Lu Dongbin. He then took Ts'ao on as his pupil so that he could learn the Tao. We notice again the element of resurrection and also of eternal justice prevailing. Also there is that slight hint of 'who pays the ferryman?' as in Greek thinking!

Li T'ieh-Kuai (Li Tieguai); He was taught the Tao by Lao Tzu himself. When he was called to Heaven, he left instructions with his disciple, Lang Ling, to watch his body and only burn it after seven days had elapsed. Lang followed instructions, but on the sixth day, he heard that his mother was dying and wanted him. Lang decided that it was nearly time-up, so he burned Li's body and went to his mother. But Li did return, only to find a pile of ashes, and nowhere for his spirit to inhabit except the body of a dead beggar. Even though the body was deformed, Lao Tzu advised Li to inhabit it, giving it a gold headband, a life-giving gourd and an iron crutch. Li went to find Lang who was sorrowing over his mother. Li poured some liquid from the gourd and revived the mother. He is thought to have special medicines, and represents the sick. He is another one who was carried to heaven by a stork. Li is often on a sign outside the pharmacist shop; his symbols are the gourd and the iron crutch. Again we see the element of resurrection and miraculous healing. Also this is an early example of the out-of-the-body experience.

Han Hsiang-Tzu (Han Xiang Zi); Han was a great philosopher and poet, a pupil of Lu Tung-Pin. He had a theory of human nature which involved three elements; the good, the evil and the balanced. Han was banished to Canton, where he banished a huge reptile that was terrorising people. He obtained immortality by being dropped from the top of the Immortalising Peach Tree and he has a magic flute that gives life. His symbol is a flower basket and he represents the cultured element in society.

Lan Ts'ai-Ho (Lan Caihe); He was a beggar who only wore one shoe and blue garments, fastened with a wooden belt. He went about as a street singer, beating time with his stick. He threw money on the ground for the poor, which is why he represents them. He also played the lute, which is his symbol. There is some uncertainty about his gender; he might have been a homosexual or a female in disguise. To achieve immortality, he got blind drunk at an inn, went unconscious, and was carried away by a cloud. He left his shoe and blue robe behind. For all his foolishness he is noted as a great healer.

Ho Hsien-Ku (He Xiang Zi); This is the only female immortal who was born with only six hairs on her head. As a young woman she is depicted as playing a reed mouth organ (a sheng), and she holds a magic lotus, which is her symbol, and she represents single women. She had the gift of prophetic dreams. One of them told her to go to the Mother of Pearl Mountains and grind up a semi-precious stone. On following this instruction, she became immortal, and spent her time picking berries around the mountains. The Empress summoned her to court, but on the way, Ho disappeared; even so, she kept reappearing in different places later on.

The Eight Immortals are shown as taking a boat trip across the sea together; this may be symbolic of crossing the divide from life to death. Although they lived at different times and there is no clear system about how they relate to one another, they are grouped together in their admittance to the next world. We notice the importance of the figure eight; it suggests completeness, the use of all elements of life, as in Taoist philosophy; it is also highly significant in Japanese mythology. Although some of their antics may seem absurd, there is rich symbolism at work in every aspect of their behaviour. They are very popular as 'gods' in China.

We notice that all these figures post-date by a long way, the main framework of Taoist philosophy as laid out by Lao Tzu. This is an interesting case of the philosophy coming first, followed by the elaborations of mythology. The Eight Immortals do not contradict Taoist thinking; all they do is give examples and show how coming to grips with the basics of Taoism, namely study and meditation, and following the simple life, will ensure its reward in the next world. Always we have the theme of resurrection, the reality of the spirit and this underscores the value of human life. It ought to last for ever; but it does not. The paradox between life and death is always a substratum in this system of thought.

The Monkey King

So far, we have seen almost all Chinese myths as a part of the Taoist traditions. In contrast, however, there is one important set of mythical sagas coming from the Buddhist infusion, which was a fairly late comer to China, about 400-300 BC. The monkey and the concept of a monkey king and a monkey god are an important element in Hindu-Buddhist thought. We only need to think of the role played by Hanuman in the Ramayana to realise his importance as a champion capable of all kinds of magnificent feats but displaying complete loyalty. In Chinese thought, the monkey symbolises imagination and ingenuity, comedy and a quixotic mind. Monkey is worked into the Chinese calendar, and his month is July, along with other animals, and his year has been, 1944, 1956, 1968, 1980, 1992, 2004 and 2016, in other words, every 12 years. It would be long-winded to recount in detail all the monkey king's exploits but a brief summary will be helpful for those who have never heard of these myths.

There was a rock lying between Heaven and earth, which split open to reveal a stone egg; from this egg came the stone Monkey. He clearly saw himself as a challenge to the Jade Emperor. Monkey played with the other monkeys and he saw a waterfall. They decided that whoever was brave enough to plunge through the waterfall would be acclaimed king. So Monkey took up the challenge and behind the waterfall he found a wonderful new world with everything in stone. The other monkeys followed him and acclaimed him as king. We notice that a 'stone monkey' is a bit of a paradox, but the symbolism in it suggested from stone, is that of permanence, firmness, indestructibility.

Monkey realised that he must die one day and wanted to find out about the Wheel of Rebirth (or the Wheel of Becoming). He went in search of someone who could instruct him and eventually he found a sage living in a cave. The sage gave him enlightenment and so Monkey became immortal. He returned to his kingdom, but also wanted to challenge the Jade Emperor. Even when he was given the title 'Great Sage, Equal of Heaven' he was still mischievous. He stole the Elixir of Life, ate the Peaches of Immortality and drank the Wine of Heaven. The Emperor's men tried everything to subdue Monkey but he beat them all. In the end, the Emperor sent for the Buddha, who might be able to calm him down. The Buddha found out that Monkey wanted to challenge the Jade Emperor himself. The Buddha thought that was a joke but issued a challenge; if you can leap off my right palm then I will take the Jade Emperor away to the Western Paradise and you can be the supremo in Heaven. Monkey thought that was a derisory challenge; he leapt through the air an immense distance and found five pink pillars stretching up into the sky. He thought that was the end of the world; he wrote on one of the pillars, 'Here passed the Great Sage, Equal of Heaven,' and urinated on the spot to prove his feat. Then he made his claim to the Buddha, but the Buddha laughed at him, pointing out the inscription on one of his fingers and a smelly puddle. Monkey realised that he had been deluded; he was pushed out of Heaven and imprisoned for 500 years. Buddha's five fingers turned into the five basic elements, Metal, Wood, Water, Fire and Earth, which are basic to Taoist metaphysics. (see later).

There came a time when the Emperor T'ang wanted to acquire the Buddhist scriptures from India. For this perilous mission, Monkey was released and with three other friends, Tripitaka, Pigsy and Sandy, they set off to fetch the scriptures. On the way they had many strange adventures.

So far, we can see that this saga is allegorical, in that it is talking about the coming of Buddhism to China, and the superiority of Buddhism to Taoism, but also, paradoxically the integration of the two. Now, it becomes even more blatant as the four adventurers come up against the Three Immortals who are called Tiger Strength, Deer Strength and Ram Strength. The stories become even more 'off the wall', as Monkey and his friends make fools of the Taoist monks. I give a précis of the essential elements in the stories.

It culminates in four contests designed to exemplify the validity of one religion over another. The Emperor allows this so that he can find out the truth. Firstly, there is the issue of making it rain, which so far, the Buddhists have failed to do. This is supposed to explain why they were not popular in China. Deer Strength begins by trying to make it rain, waving his sword about. But Monkey ran off and had a word with the Weather gods, to hold back until he gave a signal. When it came to Monkey's turn, he waved his cudgel and it began to rain. The Taoists tried to claim that the Dragons had just been delayed. But Monkey showed that he had the Dragons under his control.

The second contest, thought up by the Taoists, was to see how long one could meditate. This worried Monkey, as he could never sit still! However, it was Tripitaka who took on Tiger Strength. Both seemed to meditate motionless for ever, but after various dirty tricks, Tripitaka won.

The third contest was about guessing what was inside a coffer. A fine robe had been hidden inside, but Monkey turned into a gnat and got inside the coffer, and turned the robe into a cracked dish. Deer Strength thought it was the robe, but Tripitaka (tipped off by Monkey) gave the right answer. The Emperor was not at all pleased; he insisted on placing something in the coffer himself. It was a ripe peach. Monkey managed to penetrate the coffer and eat the peach. Ram Strength guessed it was a peach, but Tripitaka (tipped off by Monkey) said it was a peach stone. Another test thought up by Tiger Strength, was to put a Taoist acolyte, a small boy in the coffer. Monkey again used his magic, and out came a boy with shaven head, reciting Buddhist scriptures. Again Tripitaka guessed correctly.

The fourth trial was more serious and life-threatening. It entailed having one's head cut off, one's heart ripped out and being boiled in oil. Monkey rose to the challenge. As they cut his head off, a new head emerged. But when Tiger Strength had his head cut off, Monkey managed to magic a dog which stole the head and the Tiger was dead. Then the belly-ripping began. Monkey let them do it, but pushed his guts back in and healed up the wound. When it came to Deer Strength's turn, Monkey arranged for a hawk to come and carry off his guts, so the Deer died. Then came the boiling oil. Monkey jumped into the cauldron and splashed around enjoying himself until he appeared to disappear, turning himself into a tack. Then he sprang back up and beat the officer, to prove that he was not a ghost. It was now Ram Strength's turn, and he seemed to be enjoying the bath. Monkey realised that he had a cold dragon in there with him. He asked the Dragon King of the North to remove the cold dragon, and so the Ram was boiled alive. Only his skeleton was found later.

Thus Monkey and his friends convinced the Emperor that Buddhism was a good thing, and the Buddhists were given freedom and civil rights. The conclusion was that one should 'give due reverence to the three religions, which are indeed One.' By this Monkey meant the Buddhists (the priests), the Taoists, and also human abilities (which might have meant the Confucianists). This is therefore allegorically, an explanation of how Toaism and Buddhism became interrelated and mutually respectful of each other in China.

It is rather strange how Monkey does not really behave like a proper Buddhist. He goes in for violence with his cudgel, plays tricks on people and laughs up his sleeve when they are taken in. In many ways this reminds us of Loki, the trickster god of Norse mythology. Whether there ever was any interchange of ideas between the Chinese and the Norsemen, is a question that may never be answered. However, another way of seeing Monkey is to avoid taking the whole thing far too literally. If we see it as figurative, then the message is that Buddhism is more clever and enriching than Taoism. The concept of Monkey being a stone monkey ought to alert us to the symbolisms in these traditions. But then, the whole issue with mythology is the question of how literally we are to take it, and indeed, how literally these sagas were taken in centuries gone by.

Another aspect of the Monkey King is the element of the champion. This factor is seen in virtually every myth the world over. Sometimes the champion is a god, an offshoot of the supreme god. But Monkey is more in the line of Hercules, a hero who gains immortality and is in contention with the supreme god, in this case, the Jade Emperor. He wishes to displace the Jade Emperor; this is symbolic of Buddhism displacing Taoism. But this never actually happened; the two religions co-existed along with Confucianism right into modern times and have had their influence on Communism. The nearest we come to displacing the chief god, Zeus in Greek thought, would be when Prometheus defies Zeus and gives help to mankind. In Chinese thought, most of the gods are kindly disposed to the human race, and that is particularly true of the dragons.

The Sun and the Moon

Most mythologies have some kind of divine identification with the Sun and the Moon and this is certainly true in China. The tradition concerns Yi (Hou Yi) the archer and his wife Chang E. As before there are variant accounts of this myth, which may be related to regional differences. The story goes that Di Jun and his wife Xi He were the gods of the eastern sea, and lived in a giant mulberry tree (Fu Sang), where the sun rises. They had ten sons who were all suns. Their mother was strict about them taking turns to ride across the sky; only one at a time; the other nine must stay back in the branches of Fu Sang. The boys grew tired of this and decided to frolic together across the sky one day. The people on earth at first were amazed at this sight but soon realised that the world was growing far too hot. Soon everything would be parched up and indeed melt up. It was the Yellow Emperor who realised what was happening and he called upon Yi and his wife to solve the problem. Yi had ten magic arrows; he shot down one sun after another and each one fell to earth as a raven with an arrow through his heart. Yi would have shot down all ten suns, had not Yao stolen one arrow from his quiver; this meant that one sun survived (providentially).

Di Jun was heartbroken over loosing nine sons, so Yi and Chang E were banished from Heaven and doomed to live on earth. But Yi went to have a word with Hsi Wang Mu, the Queen Mother of the West. He built her a palace of jade and fragrant timbers in 16 days. She was so pleased that she gave him a Pill of Immortality; some say a bottle of elixir, but enough for two people rather than one. Yi wrapped it up in silk and hid it in the roof of his house. One day Yang E noticed a strange glow coming from the rafters, and on finding the Pill, swallowed it. She began to float upwards. Yi could do nothing to stop her. Up and up she went until she landed on the Moon and stayed there for ever with a hare for company. The gods took pity on Yi and let him build a palace on the sun. This way, the Sun and the Moon interplay with each other; when it is full moon, it is Yi visiting his wife Chang E, in her palace on the moon.

The tradition clearly predates the main upsurge of Taoism with Lao Tzu. Yi was a real historical figure, an archer, at the time of the emperor K'u (2436 BC). This is another example of how a myth has some kind of historical anchorage but has been decorated with exaggeration. The appearance of ten suns at once is not at all out of the question. It is quite possible that there were several meteorites entering earth's atmosphere and there were a series of 'air-bursts', which would explain the intense heat. But the importance of this myth for theology is that the Sun and the Moon are in balance with each other; related but separate. This explains why the T'ai Chi symbol is round, with black and white interswirled, the balance between good and evil, hot and cold, male and female. In this way, the Yin Yang sign has become the logo for Taoism, and has been borrowed and elaborated upon by other faiths. What it is saying in effect, is that the ultimate origin of all things is a subtle interrelation of good and evil.

The ravens, all of which were three-legged, must symbolise the shadow that the sun casts. The fact that they are three-legged suggests they are sinister, as indeed a shadow might be. The theologically important number, three, reminds us of the Taoist Trinity. The suggestion here is that the ravens were coming from the immortal gods but were a destructive element of the excess of suns. The symbolism is profound, and will probably mean more to one of Chinese upbringing.

Other than this myth which concerns the sun and the moon, there seems to be very little involvement of heavenly bodies in the myths of China. This is in complete contrast with Greek thinking, in which almost all the planets and stars are somehow related to gods of one kind or another.

The Silkworm goddess

There is a distinct trend in Chinese thought, to relate their special inventions and industries to their gods. Porcelain, gunpowder, silk and printing are such specialities. But the production of silk, heavily guarded against prying eyes from the west, has its own goddess.

The story goes that there was a girl whose father was often away, and she missed him greatly. One day she whispered this to her horse, adding that she would marry anyone who brought her father back. The horse reared up and bolted off. In a far country, the father realised that the horse had arrived and mounting up he rode home to check on his daughter. The horse was treated with great respect until it was realised that he was unsettled because the girl had promised to marry the one who brought her father home. The thought of her marrying a horse infuriated the father so he killed the horse and skinned it, hanging the hide out to dry. Next day, as the girl came out, the hide wrapped itself around her and carried her off. No one could find her until at last they noticed a mulberry tree with a strange worm-like being with a head like a horse and a strange white thread of silk coming out of her, with which she was cocooning herself. She had changed into the silkworm goddess. The Jade Emperor took pity on her, took her up into heaven and made her one of his concubines. Her title was Lady Horse-Head. Later on she presented the Yellow Emperor with a gift of silk, and this was the beginning of the silk industry in China.

This is another example of a very ancient myth, coming before the main Taoist inception, and clearly relating to real events in China. It seems to date back to the time of King H'sin Nu (circa 2436 BC), a time when the silk industry was in its infancy. We can see in this myth the motivation to sanctify the silk industry; this is quite understandable as fine silk is a delight to handle and commanded very high prices when traded abroad. It is in effect saying that silk is a god-given gift. There are other elements in this story. The fixation of a girl for her father is interwoven. Also the symbolism of the horse is important; there is the year of the horse. The horse is symbolic of elegance and zeal, and also of impulsiveness. For many it is a sign of good luck and peace.

There is an ancient story in which a boy, Wa Tung, made a horse of cloth and wished it were real. A magician changed it into a real one and the boy rode around the garden in delight. But the horse had no eyes, so he trampled all the flowers. The boy's father was furious and called the horse Bad-Luck. But then the magician made the horse go in reverse, undoing all the damage he had done. The father relented a bit and called the horse Good-Luck-Bad-Luck. It was a clumsy horse and kept breaking things, so the father banished it. The horse found a mate and got married; they decided to go back to Wa Tung only to find he was preparing for war. The horse thought this was ridiculous and called upon all his relatives, the other horses, to cause chaos on the battlefield so that there would be peace. Because of this, the horse was renamed Luck and his wife Luck's Wife.

Chinese culture is full of charming little stories like this. Clearly they cannot be taken literally, but as 'just-so' stories, full of symbolism, they say so much. A story like this is typical of the non-violent attitude found in most of Chinese mythology. Most of the gods are well-intentioned towards mankind. When we compare it with Japanese mythology, which is characterised by bloodshed and violence, and indeed Norse mythology as well, it helps to explain a lot how charming and helpful the Chinese can be.

Taoist metaphysical philosophy

Strictly speaking this line of thought is not actually mythology. However, much of the mythology described so far has the Taoist philosophy as its substratum. This is very well outlined in the **Hua Hu Ching** which goes back to Lao Tzu the originator of Taoism. This work, and his seminal work, The **Tao Teh Ching** makes much reference to the TAO as a basic concept in his thinking. It was not his own idea; it was indigenous in Chinese thought long before he appeared on the scene. The relevance of this to mythology is largely because the philosophy offers another approach to divinity and creation. We recall that there is the Jade Emperor and Pan Gu, the creator god. None of this appears in Lao Tzu's works, in so many words, but it would be fair to say, is somehow assumed. It would be unnecessary to describe the Taoist philosophy in complete detail, and indeed the reader may be left somewhat confused, but a general outline or overview will illustrate the point.(7)

The whole scheme is based on the use and symbolism of numbers. We start with ONE which is the TAO, or the Subtle One or the Unnamable Subtle Origin, which is represented by an empty circle. From that we arrive at TWO, where the Subtle One divides into two, the Yin and the Yang. When these two are integrated we arrive at the T'ai Chi, the symbol with black and white interrelated. Now we have THREE; the yang stands for Heaven; the yin stands for Earth; and the T'ai Chi sign stands for man. The T'ai Chi sign brings forth life. These are the three main categories of the Universe. This reminds us of the remarks made about the Taoist Trinity.

FOUR arrives from yin and yang dividing into two each; the 'old yang, young yang, old yin and young yin', added to which is Earth, making it FIVE. These are known as the Five Great Performers of the Universe, or the Unmanifested Sphere. They are called Water, Wood, Metal, Fire and Earth, the Chinese view of the basic elements in physics. We notice that this sounds uncannily like the Greek analysis of basic elements. Whether there was ever any exchange of ideas between Greece and China would be debatable, but the Chinese idea almost certainly pre-dates the Greek idea by many centuries. This provided the basis for the Chinese version of alchemy.

SIX is six Chi or six Breaths which translate into the six climatic influences; wind, cold, heat, moisture, dryness and inflammation. SEVEN is the process of change and recycling. We note from Lao Tzu's ideas that change is an essential part of the Tao. A stagnant, inert kind of world is a dying world and the opposite of the Tao.

EIGHT is the Eight Great Manifestations which are called; Heaven, Earth, Water, Fire, Thunder, Lake, Wind and Mountain. We notice that there were eight Immortals, though how they related specifically to these qualities is not clear. From this we obtain the SIXTY-FOUR hexagrams; 384 displays all the possible permutations of yin and yang. There is a diagrammatic rendering of all possible situations in the Universe, of human history and individual lives.

It is amazing that in what must have been early Bronze Age China, such an elaborate scheme could be devised. But the Unnamable Subtle Origin is clearly a kind of monotheism, roughly analogous to YHWH, followed by a kind of trinity, and then everything flows from that. It reminds us of '… all things come from thee…' 1 Chronicles 29:14

Chinese Zodiac and calendar calculation

It would be a mistake to attempt to delve into this area too deeply, as it becomes very complicated. However, though it is strictly speaking not mythological, the substratum of it is. There are many mythical assumptions as the substratum, and it shows how Chinese thinking is very different from that of the western world.

As with western thinking, there are twelve signs of the Zodiac, but they do not have one month each. Each sign covers an entire year, which means that the calendar goes in twelve year cycles. Each year is named after an animal; the first year is the **Rat** and the last one is the **Pig.** In between come the Ox, Tiger, Rabbit, Dragon, Snake, Horse, Sheep, Monkey, Rooster, and Dog. One's personality is believed to be conditioned according to the year in which one was born. So for instance, if one were born in the Dragon year, one would expect to be very lucky. Another aspect of this is that the five elements are worked in against the animals. So for instance in 1936, 24th January started the year of the Rat, with Fire. In addition to this, each year is either Yang or Yin, for instance the Yang Rat or the Yin Ox etc. Yang and Yin are related to the Sun and Moon, but apart from that the Chinese Zodiac is not related to astral constellations at all (in contrast to the Greek scheme). In addition to this, years are grouped into 'decades' except that they are twelve years rather than ten. There are Ten Heavenly Stems; these are the five basic elements doubled, for instance, natural fire and artificial fire. Also there are Twelve Earthly Branches, which are the animals as quoted above, which interweave making the whole thing very complicated, certainly for us in the west. The complete cycle with every permutation takes sixty years.

The choice of animals is explained in this way; the Buddha decided to give a feast and invited all the animals, but only twelve turned up. The rat arrived first and the pig last. There are varying tales about how and why the others arrived in the order they did. Another version of it is that the Jade Emperor invited the animals. It is difficult to be certain of the antiquity of the Chinese Zodiac, but it goes back into the mists of prehistory, possibly to the fifth century BC, at least. Intricate though this is, there appears to be no idea of a datum point in Chinese history. We now have a complete scheme of Chinese dynasties with dates, but this is because the reigns of the Emperors have been recorded, in much the same way as the Israelite kings' reigns were worked out. Even then, the dates have a certain degree of guesswork involved.

The year is divided into twelve months. New Year's day, which is the occasion of great festivities, comes on the second new moon after the winter solstice, somewhere in January or February, which means it varies from year to year. There are ten days in the week, and each day is divided into two-hour segments. This is where the Hua Hu Ching offers an intriguing diagram in which the Chinese months are correlated with the 'hours' of the day, each with its own hexagram. This is called the 'Energy Cycle'. The way this works, is, for example, the 'Pig Hour' is from 9 pm to 10.59 pm, when people are settling down for bed. But it also points to our November, a time when Nature is settling down for the winter. All twelve animals have this kind of interrelation between the time of day and the month.

The whole thing is extremely complicated and it is no surprise that on encountering western influence, the Gregorian calendar was introduced in 1912, and enforced in 1948 by the Communists. Even then, the old system is used unofficially by small groups within and outside of China.

Chinese influence within and without

Everyone has heard of the game **Mah-Jong(g)**.(8) It is an extraordinarily complicated game played with little tiles, which has become popular in the USA and Japan especially. There will be no attempt at delving into the intricacies of playing it; there are various well-written books on the subject. But for the purposes of mythology, it is interesting that elements of Chinese mythology, are worked into the rules of the game. That does not mean that vast amounts of Taoist metaphysics are assumed in the game, but the background influence is there, nevertheless.

We begin with the Dragon Kings, which are known as 'honour tiles', and which come in red, green or white. They are lucky tiles and sometimes honour tiles. Also there are references to Catching the Moon from the Bottom of the Sea (which recalls the silkworm goddess), and also the bottom of a river. These are where the Dragons are believed to reside. The Dragons are associated with the Four Winds. There are various permutations on the Dragons, such as the Ruby Jade which involves red and green Dragons.

On the subject of Jade, we do not have any direct reference to the Jade Emperor, but indirect references are numerous. There is the Imperial Jade, a hand composed of entirely green tiles. Also there are the Nine Gates of Heaven, and Heaven's Blessing; also the Four Large Blessings and the Four Smaller Blessings. All these are euphemistic references to the Jade Emperor. By contrast there is Earth's Blessing.

Also there is the Wriggly Snake, which reminds us of the goddess Nu Wa, who created the human race, and is depicted as a snake.

There is no mention of Confucius or of Lao Tzu, but the phrase The Three Great Scholars and the Three Lesser Scholars does bring them to mind. Education was given much emphasis by Confucius, and we recall that some of the Eight Immortals gave up a life of fame and prosperity to devote themselves to study with the great Sage, Lao Tzu. The Scholars are associated with the Dragons.

The Great Wall of China is the starting point of the game. Though this can hardly be mythical, since it is a historical fact, nevertheless, the Great Wall has acquired a fascination with people, which verges on the mythological. The whole of Mah-Jong is loaded with symbolisms which are rich in mythological associations. Much of this may be lost on players outside of China, but for the Chinese, it must hold much symbolic value.

Concluding thoughts on Chinese Mythology

This brief outline of Chinese mythology gives an impression of their rich and varied traditions. It is a completely different system of thought, and stands in contrast to Japanese mythology, which is characterised by violence and bloodshed, and also Greek mythology in which the gods are largely disinterested in the fate of humanity. It has been said that the Chinese are not a very 'religious' people, whatever that might mean. Nevertheless, their mythology and Taoist philosophy have a richness and independence of thinking. China has been through various violent convulsions over the last century or so, but still their cultural background is showing through. Even if their system of thought is very different from that of the West, we still see the same basic ideas and metaphors used in their mythology.

Footnotes for chapter 12

1. Hsi Wang Mu. There are variant spellings of this as with other names. The yin principle is the female element, opposite of yang.

2. The Terrcotta Army. Every statue is slightly different. Their crossbows show a very high

standard of bronze casting, amazing for what must have been the early Bronze Age in China.

3. Dragon; there are various traditions about dragons and their interaction with humans.

4. Pan Gu shows another variant on Pantheism.

5. See Genesis 2:7.

6. We have to remember that China is a vast territory with all kinds of different cultures and languages going on.

7. Various diagrams at the back of the Tao Teh Ching clarify these thoughts. Number symbolism will receive some attention in chapter 26.

8. Mah Jong; book on the subject. Play and win Mah Jong, David Pritchard.

13

The Cargo Cults of Melanesia

It is fascinating to compare the impact of western civilisation on this area, with that of the Huichol(1) people of western Mexico. It would be advisable to read both this and chapter 14 together for the sake of comparison. The area we are dealing with, called Melanesia, concerns New Guinea, New Britain, New Ireland, the Schouten Islands, Manus, the Ninigo Islands, the Solomon Islands, Fiji, New Hebrides, New Caledonia, the Loyalty Islands, the Gilbert Islands and parts of Australia and New Zealand. This is a vast and complex area, separated by large tracts of ocean. Not surprisingly, the peoples of these parts have different mythological ideas, even if they have various matters in common. What we need to accept is that these people had trading links and interchange of ideas to a far greater extent than has been conventionally thought. This is one of the main factors which form a contrast with the Huichol peoples; they were confined to a relatively small area, whereas the Melanesians were, and still are, much more spread out and diverse in their thinking.

This chapter is heavily reliant on Peter Worsley's seminal work, The Trumpet shall Sound. He also does not attempt to go into every detail of Melanesian mythology. It is such a diverse field of knowledge which would occupy an entire book itself. He concentrates on the Cargo Cults themselves, only making occasional reference to pre-existing mythology. The importance of studying this area is to see how traditional myths have been adapted with the coming of the Bible. Jehovah and Jesus Christ have been spliced in with traditional gods. The other aspect is that a political and social situation has given rise to a new, one might say, plastic mythology within our own times. This in itself must alert us to the fact that mythology is not just a feature of the ancient world. It is an ongoing factor; as one myth dies out, others come to the fore, as a replacement. This applies to us all, however 'modern' we regard ourselves as. Twenty-first century mankind is just as prone to myth-mongering as any other generation; it is all a matter of explaining our circumstances in elevated thought-levels which are on a higher level than the purely descriptive and scientific.

One of the chief differences has been the impression made by the white Europeans as they have colonised and brought 'government' to Melanesia. This has been the main impetus for the formation of the Cargo cults; they began to appear in the 19th century and are still with us to some extent now. Essentially, the natives had much resentment to the white invaders who took their land, usually the most productive parts, and reduced many of the menfolk to what must be termed as slavery. The white settlers were mostly interested in cash crops such as copra, and later, oil and gold, when they were discovered. This situation was further confused as the Europeans brought with them about a dozen versions of something called Christianity. Just about every Christian denomination managed to stake its claim in the area. Notably the Wesleyan Methodists managed to become the major influence in Fiji, but otherwise there were, and still are, competing groups, one might say 'shooting each other in the foot'. Even if the main thrust of Christianity was love, friendship, co-operation and peace, the natives could not understand why the whites would not share their consumer goods with them, or indeed, eat with them!

Another factor that baffled the natives was how or why manufactured goods of such mysterious quality could come with the white man. Their impression of the Europeans was that they never did any work, ordered people around and were generally useless. This had to mean that they could not possibly have made all those interesting goods that arrived in ships and aeroplanes. This was compounded by the fact that European economics were characterised by wildly varying prices. This meant that copra might fetch a handsome price one year but next year, the rewards were devastatingly low. Was this some kind of swindle!? It is no surprise that the natives regarded the whites with a certain degree of antagonism and mistrust. This would not be the total picture, since the Australians, with their 'matey' approach to people, were something of a contrast to the people coming directly from Europe. We must add to that the turbulence caused by the two World Wars. The natives had no idea of what was happening in Europe, and why the Germans had to leave the area. Even more complicated was the appearance of the Japanese in 1941. They were at first regarded as welcome heroes who would expel the whites; this impression was soon dispelled as the Japanese decided to treat the natives far worse than the Europeans had ever done.

It is hardly surprising therefore that the Melanesians were (and still are) keen to recover their lands and political freedoms. We see the emergence of all kinds of cults which are some kind of amalgam of traditional mythical beliefs and Christian ideas. It is not as if the cargo cults are just one unified entity; there are all kinds of variants and differences of opinion. One of the main elements is the millenarian aspect, which is almost certainly a theme inspired by the Book of Revelation. They think that the end of the world will result in their recovering their old status and happiness. Another aspect of the cults is the fertility theme; many of them are concerned with the success of the crops; this is no surprise since the white men stole most of the fertile land for the production of cash crops.

Another complication is the fact that many parts of Papua/New Guinea are not properly explored which means that there are isolated tribes that have hardly had any contact with the outside world. The same situation obtains in parts of the jungles of Brazil. Fortunately there is now more sensitivity from governments over making contact with these peoples. But it just goes to show that while we in Europe and America are in the forefront of a technological atomic age, there are still some peoples who are essentially in the Stone Age, and do not wish to move out of it. That means that they will be holding on to their traditional mythologies. There is a tendency to see the white man as dishonest, hypocritical, self-seeking and just plain crazy. Who can blame them?

It is not possible to describe every permutation of mythology in this area, since it is so diverse and interrelated. The main strands will be examined, together with the impact that Christianity has had. It would be fair to say that the area has been 'Christianised', but over optimistic to say that these countries are 'Christian'. To say that the cargo cults are Christian would be misleading. It would be less misleading to say that the collision of traditional shamanism and modern liberalistic Christianity has been a complicated matter and not always very happy. This, combined with all kinds of pidgin English, has resulted in religious expression which can be quite amusing but may not be as accurate as modern philosophical European ideas on the matter.

Traditional myths in Melanesia

It would be foolish to go into too much detail on this subject; it is highly diverse and in some respects self-contradictory. However, the main elements of it ought to be briefly described as a background to understanding the Cargo Cults. To evidence the complications in it, there is a god called Tangaroa. His name and its spelling varies from one island to another; also his role. So he might be the creator in one area and something else somewhere else. The same applies to Ngendei, who is pictured as a snake in some places, involved with fertility sometimes and in other places, with other attributes. It would be a mistake to equate him with the Devil. Even if there are evil spirits, there seems to be no Satan as such in the picture. In addition to this, there are any amount of gods and goddesses, heroes who graduated to become gods, and spirits inhabiting just about every feature of life. One might see this as akin to the Japanese concept of KAMI. Certainly, we can see it as the Melanesian version of shamanism.

With regard to creation, most myths have a creator god, and sometimes a creator goddess. Very unusual is the idea that creation just happened by itself; with this we see that modern atheism is not such a new idea after all. Most myths not surprisingly, assume that there was a primeval ocean; the sea had been there since eternity. Rarely, some picture the land as appearing before the sea. It is interesting that there are various mentions of the Flood, though not in such detail as Noah's or Utnapishtim's.(2) The sky is understood to have been resting on various trees at one time, and had to be lifted up. There are various explanations for how this came about, but normally it is a god who forces the earth and the sky apart; this has the effect of allowing the light to ripen the crops.

The sun and moon also receive various explanations, as does the alternation of day and night. The stars too are perceived as constellations with names, not unlike the Greek approach. Natural features such as thunder, lightning, ice and mist also receive some kind of 'just-so' treatment.

There is also the awareness of the three-tiered system, heaven, earth and the underworld. It would be fair to say that the underworld is not mentioned very often. At one's death, one is assumed to go up rather than down, to a better world of great enjoyment.

With regard to theodicy, this is not discussed directly, but there are situations in which the explanation for human pain and suffering are hinted at. There is the belief that humans were not destined to die; but because of some slip-up, they became mortal. Often it is the result of some failure to observe a caution, stupidity or even negligence. In one area, it was the failure of mankind to shed his skin, like the snake. Always there is the hint that life is eternal, and resurrection is a basic factor.

The origin of humanity is also highly varied, but often there is the original couple like Adam and Eve. Also there is the idea that man was created by a different god from woman. Humanity was made from such things as grass, stone, a tree, and noticeably, CLAY. A god breathed life into him; this could be by incantation, or blowing ginger on him, or by laughter or just by hitting him.

In so many features, such as race, characteristics of animals, hills and valleys; there is the 'just-so' element, as indeed we see in the first two chapters of Genesis.(3)

The Cargo Cults

It would be difficult to describe in detail every such cult, but some of the main outlines can first be cited. This will be followed by a close-up on several of them. In every case, we see a strange amalgam between traditional religious belief and the adoption of European ideas. We cannot avoid noticing that all the natives of this area have a strong impression of the world of the spirit. This is something that many in the materialistic First World will find unintelligible, but when one lives very close to the land and is heavily dependent on the success of the harvest and the attitude of White overlords, life will seem very different. The result is almost always some kind of spirit possession or ecstasy with many, what would seem to Europeans, as completely irrational behaviour. There is also a groundswell of suspicion and dislike of the Whites, not uniformly strong, but an element present all the same. In addition to this there is the element of expectation which can take the form of millenarianism, or messianism. That can mean the expulsion of the Whites and the recovery of traditional lands and social arrangements. But the chief thing is the expected appearance of ships or aeroplanes loaded with 'cargo'; this might be consumer goods, food and luxuries, but also the spirits of the ancestors coming back. In every case, we see a historical and geographical situation producing a longing for correction, and this is expressed in mythological terms. The myths become increasingly exaggerated and augmented. This means that we are looking at myth in the making in our own times, and thus it will help us to understand the myths of the past; not only that but the myths of the future.

The Tuka movement; Fiji (1870's)

This saw the emergence of one Ndugumoi, a 'prophet' with miraculous and occult powers. He had out of the body experiences. He was a hereditary priest. He gained the title Navosavakandua, which means 'he who speaks once', and he had the power of life and death. He announced the millennium, which would mean that the ancestors would soon return to Fiji, the Whites would be forced to serve the Blacks, and the world order would be reversed. The faithful would go to a Glorious Paradise but unbelievers would die and go to hellfire, or be turned into slaves and the whites would be driven into the sea. Ancient lands would be restored as some kind of paradise.

Now we see how the Fijian creation myth is blended with Biblical material. There were three brothers who survived the Flood. Ndengei the snake lived in the Navosavakandua Mountains (the equivalent of Olympus). Rokola, the carpenter married a princess and had the Twins who made war on Ndengei. They were defeated, but now they will return. The Europeans who are doing research into the coral reefs are really on the look out for ships containing the Twins. Navosavakandua also claimed to have seen flying chariots. He equated Rokola with Noah. Jehovah challenged Ndengei to make a man from clay, but he failed. Then Jehovah made a man and a woman from clay, and drove Ndengei away. This serpent was equated with Satan. We can see how elements from Genesis have been grafted into traditional Fijian mythology.

Navosavakandua renamed the days of the week after the people in the account of the Flood. He was anti-White, but even then the Twins had gone to the Whiteland. He equated Jehovah with Jesus. He would sell bottles of water, which were claimed to give immortality, for ten shillings a time. He was sexually promiscuous and heavily involved in drinking KAVA. (4) He decided to fix the day of the millennium. He went in for militaristic training, such as square-bashing and saluting.

When he came to die, no one believed it. The movement did not die out. Someone called Sailose Ratu revived it. He was plainly demented but was believed to be a prophet. He took bits from Freemasonry and the Roman Catholic Missal to embroider the basic idea of the Tuka movement.

Another variant on Tuka was the Luve-ni-wai, or the 'Water Babies', or 'Children of the Water', which ran alongside Tuka. This was non-millenarian and not so anti-White, at least at the start. However it began to show signs of violence and the authorities had to ban it. This scheme involved fairies, like fauns, as in Greek thought, and dwarfs living in the forest. To gain admission, one had to acquire one's own guardian spirit from them. Apart from that, the movement involved imitating various western features; there was a 'Home Secretary' and a ' Lord High Admiral'.

One might have thought that Tuka had faded out in the 20th century, but this was not to be. In 1945, one Kelevi decided to revive the Tuka ideas. He claimed to have the true Methodist church. But he was not strongly millenarian or anti-White. He thought that God was the snake, namely Ndengei. He and the Twins had been living in Germany, giving wisdom and MANA (5)to them, and they would soon return. Kelevi had visions, and did faith healing and did glossolalia;(6) this went hand in hand with his abuse of his coterie of females.

The Milne Bay Prophet; New Guinea (1892)

This concerns one Tokeriu, a young native who caught a spirit from a sacred tree. He had a visit to the other world, known as Hiyoyoa. He forecast that there would be a gigantic tidal wave to hit the coast; this meant that the villagers should up stakes and move inland, kill all their pigs and eat up all their food. All believers would be saved. All the white-man's goods were to be discarded, which meant, in effect, a return to the Stone Age. When his predictions turned out to be mistaken, he was not very popular.

Nevertheless, there was still the hope that a sail on the horizon would herald a ship with the spirits of the dead on board. Tokeriu would have a steamer and make a form of government. The movement was anti-White, and was an early symptom of native nationalism.

207

The Baigona Movement; NE Papua; 1912

Baigona actually means 'a snake'. It was one Maine who was killed by a snake, taken to Mount Victory, had his heart extracted, smoked and then reinstalled. He introduced new doctrines, which involved magico-medical curative techniques, as well as sorcery and rain-making. The movement turned political and nationalist; however it was not a case of millenarianism.

The Taro Cult, Buna Bay,(7) 1919 onwards

Taro is a plant giving a staple diet for many in New Guinea (as well as yams). The main movement was called Kava-keva (which means 'giddy') and began with one Buninia who claimed to be possessed by the spirit of Taro. Also there was one Kekesi whose idea went along parallel. Buninia had new ideas on gardening, control of the rain, and special magic to help the crops. Also he had a policy of getting the different tribes to make friends and sink their traditional rivalries. This unity of the natives also involved an anti-white policy. There was not much on the idea of the millennium, but the Messiah was expected. The movement was also characterised by head-jerking, spirit possession, dreams; some of this was probably genuine, but it could be self-induced for show. One of the leaders, Dasiga Giama, claimed to have had visions of Jesus and received a letter from him. There was an incantation, 'Jesu Kerisu Kaena-embo' which means 'Jesus Christ, the man for us.' It was quite normal for a leader to have a smart suit, trimmed hair and sport a walking-stick.

Dasiga also believed that the ancestors were coming back in a fleet of steamers and canoes. There were various sects of the Taro movement, the leaders of which were sometimes just plain deceivers.

The Vailala Madness; Papua, 1919

This went under various titles, such as 'Gulf Kava-kava' or 'Head-he-go-round'. The leader was one Evara, who had automaniac seizures and revelations. It was normal to see whole villages carried away with jerky movements and possession. Also there was glossolalia which they claimed was Djaman (ie, German!). This could sometimes be self-induced. This outbreak, like various others, could be related to the discovery of oil, and later, gold, in the area, and the recruitment and exploitation of the natives. Papers were claimed to have floated down from Heaven, giving them encouragement.

Evara claimed that a steamer and an aeroplane, would come, loaded up with dead ancestors, plenty of food and tobacco, and more menacingly, a load of rifles. This indicated that the Whites could be driven out. Strangely, a white missionary was believed to be someone's ancestor returned, as a white man! Also, all the natives in the after-life would turn into white men!

Someone had a vision of Heaven, 'Ihova kekere' which meant, 'Jehovah's land'. There was no forest, but plenty of food and people wearing long garments. With Jehovah were Noa, Atamu (Adam), Eva, Mari, Kori, Areru, and Maupa. He claimed visions of God and Christ. There was a faded picture of King George 5th in a martial uniform; he was claimed to be 'Ihova, the younger brother of Jesus' (!).(8)

There was much emphasis on the Return and the Millennium. There were mortuary feasts with tables and benches and relatives of the dead dressed in their best suits. There were beer bottles with croton flowers in them, decorating the tables. Peeled coconuts were supplied 'to appease the dead', as well as two bowls of rice and betel nuts. A loin cloth was used as a table cloth. The people sat waiting for the Cargo to arrive, in spite of many disappointments. They had a flagpole which was supposed to contact the spirits. These poles had names and personalities. A pumpkin might be hoisted to the top, and there would be aerials and wires so that messages could be sent to the steamer that was not quite in sight. The mention of 'Sail-ho!' would cause great excitement.

It is quite obvious that in spite of their contempt for the White man, the natives were convinced that imitating the European culture and technological gadgetry would induce the Cargo to come and solve all their problems. Traditional rituals were thrown aside and ethical standards of a Christian origin were heavily enforced. So, stealing and adultery were frowned upon, and the observance of Sunday strongly advised. Saluting and sitting out on the veranda (like the plantation owners) became the normal pattern.

By 1931, the movement had more or less faded out. Even so, the legend developed that these expectations HAD arrived, and that messages from the flagpoles HAD been received, as well as papers floating down from the sky. That Steamer HAD arrived. One of the prophets HAD risen from the dead after three days! With this we see how strong expectations and wishful thinking easily erase the truth and augment historical facts into augmented myths. This is an important clue as to how myths build up; it is an aspect of human nature.

The Mambu movement, Mandang (9) District, NE New Guinea, (1937)

Mambu was originally a Roman Catholic but reverted to a syncretistic amalgam of Christianity and paganism. He styled himself as a prophet. He claimed that the ancestors lived in a volcano on Manum Island, making goods for the natives. The Whites were stealing them as they came over to Rabaul. Now, the goods would come direct to the natives and there would be food for everyone. He was anti-tax and anti-church. He started rites for the faithful at the graves and also in new temples. The grass skirts and loin-clothes were to be removed and peoples genitals were to be washed or sprinkled. The discarded skirts and clothes were piled into graves, and Mambu would hold a crucifix over them and make the sign of the cross. Ladies now had to wear long dresses and the gentlemen, European-style loin-clothes. Mambu, who was celibate, styled himself as a king, and collected tax money. He baptised recruits and handed out rice, which was claimed to arrive by air, and fish, which was supposed to come by river, even if it was sea fish! He was arrested and gaoled, but this did not stop the movement.

The Assisi cult, Papua, late 1930's

This idea involved Jesus Christ coming in a ship with Cargo, which was to be stored in a cave so that the Whites could not steal it. There would be no more work, at least for the natives, for their skin would be turned white and the white man's skin would be turned brown. This meant that the rulers would have to be servants. There was much destruction of ancestor cults; glossolalia and shaking became common. They had an imitation of the Holy Communion, using wine made from coconut milk.

The Buka movement, The Solomons, 1932

Buka is a small island in the northern Solomons. There was one Pako, who was the main leader, but also Muling, claiming to be kin of the sun and moon. He prophesied a tidal wave, which caused a massive panic. Moreover, a ship would come with Cargo, such as tools, food, tobacco, cars and firearms.

Pako, the main leader, had travelled and seen the rest of the world. He had a European-style house. He renounced Christianity and paganism, but said that the ancestors had to be revered. Red crosses were erected at burial grounds, and pigs were sacrificed. He wanted to abolish taboos and magic, as well as money. This was an attempt at regaining a sort of primitive communism. Special storehouses and docks were constructed to receive the Cargo. He expected vehicles and aeroplanes to come from Australia, via Germany. He designed his own flag in red and black, with a letter 'P' and a white cross on it.

When Pako died, people did not believe it. There was a notion that he had risen from the dead, and people visited his house to hear his voice coming from somewhere. It was thought that someone, perhaps his brother, was speaking, to simulate his spirit.

The expectation that the Germans would return was somehow substituted when the Japanese arrived. They were welcomed with great jubilation, at first. The Coming was expected and a King. But this soon turned sour when the Japanese turned out to be a lot nastier than the Europeans had been.

But the mania continued. As seen before, the failure of a prophesy does not mean that the cult will collapse. The blame will be laid on someone else, rather than the prophet.

The Mansren Myth, Dutch New Guinea (traditional)

This account is more like a traditional myth and there is less of the characteristics of the Cargo mentality, at least in the early stages.

There was a very old man called Manamakeri with wrinkled skin. The name means 'he who itches', and Mansren is a contraction of his full name. He liked the wine made from a manes tree, so much, that he climbed up there every day to collect the juice in pots. He came to realise that someone was stealing his juice, so he stayed up all night to catch the thief. No luck; so the next night he climbed up the tree and waited. In the gloaming, he caught the thief; it turned out to be Kumeseri, the Morning Star.

The Star offered him compensation, to let him go. Manamakeri held on to the Star and refused the first offer, which was a magic wand to provide him with masses of fish. The second offer was of a tree with leaves which would make him rich and famous. This also was refused.

The third offer was really bizarre; it was a fruit from the tree, which when thrown at a maiden, would hit her between the breasts and make her pregnant. Manamakeri accepted this but still held on to the star. So the Star gave him a piece of wood, with which, if he drew a picture of anything, it would become real, if he would stamp his foot.

Manamakeri saw a beautiful maiden bathing in the sea. Her name was Insoraki. He threw the fruit at her, but missed. Even so, the fruit swerved up against her breasts, and as she fended it off, it came back to hit her again repeatedly. With this, she became pregnant. Imagine the consternation of her parents and the villagers, when she claimed she had no idea of how she became pregnant. When the baby arrived, they arranged a parade of men so that the boy would identify his father, or so it was assumed. First the young men paraded past; then the middle-aged men; then the old men. There was no result. So in desperation they made Manamakeri file past, whereupon the boy pointed out his father.

The villagers were so disgusted that they decided to abandon Manamakeri to his little island, in company with his 'wife' and child. They went off to Biak, leaving him on his little island of Miok Wundi. Soon they were short of food and the boy kept demanding something to eat. Manamakeri took his piece of wood, drew a picture of food inside his hut and there was plenty to eat.

The old man felt embarrassed at being so wrinkled, so he built a fire, stepped into it and all his skin fell off to make brass gongs and armlets. He stepped out of the fire and looked at his reflection in the water in a large shell. He was far too light in colour for his liking, so he toasted himself a little more. Then he donned the armshells and stuck feathers in his hair and went home. Insoraki was astonished to see a handsome youth, and ran off, claiming to be a married woman. She took some convincing that it was really her own husband; the boy recognised his father and that clinched the matter. The boy was termed the 'konor'.

Feeling rather lonely, Mansren decided to draw a prau (a canoe) in the sand, stamped his foot and it became real, with many rowers. They set off for the open sea and the island of Biak. He created many small islands so that his son could play on them. Now we see the reason for this myth; the peoples on these islands claim that it was Mansren that started them off, gave them their laws and instituted the men's houses. Also he provided them with food, and cured the sick. The prau is claimed to have moved under the water, like a submarine. The details of his voyages vary according to which island is in question; this indicates that each island had its own claim on his patronage. The boy is claimed to have died on Numfoor Island. Mansren's final episode was when a mother brought a child to him to be cured, and he said that she should not worry if the child died. The mother was furious with him; he was angry at her lack of faith. At that point he set off in a canoe and was never seen again.

The people look back on this wonderful Creation period. Artefacts relating to Mansren are cherished; his cooking pot, his shell-mirror, his gun (!) and not least the manes from which he derived his wine. Even the site of his house is preserved. It is interesting to see how various mythical additions have attached themselves to the basic story. There are dramatic enactments. As one would expect, Mansren is expected to come back, which would mean the restart of the Golden Age. Mansren would plant a coconut which would reach right up to heaven: notice the 'world tree' motif. The old would become young, the sick would recover, the dead would return. There would be plenty of women, food, weapons and ornaments. There would be no more work, and no more 'Company', which meant forced labour and taxation.

As expected, there were prophets who got the people excited about the Golden Age. There was one Korano Baibo. It would seem that a comet came over and he claimed it was the sign of his wondrous return. He encouraged fertility; he was keen on women and presents. The authorities were not too worried about him, since he did not preach revolution or millenarianism.

In that period there were many prophets or men claiming to be the Konor or Mansren himself. Some of them had the most bizarre ideas. Almost every year saw some kind of prophet or konor appearing with elaborate promises, or claiming to be Mansren himself. Two examples are enough. In 1934, a konor predicted the coming of a four-funnelled steamer with Mansren on board, and the coming of a factory. He made a considerable profit as large crowds from miles around came to see him. Another prophet, in 1936, claimed to have seen Mansren with the Queen of Heaven (was that Saint Mary?). He demanded that the teacher, missionary and district officer should all be killed. Also he predicted that Mansren would start a war between the Dutch and the Japanese!

Although the coming of the Japanese was initially welcomed, this soon turned sour. The natives soon were in conflict with them. They were now hoping the Americans would come. When they did arrive, the Mansren mania only received encouragement and was seen to be working, for the Americans not only brought in massive armaments, but also food which was handed out to the islanders. Cinemas, hospitals and factories were established too. After the Americans had gone, the natives tried to continue these things in imitation of the troops. They dressed up as 'doctors' and 'nurses'.

With the Mansren cult, we see how an ancient myth develops into a passive, non-millenarian movement, but then as circumstances alter, it becomes an armed force to try to drive out foreigners from Papua.

New Hebrides; Island of Espiritu Santo (1923). The Naked Cult

This is another instance of how an ancient myth became the basis of a modern Cargo cult. The myth was that there had been a native murderer; when in the end he was killed himself, all his victims came back to life. In 1923, a murder occurred, of a British planter called Clapcott, who had asked for it in fact; he had been interfering with the native women. There was a native called Runovoro, who justified this murder on the grounds that if all the Europeans were killed, the dead would arise and all the ancestors would come back from where the Whites had sent them.

He maintained that the ancestors would arrive after a Deluge, in a great white ship loaded with Cargo. This would only be handed out to his paid-up followers. They built a large storehouse for the cargo, as well as a road several miles long and a dock to help the Americans. Runovoro was believed to be able to raise the dead, not just humans but animals. He thought he too was invulnerable and did not fear execution. Many were arrested and gaoled. By 1948 there were great expectations as the Americans came with plenty of consumer goods. There was much faith in the future; there was destruction of property. Death itself was to be abolished. Separate houses were built for men and women. Many pigs were killed and there was to be equality of wealth. So equal was everyone to be that sex could be carried out in public and not necessarily with one's normal wife or husband.

With the authorities clamping down, the movement went underground, but still there were poles with creepers for 'wireless' messages, shaking fits and prophesies.

Tanna Island; John Frum (1940's)

Something similar occurred in the early 1940's, instigated by one John Frum. He was anti-missionaries, having begun as a Presbyterian. He claimed to be Karaperamun, the god of the highest mountain on the island. Even though he was arrested his reappearance seemed to be a regular factor right through to the 1950's.

He claimed that Tanna would be flattened in a cataclysm, joined to other islands and made into a plain. There would be a reign of bliss; the natives would go back to being young; there would be no more sickness, or gardening or pigs or trees. For this to happen, the Whites would have to go. Then there would be a return to old customs, one of which would be polygamy.

To induce this to happen, there was a vast spending spree to get rid of European money. They dug out their savings, which included gold sovereigns! Food was consumed at massive feasts. Friday became a holy day. Frum issued his own money stamped with a coconut. Frum styled himself as the King of America! His sons, Isaac, Jacob and Lastuan were to be kings of somewhere else.

Great excitement boiled up when some Australian Catalinas appeared; this was to be the Cargo! This was intensified as the Americas arrived with their ships and aeroplanes, generously handing out supplies to the natives. Would you believe it, some of them were Black!! This must mean that the prisoners would be released, and everyone would be paid wages. Fortunately for Tanna, the Japanese never managed to get that far.

Strangely, more John Frums kept appearing right into the 1950's, but the cult gradually died down and calm returned to Tanna.

More recent times

Up to now, we have only really dealt with Cargo cults where the native populations have been in contact with Europeans, mainly on the coastal areas of New Guinea and the small islands. After the War, with exploration going on into the interior of New Guinea, more primitive peoples, who were essentially living in the Stone Age, came into contact with the White man. It is interesting that they too began to develop cargo cults of their own, often exhibiting features in common with the coastal peoples. This is doubtless a process which is still happening to this day, as isolated tribes that do not wish to become involved with the White man, cannot avoid it.

It would be fair to say that much of the impetus has gone out of the Cargo cults. The native peoples have managed to acquire some kind of political ability of their own, and many areas have gained some kind of independence. The old situation in which the European invaders had just came in order to exploit the resources of the area and reduce the locals to slavery, is now very much reduced. The colonial days are over, for the most part. The natives are now much more likely to be running their own plantations and keeping the profits from the cash crop (such as copra and rubber).

It is interesting that the same kind of situation has arisen in other parts of the world, where shamanism and Christianity have collided. Parts of Africa, Siberia and South America could come under this heading.

We notice that the natives very quickly relate to those parts of the Bible which they understand most easily. One aspect is the element of prophesy; such people as Elijah and Elisha strike a chord with them. Also Noah is important to them, because they too have an impression of a Flood in remote pre-history. Revelation too, and the apocalyptic material in the Bible relate to them very clearly. When one is under pressure from foreign overlords and there is no other way of objecting, then a magnificent view of the future becomes important. Thus we can see how trumpets sounding, as at the Exodus and in Revelation, and the dead being raised, or ancestors returning, become a noted feature of the Cargo cults. It is no accident that Peter Worsley entitled his book, The Trumpet Shall Sound.

The most striking feature, however, is the way in which the natives take Jesus Christ into their systems of thought. They clearly relate to him, perhaps because he was rejected, like themselves, but also because he accepted all people. They even go so far as to make out that the Europeans have misrepresented Jesus; there is an element of truth in this, for which we should all feel guilty. But it just goes to show that each and every nation or race takes Jesus to itself and sees him as one of them. We do it; so do they. It goes further than that; the Bible, with all its varied material, becomes relevant to someone somewhere at some time or other.

Footnotes for chapter 13

1. The Huichol peoples, seen in chapter 14, are another 'Stone Age' society and their encounter with Christianity has been similar but different in various respects.

2. Chapter 2 contains a thorough treatment of the Flood in the Bible and in Mesopotamian Epics.

3. An example of that would by why the snake has to crawl on its belly.

4. Kava, an intoxicating drink.

5. Mana; in Polynesia, supernatural power, effectiveness, prestige.

6. Glossolalia; speaking with tongues, different languages and strange sounds.

7. Buna Bay; an important port on the SE coast of Papua New Guinea.

8. It is also claimed that some of the Cargo Cult peoples believe that the Duke of Edinburgh is Jehovah.

9. Most of these myths involve some kind of tree.

14

The Huichol peoples of Mexico

The Huichol people, who call themselves Wixarika, live in the western part of Mexico, facing the Pacific Ocean, and in a terrain which is characterised by deep ravines, deserts and small patches of fertile land. I have chosen this culture for a distinct purpose; it is one of the few areas in the New World where Christianity and the mythology that goes with it, has never really made much progress. The Huichols have held on to their traditional myths and ritual procedures with a tenacity seldom found elsewhere. This means that although certain elements from Christianity have worked their way into their patterns of religion, and some elements of Spanish culture as well, it is still possible to gain a clear picture of what their original, pre-Columbian mythology amounted to. Greek mythology, which has managed to influence so many other systems of thought throughout the world, has, it would seem, had no influence at all here. We can now see that it is a completely different system of thought; even so, many of the same basic symbols and mind-set show through. This may indicate that mythological symbolism must be something instinctive in human nature. This in turn must indicate that it is foolish to attempt to avoid or cancel off this element in human nature. It is part of our make-up, even if the details of it are worked out somewhat differently in different parts of the world. The reason for this difference is almost certainly geographical and climatic, and heavily linked to the process of producing the bare essentials of life.(1)

This chapter is heavily dependent on the classic work on Huichol mythology by Robert Zingg, who, in 1934, went to live with the Huichols and produced this seminal work. To understand this way of life, we have to realise that shamanism is a dominating element in their culture. The

218

mara'akame, (the shamans) are inextricably linked to the production of rain which is vital for the success of the harvest. For each season of the year there are specific ceremonies, which are unique. These ceremonies are designed to maintain the balance between the people and the forces of nature. We can understand their determination to hold on to their traditional patterns in the face of modernising influences from the Old World and indeed the New World. Another important element is the drink called **peyote**, which induces some kind of hallucinatory vision. It is produced by pounding up a certain cactus which grows in desert conditions. It has 28 alkaloids, one of which is mescaline. Children are introduced to it at an early age and it is an essential part of the community's communication with the gods. This reminds us of the soma which is used in Hindu worship, as described in the Rig Veda. It is highly unlikely that Hindu thought influenced the Huichols, or vice versa, since they are so widely separated geographically, but the use of intoxicating materials is, it would seem, an element in mythological experience.

The **deer**, which are common in that area, are another essential element in Huichol thinking, and are regarded as sacred. There is some sort of equation between the deer and peyote, though this is not explained. The deer horn, when ground up, is used to make a kind of magic liquor which induces a drunken stupor. Deer hairs, when dusted off one's clothing, onto the fields, will ensure a good harvest.

As a system of thought, one might conclude that it is not particularly systematic. There are all kinds of inconsistencies. One is left with the impression that many of the mythical stories are the product of some kind of dream or hallucination; many strange and illogical things happen in them. Dreaming and singing, which are a noted feature of their shamanism, seem to dominate all their mythology. In common with Greek mythology, there is the interchange between animals, plants, humans and gods, a feature which must indicate the unity of life in its various forms. The reader must forgive this chapter being largely descriptive, since very few people in this part of the world have ever heard of the Huichols, still less know any details of their beliefs.

Kauymali

In contrast to most other mythologies, we do not start with the gods. The central thread in the whole scheme (if there is a scheme) is a little boy called

Kauymali. He is the greatest shaman in the world and is very sacred. He is sometimes called the Wolf-man or the Elder Wolf. He has many dreams in which he receives instructions from the gods. He sings, sometimes all night, and this is his method for communing with the gods. He wears a shaman's plume, feathers taken from a parrot, and also the rattles taken from a rattlesnake are fastened to the end of his feathers.

Kauymali has an elder brother called Palikati, who is also good at divination. As with Kauymali, he is termed 'half-bad'; this must suggest that he is not perfect, as one would expect a god to be. It might be a way of saying that he is human, in other words, has his faults but is not completely wicked. Both of them are termed the son of the Sun, who is termed 'the Father' and his name was given by the turkey, 'Tau, Tau, Tau'. This reminds us of God in the Exodus, who tells Moses his name, YHWH. (2)

Kauymali is portrayed as human, but he seems to be integral to so many myths spanning many eras. He can change himself into a wolf and change back to a man, just as Palikati can change into a deer and back again. Kauymali appears to be the universal handy man who can solve any problem. There are many mythical tales about his intervention which saves the situation.

One such tale is about Jimson-weed man who is also a shaman, but his singing deceives people. Jimson weed is a plant of the potato family, found in Mexico, but is poisonous. Jimson weed brings sickness, so Kauymali has the task of burning him. As he burns, a stone comes out of Jimson weed's heart, and he asks Kauymali to bless him so that he will not actually die. He too is termed 'half-bad', but from his body, all the nasty animals are produced. Jimson weed is termed 'delicate', as indeed many other people and things in the myths are so termed, especially Kauymali.

What does 'delicate' mean in this context? It has a wide range of meaning and is clearly a pejorative word. Holy, sacred, powerful, dangerous, untamed, loaded with numinous power; all of these and more are implied. It could be roughly analogous to the Hebrew word for 'holy'. It applies to people such as the shamans, the Sun, water, and pilgrims who have to refrain from sex and salt for a period of time. It is also associated with young people; this is because children are especially cherished and held in honour in Huichol society. Many of the shamans are children which explains why they are introduced to peyote at an early age so that they can hallucinate. We see the situation where a boy and girl are 'intoxicated'. Kauymali, who never seems to age like Peter Pan, is an ongoing element in Huichol lore. In one sense he is a superhuman, even if he is not a god; his elder brother gets a 'god-house' and the moon goddess, Metsele, offers to marry him. But Kauymali seems not to be so favoured.

Another intriguing story comes from the earliest times, when there was a drought and everyone was dying of thirst. Kauymali was asked to find the reason. He sang all night and found out that the squirrel and the turtle had been playing at climbing a rock, and the turtle had fallen down and broken his shell. The wolves had pounced on him and all that was left was bits of shell. His mother, Nakawe, also known as Grandmother Growth, the rain goddess, who was the creator of the world and mistress of the stars, was angry at the turtle's death. The order was to piece together the turtle shell; at which, the turtle came back to life. Kauymali was commanded to dig a hole under the root of the sausa tree. (3) After several attempts, water began to stream out and filled up all the rivers, so that the drought was ended. Again we see the closeness in relationship between divinity and the created world, including the animals. Also there is the element of resurrection which is seen several times in Huichol mythology and is a perpetual theme in other world mythologies. People, animals and plants die but come back to life. That is a major fascination in human nature.

Another intriguing saga called the Corn Myth would be taken by us as humorous, but the Huichols might not have seen it in such a light. There is a boy and a widow who want to get some corn and in the course of begging the goddess for some corn, the boy gains a girl to become his wife. Eventually the girl gets pregnant but she has difficulties in giving birth. Kauymali comes to the rescue as a midwife and delivers the baby safely. He baptises the girl and the baby. But the child is ill. They are advised to go to the Lizard Atakwe but after several attempts at healing the child is still ill. It is Kauymali who goes through all the stages to effect a cure. It is interesting that the issue of brother and sister marrying surfaces; in other words, incest. It requires the permission of the goddess Nakawe to sanction it, but it leaves the way open for many other young couples to do the same. This is an interesting question which the Old Testament does not address; the sons of Adam and Eve presumably had to marry their sisters. This has been an ongoing question in the Judaeo-Christian tradition. The Huichols appear to have managed to resolve the question.

Many children appeared from this union and there was a great increase in population. Kauymali was the one who ordered them to spread out to different parts of the world. Even then, the first child who was sick produced descendants that should not have any children. So the Sun god decided that teeth were to be planted in the women's vaginas, so that when the men had intercourse with them, their penises were chopped off. This prevented them producing any children. This misfortune happened to Kauymali when he slept with a woman who had tempted him.

At this point, Kauymali began to feel that a new race ought to be started and the gods were in agreement. This is where the Huichol version of the Flood comes in, with much the same intention as with Noah, that the human race had gone crazy. First, Kauymali had to resolve the problem of the toothed vaginas. He obtain a deer horn from his brother Palikata, and used that to penetrate the women in order to break the teeth in their vaginas. Then Kauymali's penis grew again, longer and longer so that he could penetrate the women over and over again without coming too close to them. Then he found the Rock-woman and proceeded to penetrate her; suddenly she changed into a rock and he was stuck, hanging upside down. How embarrassing! It was the buzzard who came to release him; this had to be done by cutting off his penis. They burnt a squash and this healed his penis.

Now the story of the Flood is described in detail. Kauymali is living by the sea with a bitch dog, and is miraculously fed. An old woman, who is Nakawe in disguise, comes saying that she wishes to destroy the world and make a fresh start. She goes to collect all the animals while Kauymali makes a canoe out of a tree. While the animals are to be saved, his family has to be left out. A massive wind comes in off the sea, and the people turn into animals and eat each other. The sea floods in and lifts the canoe up for five days, and then it takes five hours to sink down, landing on a mountain near St. Caterina. This is dubbed the centre of the world, and a new race springs from Kauymali. The bitch god turns into a woman and he gets her pregnant. Kauymali is renamed Kauimali Tsaolikame; this reminds us of how Abraham and Jacob had their names altered.

Another intriguing saga concerns 'Duck-boy' whose name was TumuSauwi. He is styled as the first of the Huichols. He is described as an innocent boy, with the implication that he might have been a shaman, who dived into the sea and came out as a duck. He cannot catch a deer, so Kauymali comes to help him and advises on what offerings he should make.

Kauymali keeps appearing in the saga. When Duck-boy's wife is in trouble with her labour, Kauymali comes to the rescue. When some men take advantage of Duck-boy's wife, it is Kauymali who divines that she has been unfaithful, and induces her to confess to the gods. He cuts grass and rubs her all over to cleanse her; then it is burnt. That ritual occurs often in the myths. Mrs. Duck-boy leaves him and now Kauymali wants her, trying to bribe her with feathers,(4) but this does not work. In the end he shoots her in the heel with a magic thorn and she becomes a mosquito, which he catches in a hollow reed. She appeals for release and he lets her out. She flies away and he chases her. She climbs up into the sky to the eagle goddess. Again he shoots her and takes her away. She changes into a rock crystal. With this, Kauymali establishes funeral customs which prevent the soul coming back to annoy the family which is left behind. Souls go to the Pacific Ocean. When Duck-boy takes another wife and she has a 25 day pregnancy, Kauymali comes to help. He establishes a ceremony with a rubber ball (this might have been derived from the Aztecs). After another pregnancy, Kauymali performs a baptism. When the children are sick, they send for Kauymali. He orders drums to be beaten and singing. He finds a hollow tree and makes a drum, and sings the myths; so the children are saved. These become the Huichol people.

It makes fascinating reading and one can see the symbolism in it. Much of this would have been obvious to the Huichols, but for us it is less than obvious. Just as we have difficulties in appreciating the symbolisms in Revelation, so too with Huichol mythology.

It is also fascinating how Kauymali becomes integrated with the coming of Catholicism with the Spaniards. This does not mean that the Huichols embraced Christianity in its orthodox form; far from it; they adapted it to work with their mythology and symbolisms. We shall explore the Christian myth cycle in more detail later, but here, we just need to see how Kauymali, the everlasting ultra-shaman, works in with Christianity.

When a picture of a Catholic saint appeared, Kauymali painted a copy of it. That in itself is suggestive of Huichol culture imitating Christianity. In a scene where Christ hid in a church tower to avoid the Jews, the bell fell down and broke in pieces. It is Kauymali who salvages the pieces and turns them into silver. This he presents to the government (presumably in Mexico city). Jesus Christ is pictured as working with Kauymali. As Jesus is changed into an eagle, the Sun tells Kauymali to notice where he comes to land; wherever he lands, Kauymali finds golden statues of the saints. The symbolism in that is just a little more straightforward; Jesus becoming an eagle suggests that he becomes the god of the skies (heaven), and wherever he exerts his influence, there are the Christian saints. Incidentally, this is the only reference to gold in the myths; silver is rather more common, but is thought to relate to the Spaniards opening up silver mines in the area.

When Nakawe, the original creator of the world, had the urge to have another Flood, it was the Sun, Jesus and Kauymali who together manage to calm her down. Jesus even shows Kauymali how to brand cattle so that they cannot be stolen so easily (by the Mexicans!)

Gods, devils and other spiritual entities

In contrast to other mythologies, we do not start with one primal spirit which could be analogous to YHWH. It is rather more complex and vague than that. But there is certainly a strong awareness of the world of the spirit, and we are left wondering where the Huichols drew the line between this world and the next; perhaps they never did, unlike us.

We begin with the Great Grandfather Deer-tail, **Tatotsi,** who is one of the great gods, and this explains why the deer is regarded as sacred and it is important to kill a deer to make any progress with the harvest or other matters in life. Then there is Grandfather Fire, **Tatevali,** who came as a spark out of a hole in a rock. This was before there was any fire or sun, but the moon and darkness were there and people were tired of eating raw food. The Huichols regard themselves as the family of Grandfather Fire. With a slight contradiction, the Huichols also see themselves as children of the sun. **Topina** is stated to be the father of the Sun. His name is TAU, and he produced people in his own image. Also the animals belong to the Sun, especially the rattlesnake. The Sun was understood to be 'delicate'; he came too close to the earth and had to be 'tamed'. The Sun came to replace the moonlight; this was as a result of the deer hunt. Also, the Sun would not arise in the morning unless Kauymali had made vessels for him. The relationship between these gods is never clarified, even if the term 'father' is used.

Other great gods are as follows: **TsipuSawe, Tsakaimuka, MaSakwaSi (deer tail), Takalao Iwamaleame, and Suluwiakame** (mother of the deer). These are the gods who told the moon to rise up at night on his monthly cycle; he (or she) was originally one of the sea goddesses. There is **Kaciwali**, the water and corn goddess, who appears as a parrot, and is the mother of fishes and snakes, and also appears as an eagle.

The actual task of Creation is the work of **Nakawe.** She managed it in five days,(5) founding the earth, and is mistress of the stars. She is the rain goddess. Her daughter is **Keamukame**; her mother baptised her, and she climbed up into the sky and caused the rain to fall. Nakawe continues to appear in the Christian myth cycle, and there is some notion that she became dubbed as Maria Santigissima (most holy Mary). As a very significant touch, Nakawe is claimed to have arranged the world, but Christ came and improved on it. The symbolism in that is lovely. There is also **Ereno,** the goddess of love, who later became equated with the Virgin Mary.

The relationship between all these gods is not clarified, as it is in Greek mythology. They appear to co-exist but also seem to agree with one another. There are assumed to be lots of gods out in the Pacific Ocean.

We now turn to the Devils. While the gods are generally speaking well-intentioned towards mankind, there are evil influences at work. It would be misleading to say that there was one such spiritual influence which could be equated with Satan, but there is an assortment of nasty spirits interfering with this world.

There is someone called **Hortiman** who is a wind, or air devil. He is a deceiver. There is an amusing saga about how Kauymali was 'sold a pup' three times over by Hortiman. Also Kauymali was doomed to have only one foot and one eye, but he got his revenge in the end. There is also **Tekuamana,** another sort of devil or bad spirit, but information on him is somewhat sparse.

More noticeable are what appear to be the human bad influences. There is a wizard called **Hiwas**, and the gods have to catch the evil-doers and burn them. We have already related the saga of Jimson-weed man. There are also the snake people, **Haiku** who are born in the sea, and come out on land to beguile innocent Huichol girls. The result of one union was a 'snake-man' called Kutomai; although he seemed human, he had shining eyes and a forked tongue, and was a sorcerer. There is also **Tutakame** who is a bad ghoul. None of these entities seem to relate to one another.

This brings us to consider the cosmology of the Huichols. One might have noticed that the figure five is of great importance in Huichol thinking, just as seven is in Biblical and Christian thinking. The reason for this is the Huichol conception of the world. There are five regions; here, the centre of the world near the mountain of Santa Caterina, then north, south, east and west. Five appears repeatedly as a single digit or in many compounds such as fifteen, fifty, 500 and so on. Also there is a sixth region, the upper world, or the sky world. The eagle is the god of the sky world, but one can also hitch a ride on a buzzard to get there. Also there is an underworld and people living at the bottom of the sea. A ladder can be used to go down below, but there is no mention of a ladder going up. A message can be sent to the gods using an arrow. Not that the arrow has any writing on it; written messages only appear in the Christian era. The arrows themselves are capable of 'talking' to the gods. When one is ill, one sends an arrow up above. It is very unlucky to drop an arrow on the ground. A Huichol 'god-house' would normally have lots of arrows made of Brazil wood.

However, the main method of contacting the gods and finding out their intentions, is through the shaman. Kauymali is the archetypal boy shaman but there are many others. They will sing and go into a trance or a dream, and then issue an oracle with instructions on what sacrifice is to be made. One might be instructed to fast for so long, desist from sexual intercourse, or keep off salt for a time.

The division between this world and the next is not particularly clear. Often we have the phrase 'on this side' or 'on that side', which appears to be euphemistic way of talking about life and death.

Neither is there a clear distinction between gods, humans, animals and even stone. People change from one to the other and back again without any clear logic to it, or at least, logic in our sense. It may have seemed logical to someone of the Huichol mentality, but that is something that modern western minds will find difficult to analyse, if indeed it can be analysed. There are 'ant-people' living in the sea, and bee-people, with a queen bee, created by the gods of the sea. It is a strange spiritual world in which one can be turned into stone and yet still be 'alive' in some sense. It reminds us of Lot's wife being turned into a pillar of salt. But we can approach it from the point of view of symbolism. The main message to be appreciated, is the unity of creation; something that was obvious in Greek mythology and can hardly have been communicated to western Mexico before 1492. Thus must indicate that it is something instinctive in human nature, to see the created world as the product of one creative mind, with everything interrelated. In a strange way, even the theory of Evolution is saying the same thing; that everything natural is somehow related. The main difference is that evolution tries to omit the spiritual element, and the reality of the 'other world'.

The Coming of Christianity

It is interesting to see how the Huichol mythology is adapted to cope with the coming of Roman Catholicism in the wake of the Spanish invasion. It would be fair to say that the Huichols simply took Catholicism and worked it into their pre-existent system of thought. One important aspect of it is the appearance of metal. It looks very much as though the Huichols were in effect in the Stone Age before the Conquistadors appeared. There is never any mention of iron or steel, and silver and gold begin to be mentioned. This is because the Spaniards began to open up the silver mines in the area and introduced silver coinage (pesos); before that the Huichols had no idea of money as we know it. Many of the Huichols were recruited to work in the mines. Because of this, the coming of Jesus Christ was associated with metal, money and also cattle. It is not entirely clear about the use of candles; it is possible that the Huichols knew about beeswax before the Spanish invasion. At least, candles of some sort were much sought after in the pre-Columbian system. But it is fascinating to see how the Huichols viewed the whole process of an entirely different culture interrelating with their own.

We begin, not with Jesus, but with the Saints. The sea water boiled and produced green foam. This is where the Virgin of Santa Guadalupe,(who is equated with the goddess Ereno), and Santo Jose enter the picture; Kauymali ordered them to get engaged and then copulate. The result was Santo Christo (Holy Christ, ie. Jesus). We notice that there is no attempt at understanding the virgin birth; the Huichols may have thought that was impossible.

But the saints are certainly 'born'. St. Jose (Joseph) is noted for having a violin(!). Music is seen as an important way of communicating with the gods. There is St.Juan (John); Kauymali ordered him to live 'on that side'. Santo Kaytano is placed 'on this side'; he is the equation between Father Sun and the Christian God. Kauymali found St. Miguel; he was a saint who had been an eagle, plunged into the sea and found the cross of Christ at the bottom. Two lady saints, Santa Paulina and Santa Magdalena were born.

We have the intriguing story of how a very poor boy became beloved of one of the rain goddesses. Her ten brothers were furious and attacked him. But he was protected by the gods and his wife. After many tribulations, the man was offered a wild mule to tame, which he did, so winning the contest. His name was St.Iago (James)(!)

San Jose wanted to have a bow for his violin, so Kauymali made him one. In five days it turned into flowers and made beautiful music. The Virgin also wanted flowers to hold on her breast. The flowers went into their bodies and became their real hearts, and from that they could produce children, one of which was Jesus.

A good violinist was needed for the god-house, so Kauymali held a contest with ten players. Ereno was to be the judge. The last contestant was a little boy, Jesus, with a tiny violin (only six inches long). But the sound was so beautiful that he won the contest outright. But the losers were jealous and plotted against Jesus. He knew what was happening, so he suggested another contest outside the temple. This time there were fifty players and they played five times each, with violin and guitar. Jesus appeared as an old man this time and pretended to be lame; he played the violin with his hands and the guitar with his feet! Ereno was thrilled, got up and danced with him and proposed marriage to him. The losers were furious but Jesus was protected by the gods, especially the Sun. The losers were actually the **Jurilos** (the Jews) who were bent on killing Jesus. He went into the sea and found that great shining cross on the seabed.

The story is now characterised by the Jews hounding Jesus and he goes to all kinds of lengths to avoid them. While this is going on, he founds many towns in Mexico, starts irrigation projects, blesses the fields and plants, shows Kauymali how to brand cattle, orders musical instruments, provides bells for all the churches, provides a shoe factory, shows how to provide shoes and sandals, shows the Huichols how to do carpentry, organises pillories and stocks, and establishes Holy Week, which is dubbed as a 'delicate' time. In all this, he does not touch women and remains celibate. There is the ongoing problem of avoiding the Jews; he has a habit of hiding in church towers, or climbing up the Sierra Moron, or hiding up various pine trees. Sometimes he changes appearance to become a child, or a cripple, or a blind man, a dwarf, a fatman, even a one-eyed man or a one-armed man. The hint in that is that he is being equated with Kaymali, who lost an eye and a foot.

Eventually, the Jews do catch up with him, since he is betrayed by the heron. Jesus only allows himself to be caught because he feels his work is complete and the world is perfect. They put him in the stocks, but he escapes only to be recaptured and beaten. He escapes again but he knows the inevitable has to happen; he orders a cross covered with tinfoil. There is an eclipse of the sun lasting five hours, but this is not specifically related to Holy Week. The Jews get thirty piles of silver money from the National Palace of

Mexico and give it to Santo Nicario (Pontius Pilate?) for permission to kill Jesus. At four pm they nail him to the cross in the plaza and raise him up high. The great gods of the sea cannot bear to see this so they send an old blind god who accepts a sabre from the Mexicans. They help him to place the sabre right on Christ's nipple and push hard. Thus Jesus dies without the killer knowing what he is doing; however the blind god receives his sight and sees his God, dead on the cross. Jesus' soul flies up to 'Gloria'; also the saints die, and that is the completion of the Christian work. Amidst all these strange ideas is the fundamental truth that the completion of Christ's work on earth was the completion of creation; a profound thought.

We can see how the Gospel stories are cleverly integrated with life in Mexico at that time. What is strange is that there is no mention of the Resurrection; one would have thought, with all those people, plants and animals coming back to life in the original myths, that the Huichols would have sprung on to the Resurrection. One might complain that this Christian myth is all too fanciful and takes too many liberties with the Gospel stories. However, as with so many matters in mythical sagas, we need to look for the symbolisms in it.

One such example is Joseph and Jesus as violinists! The violin is almost certainly a European import and can hardly have been known in the Americas before 1492. But what does it signify? Jesus plays a beautiful tune which entrances everybody, even the gods, but enrages the Jews. In the Gospels, Jesus' teachings and miracles do enrage the strict legalists of Judaism; but the 'music' is a thing of great beauty, like a bouquet of flowers. We notice that St.Joseph does not have a bow for his violin; it is Kauymali who makes him one. This suggests that although Joseph and the saints had the truth, it needed a certain amount of input from Huichol mythology to make it work in that part of the world. In many ways, Kauymali and the great gods are in agreement with Jesus and the two work together. This is an indication that the Huichols think that their religion and the new faith from Europe are essentially in agreement. It is interesting that twice a shining cross is found at the bottom of the sea; in other words, the great gods of the sea are protecting the new faith of Jesus.

What do we make of the 'Jews' in these myths? There can hardly have been any Jews in Mexico in the early years of the conquest, and probably still are not many even now. What do they symbolise? Perhaps they symbolise elements from the old religion who were jealous of Jesus. This could be an admission that the original paganism of central America could not countenance the new faith from Europe and wanted to destroy it. So in a sense there is a paradox going on here; on the one hand, Kauymali and the gods are co-operating with Jesus, but there are elements amongst the natives that are antagonistic to the new faith from Europe.

Another symbolism is Jesus climbing up a tree or a mountain. He is getting nearer to God for protection, and indeed it states that the gods, including Nakawe, are defending him from being attacked and killed. Climbing up a church tower suggests that the church, the Christian people whom he has converted, are looking after him as well. It is worth mentioning that the concept of the ' World Tree' is missing from Huichol thinking.

It is strange that the National Palace in Mexico City is drawn into the myths. In general terms, the Mexicans are seen in a somewhat jaded light by the Huichols. We can understand that since it was the lust for silver to be sent to Europe that inspired the Mexicans to force the Huichols into the mines, in virtually slave labour conditions. It is Jesus who orders the Mexicans to give the Huichols a proper title to their lands, and possibly the right to be left alone. In this instance, we can see actual history being turned into mythical proportions.

What do we make of Jesus turning into a blind man, a cripple and other things? Apart from being a ploy to avoid the Jews, could it be an indication that Jesus associated himself with all the poor, the casualties and misfits in society? We notice that St.James starts as a poor boy, beloved of the rain goddess; could this be a reflection of the Franciscan friars who were evangelising in that area? They were popular with the Aztecs and other indigenous peoples, because they were gentle and helpful, in contrast to the Conquistadores. This must indicate the humility of the genuine Christians, something that the Jews found confusing?

On the face of it, if we take these sagas literally, they do seem absurd. But there is much more to it than face-value truth. In general terms, we can see the European influence, with its superior technology and agricultural methods, coming in to improve the standard of life for the indigenous peoples of the Americas. This does not really take into account the thousands of people who went down with smallpox because they had no resistance to the germ. It is not clear at what point smallpox enters the picture; if we follow the Huichol scheme of things, it suggests that smallpox was present before the Spaniards arrived, but this must be some kind of retrojection, (just as the mention of pesos must be). The Huichols attributed smallpox to marital infidelity, the result of which was that the children caught it. There is no understanding of infection here. What is interesting is that in one scene, Kauymali is seen to take pus from a smallpox victim and perform what we would see as 'vaccination'! How and when this idea came in is a matter for debate, but it could suggest that the European influence cannot have been all bad.

What is missing from Huichol mythology?

Because of their isolation, it is only to be expected that various elements of mythology seen in other parts of the world, are missing. One such aspect is the matter of jewels and translucent stone of any kind. This must indicate that the Huichols did not have such things. However there is one mention of crystal. Nevertheless, we can see in the fascination for parrot feathers, the same kind of symbolism. The shamans dressed themselves with parrot feathers, which would be green and red. There is one account, during the corn ceremonies, when Tatevali, the Grandfather Fire, takes out his plumes and gives them to Palikati and sends him off to the fields. The feathers spontaneously catch fire and burn the field to remove all the pests, before it is baptised and planted. In another situation, the shaman's plumes represent the grasshopper's wings. In the peyote country, there is a grasshopper with no wings (it would seem) and this is because the wings were taken off their children. In addition, there is a fascination for the firefly which is associated with Tatevali.

It would be wrong to think that there was nothing shiny in Huichol lore. There is a mirror, like a relic, which is seen hanging round the shaman's neck. It represents the Sun god. It is about one and a half inches in diameter and is alleged to be made of stone with tinfoil stuck to it. Quite how far back this idea goes is debatable, but it is not impossible that the Huichols could have had bits of shiny metal before the coming of the Europeans.

With regard to precious metals, silver and gold, these do not seem to play any important part in Huichol mythology. Silver is clearly associated with the coming of the Spaniards, but is not essential to Huichol thinking. Gold only receives one mention and seems to be of no importance at all. This is a surprise, since the Aztecs and the Incas had such metals; the Huichols appear not to attach much significance to them at all. This is in contrast to most other mythologies. Mercury is never mentioned and was probably not known about.

With regard to Creation, it appears that there is no mention of 'Adam and Eve'. It is slightly misleading to say this. Several times we have mention of 'an innocent boy and girl', which means that they have not had sexual intercourse. They appear in various permutations and are suggestive of the start of humanity. They are not given names in the way that the Bible and Greek mythology do. But it is a way of emphasising the importance of virginity and innocence, and by extension marital fidelity, which must have been an essential element at the start of all things. In certain ceremonies, a boy and a girl are dressed up to lead the procession.

One might conclude that there is no mention of the 'World Tree' which so often appears in world mythology. This too is slightly misleading. We recall that Jesus more than once hides in a pine tree, and there is also a Sausa tree which produces water to end the drought. The shortage of trees may reflect the conditions in Huichol territory, which is characterised by patches of desert and cultivated land. The idea that the tree is the connection between heaven, earth and the underworld is not really present in this mythology. The existence of the underworld is quite heavily understated; there is far more interest in what goes on in the deeps of the sea (the Pacific Ocean).

Another missing element is the sword; this is understandable since swords as we know them were not known until the Spaniards arrived. The Aztecs had a clumsy weapon with obsidian stuck in it, and there is one possible reference to such in Huichol mythology. By and large, it must have been a peaceful, non-aggressive community. The substitute for the sword is the arrow; the Huichols have any amount of them, but they are used for killing the deer and sending messages to the gods. The symbolism in it is that of establishing justice and equity; the arrow is intended to counteract sickness and children dying.

One interesting omission in Huichol thinking is the importance of the stars. The Sun is central to their system and the Moon, even if it did come before the Sun, is also significant. But the stars receive scant mention. Although Nakawe is the mistress of the stars, that is the limit of their mention. There is no attempt at describing constellations and their significance, as in Greek thought. Consequently there appears to be no Zodiac or its equivalent and hence no calendar. This is something of a surprise since the Incas did indulge in constellations,(6) albeit different ones from the Greeks. The

Huichols appear not to have had any contact with the Incas. The end result of this is that there seems to be no system of prophecy, in spite of there being shamans. This too is a slight surprise since the Aztecs certainly did have the Jaguar prophets who were quite successful. But then the Huichols were quite scornful of what they term 'the Mexicans.'

Another omission is the terrifying struggle with an assortment of monsters. This requires a champion, such as Hercules in Greek thinking. Kauymali is clearly the champion, but he does not have to go to extremes of violence with aggressive and overwhelming misshapen creatures. In fact, the Huichol system is a much more peaceful one. Admittedly there are people who are bent on violence, but that appears to be when the Christian era breaks into their scheme. This was not exactly the finest advertisement for Christianity, but then the Conquistadores were not the finest examples of Christian virtue, with their killing and thieving.

What is in common with other mythologies?

Some of this has already been seen, but to sum it up is worthwhile. There is a heavy emphasis on snakes. The Pacific Ocean is riddled with them and rattlesnakes appear to be valued. There is an instinctive fear of death in human nature, with regard to snakes; also they symbolise fecundity and everlasting life. The paradox in this produces an ambivalent reaction in virtually all people and that would be true of the Huichols.

Fire and water are also important factors in Huichol thinking. Both of them symbolise cleansing. Interestingly, blood too is brought in as a third element; this is also seen in St.John's epistle.(7) Baptism can be with water but also blood may be used, largely on cult objects. The word 'baptism' almost certainly was supplied by the Spaniards, but the actual ceremony itself can be seen as pre-dating the conquest. We do not know what the Huichols called it, but the idea of cleansing and a fresh start, not just for people but for anything else, is important in their system. It is symptomatic that the need was felt for the world to be cleansed of evil; this helps to explain the Huichol version of the Flood, with Kauymali as the 'Noah' of the story. This is by no means saying that the Flood is purely mythological. We are left with the impression that there must have been some kind of inundation in the distant past, since so many cultures around the world make mention of it.

The three-tier universe is there, but the operative number five relates to it in a different way. It would seem that each mythological system has its own idea about a key number; nine in Norse lore, eight in Japanese and Chinese, seven in Christian thinking and five in the Huichol world.

Another element found in many mythologies is the question of free will and predestination, a philosophical matter which has haunted mankind since its first beginnings. Time and again in the Huichol myths we have the phrase, 'the gods have ordained' or 'it has been ordered that' which is a fairly obvious indication that they believed in predestination. At the same time, there seems to be an element of freedom in which people can go against the will of the great gods. So the Jews are bent on destroying Santo Christo; whether they realised they were working against the great gods is not stated, but the shaman, Kauymali does know.

Final comments on Huichol mythology

This is a fascinating look at a culture that has altered very little since the Stone Age and is resistant to other influences. The exception to this is their acceptance of the Saints, Jesus and Holy Week. We are of course seeing it through the eyes of an American, Robert Zingg, who might just have been a Protestant and not totally happy with Roman Catholicism. As evidence of this, so often we have the use of the word 'paraphernalia' when talking about cult objects used by the shaman. The word 'paraphernalia' is a pejorative word with a negative feel to it; it is suggestive of being fussy, having too much in the way of superstitious bric-a-brac. One wonders what the Huichol word for such things might have been; possibly something with a more positive ring to it. Admittedly Zingg obtained his information direct from a Huichol informant, who may have been speaking Spanish. A lot can be conveyed in translation, either with a negative tone or a positive tone.

Even with this caution, we can gain a helpful impression of pre-Columbian Huichol mythology, and we find it fascinating how the coming of Christianity has impacted on it. The general impression is that they understood some of the best elements in Christianity and loved Jesus, Mary and Joseph, and drew some sort of equation between Jesus Christ and their chief shaman. Also the Christian God was equated with the Father sun. But going further than that, they resisted any attempt at destroying their ancestral faith and ritual procedures. How much this is still true to this day is beyond us to say; we have to recall that Robert Zingg was writing in 1934 and a lot has happened in the world since then. Even so, with this caution, it is a fascinating look into the thinking of what must be regarded as the 'Stone Age' mentality. We shall see that the African myths in chapter 15 are also fascinating for their traditional content and collision with Christianity.

Footnotes for chapter 14

1. Huichol myths are related to the dry and wet season, and all their rituals are relevant to producing a good harvest. It cannot have been easy to wrest a living from the western desert of Mexico.
2. YHWH, a contraction of 'I am that I am', is the name of God given in Exodus 3:14.
3. The sausa tree is one of the few drought-resistant trees in that area. It is like a willow tree.
4. The shiny feathers of the parrot seem to be a substitute for jewels which were not known in that area.
5. Five is that significant number in Huichol thinking, analogous to 9, 7 and 8 in other parts of the world. Five appears in all kinds of compounds, such as 500 or 50,000.
6. The Greeks attached theological and mythological significance to vast numbers of stars and produced the Zodiac and the calendar that followed from it.
7. I John 1:7 'the blood of Jesus cleanses us from all sin'.

15

African myths

With Africa, we are dealing with a massive land area with a vast number of different languages, cultures and myths. This is in contrast to the Huichols (chapter 14) whose land area is very small and their culture unified. Also it is interesting to compare it with the Melanesian Cargo Cults (chapter 13) which occupy a varied area separated by large tracts of sea. It would be unrealistic to attempt to describe all the African myths, as they would occupy a very large book. We will concentrate on the creation myths, with some mention of myths of origin for each tribe or cultural group. It is worth remarking that those areas that have had a strong Muslim influence, seem to have very largely lost their creation myths; this would be North Africa, Egypt and the Sudan, and many sub-Saharan areas. Other, more southerly areas which have received much Christian influence, seem to have retained their myths, albeit with an element of Christian influence. We do not seem to see the 'cargo cult' collision between traditional myths and the coming of Christianity. This may indicate that the colonists were rather more careful about how they shaped Christian doctrine. This information is gleaned from Stephen Belcher's book, African Myths of Origin. It is worthwhile to find the ideas that are in common across the continent, and make a few comparisons with what might be termed 'unusual' ideas. As one would expect, with tribes connected geographically by a continuous landmass, many ideas must have circulated in the past, and each tribal group has kept its own traditions. Many of them were found, by the missionaries, to be essentially living in the Stone Age, and some seem intent on remaining so to this day. This much they have in common with the Huichols.

One God

Virtually all the myths begin with one god up in the sky. This god goes under various names; the Bushmen call him Khaggen; the Pygmies call him Khvum; in Ethiopia we have Waqa the sky god; and in Kenya it is Mogai. There are many other names. Sometimes the god is female, so for instance, in Dahomey, Mawu, a goddess is the creator, and she had a consort called Lisa, forming a dual deity. Both of them live in the sky, but Mawu is the moon and Lisa is the sun. This may be an elementary way of approaching the problem of Theodicy. This is more obvious with the Sara peoples of Lake Chad, who also have a dual deity, Loa the female and Sou the male. Loa lives in the heavens and does careful work, such as a beautifully carved canoe, but Sou is a careless workman who works on earth and produces a sloppy canoe, and other artefacts. This is more obviously a way of dealing with Theodicy, in picture language.

Sometimes, the original god has agents or deputies which he sends in to do the work of Creation. So, with the Bamana people of Niger, the sky god (unnamed) sends in Pemba to create the earth, and another god called Faro to create the heavens and cause rain to fall. Pemba produces a creature that is part human, part fox, and she becomes his female double called Muso Koroni. It is she who creates all the animals. She is also his wife. The Ashanti have another interesting permutation on this. The sky god, Nyankopon, enlists a spider called Nanni in creating humans. She spins out the thread and the god weaves it into humans. In Buganda we have the intriguing story of how Kintu is the first man in that area; a woman called Nambi comes down from heaven and wants to marry him. Her father, Ggulu, in heaven is not too keen on the match and puts Kintu to the test three times, but he prevails and wins Nambi. Another god, Walumbe now enters the scene and represents death; his brother Kaikuzi comes to fetch him back, but he refuses and Death still stalks the world. Again, this is an attempt at Theodicy.

In case one were thinking that the Africans were originally monotheists, that would be a mistake. The sky god may have been the original deity but very soon we have other subsidiary gods appearing, some associated with the creation and others representing Death. Usually the original god is seen as masculine, but not always; sometimes she is feminine. Almost always the original god is understood to inhabit the world up in the skies; in a very few cases, he lives in the underworld. Very unusually, there appears to be no god to start things off; life on earth, including humans, just appears. So for instance, in Dahomey, the Allada people say that people just come down to earth from the sky, as if there were no Creator. Another unusual configuration is found in west Aftrica. Someone called Sanen, comes into being by herself; she is not born. She bears a son called Kontron who becomes a great hunter. He is one-eyed; this reminds us of Odin in Norse thinking and Math in Celtic lore. Kontron is a virgin, but he has a swelling in his thigh and out comes a baby girl. This is enough to see that god or gods have many interesting permutations in Africa, and the dividing line between deity and humanity is not particularly clear. Some of these ideas might have been influenced by contact with Europeans.

Creation

Every myth makes the assumption that there must have been a beginning to all things at one time. It is interesting to note that that idea still persists among our scientific community even today. Almost always, we begin with an ocean or waters of some description and the land is formed later. So for instance, with the Igbo peoples, they believe that Ale, the mother of earth, gives her body to form the earth, and the land appears from the water. This sounds like a kind of proto-pantheism. Very rarely, the land is believed to have been formed before the waters. This occurs in Dahomey with the Fon peoples. The notion that the sky and the land have to be separated is a common motif. In Buganda, the Bunyaro believe that Ruhanga and his brother Nkya separated them using a pole, a tree and an iron bar. Even more graphic is the account from central Mali, in which Amma, the creator made the world in layers and separated them with a metal post. After creating animals and humans, he decided to knock the post down. This crushed everyone except the spirits and the old people (who were actually snakes). The earth came to admit the supremacy of the sky and the metal posts are restored, but now the sky is not very high. This explains why humans do not grow to their full height. It is the women, with their pestles and mortars, that bump the sky and also an old woman pushes it off. The sky goes back to its normal height. This can be seen as a way of saying that the world of deity is superior to that of humanity, and yet, humanity has some kind of influence on it.(1)

In many cases, creation is accomplished by the production of an egg. (2) So in Mali, the god Mangala provides an egg with seeds inside it, the potential of all life. From Zaire, a hero called Bokele is hatched from an egg. It mentions his father and mother, but there is no indication of a creating deity or how the egg was produced. It is the old question of the chicken and the egg. But the egg motif is also seen in Greece and China.

It would be fair to say that the three tiered system of heaven, earth and the underworld is assumed just about everywhere. The underworld is not mentioned very often and does not play a prominent part in African thinking, at least nowhere near as important as heaven and earth. To match this, it would be reasonable to suggest that there is no notion of 'the devil' as in Judeao-Christian thinking, and sin is not at all a major factor. There is such a thing as human misbehaviour and gods or spirits reacting to it, but it is nowhere near as heavily emphasised as in European thinking.

Connecting heaven and earth

The need for some kind of connection between heaven and earth is seen in virtually every myth in the world. The motif of the 'world tree' is most commonly encountered, and it is also seen almost everywhere in Africa. The tree does not always seem to have quite the same significance, but it does appear in virtually every myth. The Fang people of Gabon and the Cameroon know of an enormous tree, called an AZAP tree.(3) The Pygmies showed them a way through the tree, via a narrow passage. The Fang needed to escape because a race of red giants was threatening them. The symbolism in this could be that knowledge of God in heaven is the way to escape evil. For the San people of South Africa, there is a N=AH tree,(4) whose seeds are poisonous. With the Songhay hunters of the Niger River, there is a tree of spirits. Nyame's mother became pregnant after sleeping near this tree. Very often a tree has spiritual or magical properties. The Fon of Benin believed that trees were the first things created and that one of them produced seeds that could be used for FA(5) divination. In Kenya, the Creator god Mogai regarded mount Kenya as his resting place, but also designated a grove of fig trees where he would settle when he came down from the mountain. The Mongo peoples of East Africa had their champion Lianja trying to cut down a Safu Nut Tree(6) which had caused his father's death. At first they tried to cut it down but with no success; it was too tough. Then Lianja advised them to put a bit of water on their axes; then the tree was cut down. One wonders about the symbolism in this; does it mean a breakdown in relations between heaven and earth? For the Bamana people of middle Niger, the Balanza tree(7) is of significance. The god Pemba took the form of this tree so that he could keep an eye on things in the world; this acacia albida is the only one that remains green throughout the dry season. The humans came to worship this tree, and it instructed them in the arts. There was also the Karite tree,(8) whose oil gives a savoury moisture, and Pemba asked for more. In this case there are two important trees with a spiritual significance.

A scene reminiscent of the Tower of Babel comes from Zambia. Three sons of a man called Mukulumpe, decided to build a tower by which they could reach heaven, but the tower became unstable and collapsed on them, killing many people. This is the same motivation as with the Tower of Babel; to peer into God's eternity. But they find that it is not possible for mortal man to do that; it is the other way round, that God shows his eternity to certain selected people as and when he chooses.

We have already seen that some people know of a pole between heaven and earth. A rope too is seen. For the Igbo people of Nigeria, the creator god, Chukwu, let down the first man, Eri, from heaven on a rope. He landed on an anthill which was the only dry patch available. A blacksmith came with his bellows to dry out the land so that Eri could walk on it. The Chaggas of Tanzania believe that Murile, their champion , sang a song to his stool, and it lifted him up right into the clouds. There he met people who gave him instructions about cooking and other skills. To return to earth, he made an agreement with a bull, and came down on the bull's back. Clearly the bull symbolises strength and virility, and exacted a promise from Murile, which he inadvertently broke. The result was that Murile sank into the ground and was swallowed up by the earth (like Sita in the Ramayana).(9) The most intriguing connection comes from the Yoruba peoples of Nigeria. A god called Obatala got permission from the chief god, Olorun, to go down to earth and make things more interesting. For this he acquired a gold chain and climbed down it. When he reached the waters, he poured sand out of a shell to form the land. This is a rare mention of gold in African mythology. This is not really surprising, since most of the peoples might not have had any gold; however, living near Ghana, the Yoruba may have had access to gold, since this was the Gold Coast (until recently renamed). However, the symbolism in it is good. It suggests that Gold, symbolising eternity and indestructibility, is the link between heaven and earth. In other words, God and Mankind are permanently linked, even if separate.

With regard to the underworld, which is understated in African mythology, there is very little said about how it is connected to the earth. People are said to go down into the lower layers, but there is little information about how this happens. Obatala is the only person where it is actually described; that he sank into the ground and disappeared. This was because he broke a promise.

The Snake

The snake is a universal symbol in mythology; it is paradoxical in that it symbolises both life and death. In Africa, virtually every myth has at least one snake, if not hundreds of them.

The Ethiopians have a fascinating story of how a massive serpent ruled the land and demanded sacrifices from the people. A stranger came and on seeing the plight of the people, decided to kill the serpent. He stuffed a goat with poison and served it up to the snake, whereupon it died. The people made him king, and his only daughter, Makeda, became the famous Queen of Sheba. More of that later.

The Massai of East Africa have a story about the origin of cattle. There was a hunter called Dorobo, a snake and an elephant living together. The snake had a habit of sneezing (!) which sprayed venom into the air. The elephant did not mind as he was very thick-skinned, but Dorobo developed a rash. In the night, Dorobo crushed the snake's skull; later on he killed the elephant too. The story goes on to show how the Massai got their cattle. One wonders at the symbolism in this story. Clearly, the snake depicts someone human, who sneezes, but is also very nasty, spraying poison around. Dorobo kills him, which means that evil has been defeated.

In Buganda, the champion, Kintu, who managed to marry the daughter of the chief god, came up against a king snake called Bemba, and prepared to fight him. It was the tortoise who helped to defeat the snake. The fact was that the tortoise pulled in his head and legs at night and this, he maintained, was the secret of eternal life. Bemba was taken in by this idea and offered to have his head cut off in the evening, so that he could live for ever. So the tortoises obliged by cutting off not just Bemba's head but all the other snakes' heads. So the enemy was defeated.

An amusing story comes from the San people of South Africa. The animals lived together, including the python, but the jackal hoped the python would die. One day, the two of them went down to the water hole and saw the berries on the N=AH tree. The jackal could not climb it, but the snake could. The jackal temped the snake to slide out on to a thin branch overhanging the pool. The result was that the branch collapsed and the snake fell into the water. The jackal was delighted to think that the python and the baby inside her, had drowned. However, later, the giraffe, who had long legs, investigated the water hole and found the snake, or rather two of them, at the bottom, and brought them out alive. The other animals were delighted. One could see the symbolism in this, that one may think that evil has been defeated, but it is only lurking deep down until fetched to the surface again.

One incident that reminds us of Noah's flood comes from the San peoples of South Africa. The snakes had been attacking Cogaz who was the son of the first person, a sort of Adam only somehow divine. The chief of the snakes realised there would be retribution, so he built a platform which would be high enough to withstand a flood. The chief snake and his followers survived the flood but the bad snakes were drowned. Khaggen struck the good snakes with his walking stick and they lost their skins and became human. This ties in with the idea from Mali that the old people are actually snakes. In general terms, there is no firm dividing line between humans and animals.

The creation of the human race

There are various ideas on how mankind was created. Seldom do they just appear without an explanation. The most common one is that of clay being used by a god to form a man. In Rwanda, the god Imana made people in the upper world; it was a life of bliss but one couple was childless. So Imana fashioned a tiny clay figurine and this eventually became the first humans on the lower earth, but it was not to be a life of bliss. So also the Yoruba people of Nigeria, the god Obatala made figures of clay and breathed life into them. He got drunk on palm wine and so the figures became deformed or incomplete. Both these accounts are an attempt at explaining human failings or disease. The Fang people of Cameroon have someone called Mebege, the first being who made a lizard out of clay and placed it in some water. After eight days it emerged as the first man and was named Nzame. From his big toe, a woman was formed, and was named Oyeme-Mam. She was strictly speaking his sister, but this did not prevent them going in for incest and producing eight pairs of offspring which now represent the various tribes of the Fang, as well as the Pygmies, the coastal peoples, the whites and the chimpanzees. We can compare these ideas with Genesis chapter 2. In Southern Africa we see some variations on these ideas. The Zulus and the Swazis think that the god made men out of reeds of different colours, which explains the different races of mankind. The Xhosa think that all humans and animals came out of a cave; this again indicates the idea that humanity and the animal kingdom are not very clearly divided.

Sometimes, the creation of a man is not described. So, for instance, in Kenya, the first man Gikuyu is just made by the god Mogai. When Gikuyu came down to earth, he found that Mogai had already provided a woman for him, and she was named Mumbi. We notice that the issue of incest is avoided in this story. They had nine daughters; this was a matter of concern, but after sacrificing, they found that nine sons had mysteriously appeared by the special tree. This is the basis of the nine tribes of the Kikuyu.

A very unusual and amusing account comes from the Pygmies of Zaire. The creator, Khvum felt lonely so he decided to create people. He collected a lot of Nkula nuts,(10) then went to his canoe and harnessed his crocodile to it, to pull him out well into the river. He took a nut, rubbed it, blew on it and threw it back on to the land. 'You shall be the first man,' he said. The second nut became the first woman, but he did not stop until all the nuts had landed on the shore, so that there was a crowd of people waiting for him in the village when he returned.

Life as eternal

Although most African myths have their own ideas about the permanence of life, there is the suspicion that the Epic of Gilgamesh, stemming from Mesopotamia, has had its influence in parts of Ethiopia. This tale has been examined in chapter 2, but the gist of it is, how do we sidestep death? This question is still an issue now, with scientists trying to devise methods of extending life artificially, or arresting aging, or even the 'Rip Van Winkle' motif.(11)

The Zulus have a tradition that the creator decided that humans ought to live for ever. A chameleon was charged with the message to tell the humans that they would not die. As the god watched, he noticed that the humans were multiplying rather quickly, so maybe it was not such a good idea to let them live for ever. He sent off a lizard to inform the humans, but the lizard moved a lot faster than the chameleon and arrived to tell the humans the bad news. Only later did the chameleon arrive with what would have been the good news, but that was a little too late. The Bamana of middle Niger have another intriguing story. Pemba, the god, made humans immortal at the start. It began to go wrong because Pemba wanted to copulate with the women, and Muso Koroni, who was his double and also his wife became jealous. She turned nasty and ran off, mutilating her genitals. Through this, the earth lost its purity. In the end, the balanza tree,(12) which was actually Pemba decided not to protect men from death. Therefore death came to be a factor of human life.

However, there are many instances of people being brought back to life. The Bushmen of South Africa have a god called Khaggan, the creator, and Cogaz is his son. The baboons caught Cogaz and killed him, placing him in a tree. Khaggan found out and took his revenge, sending them off to the mountains. Then he brought Cogaz back to life, using magic. In Mali, the sky god discovered that during a drought, there had been a fight over some water. Two hunters and their dogs had been killed. The god brought them all back to life. The Mongo people have a hero called Lianja who had a war with Sausau. In the end, in a one to one combat, Lianja cut off Sausau's head. But Nsongo wanted Sausau brought back to life. Lianja took out a magic powder and sang a spell with the result that Sausau came back to life and became Nsongo's slave. The Shilluk of Southern Sudan have a story which describes Nyikang, one of the sons of the creator, and he arrived at a battlefield to find many dead men. He sprinkled them with water and touched them with his silver bracelets, whereupon they came back to life.

An understanding of death is often seen in the myths. An interesting example comes from the Kororofa peoples on the upper Benue river. Chido was the male celestial god and Ama was the female earthly goddess. She created mankind and also the animals and spirits found in the world. One of those spirits was Aki, death, and he wandered around trying to overpower anyone he met. If one could defeat him, one would survive. However, an ant told him to use better tactics; he should work underground, unseen, and making tunnels, like the ants. This way, people would collapse into the tunnels quite by accident. Aki took the advice and that is why he does not attack one openly; he kills from within, craftily. This is a kind of 'just-so' story, but it contains a lot of truth.

From this selection of examples, it can be seen how life is of great value to people and death has to be avoided, sidestepped and delayed as much as possible. It is only human instinct, but typifies how instinct can easily produce all kinds of mythical stories.

Different species

The San people of the Kalahari desert have a tradition which is an interesting 'just-so' idea. At one time all the animals and people were together with no distinctive markings on them, still less, no names attached to them. They decided to differentiate one from another. They lit a fire and warmed up a branding iron. All the animals received different markings, the zebra, the giraffe, the kudu,(13) the wildebeest, the gemsbok; some of the humans tried to mark themselves in imitation of the animals. This idea persists today, when a boy becomes a man, after having killed a large game animal, such as an antelope. The boy receives markings. The hyena, however, as yet unmarked, lay down by the fire and waited. They rammed a red hot iron up his bottom; that explains why to this day, the hyena walks awkwardly with a hunched back. That is how the animals all came to have different names. We can compare that with Genesis, where Adam gives all the animals names.

An intriguing story comes from the Songhay hunters of the Niger Valley. There was a magical beast called a Hira which was terrorising the area. Musa and Meynsata were courting at the time, but Meynsata took it upon herself to defeat the beast. A terrible battle took place and Musa had to intervene or she would have been killed. The beast transformed itself into an elephant, then a lion, then into a hyena, and then a leopard. The girl managed to break its neck each time and the beast was killed. We notice that the monster, as in Greek mythology, is defeated, but this time it is a team effort. The substratum of it is that the women claimed it was Meynsata who was the champion and the menfolk acclaimed Musa as the champion. Clearly there was some kind of struggle over sexual dominance in that area.

The Shilluk of Southern Sudan have a strange tradition concerning crocodiles. A man called Okwa spotted two maidens on the bank of the Nile. They were human at the top but the bottom half was crocodile, something like a mermaid. He tried his luck with them but they escaped and called on their father. He was human on the left side but crocodile on the right side, but he agreed to the arrangement. This is why the humans and the crocodiles were friends at the start, but enmity soon emerged. This is why the crocodiles will kill the humans if they go in the water, but vice versa, the humans will kill the crocodiles if they come out on to the land. This is another idea not unlike Greek thought, where therianthropism (14)is quite common. This involves some kind of amalgam of human and animal, an example of which is the centaur.

In the Kuba kingdom of the eastern Congo, Mboom is the great spirit who spat out all kinds of animals and designated their way of life. It was a kind of dualism for there was another spirit called Ngaan and they quarrelled. Ngaan created all the nasty animals such as snakes, iguanas and crocodiles. They are termed, 'the creatures of Ngaan'. From this we see that humans and animals began in harmony and in an ideal state of peace, but this did not last very long. There is distrust and enmity between them.

Number symbolism

As compared with some mythologies, there is very little in the way of number symbolism in African thought. The number nine seems to occur quite often. In the story of Wamara by Lake Victoria, Kintu the god of the underworld, invited people down into his caves for a nine day visit to learn about agriculture, and sent them back up with a herd of livestock. Mboom, of the Congo area, had nine sons, all called Woot, each of them was in charge of some aspect of creation. The Kikuyu of Kenya have nine tribes and this is explained thus; that Gikuyu and his wife Mumbi had nine daughters. This was a matter of concern, so the god Mogai prescribed a sacrifice, after which nine young men appeared, one for each of the girls. Apart from this being a kind of 'just-so' explanation for the Kikuyu tribal arrangement, there seems to be no rationale for the number nine. That number appears as quite significant in Norse tradition, but it is difficult to see how the Africans could have gleaned the idea from Northern Europe.

Biblical influences

It is not too difficult to understand how Judeo-Christian ideas could have worked their way into Africa. After all, the kingdom of Ethiopia has been a Christian empire going back almost to the 1st century AD. The story of Kelimabe and Kelikelimabe, two brothers, from the Songhay hunters of the Niger valley, has various aspects reminding us of Jacob and Esau and also of Joseph with Potiphar's wife. It may have come into Africa via Egypt where we find the Tale of Two Brothers as described in chapter 2.

The king of Bornu, near lake Chad, called down fire from heaven, and this terrified the attacking army. Elijah is recorded as producing fire from heaven, but for a different purpose.

However, the most obvious connection with Biblical tradition concerns The Queen of Sheba. This is recorded in the Kebra Negast, 'The glory of Kings', dated about 1200 AD. It is interesting to compare this with the Biblical account of Solomon in the book of I Kings. Makeda, the Queen of Sheba, heard of Solomon's fame and glory and decided to visit him. They were so impressed with each other that they slept together. The result was a boy called Bayna Lekhem. He wanted to know who his father was, and on learning the truth, he set off to Jerusalem. He was so like his father that Solomon wanted to make the boy his heir, but Bayna Lekhem declined the offer. What he did do was to make a copy of the Ark of the Covenant, and then craftily did a substitution so that he could take the real Ark home to Ethiopia and leave the Jews with the fake! That is the basis of the claim that the Ark is now hidden away in the bowels of the Ethiopic Church.

We can see in this that it is a picture-language way of saying that the true faith resides in Ethiopia and not in the land of Israel.

In general terms, the relationship between Judeo-Christianity and the pagan faiths of Africa works out in quite a different way compared with what we see in Melanesia with the Cargo Cults. One has the impression that the Christian missionaries were eager to record and understand the native African myths, rather than just blot them out, which is what happened in Wales. After all, if one is going to convert people to a new religion, it is common sense to attempt to gain an understanding of what these peoples believed in the first place, and work on it from there.

What's missing?

The African myths are in many ways heavily centred on climate, especially rainfall. However there are some elements of mythology which are notably understated if not absent altogether. There seems to be no mention of jewels, translucent stones such as onyx or alabaster. This may be because they never saw such things. Gold and silver are rarely mentioned, possibly because they were not widely available, but also because no great significance was seen in them. The sword is mentioned rarely, as is the rainbow. The aurora is never mentioned, but that is no surprise. The important element of exaggeration is seldom seen; all the myths are very down to earth, even if the element of magic is quite commonly seen. In contrast to European mythology, there is no sense of eschatology; there is no apocalyptic material in it at all. Actually describing the gods is not overdone. We do not see the outright crudities as seen in European thought. The crudities tend to be related to humans. Also the trickster element is present with the gods, but not overdone; it tends to be applied to the early heroes or champions.

Myths of tribal origin and leadership

Many African myths are concerned with how tribes came into existence and their leadership. We have to realise that many areas were kingdoms and still are in spite of European interference. One important element in tribal leadership is the tussle between male and female dominance; this is something that has already been seen. However, here is another interesting example.

The Darassa people of Ethiopia, in the early days, had very few women. The men had to do all the menial tasks. The rulers and officials were women. Ako Manoya was the name of the queen. The menfolk became uneasy about this arrangement. They had a leader who fomented sedition. He also had a mistress in addition to his wife. The queen came to know of this and told the wife about his infidelity and the plot. She promised that if the wife could bring in his head, she would make her the heir to the throne. The wife managed to do this and was appointed as heir. The menfolk were disheartened by this and decided that the queen must die. They knew of a road along which she must pass, dug a pit in it and concealed the hole. The men made sure that the queen fell into the trap and was buried. The young wife who had been named as heir, climbed a tree but was speared by the men. After that, men ruled the kingdom.

It is interesting to note that ancient Egypt's system of monarchy had the arrangement that the claim on the throne ran through the female line. Literally anyone could become the Pharaoh as long as he married one of the royal ladies. That would legitimise his claim on the throne. To prevent another enterprising man mounting a claim, Pharaoh had to marry all the other royal ladies as well. It is true that in some parts of Africa to this day, there are some people with this female ascendency arrangement. We in the Western world normally assume that the claim on the throne or indeed any property, runs through the male line.

There are so many fascinating mythical stories coming from Africa. It would be impossible to describe them all in a work of this scope. The reality is that we all need some kind of myth to underpin our tribal, family or national identity. It is another of those instincts which are important to us all.

A Swazi story of a king

With so many different peoples with no clear geographical divisions, there have been disputes over rulership and possession of land. This is no less true for Southern Africa. In Swaziland there was a king with many wives. The chief wife had a son called Madlisa; other wives had sons too; the cadet wife had a son called Madlebe. He was different from the others; when he wept, he wept tears of blood and he was born with a silver bracelet on his arm, which cried when he did. Then the king decided to select his heir by a trial session. The boy that could spit the furthest would be the winner. All the other boys did not manage to spit very far, but Madlebe's attempt was by far the furthest. Also the thunder rolled overhead and the silver bracelet cried out. The king was not quite convinced so he gave Madlebe a gourd, a clay pot and a wooden spoon, and charged him not to break them on pain of death. Some time afterwards, Madlebe clumsily broke the pot. This meant that the guards would have to take him out into the savannah and kill him. Out in the countryside, the guards were pointing their spears at Madlebe when there was a roll of thunder and a bolt of lightning. Madlebe was weeping tears of blood and his bracelet was crying. The guards took this to indicate his royal power and saved his life. Later on, he became the king.

In this we can see how a royal claimant substantiated his inheritance by quasi-supernatural happenings. Although there are no gods involved in this story, the mythological symbolism is every bit as acute. The thunder and lightning indicate that the gods are taking an interest in the matter. The spears, which are a substitute for a sword, indicate truth, the righting of wrongs. The silver bracelet, made of a precious metal, indicates eternity and royalty. The bracelet was in sympathy with the boy, who wept blood. Blood also indicates life. So often in mythology we see an earthly king justifying his authority by recourse to supernatural phenomena. We think of King Arthur who was the only one who could pull the sword out of the stone. This is where mythology underpins politics and whole dynasties.

Footnotes for chapter 15

1. The separation between the earth and the sky is a common feature in mythology. It includes the assumption that the sky is a shelf upon which the gods live.
2. The world egg is another common motif, and betrays the idea of fertility.
3. The Azap tree. A kind of olive tree, clearly with mythical overtones of reaching up to heaven.
4. The N=AH tree. The Noah tree. A tree of life.
5. FA divination. A method found in Dahomey, making patterns after passing nuts from one hand to another, associated with the god Mawu.
6. Safu Nut Tree. In Swahili-land, an engaging story of how this tree was guarded by Fetefete and Ilele climb up to gather nuts, and pelted Fetefete.
7. The Balanza tree. Like a cedar, the connection between heaven and earth.
8. The Karite Tree. The source of Shea butter and also skin cream.
9. Sita, the wife of Rama, is swallowed up by the earth, in spite of the fact that he and she are in love and both on the side of goodness. It may indicate some kind of collusion between heaven and hell.
10. Nkula nuts. Kola, the bitter flavouring in coca-cola, found in African rainforests, contains caffeine.

11. Rip Van Winkle. H.B.Stow gives us an account of a man who went to sleep for a hundred years and woke up to find the world a very different place.
12. Balanza tree. Acacia albida, like a cedar. Symbolic of the male component in creation.
13. A kudu; a kind of antelope.
14. Therianthropism is a common idea in mythology. It involves an amalgam of animal and human features, such as a centaur. It may be symbolic of the unity of creation.

16

Mythology and Freemasonry

People's conceptions of Freemasonry are very varied. Some regard it with deepest suspicion; others see it as a force for good. As a closed society with its own rules and procedures, it has always attracted a certain amount of criticism, but for the purposes of this book, there is a wealth of symbolism and mythology. This time, the connection to ancient Greek mythology is not particularly strong; the same would be true for Egyptian mythology. But paradoxically, freemasonry has shown itself willing and capable of absorbing ideas from many religions and philosophies. One might almost see it as a syncretistic system of thought, except that there is no attempt at a major amalgamation of two or more religions, as for instance with Sikhism. But as a widespread international brotherhood which is a force for peace, co-operation and friendship, it has to be commended.

The modern expression of Freemasonry is traceable back to the late Middle Ages, but the mythical theory of it is rooted in the reign of King Solomon and the building of the Temple in Jerusalem . This event is well-authenticated in the first book of Kings(1) in the Old Testament and there is no reason to doubt that such a building was erected. Just as ancient Troy began with a certain degree of historical truth, which then became decorated into the mythical book, the Iliad, so too the Temple becomes elaborated into an entire system of thought most of which does not appear in the book of Kings. The same is broadly true with the Atlantis mentality. The Atlantis idea gave the Nazis much impetus; the Iliad served to justify the Roman domination; the Temple inspired the Freemasons.

The bald facts about the Temple are straightforward enough. King David, having fought off all his enemies and established a generous Hebrew Empire, wanted to create a permanent home for the Ark of the Covenant. The obvious place was Mount Moriah on the eastern side of Jerusalem, the site on which it was believed that Abraham nearly sacrificed Isaac. But God's word via the prophet Nathan, was that since David had been a man of violence, it required another man actually to build the Temple. Solomon, as his successor fell into that role, combined with his wisdom, which had become legendary, was the ideal person to fulfil the task. But the Hebrews were not skilled in architecture or artwork. So Solomon enlisted Hiram king of Tyre (an ally of David), to provide materials and skill to accomplish the task. Thus far, are the bare bones of the facts; but now come the Masonic elaborations.

According to Masonic myth, Hiram enlisted someone called Hiram Abiff as chief architect and Adoniram and Titozadok as artisans. Hiram Abiff was later murdered, much to Solomon's sorrow.

Two enormous bronze pillars, which were actually hollow, had lilies on top, and they symbolised Judah and Israel. Across the top was a lintel to give them stability; it was termed 'Jehovah'. There was a molten sea holding 10,000 gallons of water for the priests to wash themselves. Solomon had built vaults under the Temple, into which were placed sacred objects; a cubic stone with a triangular plate of agate and gold with jewels adorning it. The name of God, YHWH was inscribed on the plate. This was explained as the foundation stone installed by Enoch.(2) This stone was placed in the Holy of Holies, as a pedestal for the Ark of the Covenant. Later the stone was moved to a safer place. Once a year on the Day of Atonement, the High Priest would enter the Holy of Holies and speak the name of God.

We find that much of this is not found in the book of Kings, and one wonders where this information came from, or who invented it, but we shall see later how much of this is basic to the symbolism of Freemasonry in action. It is interesting that the Bible records that the materials were prepared away from the Temple site so that the sound of hammering was never heard on site; now comes the augmentation, the non-biblical element, that it never rained during the daytime but only at night, so that the work was never interrupted.

Now we come to more recent times and supposedly less fanciful historical information. There is a document called the Regius Manuscript of 1390 which records Athelstan establishing a stone masons' guild at York. Thus we have the basis for calling the Masons, 'the Masons'. The Cooke Manuscript of 1450, written by a mason, makes reference to the symbolism and thought, including the various aspects of the Temple; also various mentions of liberal arts and sciences. Thus we see that the raw materials for Masonic procedures were present in the late mediaeval period. The real emergence of Masonry comes in Scotland with the Schaw Statutes of 1598 and 1599. These formalised the duties of lodge members; it was not just about high standards of building, but also about spiritual knowledge and the keeping of written records. So it would appear that the main impetus and inception of Freemasonry began in Scotland, but it did not stop there for long, as many other countries soon took up the idea.

In England, we see the inception of the Royal Society.(3) Many of them were Masons. In 1717 four lodges in London combined to form the Premier Grand Lodge of London. The Roman Catholic church condemned Freemasonry in 1738, but Masonry thrived on the culture of the Enlightenment; this was the ethos of being critical of the old ways, or irrationality, religious dogma and tradition. The drive to acquire knowledge and facts and develop the arts and sciences became important. The masons did not have a monopoly on Ideas about social reform and political liberty, but they were an important element in such trends at that time. Now we can see how the French Revolution, the American Independence, the constitution and Bill of Rights, and in Britain the move towards enlarged suffrage, were connected to Masonic ideas. Many of the activists behind these developments were actually masons. Thus far, are the less mythical and symbolic aspects of Freemasonry. It extends a long way back into the mists of late mediaeval times, but how far is a difficult question; it was certainly tied in with the socio-economic methods of the Mediaeval Guilds, and may even go back in a rudimentary fashion to Saxon times.

Now it becomes rather more sketchy. It is claimed by the Masons of Edinburgh, that Solomon's Wisdom was absorbed by the Dionysian Artificers of Tyre, and this was passed on to Pythagoras, and from him to the Roman Collegia. This was mainly architectural skills. When the Roman Empire fell, the Collegia survived as the Comasine Masters, situated on Lake Como. They sent masons to England with Saint Augustine (not the St. Augustine of Hippo), and taking ideas from Noah's Ark, this resulted in the Gothic Cathedrals of England. This idea is speculatory; some would call it mythical, but that might be a misuse of the word 'myth'.

From the 18th century onwards, it is also claimed that the Knights Templar, on their occupation of Jerusalem, brought back various ideas which worked their way into early Masonic notions. When the Templars were put under persecution, many found refuge in England and especially Scotland, and infiltrated the guilds. It is claimed in some systems of Freemasonry, that modern Masonry is the child of the Templars, but this is hard to evidence. There are even claims that Rosicrucianism (4)has had its influence on Masonry.

Rather more convincing is the idea that the Kabbalah, the mystic element in Judaism, has had a considerable influence on early Freemasonry. This strand in Judaism has been an ongoing matter for 2000 years; just as there is the mystic aspect in Islam, the Sufis, and also various Christian mystics, so too, Judaism has this aspect. The theorisings of the Kabbalah state that creation is divided into four worlds; the divine, the intellectual, the emotional, and the instinctive.(5) The Light of God emanates from ten different spheres (Sephiroth), and is channelled down a system of 22 paths (Nativoth).(6) This means that God's light, which is unbearable for humans, is diluted down to the tenth sphere. Each of the four worlds descends from the one above, and each has a tree of life of its own. To reach a certain level of awareness, one must master the level beneath it. Animals are stuck at the first level, the instinctive. Humans can rise up, using speech, to the emotional level, whereupon some get stuck at that. Others however can rise up to the intellectual level, and perhaps even further. The implication in this is that one can become 'divine' in some sense, and be reborn into the divine and light. This is the route to perfection of the soul, a process we see in Freemasonry with its three degrees. The first degree is the ethical, the second is the intellectual and the third is death and rebirth into spiritual awareness. At what point this influence came about is not clear, but it must predate the 17th century. We can see that this has certain affinities with aspects of Gnosticism.(7)

With the Kabbalistic idea of 10 Sephiroth and 22 Nativoth, that gives us 32 elements; the same number of degrees appears in the Scottish rite. With the four worlds, we can compare it with bodies represented in the York rite. Although there is a certain element of syncretism in Freemasonry, it is rather more obvious that Judaism plays an important part in their thinking and procedures. The Masons have attached themselves to the Davidic covenant, which relates to the status of David, Solomon and the Temple, with the additional element of Kabbalistic thinking. One could almost call Freemasonry another permutation on Judaism, but one must recall that many of them are ardent Christians at the same time, and that a part of their rituals involves bringing in the King James Version of the Bible. The sacred book may vary from one lodge to another.

It is with the symbolisms within Freemasonry that we come the closest to mythology in the true sense. Mythology is full of important symbolisms which connect with the human soul. However, Masonic symbolism has a number of features which are independent of normal mythological symbolism; this is not to say that they have a completely different pattern of thought, but many aspects of it are different.

At one's initiation, one is walked round the lodge; this is symbolic of the sun's path through the sky. If this reminds us of Egyptian mythology,(8) that might be fair, but the masons may not have thought of that at the start. Then one comes to the altar, upon which there is the Bible, or if one is from another religion, a copy of its sacred scriptures. Also there is a square and compass. The square stands for honesty, truth and morality; this has worked its way into English phraseology with such remarks as 'square dealing' and 'fair and square'. The compass represents skill, knowledge and restraint, and the exclusion of harmful things. These are conjoined with a capital 'G' standing for God, or geometry. This is symbolic of God's will in the creation of heaven and earth. Also the three degrees of body, mind and soul are symbolised.

There is the Apron, which they all wear. This is derived from the mediaeval stone masons. It stands for innocence, virtue, rebirth, the builder's craft, purification, sacrifice, energy and growth. Also this connects Freemasonry to the ancient mystery cults of Greece and Egypt, especially to Mithraism.(9) One could see the apron as a reminder of the embarrassment in the Garden of Eden.

The apron is a simple rectangle surmounted by a triangle. This is symbolic of four plus three, which makes seven. These are number values that recur many times in Masonry.

The new apprentice is shown the set of working tools. One of them is the 24 inch gauge in three folding sections, representing the division of the day into three portions of eight hours; one for work, one for worship, charity and self-perfection, and one for sleep. The other tool is the gavel, a stone hammer with which rough edges can be chipped off; thus the apprentice can smooth off his own rough edges and remove vices. The first tool is passive and the second active.

The apprentice is then placed in the north east corner of the Lodge, which is where the cornerstone is laid; he then becomes his own cornerstone. In that corner, he is approaching the light but has not fully achieved it. The Worshipful Master sits in the east, having found the light, and is the source of wisdom and instruction.

There are three supporting pillars in the Lodge, wisdom, strength and beauty. They also represent three main officers; the Worshipful Master, the Senior Warden, and the Junior Warden. Also, the symbolism is compounded as there are three Grand Masters; Solomon with his Wisdom, King Hiram as a builder, and Hiram Abiff the skilled artificer. This also gives us the three immovable Jewels; the square which represents morality, the level which points to equality, and the plumb line which indicates goodness.

There are also three movable jewels; the rough ashlar (building stone) which represents the raw apprentice or recruit; the smooth ashlar which means fellowcraft; and the trestleboard which applies to the master mason who is building the Temple in his own soul. Thus we see the relevance of calling the movement 'freemasonry'.

But the symbolism goes further. On the floor of the Lodge, is a mosaic pavement which is symbolic of the world with good and evil interwoven. This is possibly the only reference to the question of Theodicy in Masonic thinking. There is the indented tassel, usually seen on the Apron. This indicates the blessings and comforts in life, which make this world bearable, but we have to earn them. There is also a blazing star, normally a pentangle, with an eye or a capital G in the centre. This speaks of God's providence. The star has nothing to do with witchcraft, and can sometimes be the Star of David, with six points.

The two bronze pillars at the entrance to Solomon's Temple, are depicted in all Lodges; they imply power channelled into effective action. Power, if not brought under control becomes anarchic and destructive. If control has no power, it becomes ineffective. The two need to interact with one another for life to proceed. The Pillar of Cloud and the Pillar of Fire as seen at the Exodus,(10) are also implied. This does not exhaust the possible interpretations of the two pillars. Often they are surmounted by globes and these represent the two worlds of heaven and earth.

In some Masonic systems,(11) there is also a winding staircase at the Lodge; this gives access to higher levels and alcoves. It is used in inducting candidates to higher levels, and the implication is that one is getting nearer to God, or the light. At this point it is worth referring to Jacob's Ladder. The first three steps indicate the three degrees and almost everything else that involves three, even faith, hope and charity. The second set of steps, five in number, correspond to the five orders of classical architecture. The Doric, Ionic and Corinthian were the original Greek ones, added to which were the Roman ones, the Composite (like Corinthian) and the Tuscan, a simpler version of Doric. Five also indicates the five senses; sight, sound, touch, taste and smell. Five also reminds us of the pentangle.

The third group of steps, seven in number, indicates the seven liberal classical arts and sciences; grammar, rhetoric, logic, arithmetic, geometry, music and astronomy. Geometry is particularly prized by the masons, as an essential element in architecture.

At the first degree initiation, there are three tenets; brotherly love, relief and truth; also the four cardinal virtues; temperance, fortitude, prudence and justice. The candidate is presented with chalk, charcoal and clay. The chalk symbolises freedom; it leaves a mark on any surface. The charcoal stands for fervency; it can produce enough heat to melt any metal. The clay stands for zeal; clay of the earth supports us with food and reminds us of our mortality.

At the second degree initiation in the middle chamber, one is given corn, wine and oil, which were the wages given by Solomon to Hiram. The corn means plenty and giving of service. The wine means refreshment, and health, ease, peace and blessing. The oil means joy, happiness and glad times. The three jewels given are an attentive ear, an instructive tongue and a faithful breast.

At the third degree one becomes a Master Mason. The candidate is made to symbolise Hiram Abiff. He lies on the floor and swords are pointed at him. He is 'slain' and then comes back to life; this recalls the ancient mythology of sacral kingship. He is symbolically put in the grave and then raised again. He is presented with skirret, a pencil and a compass. The skirret is a pin used for making straight lines, the straight line of good conduct. The pencil is for giving instructions to the builders. The compass is for calculating limits, proportions and arcs. A trowel too is offered, for cementing ties and spreading brotherly love.

Further symbols used are as follows; an incense pot, for purity of heart and sacrifice. A beehive, for hard work and co-operation. A sword, for being cautious and divine justice. The symbol belongs to the Tyler, who is the guard who stands outside the lodge to ward off intruders. An ark and an anchor, means a life well-lived, also Noah's Ark and also virtue which brings safety. An hour glass and scythe remind us of the shortness of time and life.

A maul stands for accidents and diseases. A spade is for digging a grave, and a coffin is one's last resting place. An acacia sprig reminds us that mortality is only for the body; the soul lives on.

It will be seen from this that the symbolisms are quite heavy and often multi-faceted, and to some extent artificial. One important symbolism seen in every world mythology, the snake, seems to be missing from this all-inclusive list. The snake is important because it symbolises life and death; it is a paradoxical figure. Other symbols which are present but somewhat underemphasised would be the sword which indicates truth, justice the righting of all wrongs; also the tree which implies the connection between three worlds, heaven, earth and hell. While the masons are quite happy with earth and heaven, hell seems not to receive a mention. Does this mean that they believe there is no hell? If this is so, it would make it a very modern system of thought.

Compared with other mythologies and symbol-systems, Freemasonry appears rather contrived and overdone. It is however an interesting example of how a historical situation has become the basis of an entire theology which is not quite the same as the Judaeo-Christian system. It would be true that the Jews particularly value great builders; Solomon, Nehemiah and Herod the Great, but this is not spun into an entire ritual and ethical basis for life.

Another important element in mythology is the factor of life and death, and resurrection. The assumption in the human mind is that life is precious and indestructible. It ought not to be the end when death occurs. Some would say that this is wishful thinking, but there is much evidence to indicate the survival of the soul beyond death. Many of the symbolisms which occur in virtually every mythology the world over, relate to the wonder and eternity of the soul. The snake is a case in point, for paradoxically it means life and death, the two factors in the one creature. Another way of symbolising this factor is the reference to gold and jewels. It is noticeable that there is not much mention of these in Freemasonry; diamonds, precious metals and the like are not really included. However, there are jewels mentioned, the movable and the immovable ones, but they are not gemstones in the accepted sense. They are materials and signs relevant to building.

The whole matter of Theodicy, why do we have to suffer, is present in Freemasonry but is not a particularly prominent issue. The main theological strand is about merit; to advance towards the Light and come nearer to God, is a simple matter of controlling one's conduct and acquiring virtue. The assumption in this is that the more virtuous one is the more one will be rewarded in this life and the next. While this would accord well with the thinking in the Mosaic Covenant, as hammered home in Deuteronomy 28, at the same time this does not always work out as simply as one would hope in real life. What about the person like Job, who was very virtuous, never did anything wrong, and yet it all went wrong for him? We can all think of someone like that, who did not get what he appeared to have merited. This is where the Mosaic Covenant, essentially the Old Testament, has its shortcomings. The Masons appear to have centred their thinking on Old Testament theology but have not really come to grips with the New Testament.

Symptomatic of this is the lack of mention of Jesus Christ in their system. It would be fair to say that they place much emphasis on the King James Bible in the Masonic ceremonies, but like every system of theology, sacral or secular, it is selective when dealing with the Bible. We all like to choose the bits that suit our thinking and ignore the bits that do not fit somehow. In fairness, there is mention of sacrifice, in the sense of one giving of oneself and caring for others. That caring is not confined to fellow masons, but in theory to all people. That is very much in line with New Testament thinking. However, we do not seem to see the motivation for it coming from the ministry of Jesus Christ, whose entire life and death was a complete sacrifice.

Another interesting aspect of Freemasonry is the lack of emphasis on the factor of Evil. It would be fair to say that the symbolism of the black and white squares on the floor indicate the interplay of good and evil in life, but beyond that there is no apprehension of the powers of evil. Satan and the Devil are never mentioned; a factor often seen in the Bible, particularly the New Testament. One could maintain that Masonry is on this issue a demythologised system of thought. How far back this goes in the history of their development, would be a good question, but it looks as though it predates the modern trend, instigated by Bultmann and others,(12) to demythologise just about everything in the Christian tradition.

From the point of view of equality, one would have to hand it to the Masons that they were far in advance of most other systems of thought. Originally, it was for the menfolk only, but that was only because it had not occurred to them that women might be interested. When it was realised, some centuries ago, women's lodges were inaugurated, and they now have their own ceremonies and costumes. On the racial question, there seems to be no problem, for in many countries people of different races or colours are able to become Masons.

This resume is intended to give a general impression of Freemasonry. It must be remembered that different Lodges in different countries have slightly different rituals and procedures. To become a Mason does not entail renouncing one's religion or philosophy; one can continue as a Christian, Muslim, Sikh etc. In that respect, the Masons offer a basis for unity and cooperation for humanity. The other organisation working on the same lines would be the Baha'is,(13) but they attach themselves to another version of mythology and set of symbolisms.

Footnotes for chapter 16

1. I Kings 6 to 8; the passage goes into great detail about the construction and decoration of the Temple.

2. Enoch, one of the forbears of Noah, is recorded as 'assumed'; the Book of Enoch was written with this in mind. There is no mention of Enoch being involved with the building of the Temple.

3. The Royal Society, a group of scientists who were keen to advance scientific progress in the 17th century.

4. Rosicrucianism; a 17th Century group of mystics who studied the metaphysical laws governing the Universe. It is related to Hermeticism, Jewish mysticism and Christian Gnosticism.

5. This seems to predate Freud and Jung with their analysis of human nature; the difference is that they tried to omit the divine element.

6. See chapter 26 on symbolism and the Kabbalah.

7. Gnosticism, see chapter 5, was also a system of spiritual promotion.

8. The Egyptians believed that the Sun rode across the sky in a boat, went under the earth and went round endlessly. See The Egyptian Book of the Dead, in The Theology of Truth.

9. Mithraism was a cult much favoured by the Roman army. It involved wearing aprons; this goes to show that there is nothing new in this life!

10. Exodus 14:19.

11. Jacob's Ladder; this was a vision of angels that Jacob saw. Genesis 28:12.

12. The tendency to demythologise; Bultmann and others, see chapter 24.

13. For information on the Baha'is see my chapter on the Kitab-i-Aqdas, in the Theology of Truth.

17

Erich Von Daniken. The Chariots of the Gods

It would be a mistake to think of mythology as a thing of the past. We have plenty of modern mythologies filling the gaps left by the demise of ancient mythologies. One of these ideas is the notion that there are intelligent beings somewhere else in the universe; this is in itself is not a new idea as we can see it in the thoughts of Emanuel Swedenborg (see chapter 25). The new element is that it is imagined that people from other planets have visited this world at various times in the past. One could see this idea as a substitute for the way in which belief in Almighty God has been fading in the western world. Something has to take its place.

One notable example of this modernistic mythology is **The Chariots of the Gods,** by Erich Von Daniken. When it first appeared in 1969, it caused quite a stir and it is quite likely that many people took it seriously. It went through various reprints. It is difficult to assess the impact of this book on the long term; it is now largely forgotten. Even so, some of its main claims appear to be still having a considerable impact on thinking today, and that includes the scientists. To read it now, it comes over as somewhat dated; also rather emotional and sentimental.

What are the main assumptions in this book and how are they worked out? Firstly he makes the grand assumption that people living in the remote past were all idiots. How often do we have a remark that dubs them all as savages or barbarians, which implies that they would not have the intelligence to produce anything clever. The idea that they could have achieved something cleverer than us simply does not occur to him.

The second assumption is that since there are millions of stars in the universe, each with its own solar system, there has to be not just one, but probably many other worlds in which there are intelligent beings. These beings are assumed to be a lot cleverer than us. We never seem to have the idea that they might be more stupid than us. We have seen in recent years, indications that there are 'exo-planets'.

The third assumption follows the line that there are many drawings, artefacts, effects and understandings of the world which could only have been inspired or produced by alien invaders who had superior knowledge and technology as compared with what we are assumed to have had in those days.

One of the most prominent effects of this line of thinking, is the present mania for seeking life on other planets. We have ruled out Venus as a possibility because of its very high temperatures. Mars is still in the frame; there is a frantic search for water on this planet, since water is the basis for any kind of life, as we know it. So far nothing conclusive has been found to support the idea of life on Mars. Beyond that, are the major planets which are thought not to be able to support life. Even so, Jupiter has satellites which if investigated, might become candidates. All this is evidence of the self-convincing wishful thinking of the present age. It may easily turn out to be a complete red herring. Even so, vast sums of money are being expended on this kind of research.

Taking the first assumption, namely that early mankind was all stupid and incapable of any bright ideas, this takes no account of several factors. Firstly, as we all know, there are such people as Einstein who are exceedingly clever. Whoever it was that devised the Antikithera mechanism must have been in that league; one thinks of Archimedes.(1) We know that a prodigy occurs sometimes, not often, but enough to alter people's thinking and procedures. On a lower level perhaps, there are people who just have an inspiration when they are experimenting with something, and a new idea or method is found. Why can there not have been such people in the ancient world? The person who devised the Pyramids must have been in that league. Whoever he was, he must have been much cleverer than anyone nowadays. As evidence of this, I can quote the example of a recent attempt at building a scale model replica pyramid; the experiment failed, even with all the modern gadgetry available. Do we really have to think in terms of 'gods' arriving from outer space to show us how to do these amazing things? After all, somebody had to have thought of these ideas at some time in the past and somewhere; how did these so-called 'gods' manage to think of it far, far away?

In fairness, Von Daniken provides all kinds of intriguing examples of inventions or artefacts from the ancient world, which are a puzzle to us. There is an iron pillar about 12 feet tall, in India. It does not rust. We have no idea of its age or how it was produced. It is strictly a 'one-off'. In the Baghdad museum is a clay jar with 'electrodes', which appears to be a kind of electric battery. Also there is an Assyrian crystal lens which has been finely ground; how could this have been achieved? Many more such examples could be found; they are beyond present-day explanation, as yet. But does it really have to involve clever beings arriving from outer space?

Even more challenging are the strange markings in the Nazca desert in Peru. These are accurately marked out stretching over many miles, and one can only really appreciate them by going aloft in a helicopter. No one has any idea of the purpose of these markings. Von Daniken thinks that it might be some sort of runway for a space ship to take off; many hundreds of years ago! For the pre-Incas, the purpose of these lines would have been quite obvious; that is because they were almost certainly assuming an entire list of different assumptions from us. The mistake we make is to superimpose our modern assumptions on to prehistoric ideas and artefacts, and then complain that it does not work. Is it possible to get inside the mind of these ancient peoples and reach a more moderate understanding of their ideas and methods?

One assumption which I bring to this discussion, is that ancient mankind were not stupid; in fact, some of them appear to be a lot more inventive than we are today, in proportion to the technological developments we have available. That is not to say they were all geniuses; there were idiots then just as there are idiots now. Going further, I am going to assume that there was no invasion from outer space, any more than there is nowadays, and that mankind, in close communion with the world of the spirit, developed all kinds of clever ideas, some of which have been lost over the centuries because of the stupidity of others.

One puzzling artefact cited by Von Daniken is the Piri Reis map found in the Topkapi Palace, Istanbul. We are not favoured with a date for this map, but it must predate the 17th century. What is extraordinary is that the map gives a very accurate outline of the continents, not just Africa and the Americas, but also Antarctica. Also, the relief features such as mountains are shown, and also the mountains beneath the ice shelf of Antarctica; these have only recently been plotted with modern gadgetry, since they have always been covered with snow. How could that have been done? Von Daniken thinks someone in a space ship looked down from outer space. Indeed, the way the projection is done, using Cairo as a 'pole', produces a very accurate impression which matches well with a photograph taken from Apollo 8.(2)

Much of Von Daniken's argument relies on curious cave drawings found in various parts of the world. From Rhodesia is found a reclining figure appearing to be clad in chainmail and wearing a curious headgear. This is thought to be an astronaut receiving supplies. From South Africa there is a drawing of a figure looking remarkably modern with shorts, garters, gloves but carrying a bow and arrow, and sporting a white beard. Von Daniken is surprised by this, assuming that primitive mankind all went about naked. There are various figures with unusual headdresses and wearing suits of some kind. Val Camonica in Northern Italy, Navoy, Fergana in Uzbekistan, and Tassili in the Sahara are all examples. The last one strongly resembles one of our astronauts in his space-suit and helmet. Again, we see the tendency to interpret these things in terms of our own experiences and assumptions. The artists who drew these things may have been having completely different thoughts.

One way to approach these matters is to take the symbolism route. As we have seen so far with mythology, symbolism plays a very important part in early man's thinking (and still does today). The so-called headdresses may be an early attempt at a halo; in other words the figures are intended to be gods. This could tie in with the fact that they appear to be naked, a feature seen in Greek mythology. There is one scene (from Navoy) where the halo is on top of some sort of contraption supported by men and figures who appear to be bringing offerings. In other words, it is a sacrificial scene, which is perhaps less reliant on symbolism and more inclined to reality. But the halo effect may indicate the presence of deity. The figure from Tassili, resembling a space man has curious markings on his head and only one eye. Again this may portray some kind of symbolism which is lost on us. Odin, the chief Norse god, and Math, one of the Celtic gods, only had one eye; that probably conveyed the idea that he could concentrate his gaze on people and not be sidetracked. Clearly, there were various kinds of symbolism at work in various parts of the world, which worked in with the mythology of early mankind, much of which is lost on us nowadays. There is no need to explain it all as space invaders.

Another approach is as follows. We all know that shamanism was a strong feature in early times (and still is in some parts of the world). Shamans were capable of going into trances and some were, and still are genuinely psychic. What would be to stop them seeing into the future? There is also the phenomenon of Nostradamus, a prophet of the 16th century, who was able to see four or five hundred years into the future and describe 20th century features such as submarines, aeroplanes and actually the names of important people. This is a possible explanation for the drawing from South Africa which shows the archer in remarkably modern attire. How he is supposed to be a space invader is a mystery! Again, modern preconceptions do not readily tally with ancient artistry. After all, they could have been just as keen to do 'modern art' as some of us nowadays.

Another factor raised by Von Daniken is the shaping and transport of massive stone blocks in ancient pre-history. One such example is the Gate of the Sun at Tiahuanaco,(3) which is carved out of one massive ten ton block. It has a flying god and 48 mysterious figures, and there is a legend about a golden space ship coming from the stars. Again, ancient symbolism and mythology, which is lost on us, may underlie this feature. How a ten ton block could be shifted would be a problem for visiting astronauts as well us humans. Much experimentation has been tried to explain how large stones could have been moved. Much of this centres on Stonehenge, for some of the stones must have come from the Prescelly (4)Mountains in South Wales. One can see that wooden rollers would have presented quite a problem, but someone has suggested that stone 'ball-bearings' in a trough could have been used. It would be fair to say that some of the masonry in Sacsayhuaman (central America) displays an amazing accuracy in the jointing, but then it would have been just as difficult for space men to accomplish as for humans. What early man had was plenty of time and patience to accomplish these feats; something that we nowadays do not really understand.

Another feature Von Daniken uses is the rock vitrification found in various parts of the world. It would require very high temperatures to give this effect; since we have exploded atom bombs which have given the same result, he concludes that someone in the remote past had an atom bomb and since primitive man could not possibly have had one, it has to be space invaders. However, since this book has been published we have seen for ourselves how this effect can occur. A meteorite, not necessarily very large, coming into the earth's atmosphere, creates massive heat and can explode before actually hitting the ground, but causes devastation over a wide area. This is now termed an 'air burst'. The incident of Sodom and Gomorrah in the Bible is now seen as a good example of such a phenomenon. Fortunately for Lot and his family, someone who was psychic, termed here as an angel, warned him in time to escape. Rock vitrification does not necessarily have anything to do with ancient space ships taking off!

Another issue which Von Daniken raises is the UFO's. He admits that he does not know what they are (page 142). He cites many examples of people seeing these things; reliable witnesses and observers such as policemen are known to have recorded these incidents. Also there have been all kinds of spurious sightings which can easily be explained away as some kind of optical illusion. However, it would seem that during the Second World War, British bomber crews became aware of something strange encountering their aircraft.(5) Von Daniken does not mention this matter. The conclusion could fairly be drawn that the Nazi's who were full of clever scientific ideas, had developed some kind of 'flying saucer'. It is quite possible that the idea went to America, along with Werner Von Braun and many other important scientists and has been the subject of experimentation ever since. Obviously such a technology would have to be kept top secret.

Much air space and speculation has gone into this issue of UFO's and some people are convinced that it is aliens interfering with our world. Some people are quite hysterical about it. However, I am of the opinion that there are genuinely such things but they do not have to be invasions from outer space. They could be some kind of futuristic technology which is being tested but kept as highly top secret for obvious reasons. One can remark that as far as we know, the gentlemen in the artificial satellites which circle the earth do not seem to have noticed any such things coming in from outer space. I suggest that UFO's are terrestrial. One might also remark that these sightings are very often in proximity to military bases of one kind or another. Whether or not they are any sort of threat to humanity is another question, but that has nothing to do with outer space.

What we can say is that all this excitement is excellent fodder for modern mythology. In common with many of our ancient myths, we start with an historical event or fact, or even a legend, and then it becomes decorated with speculation and augmented excitement. Eventually we see a full blown myth with 'gods' or 'devils' or strange creatures. But beneath it all is the factor of symbolism. What does all this convey to the mind of modern western mankind? It conveys the idea that there are intelligent beings which are superior to humanity. Just as the ancients had any amount of gods to worship, so now people are in fear of modern 'gods'. It is the same paganistic impulse in human nature displaying itself as in times gone by, even if it is decorated with technological and scientific invention. The need for some form of god is still there in human nature. It is interesting that since, in the modern world, the awareness of God is somewhat diminished (although not for everyone), there is instead the urge to invent 'gods' far away in the space, living on distant planets. Human nature may have changed a little, but not too much really.

Flying Saucers and UFO's

Much excitement and elaborate speculation has been occasioned by the modern feature of strange objects seen in the skies. This has clearly given much stimulation to the notion that there must be other people living on other planets and that they have the idea of visiting us in their flying machines. My view is that this is a lot of hysteria and has nothing to do with outer space. The lights seen in the skies may be real enough, but they are caused by something other than spacemen.

This puzzling matter goes back to 1943 when British bomber pilots began to see strange lights in the night sky over Germany. These seemed to be hovering silently in mid-air, but nothing showed up on the radar screens. The lights would vanish and reappear, and sometimes follow the aircraft. A pilot called Lumsden seems to have been the first person to see them, but many others began to see them also. When the Americans saw them, they dubbed them as 'foo-fighters'. It was investigated under the assumption that this was 'autokinesis', but that did not really answer the question. (6)

It was suspected that the Nazis had some kind of wonder weapon. This would not be out of the question. We know that they had some amazing technological ideas, including the development of the atom bomb, and if they had been given more time, they might still have won the war at the last minute.

The whole matter now becomes a little more certain. As the Allies invaded Germany, they discovered in the Wroclaw area a place called Riesa where some kind of anti-gravity propulsion vehicle had been in the process of development. It was called 'The Bell' or 'Die Gloche', which could spin round in contrary motion and do vertical take-off. This was the 'flying saucer'. British pilots had seen some sort of flying thing in daylight. How this relates to moving lights in the night sky is not clear. The Nazis gave it the name 'Feuerball' which means 'Fireball.'

However, as Germany collapsed, the Americans had a scheme called 'Operation Paper Clip' which involved rounding up all the German scientists, including Werner Von Braun and Victor Schauberger, and taking them back to America. One known project was the Avrocat 115, which was an attempt at making a flying saucer. It gave only a poor performance. Apart from space rockets, we do not know what else was developed in secret in America. Obviously the whole matter is top secret. It is not unreasonable to say that UFO's are some kind of secret facility which is a spin-off from the Second World War.

In addition to this there was an aircraft factory at Gotha, which was attempting to produce advanced stealth aircraft. Also vertical take-off machines were being designed. The Nazi technicians had a thing called the flying triangle, termed HO229, and this again was under Victor Schauberger. If the Germans had been allowed more time, they might have gained the advantage and turned the tide of war in their favour.

In July 1947, there was a curious incident at Roswell, New Mexico. Some kind of flying object, dubbed as a 'flying saucer' crash landed on a ranch near a military base. The metal debris was very strange and was retrieved quickly by the military. The whole incident received a clamp down and cover up . Only thirty years later has information begun to emerge from records being released, but we are not being told the full story. This is for obvious reasons; if the Americans have managed to develop some kind of advanced weaponry, via the Nazi scientists, it would be foolish to inform the entire world of what they had available.

Of course, Hollywood sprang on the idea of flying saucers and thrilled us all with science fiction derived from these UFO incidents.

The latest twist in this kind of mentality is the supposed discovery of exo-planets orbiting far away stars. Some people are absolutely convinced that some kind of life has got to be existing many millions of light years away. But the truth of the matter is, that no one has ever actually seen even one of these alleged exo-planets. We only infer their existence from the way the stars appear to lose brightness and then regain it, which would suggest that something sails across to cause this effect. No one seems to suggest that something else could cause this effect.

The whole matter of other life out in space is the modern mania and has become one aspect of the mythology of the modern world. Like almost all the other mythologies, it begins with some kind of historical incident or legend and then gets exaggerated and augmented into a full scale self-frightening matter. All this indicates is that we have to have some kind of hysteria in life, to make life liveable.

Signals from outer space?

Complementary to UFO's is the issue of radio messages from outer space. There have been various attempts at sending out radio signals into outer space in the hopes that someone out there will make a response. This idea rests on three assumptions; firstly that there is someone out there with some sort of intelligence who might be inclined to respond, and secondly, that if there were someone out there, they would be able to decipher whatever message had been sent in our language, assumedly American slang! Thirdly, if the recipient were many light years away, the message would take several years to arrive and then the same time span to be responded to; we might still be waiting for a reply for many years to come. As yet, no reply has been received, except to say a lot of static; have the scientists wondered if the static is some sort of answer? We are still left with the 'Great Silence' as it is termed.

In recent years, something exciting has occurred. It is termed the 'Lorimer Burst'. A very bright signal, never seen before, appeared to have come from a very great distance, and it was not produced by any normal phenomenon. This puzzled everyone, and was thought to be a signal from another civilization far away. Some years later, (2013) it was noted that there were six detections of such radio bursts, regularly spaced but coming from different places. Again, the source was unknown. It was very anticlimactic when it was realised that the use of the microwave in the observatory office seemed to correlate quite well with these traces on the screens! When this factor had been allowed for, there were still some questions to be answered. It is now thought that such radio bursts might be the result of neutron stars colliding with each other. What this indicates is that all these amazing observations may be the result of terrestrial interference, and have nothing to do with outer space. Just as mankind at one time projected its own failings into the skies and imagined all kinds of gods with moral defects, so too now, we are projecting our own technical clumsiness into the skies and calling it little green men from far away!

In spite of this, there is a group called the Order of the Dolphin, twelve 'experts' who are convinced that there is life somewhere out in space. Vast amounts of money are expended on this kind of research. There is a thing called the 'Drake Equation', a very complicated mathematical probability expression, which tells us that there are ten thousand detectable civilizations out there. It is notable that this equation uses all kinds of suppositions, guesses and wishful thinking, and can not be held up as evidence of anything, except the wild imagination of a certain Mr.Drake.

As if all this modern mythology were not enough, the 'scientists' are also embarking on their own version of eschatology. The main assumption is that the more advanced a civilization becomes, the more energy it will need. There will come a time when this earth's resources will be unable to sustain the energy needs for our so-called advanced life. Putting it crudely, we shall not able to produce enough electricity to support all the clever gadgets we have invented. If this happens, it might bring about the end of civilization and indeed the end of time.

Somewhere we have read something similar. Karl Marx thought that Capitalism would develop too far and bring about its own collapse. Is that so different from the previous thought?

E.T. The Extraterrestrial

Relevant to Von Daniken's thoughts is the feature film E.T. which was all the rage in the 1980's. The following remarks are derived from William Kotzwinkle's novel, E.T., which is based on the film produced by Steven Speilberg. It is quite possible that the inspiration for the film was derived from The Chariots of the Gods; it is certainly the same motif and speculation.

In brief, a space ship comes to land in a forest in America, and aliens come out to do some research, but avoiding any contact with humans. One such 'scientist' who is a biologist trying to take samples of plant life, gets left behind. This is because the American police have closed in on the spaceship and there is a mad scramble to take off before being apprehended. A little boy called Elliot finds E.T. and takes him home, hiding him in the closet.

It is interesting that the plot assumes that there are such creatures far away in outer space; many people, we suspect, would take that as literally true. As yet, this is all the stuff of imagination and wishful thinking. Other assumptions are often referred to or assumed. The effect of earth's gravity on E.T. is a matter of concern. Since it is different from his home planet, it will in time have a damaging effect on his physique. Another assumption is that he can eat and drink earth comestibles without any undue harm to his constitution. Something as mildly alcoholic as beer renders him seriously inebriated. There is no mention of any sort of toilet routine or evacuation. Breathing is not really explained. He can hold his head under water for a long time and can lie inert appearing to be dead. But he does inhale and this would assume that his home atmosphere is more or less the same as that of earth. He is termed a 'monster' and so ugly that one might find his appearance repulsive. He has a pot-belly, duck-shaped feet, squat face and elongated fingers with which he can do all kinds of things like Harry Potter's magic wand.

Not surprisingly the children go to great lengths to keep E.T. out of sight of adults. He is hidden in Elliot's closet most of the time, only to emerge when Mary , the mother, is out. There is an interesting contrast here between the American-earthling family and E.T. with his family ties in the sky. Mary is divorced and trying to raise three children. They are plainly beyond her control and behave like hooligans; she is verging on a nervous breakdown. Her only hope is to find another husband and thus stabilise the situation, but this never happens. E.T. would like to take on this role but being realistic this would never work. In contrast, E.T. is from a highly developed culture which is technically well in advance of anything found on earth. He has an intelligence and sensitivity well in advance of humans, but does not appear to be scornful of them. It is interesting that the children relate well to E.T. Elliot comes to love him and can hardly bear to part with him at the end. Gertie, who is under school age, seems to relate best to him, and she is the one who introduces him to her Spell Check and thus teaches him to speak English. Harvey, the dog, probably relates the best to E.T.; the dog instinctively tries to conceal E.T. from the adult world. There is almost certainly a symbolic message in this, that youth and innocence relate more readily to something completely new and alien.

The contrast is augmented by the frantic machinations of the American authorities. They are aware of the visit of the spaceship and that one of its occupants is stranded and in hiding. They bring in all kinds of 'experts' with an immense warehouse full of gadgetry with the intention of analysing this alien being. There is the contrast between the detector van which is trying to gather evidence of E.T.'s whereabouts, and the Heath Robinson contraption that E.T. devises for attracting his space ship back again, in order to be rescued. When finally, E.T. is cornered and 'arrested', he is smothered with experts trying to probe into his workings. They do not manage to understand much, because he is fundamentally different from humanity. The irony is that Elliot understands him but the scientists do not. There must be a lesson in this, somewhere.

One important undercurrent in this story is the assumption of Evolution. Although not much play is made of this, the word occasionally breaks the surface, but it is not enlarged upon. The insinuation from this is that E.T.'s culture is a much higher version of evolutionary development than ours. This is an assumption that runs through many, if not all, science fiction productions. We never seem to hear of a culture that is a long way behind us.

In a way, E.T. reminds us of Frankenstein's monster,(7) who is so frightful that he has to keep out of sight. He does not kill anyone, except to say that Elliot comes close to collapse as he takes on some of E.T.'s traits. In this way, he reminds us of Dracula, a monster that actually recruits innocent people into his mode of living. But E.T. never embarks on bloodsucking. He is peaceful, loving and has a healing influence on anyone with a bleeding finger.

The mythological aspects of it are present, although they are not quite as obvious as in some modern mythologies. 'A beam of golden light shot through inner space,' (Page 231) is a rare mention of gold. Such elements as gold, jewels, crystal, and mirrors are played down, and the world tree never appears at all even if he is a botanist! However, strangely, the plants in the garden are growing at a much faster rate, much to Mary's puzzlement. As far as snakes are concerned, there are none, except to say that E.T.'s fingers are elongated and snaky. Questions concerning life itself are abundant. E.T. has a heart that glows but does not behave like a human one. This raises the question of how he keeps alive; it is clearly a different version of life. We understand that he is millions of years old which means that life on his planet must take a very different permutation. When it comes to E.T. dying, this comes as something of a surprise, even if the doctors are fumbling around to keep him alive. Then comes the expected resolution of this; E.T. comes back to life as Elliot and the other children exert their numinous power. This means that the motif of resurrection is included as it is in so many other mythologies. It implies that life is everlasting; it is precious and ought to last for ever.

Like all good modern mythologies, scientific or science fiction, it all swings round to eschatology. This comes mainly in the closing parts of the book. It is feared that E.T.'s death will bring about the destruction of the world.

'Others say the Earth was doomed and could not save itself, that the saving force had come from a sister planet, to lend a hand in pacifying the dragon of the nuclear force.' (Page 231).

However it never comes to the end of the world, since E.T. is safely restored to his spaceship.

The book is characterised by a strong sense of poking humour worked in with the banalities of American life and sloppy sentence construction. There is also that sense of despair running through the plot, as we wonder whether this dysfunctional family will ever find some kind of resolution.

More serious however, is the question of E.T.'s significance in relation to the human race. He is called all kinds of titles, for instance, 'the ancient voyager', and occasionally the word 'god' breaks the surface. 'The god had to go'. How literally we need to take this is a matter for discussion. E.T. may be intended to be symbolic of God, and coming to earth to be with the children reminds us of Jesus. But he was frightened and lonely, which means that the equation is not a complete one. He can hardly be taken literally as God, even if his fingers can do all kinds of inventive deeds, including restoring people to health.

But the message from all this is unmistakable. There is great power involved, numinous power and restorative power. But even more importantly, there is love. Elliot and E.T. love each other and parting is a difficult matter. E.T. points to his heart and says, 'I'll be right here.' (page 246). How appropriate! So love is the fundamental quality which overrides all the scientific clutter and fuss. That is the message we can learn for today, that all our clever methods and futuristic speculations are as nothing when we consider love as the vital building block of life.

Footnotes for chapter 17

1. The Antikithera mechanism was recently found in a wreck of a Greek ship off the coast of Greece. It is dated as something like the first to second century BC. It is a series of brass sheets with markings on, from which eclipses and other predictions can be made. Everyone has been stunned by the kills in making it and the astronomical knowledge involved.

2. Apollo 8; in the period 1959 to 1972, fourteen Apollo missions have probed the Moon and taken pictures of the Earth from outer space.

3. Tiahuanaco; a gateway made of enormous stone blocks in west Bolivia, near lake Titicaca.

4. The Prescelly Mountains in South Wales. Rock cut from them was used in the construction of Stonehenge. No one has yet convincingly explained how the stones weighing several tons, could have been transported all that way.

5. UFO's; it is now being claimed that such strange lights in the sky have been observed since the 1890's.

6. Autokenesis. The effect when a small stationary point of light in a dark featureless environment appears to move.

7. Frankenstein's monster and also Dracula; see chapter 22.

18

The mythology of Economics

The science of Economics is a particularly modern discipline and on the face
of it, would seem to have nothing to do with mythology, whether ancient
or modern. However, there is a substratum to it which does connect it to
economics in more than one way. Doubtless I shall be condemned as the
worst kind of heretic by the economists, but I maintain that economics is just
as dependent on mythological assumptions as any other of the 'sciences' of
modern times.

Essentially, Economics is about the distribution of goods, services, raw
materials, labour, transport and money. The inescapable fact is that this planet
has abundant resources for the purpose of earning a living, but the problem is
that these resources are not evenly distributed from one country to another.
There are some countries which have very little in the way of mineral wealth,
for instance, Japan, and others, like Canada, that have an abundance. Similarly
the distribution of population is not even; some countries such as Namibia
are sparsely populated and others like the Netherlands, heavily populated.
Also, the quality of the soil varies significantly from one part of the world to
another. If every country had the same endowment in resources and the same
spread of population, and nobody lacked anything or had a superfluity of
anything, there would be no need for economics or international trade. The
climatic and geological reasons for this we need not delve into; they are just
facts to be grappled with. But the result has always been discontent between
nations and smaller areas, envy, land-grabbing and violence.

The underlying assumption in Economics, is that there ought to be
equality and fairness in the distribution of resources. This is where a certain
aspect of mythology enters the picture and conditions the whole matter.

Everlasting justice and fair play, which is usually symbolised by the image of a sword, and also the concept of 'Nemesis' are an ongoing assumption in the human instinct. If there is some kind of imbalance, unfairness, onesidedness, the instinct is to redress it somehow. If one were to imagine that economics tends to favour a Socialist frame of mind, in the sense of international co-operation and fair allocation of wealth, that would be very largely a fair assumption. However, economists of various kinds are to be found attaching themselves to other 'isms', not least Capitalism. Economics largely divides itself into two main camps of opinion; the Keynsian idea and the Monetarist idea. Each of these have been tried in modern times but with mixed results. At the moment, no one really knows how to solve the inequality problem, whether it be within one's own nation or internationally. Perhaps the world is waiting for a third theory. The details of these two theories need not be delved into here, but both of them assume that government intervention or interference has to happen to stabilise the situation.

The instability of the situation can be summed up in the 'boom and bust' situation which is an ongoing problem in economics. There are times when all is well, with no unemployment, hardly any poverty, steadily increasing prosperity, stable value of money; this we call boom times. But then it falls back into recession and there are serious social problems. An attempt has been made to iron out this kind of problem; the Communists in Russia attempted to remove the boom and bust situation, but this barely succeeded, and the result was a sterile economy which was a long way behind the rest of the world in terms of technological advances.

The fact is that no one so far has found the ideal economic system, still less the ideal political system. It would seem, so far, that a delicate balance between personal freedom and government control is the best we can do, but this situation always remains fragile.

This is where another mythological element enters the picture, that of governmental control. Economists of all shades of opinion would accept that governmental interference of some kind cannot be avoided if we hope to moderate the extremes of failure or success in prosperity. Even if Economics is a relatively recent discipline, the rudiments of it have been the substratum of civilization since very early times. I refer to the phenomenon known as Sacral Kingship.

Sacral Kingship means in effect that one's ruler, whether it be king, queen, emperor or whatever form the top of the pyramid happens to be, is equated with or synonymous with one's god. The most extreme form of this was seen in ancient Egypt, where the Pharaoh was actually accepted as god. His life and religious activities were essential for the rising of the Nile for its annual inundation which ensured prosperity for another year. This kind of thinking has been noted in so many different parts of the world, in which the fertility of the land and the success of the harvest is dependent on the correct ritual procedures of the monarch. The assumption is that the top man is divine; not necessarily the top god, but near enough to the top god to influence the weather, the climate and any other factors influencing the food supply. One may say that this is a lot of nonsense, to say that one's ruler must take the blame for a failed harvest; it would be fair to say that this is some kind of delusion. But that is what people in the ancient world took very seriously. Just in case one were to imagine that this strand of thought had faded out in recent times, consider this. Just before the French Revolution, there was a series of failed harvests in France; King Louis was blamed and that was a major contributory factor for the explosion of 1789.(1) Human nature may have altered a little, but not completely.

In today's world, the monarch, if there is one, is not quite so acutely blamed when things go wrong. However, the government almost certainly is. When there is a downturn in trade or a recession, the first target for blame is almost always the government. The government is expected to do some clever manoeuvring with taxes and incentives and solve the problem. Sometimes it works, more by luck than judgement. The truth of the matter is that the idea that the government can solve these economic problems is just as much a piece of self-delusion as Sacral Kingship was.

What solutions did the ancients have for an economic downturn, such as the failure of the harvest? The answer was to sharpen one's sword, get the army together and attack another country where there was something to be stolen. To put it bluntly, international mugging! When it succeeded, the mugging was augmented into 'empire building', which very often took the form of an elaborate protection racket. How many empires arose and fell in the ancient world? Too many to count. This has been going on right up to the present day. The difference now is that aggression is right out of favour; it is politically wrong. We all know why; it is because the weaponry now is so fearsome that another world war could spell the end of civilization altogether.

In a world where thieving could be justified by claiming that one's god (one's king) was in favour of the idea, and whole populations could be turned into cheap labour or slavery, it is easy to see how one's economic problems could be solved. We saw a very clear example of this with the Third Reich; Germany set out to reduce the eastern European countries into colonies of cheap labour. But this was always a temporary expedient. The boom and bust configuration is always in the background; this applies to empires as well as economies. Empires rise and fall with a sickening regularity. The Third Reich, which was supposed to last 1000 years was cut short because of its hyper-aggressive attitude which threatened the whole world. If one were to think that not such extreme empires had faded out long before, as this was a peculiarly ancient pattern, we could recall that this was happening right into the 20th century. The British Empire as indeed the French Empire prevailed right into the middle of the 20th century, only to be overtaken by the American and Russian Empires. Admittedly, we do not see justified thieving on quite the same scale, and perhaps not the levels of human exploitation as was seen before. Even so, it is still not possible to pay everyone for all of the work done. There is still a certain amount of slave labour going on in various shapes and sizes across the world. In this country it is dubbed as 'volunteering', but the truth of the matter is that if the 'volunteers' decided to go on strike, all kinds of institutions would grind to a halt. It is an uncomfortable thought; slave labour or exploitative labour may be an inevitable factor in the world economy.

The illusion is that government can solve all these economic tensions and problems. The truth of the matter is that governments, rightly or wrongly, try to cope with the situation but with mixed success. The attitude and sense of responsibility varies greatly from one country to another. The answers which were employed in the ancient world can no longer be justified, even if one does picture one's head of state as some sort of divinity. It is instinctive in human nature to regard one's ruler as 'divine' in some respect; less so than it was before. This is the mythological aspect of it. The illusion, or rather, self-delusion, is that government can wave some kind of magic wand and resolve all our economic problems. The reality is that, just as the waves on the sea are beyond our control, so too are the waves of prosperity and shortage. The times of prosperity are a temptation to less wealthy countries to invade and steal; the times of shortage are a temptation to go and pillage someone else's country. The substratum of all this is conceit, greed and envy; all these are essentially wicked responses in human nature.

The modern attempt at coping with these problems across the world has been the inception of the United Nations since 1945, and the operation of UNICEF. This was a direct result of the horrors of World War 2. The importance of world peace was admitted by almost every nation; in addition, it was seen that an attack on world poverty and the interchange and sharing of resources was a firm basis for peace. Now we have international aid agencies. This policy has so far met with considerable success, but there is still much work to be done. We have a phenomenon called 'climate change' as our latest challenge. This means that some countries, largely in the so-called Third World, are facing devastating crop failures and food shortages. This is on a scale which may in the end overwhelm us all, even the highly prosperous countries. The challenge is to maintain world peace, and through trade and international aid, offset the worst aspects of boom and bust.

The importance of GOLD

There is another way in which economics connect with mythology; that is over the matter of gold. Gold has an extraordinary hold on the human mind; people will go all out to obtain it and hold on to it. This is surely an instinctive response which applies to all peoples of whatever nationality. It exerts a fascination on people, that other commodities do not, with perhaps the exception of silver. From the mythological point of view, the explanation is that gold is lustrous, durable, incorruptible, and has become a symbol of indestructible life, eternity; also it is associated with deity and royalty. The symbolism does not stop there; silver, by association, is also highly valued, even if it is usually reckoned as one tenth of the value of gold. Other metals such as mercury, and jewels and translucent stones are also seen as indicating everlasting life. Strangely, platinum,(2) which is rarer than gold, has never been seen in the same light. It is no surprise that great efforts have been made to turn base metals into gold; this is not just a mediaeval fad but has been going on since ancient times, and is not confined to the western world. Now that we have a better understanding of atomic theory, it ought to be theoretically possible to turn a base metal into gold, but the expense of the process would almost certainly render it uneconomic. It is still cheaper to mine it from natural sources. Every time there is a new deposit of gold discovered, it produces a gold-rush, or gold fever, and this almost always disturbs the value of money, causing inflation.

There is no need to go into too much detail about the history of gold, but we can trace it in mythology going back to the legend of Jason and the Golden Fleece. This is a good example of the lust for this precious metal. Other myths from round the world almost always work gold (and silver) into their framework, with the same basic assumptions about symbolism, namely that of deity and royalty.

Coming into historical areas, King Midas, who lived in Phrygia in about 750 BC, was granted a wish that whatever he touched would turn to gold. The literal outcome of this was that everything, including his daughter, turned to gold. Midas had to have the wish reversed; he was told to bathe in the river Pactolus. This explains why that river became a valuable source of alluvial gold which was exploited by the Phrygians and Lydians. How literally we need to take this story is a good question. But there are people who seem unable to fail at making a fortune; it is termed 'the Midas Touch', or more prosaically, it is called 'business acumen', which is a natural gift. This is a good example of a legend acquiring mythical additions and then extending into a 'just-so' kind of account.

This follows on into the beginnings of actual coinage in the age of King Croesus.(3) This occurred in the same area, namely Lydia, where alluvial deposits of electrum (or 'white-gold') were found. It was the Lydians, centred on Sardis, who devised a method for refining gold out and also for assessing its purity. They had a thing called a 'touchstone' which was actually made from a piece of local black stone. Then they had 24 needles with varying proportions of gold, silver, gold and copper, and all three metals. This is why to this day pure gold is termed as 24 carats. There was always a problem over the purity of the metal when offered for exchange. Actual coinage began with something called 'dumps'. These were bean-shaped lumps of electrum, but they varied in size and shape and had no values stamped on them. This is where the idea of state monopoly over money comes in. King Gyges, who came before Croesus, brought in a law by which all metallic 'money' was issued by the state. This is a procedure which has persisted to the present day and is assumed to be the normal thing by everyone, that is apart from forgers.

Actual coinage, as we know it, began with Alyattes, the father of Croesus, as the dumps were stamped, marked with values and became more like regular coins. But it was Croesus who minted pure silver and gold coins of regular size and weight with stampings to indicate their value. This is where the 'stater' enters the picture, with smaller denominations of thirds, sixths and twelfths. The twelfths became the father of the English shilling. This new idea quickly spread to other neighbouring countries, particularly Greece. The Greeks, who were artistic people, quickly realised that coins could be a work of art and also of propaganda. At the same time, gold and silver as the basis for jewellery and symbolism did not fade out. On the contrary, rendering them as coinage simply augmented their mythological and religious implications. It was the Greeks, under Philip of Macedonia who thought of putting a head on the coin; it was that of Zeus. Alexander used the head of Hercules, a face that strongly resembled Alexander himself. Now we see the propaganda element in coin design!

One would think that using precious metals for commercial transactions would avoid the problem of inflation. To some extent this would be true, but not entirely. There have been times when prices have remained stable for several centuries. But this can go wrong when the supply of gold and silver alters. The demand for coins constantly grew in the Roman era but the supply of metal was always lagging behind. There were various ways round this problem. One of them was to take a coin of say £1 and stamp £2 on it instead. This reminds us of the way in which postage stamps were overprinted during the serious inflation in Germany in the 1920's. Another trick was to reduce the gold content by adding something like copper, so that the gold would spin out further. Another trick was to go in for 'clipping' which meant that a tiny amount of gold could be snipped off each coin, so as to make more coins. This was the forgers' paradise. All this kind of trickery does not delude the public for very long. In the case of the Roman Empire it stimulated roaring inflation. When Diocletian came to power in 284 AD he spent twenty years trying to bring inflation under control, but the basic problem was that people had lost faith in the currency.

Constantine (306-337 AD) decided that a new gold coin, the Solidus, later called the Bezant, would stabilise things. This coin was 98% pure gold, which is good sense because pure gold easily erodes, so a small addition of say copper, reduces this tendency. The Bezant was a highly successful coinage; it went on for 700 years, which must be a record, but it also indicated the strength and stability of the Byzantine Empire. It was a constant problem to retain the gold within the Empire, since the Bezant was acceptable and the object of desire everywhere. At first, the Byzantines could rely on the mines in Nubia, but this was lost because of the Muslim eruption. The Bezant was an important symbol, verging on the mythological; this was augmented by the use of the emperors' faces on the coins, and even more so, the face of Jesus Christ.

The other side of the coin, so to speak, on the stability of prices, is when the supply of metal suddenly increases. All through the mediaeval period there were various moves to issue pure coins or reform the currency. But a major disturbance came when the Spaniards discovered the New World with its vast amounts of gold and silver which could be stolen from the Incas and the Aztecs. As shiploads of it came back to Spain in the 16th century, the effect was twofold; the value of silver and gold went down drastically, which is the other side of inflation. The other effect was, in England at least, but in other countries, that there was a constant threat from an overpowering Spain with far too much money. Henry 8th had two answers to this; firstly he pillaged the monasteries and secondly he debased the coinage. In this we see that the religious and mythological aspects of gold actually backfired on those of a religious inclination. As far as Spain itself was concerned, all that 'wealth' in the long run, ruined the Spanish economy. There must be a lesson in that somewhere.

The strange thing is that gold and silver, though being attractive to the eye and connected to mythology, are actually of very little use when it comes to the basic necessities of life, such as food, clothing and finding shelter. It would be true that jewellery and table utensils are wonderful as works of art and indications of status, but gold and silver can become valueless if there are no commodities to be purchased. The coins are only of any value as long as people value them; if and when they cease to value them, they become meaningless.

The same is even more true when we come to consider paper money. It is thought that this idea stems from China. It was Marco Polo who discovered to his amazement that the Emperor Hien Tsung (806-821 AD) had issued sheets of paper, printed with the names of officials and stamped with the seal of the Great Khan. This must have seemed just like our modern bank notes. So convenient was it that the Chinese realised that all the bronze coins could be rounded up and sent off to Japan. The paper money was in reality some kind of pretence, a fiction, but as long as everyone believed in it, there was no problem. It was very convenient to carry large sums of money around with a medium as light as paper. But the problem eventually emerged, as was found in modern times, that if paper money were over-issued, it would cause runaway inflation. In the end, the Chinese had to return to metal-based money. The idea of paper money is a clever one as long as it is carefully controlled. Since the Middle Ages, we have seen various types of paper issue; bills of exchange, promissory notes, bank notes, stocks and shares, debentures, traveller's cheques, postal orders and even postage stamps. Apart from the fact that paper money, as the age of printing came in, was relatively easy to counterfeit, it has made life much easier for us all. There is no need to cart wagons loaded up with coins for hundreds of miles, still less over the oceans. This will work as long as there is trust and faith in the currency. It was soon realised that although a paper currency had to be backed up with a gold reserve in a bank vault, there was no need for the exact amount of gold to match, pound for pound, the paper issue. There could be twice the amount of 'pounds' in circulation as paper, as there was real gold pounds in the vault. As long as people did not start a run on the bank, there was no problem.

Problems did arise when a foolish government issued far too much paper with no metallic backing. This happened in the French Revolution. The government issued the 'Assignat' but it was (5) based on land which had actually been stolen from the papal enclaves in France. The value of the Assignats went down so drastically that they were actually not worth the paper they were written on. It was Napoleon who took a strong hand and reformed the currency, basing it on metal again. Another similar situation arose in Germany in the 1920's when roaring inflation reduced the Mark to something virtually worthless; to buy a loaf of bread required a wheelbarrow full of paper. In such circumstances, people revert to barter and abandon money altogether. Since Britain, and virtually every other country has abandoned the gold standard, inflation has become an accepted fact of life. Even so, each country has still retained its gold reserves as a stabilising basis for its currency. The issue of paper money has to be carefully controlled so as to keep inflation within reason. In addition to this, we now have the phenomenon of 'plastic money', which is a very clever device, but once someone discovers how to counterfeit the credit card, we shall have big trouble.

What it means is that 'money', in whatever form it takes, is only 'money' as long as everybody accepts it as such. Once confidence is lost, it causes panic and loss of faith. This is another factor which makes economics relate to mythology; it all depends on what you believe in and how much you are prepared to indulge in self-delusion. There are many aspects of mythology which are pure self-delusion tinged with superstition. This reminds us of another element linking money to superstition; every time one sees a 'wishing well' there is the urge to throw coins into it. We note that paper money and credit cards do not receive a ducking! But the superstition is that if you throw a coin in the water it will fulfil your wish. That is why we are well endowed with coins from the past; people threw them into places like the warm springs at Bath.

The modern world is dominated by a frenetic paper-chase with massive international and personal debts, and currencies which are assumed to be solid. As long as this kind of self-deception persists, we shall probably thrive and muddle along, papering over one crisis after another. But as soon as we have something like the Wall Street crash, then we will have chaos. Business confidence is a strange and fickle thing; it is like the boom and bust situation. No one can control it but it is real enough in its own way. Once confidence is lost, it spreads like an infection and results in a downturn in trade.

It is rather like believing in God; as long as you are confident about God, your life can run along quite smoothly, coping with the occasional crisis. But as soon as some cruel person manages to demolish your faith, your life can crash in disarray. Let us remember that the prosperity of the 21st century, which does not extend to the Third World, is like skating on thin ice. It only needs someone to make a crack in the ice, and the whole thing could collapse.

The allure of Gold; Goldfinger

The early 1960's saw the rise of the author Ian Fleming, and one of his most notable publications was Goldfinger, which was made into a highly popular feature film. We begin with the book, since the film introduces various elements that Fleming did not envisage.

The book clearly taps into that basic allure that is instinctive in human nature; the snobbery surrounding gold. There is no need to go into every detail of the story but the essentials are as follows.

An American gambler is puzzled by the fact that Mr. Auric Goldfinger always manages to win at Canasta.(6) Normally the odds would work out at more or less even; therefore there is something strange going on. Bond manages to uncover the swindle by invading Goldfinger's apartment and finding a girl, Jill Masterton, with a pair of binoculars and a radio set tipping Goldfinger off over the contents of the American's hand. From such an insignificant beginning the story develops into a complete quest to apprehend Goldfinger for gold smuggling on a grand scale. The irony is that since he was vastly rich from illicit gold dealing, he still finds it necessary to cheat at cards, and also at golf, for paltry sums of money.

We are treated to a technical lecture at the Bank of England by a Colonel Smithers on the subject of gold. This has the effect of heightening the fascination. Bond is now sent out to try and find out what Goldfinger is up to, draw him into a game of golf and work his way into the man's confidence. Again, the irony of it builds up as Goldfinger, like an ill-principled schoolboy, cheats at golf, thus building up Bond's determination to unmask him. The fascination in the story builds up over the Rolls Royce Silver Ghost, as this is suspected of being the means of smuggling vast amounts of gold, firstly to Switzerland and then on to India. Also the fascination surrounds Oddjob, the tough guy Korean who can smash anything, like Desperate Dan. It is only when Bond manages to pry into the secrets of the Swiss factory that we find that all the body-work of the Rolls is actually solid gold; what an ingenious scheme! A girl called Tilly Masterson enters the story; she too is chasing Goldfinger because he murdered her sister by covering her all over with gold paint. This element also adds to the allure of the gold. That fact that he made a habit of doing this with pretty girls all adds to our hatred of the villain.

But then Bond (Tilly Masterson) is caught by Goldfinger and narrowly avoids being horrendously put to death. Goldfinger decides to take the two of them to America as his secretaries, to help with his master crime, an assault on Fort Knox, the main gold reserve of the USA. The whole scheme, which includes gangsters from other parts of America, seems quite preposterous but just within the bounds of credibility. It is so well planned and resourced that one almost hopes that it will work. The only reservation in the reader's mind is over the ruthlessness of Goldfinger; he has no respect for human life. Gold is his one obsession in life. From that we deduce a moral in the story; that all-consuming greed is in the end self-destructive.

Mercifully, Bond manages to slip a message to the American authorities, and they have just enough time to take preventive measures. When

Goldfinger and his team of criminals arrive at Fort Knox, the balloon goes up and the plan is thwarted. The Americans are not deprived of their gold after all. But Goldfinger and some of his crew manage to escape arrest; this is ominous.

On the way back to Britain, Bond and his new girl, Pussy Galore, find that their airliner has been hi-jacked by Goldfinger and Oddjob. On board is also Goldfinger's moving supply of gold bullion. Bond manages to depressurise the cabin which means that Oddjob is sucked out through the window into space. Then Bond thrashes Goldfinger to death; we all cheer inwardly! As the aircraft hits the water, it breaks in half and all the gold tips out into the ocean. Bond, and his new girl, are rescued. We see the irony in that the gold, which Goldfinger has illegally acquired, goes back to mother earth where it came from originally. In this way, the story ends on a very appropriate anti-climax. However, the real end comes when Bond cuddles up with his latest female conquest, Pussy Galore, a converted gangster and lesbian. So we see that the true value in life is love as opposed to the yellow metal.

The question has to raise itself in our minds about the impracticality of removing all that gold from Fort Knox. Even if one did manage to break into it, how long would it take to empty the repository and how many lorries would be needed to transport it to somewhere 'safe'? This is where the film-makers make a clever alteration to Fleming's plot. There are other minor amendments which need not concern us. But the essential thing in the film is that Goldfinger does not intend to remove the gold at all; he has a nuclear bomb which will explode in the vaults and render the gold stock radio-active for hundreds of years! This, he hopes, will have the effect of doubling the value of gold all round the world, including his vast stocks in various locations. One wonders if this effect would really be seen, or would the economists find a way round the problem?

In the film, the climax comes when Bond and Oddjob are trapped inside the Fort with the bomb about to go off. It is a heart-stopping scene, as Oddjob manages to electrocute himself with his own murder weapon, the bowler hat; everyone sighs with relief. But now the bomb is seconds away from detonating; Bond frantically smashes the casing with a gold brick, but has no idea of which bit of wiring to disconnect. A hand suddenly appears and switches the device off; the dial shows 007; everyone sighs an even bigger sigh of relief. This means that the gold reserve is not disturbed. But the irony of Goldfinger's travelling stock of bullion falling into the sea, is lost.

It is an ingenious story, whichever version one takes. It all plays on that instinctive fascination for gold and the greed that goes with it. But that is not the only mythological element in the story. There is the element of eternal justice; in spite of all the odds, Bond, the hero, prevails against the gangsters. So right wins through against wrong in the end. At times, (in the book) it looks as though Goldfinger and Oddjob are going to escape justice. This has the effect of increasing the tension. In the end, it is their mania for exacting vengeance on Bond that finally seals their doom. This is the final irony.

The whole story, whether of film or book, is just a little far-fetched but not totally unbelievable. It does not go so far as the 'blockbuster' mentality of later James Bond films, which really do go beyond the realms of common sense and reality, and which do much more strongly tap into the mythological instincts of human nature. But the common basic theme of the champion hero who establishes justice and fair-play is common to all of them. It does not matter whether the villain is linked with SMERSH, the Russian spy organisation or not. Actually, the book does link Goldfinger with SMERSH but the film does not, which is rather strange. But the champion tough-guy is such a common theme in mythology the world over, that this plot can reasonably be claimed as one aspect of the mythology of the modern world. Certainly, James Bond himself has become some sort of mythical super-hero in the popular imagination. This is not very different from people like Baal, or Hercules or Thor.

Footnotes for chapter 18

1. See The Oxford History of the French Revolution, William Doyle, 1989. The run of failed harvests in France made the exchequer bankrupt and this was a major contributor to the failure of the French monarchy.

2. Attempts at making platinum the basis of currency, such as the Kruger Rand experiment, have failed.

3. The Kings of Lydia; Gyges 608 to 648 BC Sadyattes 648 to 619 Alyattes 619 to 560 Croesus 560

4. Gyges was an ally of the Assyrian, Sennacherib. Gyges is reported to have had an invisibility ring (this sounds like Harry Potter and Bilbo Baggins!)

5. The Assignat was a paper currency which lost value to such an extent that no one would use it.

6. Canasta; a card game, using two packs of 52, not unlike Rummy. It originated in Uruguay and became popular in the USA in the post war era. It does not command much popularity in Europe.

19

Instinct and Psychology

It is an interesting question as to how mythology has circulated amongst the human race. One could maintain that it started with the first stirrings of humanity as human consciousness began to appear. That would go so far to explain why there are so many features of mythology in common across the whole of humanity. There are peoples, races and cultures very widely dispersed into the remote corners of the world, and still there are largely the same features of mythology in evidence. This must surely indicate that mythology is a matter of instinct in the first place. Obviously there has been a certain amount of borrowing, cross-fertilisation of ideas and imitation, but this is not the entire answer to the question. The main example of 'borrowing' has been the way in which the coming of Christianity has shown elements of the Bible being grafted into the original scheme of mythology. We think of the Huichols, the Melanesians and various mythologies in Africa.

When we start to talk about instinct, this clearly implies that we should consider modern psychology. This discipline was, and still is, concerned with human instinct, as well as other aspects of human nature. We shall see that from this perspective, mythology is far from dead in human affairs. One obvious example is the way in which people are fascinated by the heavenly bodies, the sun, moon and the stars. As we have seen, in the Ancient World, all kinds of fanciful speculations have been produced in this area of knowledge. But this fascination has not died down; if anything, it is more alive than ever. The difference is that we have all kinds of clever gadgets for probing into outer space, and all manner of speculation (some of it just as fanciful) as to what is really out there. The chief mania at the moment is the question of whether there are other forms of life living on other planets. Vast sums of

290

money are being spent on investigating this question. It is possible that this quest may turn out to be a complete waste of time and money; who knows?

When talking about Psychology, the obvious starting point is with Sigmund Freud.(1) His main contribution was to talk about the 'unconscious'. This could hardly be called an invention, or a discovery; more likely a 'realisation' or even 'speculation'. There is no way that such a thing as the unconscious can be proved to exist. Even if we take someone's brain apart, there is no way that the grey matter can be shown to contain a thing called the unconscious mind. Freud's theory went thus; the human personality consists of three elements; the **id**, the **ego** and the **super-ego**. The id contains all those instinctive responses, including reflex actions. This will include all those basic urges towards violence, supplying oneself with food and very importantly, the sex urge. These urges cannot be allowed to play havoc in society, or we should have murder, rape, cruelty, and all manner of bad behaviour going on. This is where the Ego comes in; this is the element of reasoning, or common sense. We all know that our urges have to be kept under control, and if they are not, then we have chaos in society, some might call it 'the law of the jungle.' The Ego is that element of rationality which says we shall achieve much more by using common sense. Then there is the super-ego, which equates to the conscience. Like the ego, the super-ego has to be learnt as we are taught by our parents and teachers. It controls and modifies all our urges and reasonings, like a ghostly policeman with his notebook out. Essentially it is about a sense of fair play; being reasonable with other people on the basis that they should be reasonable to oneself. Freud claimed that if these three elements are in balance in a person, then we have someone who is well-adjusted. If one element is over-powering in relation to the others, then we have someone who is maladjusted.

Freud's framework of thought made quite an impact on the world when it became known, and his terminologies are still current in today's world, even if people do not completely understand them; such words as complex, identification, regression, fixation, and repression, for example. It was all very elaborate but also pure speculation. What concerned people then and now, was the notion that practically every human thought or action was somehow based on sexual urges. This might be true with some people, but to generalise and make out that everyone is so motivated is a big assumption. Today, Freud and his theories are now seen as largely outdated. I have to confess, as a late teenager, to being bowled over by Freud's analysis of human nature; now I can see the pitfalls in it. One serious shortcoming in his analysis of personality, is the absence of religious belief in the many forms it can take. Mythology too is hardly ever mentioned. Even so, many psycho-therapists still to this day use his methods. One such is the 'free-association' method whereby a patient sits back in a relaxed state on a couch and responds to a random collection of words thrown at him. This is supposed to defuse neuroses. Another approach was to hypnotise the patient and then allow him to say anything he wanted, on the assumption that this was seeing into his unconscious mind and relieving tensions. Freud's disciple Jung took up many of his ideas and developed them as well as disagreeing with some of them. It was a useful starting point for this new discipline of psychology, but also highly speculative. Today, psychologists embark on what is known as Behaviourist methods; this means testing with scientific experiments such things as memory, and intelligence. (2)

How is this of any relevance to mythology? For a start, we notice that the significant number three has crept into the analysis. He may not have realised this, but this is a very important element in mythology, as in a way, it matches up with the three levels of the universe. There is the id, which would correspond to the underworld where there is wickedness, disorder, and the torture that goes with it. The ego corresponds to the earth plane in which rationality has to rule the day. This world has to function on the basis of common sense, hard work and human logic. If and when these things break down, then those instinctive impulses from the id break through and lead to chaos. It is only common sense to steer clear of crime and misbehaviour. The superego corresponds to heaven, the abode of God (or gods). They are the ones who give us law codes, either written or oral, and make us feel guilty. That conscience tempers common sense. In a way, that three tiered system of Freud is the internalised or subjective version of the ancient universe; heaven, earth and hell.

Another way of seeing it is to turn the whole thing upside down. We could say that the id, all those irrational urges, violence and sexual misbehaviours are writ large in the skies when the gods behave like hooligans, especially the Greek ones. This would apply to the pagan pantheons but not the monotheistic pattern of thought. If the id is up in the skies, then the superego would match hell; the place where we go if we cannot behave ourselves. In other words, it is conscience catching up on us! That leaves us with the ego being equivalent to normal life on earth, where we have to function according to rationality. Laziness will not do; hard work is the lot of virtually everyone, on the assumption that we have to eat, sleep and take relaxation.

In a way, Freud's analysis of the personality is just an internalised mythology, which has been current in virtually every culture throughout recorded human history. I wonder if he realised this?

Another aspect of his theories was the element of dreams. He maintained that all dreams are wish-fulfilments; we dream about what we want. One can reduce the tension over something that one wants, by reviving memories of things that one used to enjoy or used, to reduce that tension. So for instance, someone who is half-starved might dream about the meals he used to enjoy, and find some sort of fulfilment out of it. There is clearly a degree of truth in this, but can hardly be seen as the total truth about dreaming. He does not seem to consider the factor of nightmares! But this is one area in which basic mythological impulses in human nature can connect with psychology. We have only to recall that the Huichol culture and the Cargo cults have shamanistic dreaming as an important part of their systems. Also the great prophets in the Bible had dreaming as an important substratum of their message. This is particularly seen with Daniel and Enoch.

This is where the work of Jung becomes significant. He decided that mythology and dreams were not a lot of nonsense, but were to be taken seriously. He found that exploring people's unconscious gave evidence of a thing called 'archetypes'. The same kind of images were mentioned by many people, and they cannot have been merely the day-to-day experiences in normal life. In other words, they were experiences common in the back of people's minds. This is coming very close to myth; in other words, the instincts which produce the myths of this world are much the same for all of humanity. This will go back in time as a sort of collective memory or folk recollection. We have already come across one such image; that of the World Flood, which is found in the mythology of so many peoples in different parts of the world. That is not to say that the Flood is just a lot of imagination and neurosis; it looks very much as if the Flood motif is based on a real disaster in the remote past, and the impression of it is still there in people's unconscious. If it is deeply ingrained in people's minds, that explains why the story of Noah's ark connects with something in people's minds. Related to this is the Atlantis phenomenon, which appears in chapter 7. As we have seen, this too is almost certainly more than just a vague legend. It gives the impression of being a real event in remote history, but the 'folk recollection' of it explains why people are still obsessed with it now. We can go further than that; precious metals and jewels exert a fascination on people's minds. This must connect with some kind of human instinct which speaks of eternity, indestructible life and deity in relation to royalty.

It is interesting that Jung, much more than Freud, came to grips with the factor of mythology. This is now where the importance of dreams comes in. Jung regarded them as a way of bringing back archetypal memories. This goes a lot further than Freud did; it was a much more positive and constructive view of dreaming. He could see how ideas that people described in their dreams actually connected with the content of mythologies. He studied all kinds of areas such as Gnosticism, Alchemy, Astrology and Taoism, on the assumption that these would support his analysis of the human unconscious. It can be seen that these matters have already arisen in the mythologies described in earlier chapters. The precise relationship between them all is not easy to determine, but a few remarks about them will be helpful.

Gnosticism. As we have seen, this was a philosophico-religious movement which took ideas from Egyptian and Greek mythology and sanitised them. It must have occurred to someone in the late Hellenistic era that the Greek and Egyptians gods not only could be syncretised but also tidied up, leaving out all the crudities and human failings. So a system of one primal, original god, with principles and spiritual realities emanating from him was devised. It was all very elaborate and speculative; this reminds us of the early psychologists with their ingenious schemes about the human mind. In a way, modern psychology, in its early stages, was just another outburst of Gnosticism, even if it was internalised as opposed to projected into the skies. Just as each psychoanalyst had his own individual ideas, so too did the Gnostic speculators. Another important aspect of Gnosticism was the idea that human flesh and this world was unworthy; it was tainted and beyond redemption. To achieve salvation, one had to find that essential factor called 'gnosis', which meant knowledge. This would free one from the world and connect one directly to the one primal, perfect god. How does this work with modern psychology? Given that we all have neuroses, mental problems, fears, guilt, angst, however one might term it, the way to free oneself from this is through coming to terms with one's unconscious mind, where all these problems are lurking. This can be done by psycho-therapy. In other words, modern psycho-therapy is just another version, albeit internalised, of the ancient Gnostic method of salvation. What is missing of course, is

God, but that would be typical of the twentieth century, in which we have difficulties with the reality of God. But even that is nothing new. When we look at Buddhism,(3) which arrived slightly before Gnosticism in the BC period, there too we find that escaping from the pain and toil of this life involves coming to grips with the urge to want things, and thus achieving Nirvana. This does not involve any sort of god, but Nirvana can be seen as a demythologised or secularised substitute for God or heaven.

Not that there were no other versions of Gnosticism in evidence. We have seen (see The theology of Truth, chapter 9) that Mary Baker Eddy's ideas on Christian Science, are just another version of Gnosticism. There is also Scientology; not that its ideas are generally known but what seems likely is that it is another version of Gnosticism. The same could be said of Swedenborgianism. The same tendency appears in many ways. Every time someone tries to explain God away as some sort of principle, philosophical construct, expanded logic, or notion in the back of people's heads, this is essentially another outburst of Gnosticism.

Jung eventually decided that trying to analyse Gnosticism was problematical, since all the evidence for their ideas were only reported through the eyes of the early Christians who were hostile to them. One wonders if he managed to study the Corpus Hermeticum, an ancient Egyptian document which is full of Gnostic thought. If he were here to today, he would have the benefit of the recent discoveries at Nag Hammadi (in Egypt), which have unearthed a treasure trove of Gnostic literature.(4) Some of this is non-Christian; some of it is Gnostic with mild Christian influence and some of it is outright Christian with certain Gnostic influences. It is fascinating to see how the coming of Christianity in the mid-Roman empire has impacted on Gnosticism and vice versa. Gnosticism as a train of thought did not die out even if the Christians dubbed it as heretical. It had its influence on the Renaissance and on the Age of Enlightenment in 18th century, and even on the Flower Power movement of the late 20th century.

As a mythological system of thought, it has difficulties with seeing God as 'personal'. This is an essential element in Biblical teaching and the traditions of Judaism and the Christian Church.

Alchemy. This is another area that fascinated Jung, but also connects with mythology. For many people now, alchemy is seen as a cranky, far-fetched discipline which achieved very little, if anything. This is unfair, as the mediaeval alchemists did make some interesting discoveries which led on to the modern science of Chemistry. We have to try to see into the mindset of a pre-scientific age in an appropriate light. They had no atomic theory as we have now; they were working on the ancient Greek principle of the four elements, namely earth, fire, air and water. This was taken to be an unassailable doctrine right down to virtually modern times. It is interesting that the Taoists in China thought much the same thing except that they had five elements, adding in metal! Before we sneer at what might seem ignorance, let us just beware that in ten centuries time our next generation of scientists might well be sneering at us for our clumsy ideas in the 21st century.

The best-known aspect of alchemy was the attempt at turning base metals into gold. This was not the only thing they were trying to achieve. We have already seen that the factor of gold, and by association, silver, is a basic mythological response in virtually every mythology the world over. Where the gold-mania is missing can be explained by there being no gold in that area (for instance, the Huichols). But silver easily takes its place. Also the plumage of exotic birds is a substitute. This is one reason why we can see alchemy as an aspect of mythology. Because gold is lustrous, non-corrupting and is easily associated with royalty and deity, it was thought to be the key to extending human life. Now we see that basic urge in human nature to cheat death, or live for ever.

It is also worth noting that the mediaeval alchemists in Europe were not the only people trying out the same sort of ideas. Alchemy can be traced back to Ancient Egypt, but also the Chinese and the Indians were working on the same lines. We know that the Yellow Emperor had the idea that if he swallowed mercury it would prolong his life; little did he know that the opposite effect would be seen! Interestingly, mercury does come into western experimentation. It would seem that in one of their processes, they had a white stone and when mercury was added to it, it went green and then red. This was supposed to result in the elixir vitae, the elixir of life, which would extend one's life or even give immortality. We have seen that the element of resurrection or nearly dying and yet coming back to life is an ongoing theme in mythology. It all indicates that we see life as precious; it has to last for ever.

How does this work in relation to Jung's ideas? It would seem that alchemical thought coincided with his own ideas about the unconscious mind. Alchemy was full of weird fantasy images, and Jung could see these as archetypal. He was intrigued to find that alchemical imagery would appear in his patients' dreams, while they were going through the process of 'individuation'.(5) He studied the alchemical process only to discover that it went through a series of stages, and these stages could be matched by the development of the maturing psyche.

Here, in outline is the process. Firstly, there is the Nigredo ('blackness') stage. The alchemist heats up the material until it goes black. We might term that as oxidation, possibly. This coincides with the first stage of individuation, in which the patient breaks down the barriers between the conscious and the unconscious mind. This might result in depression as one is confronted by one's own deep-down (repressed) emotions. This has been termed 'the dark night of the soul'.

Secondly, there is the Albedo ('whiteness') stage. White flecks appear in the mixture which eventually crystallises into a white stone. Is this the famous 'philosopher's stone'; we have had something of this in the Weirdstone of Brisingamen (see chapter 8), and we shall see it again in Harry Potter's chapter 23. As the inner darkness is faced, this represents the cleansing of the psyche. The patient comes to confront the archetypes at this stage, and it has a healing effect; this means coming to terms with one's own 'id', something that many people cannot bring themselves to do. How often have we seen, in the myths, the need for cleansing, either by water or fire, the feeling of unworthiness and shame. With the Huichols, it was the blood of a deer that brought cleansing; how well this ties in with St.John who talks about the blood of Jesus cleansing us.(6)

Thirdly, there is the Rubedo ('redness') stage, which has been referred to earlier. As mercury is added to the white stone, it goes green and then red. This represents the union of opposites and the production of the elixir. This is the resolution of psychic conflicts and the balancing of opposites. Jung's work was much concerned with a balancing process. This can be seen in people's personal dreams and fantasies, and also in the shape of religious systems, their symbols and their mythical material. This balancing of opposites, the id with the ego, and the development of the psyche he termed 'individuation'.

What did he mean by individuation? We begin by assuming that deep down in the unconscious mind (the id), there are nasty, violent, hurtful urges, which most people do their best to ignore. Some have more success than others. But ignoring this element in one's nature is to no good; one needs to face up to it and confront it. If it is repressed too much it can cause all manner of problems such as neurosis or psychic disturbances. The first step in the process of individuation is to take responsibility for these nasty elements or 'shadows' in our nature. This then helps us to become more peaceful people and able to relate more effectively with others. The next step is to begin to understand one's 'anima', which means the opposite sex image in the psyche. Once we accept our anima, it results in achieving a balance between the inner and outer aspects of oneself. The third stage comes when we integrate the positive and negative aspects of our psyche. The end of the individuation process, which might not actually be achieved in one's lifetime, is to find that sense of balance, which gives wholeness. He called it the 'Self'; it is a transpersonal, transcendent state, in which we have come to terms with ourselves. It was very clever to match this up with the processes of the alchemists; they did it with chemicals in a laboratory; modern psychology does it with a therapist and a couch! This is another example of internalisation of mythical material.

If this idea of balance reminds us of ancient Taoist theories, as outlined in the Tao Teh Ching, one would be right. This is where Jung drew in Taoist ideas to connect with his own theories. It may help to refer to my chapter on the Tao Teh Ching in my previous book, the Theology of Truth (chapter 10). In short, Lao Tzu, the founder of Taoism, understood that a harmonious relationship between heaven and earth was the original state of things, but this went wrong somehow in the remote past. This caused an imbalance between heaven and earth, and also between different people. To restore the balance, which is what we ought to work towards, we all need to be nice to one another. That means minimising all the nasty elements in human nature. It is all a question of balance; how close this was to Jung's ideas, or rather how close Jung's ideas were to Taoist mythology.

Astrology

It may seem strange that astrology would command the attention of a modern rational thinker, but Jung was fascinated by it and saw it as connected to his idea of archetypal symbolism. This would connect with mythology. (7) He believed that the events in the outer world of material things were reflected in the inner world of the psyche and vice versa. This would make sense if important events in the past had somehow embedded themselves in the corporate consciousness of the human race, and such 'memories' kept coming to the forefront of people's minds. He went further and suggested that someone observing an event can actually affect the outcome of the event, as well as the event affecting the observer.

He studied birth charts and compared them with the actual course of people's lives. He found that there was not a complete correlation, which would have shown some sort of causal link between the planets and actual events. However, he did find that the results of the analysis varied according to who was doing the analysis. In other words, the analyst's expectations somehow influenced the results. This ties in with the claim, made by some, that the predictions can be 'tailored' to apply to one particular person and thus impress and influence them. The horoscopes seen in the newspapers are to no purpose for they are far too generalised.

As we have already seen, the Zodiac was a direct product of mythological notions going back to Ancient Greece and further back, to Mesopotamia. From that we can conclude that it is instinctive for humanity to see some sort of meaning in the planets and the constellations. While there are still those who work on the basis of horoscopes, there are others who think they are more scientific, who make the assumption that there is something analogous to human life in deep space, and that if this is true, it will alter our thinking about the value of humanity and many other factors. The difference between these two approaches is not very great; both of them employ a generous amount of speculation and wishful thinking.

Dreams

Jung took a far more positive and sensitive approach to dreaming, as compared with Freud's ideas. Jung could see that dreams were much more than wish-fulfilment. They might be something to do with indigestion, or recalling something from the past, or compensation for something lacking, or looking ahead, or what he termed 'oracular' dreams. This last one means when one has a really highly significant dream, with a numinous quality and particularly vivid. This would include what we have seen with Kauymali the Huichol and also the Cargo Cult prophets. There are certainly several like this in the Bible, which we shall study further on, but Jung cannot bring himself to call them 'messages from God'. Why is that? Because 20th century 'scientific' analysis fights shy of such an admission!

To his credit, he resisted the temptation to force an interpretation on anyone's dream, simply for the sake of some sort of instant analysis. He was right to see much of the content of dreams as symbolic, and those symbols almost certainly would relate to instinctive, mythological impulses. If it came to recalling the past, that 'past' might include going back further than one's own life. He was interested in Karma, but that is not the entire picture. He assumed that there would be some kind of collective unconscious planted in everyone's mind. That would help to explain why not all dreams are obvious at first experience, but can be recurring with slight alterations.

We can commend Jung for his sensitive and positive approach to analysing the human mind. If what he says is true, it will help us to understand why such matters as Atlantis and King Arthur have such an influence on people's minds. The issue of Noah's ark is a case in point. But there are many other factors, which we have already seen stand as important symbols for all people; the tree, the snake, precious metals, jewels and translucent stones, just to mention a few. These factors seem to be understated, if not omitted altogether from the psychologists' analyses.

The importance of modern psychology

To sum up, it is significant that in the modern world the issue of the unconscious mind is taken seriously. To term it the **id** is somewhat idiosyncratic, but it has to be called something. The mistake comes in saying that if everyone has got an id, it must therefore be the same in everyone. Surely there are elements in it that are stronger or weaker, just as for instance physical strength varies enormously from one person to another. To say that everyone is basically motivated by the sex drive is a massive generalisation; it would be hard to demonstrate this objectively.

It is worthwhile to agree that the id contains much material that is symbolic. Symbolism is an important factor in mythology regardless of which part of the world we are talking about. We have already seen that certain symbols are universal, such as the snake and the tree. Other symbols of lesser importance can also be found; sometimes this is related to the absence of certain factors in some countries, such as gold and jewels. But the substratum of it all, no matter what culture is involved, is that element in human nature which says, 'life is precious; it ought to last for ever; how do we sidestep death?' And the other one is in these lines; 'what does human life amount to? I know there are divine beings (gods), but how do I relate to them; how do I maintain a good relationship with them?'

This is the major weakness with modern psychology, especially the early thinkers like Freud and Jung; there is a serious failure to cope with the divine. They steer clear of talking about God and the world of the spirit. But this is a factor that so many people have an awareness of, something that is deep down in the unconscious mind, as an instinctive response to life. Mythology, however, does not duck the issue over God (or gods); there is a strong admission that nothing makes sense unless we see the universe as three major compartments; heaven, earth and the underworld. This used to be a literal geographical reality, but this has died the death with the exploration of outer space. Even so, the spiritual conception of the three-tiered universe with God 'up there' still rules people's minds. It is not possible to think oneself out of this system of thought. Hell is now politically wrong, but people still assume something like that anyway. We can call it mythological if we like, but the spiritual reality is that everyone's unconscious mind carries this notion around all the time. It is one thing trying to deny it; another thing to erase it from one's id. The impression of it may be stronger in some people and weaker in others. This will account for why some people take religious belief more seriously than others.

One could say that the atheist is someone who has managed to expunge this system of thought completely. I wonder if it is possible to achieve it; still less if it is worth the bother. If it is true that mankind was created in the image of God, then that element of divinity will be there somewhere in everyone's unconscious mind, even if they are trying to deny it. I am impressed by the fact that every known culture or race in the world has got some sort of mythology and also some form of religious expression which is based on that mythology. This must indicate something essential about human nature; that awareness of the divine.

Another aspect of modern psychology is that as the theory of Evolution became a major assumption towards the end of the 19th century, it became the substratum of Freud and Jung's theorisings. If it is true that mankind is nothing more than a highly developed monkey, as the evolutionists would have us believe, then the instincts that the animals have would be the same in the unconscious of the humans. This very largely explains why so many experiments are done on small animals, such as rats. The assumption is that if a rat can learn and unlearn things and this can be recorded and the data used to predict behaviour, then the same frame work can be used with humans.

This is very big compound assumption. The first assumption is that Evolution is correct and will apply to all aspects of human life; what happens if someone manages to disprove Evolution? Secondly, the assumption is that human instincts function in the same way as that of animals. It seems to me that rendering the human mind down to the level of small animals does not carry conviction. We may indeed have an ego and a super ego, maybe the animals do also. But most people do not function purely and simply as some sort of mental machine. There is inventiveness, and ingenuity, and kinds of emotions that we assume are missing from the animals' make-up. Another element is determination and motivation. It is one thing to record someone's intelligence with a piece of paper with symbols on it, which is what the IQ tests amount to; but to assess someone's outlook on life in conjunction with intelligence would be a far better indicator of that person's future.

In addition to this, modern psychology makes no attempt at assessing one's inspiration level. What about all those bright ideas that have led to all kinds of new processes? The ancient Greeks had the god Hephaistos putting ideas into the heads of the humans. Mr.Von Daniken has helpful little men coming from outer space to put ideas into people's heads. Modern psychology has no answer to this. The theologian does have an answer; that God gives people inspiration; but then, God is not too popular nowadays!

Footnotes for chapter 19

1. Sigmund Freud, an Austrian psychotherapist working in Vienna.
2. One of the early experiments was done by Pavlov using rats to assess the faculty of memory.
3. To read the Dhammapada one sees the same line of thought as with Jung. See my chapter on Dhammapada in The Theology of Truth chapter 14.
4. Our knowledge of Gnosticism was somewhat sketchy until in 1946 at Nag Hammadi in Egypt a cache of Gnostic literature, mainly 'gospels' was found.
5. 'Individuation' is Jung's special term for psychotherapy, in which one comes to confront one's own id.
6. I John 1:7.
7. Strangely, Jung does not seem to indulge in numerology, as we see in chapter 26.

20

Star Trek and Star Wars

The late 20th century saw the production by Paramount of the famous TV series Star Trek. I include this material because it is futuristic mythology; in other words, the eschatology of the modern age. We are accustomed to thinking of eschatology as something biblical or at least well rooted in the thinking of the Ancient World. But the modern world is just as eager to provide modernistic, technological eschatology as the ancients were. It is interesting that many, if not all, of the metaphors and motifs used before have been used again. The film makers, with their special effects have had a wonderful time frightening us all, but very few of the ideas are entirely new. Most of them are the same old ideas just rehashed. One wonders if they realise this!

There is no need to recount in detail all the exploits of James T.Kirk and Mr. Spock, since they are well known and can be seen again on disc. Essentially, they are living in an age 300 years into the future, at a time when the Americans (not the Russians, we note!) have constructed space craft which are capable of travelling at massive speeds so that they can cover millions of light years in order to visit faraway planets. We learn later that it is an earthling scientist called Dr.Zephon Cochrane, who is mostly drunk, that invented 'warp' speed, which means going faster than the speed of light. Later in the series, we are confronted with a new captain, John Luke Pickard who has a second in command called Data. While Mr. Spock is a cross between a Vulcan and a human, and is entirely logical and has no ambition to be anything 'less', Mr. Data is an android, but does have a faint inkling that he would like to have emotions. It would seem that he is capable of feeling anxiety but has the facility to switch it off when ordered to. While Jim

Kirk and his crew very easily carried conviction as a working community, this was less true with John Pickard. The other positive thing with Kirk's regime was that it was a multi-national group which worked in wonderful harmony; people from all parts of the world, including Scotland. This brings us to one of the difficulties with Star Trek; the speech is usually so slurred and unclear that we have difficulty in getting people's names right. There is a chap called 'Scaddie', the chief engineer; we take that to be 'Scotty'. Mr. Data, the android who might be spelled 'Dater' (!), only receives clarification after about three episodes. The same applies to all those technological and pseudo-scientific matters referred to in the story. They are mentioned at such rapidity that one cannot normally grasp what is being said.

There are massive assumptions in these stories. Firstly, that such a spaceship as Enterprise could be built, bearing in mind the resources available on Earth. That factor is actually commented on by Ellie, an earthling of the 20th century, who cannot understand how so much titanium could be sourced on earth. Secondly, that another method of propulsion capable of 'warp-factors' could be developed. Thirdly, that there really are 'exo-planets' which are somehow compatible with our conditions on Earth. We notice that normally, when the spacemen visit a new planet, they have no difficulty in breathing; does that mean that all these alleged planets have the same atmosphere as Earth? Fourthly, that there are forms of life which are strangely similar and even biologically compatible with the human race. Even the androids and the Borgs, who are some sort of technical machine, have a form similar to the human frame. Beneath it all is the grand assumption that Evolution is a reality; remarks on this line often break the surface, but usually it is a tacit assumption that the human race will develop to greater things and that other planets have 'humans' at a different stage of Evolution. This explains why star fleet command forbids visitors to interfere with the culture of any newly-discovered planet. This is something that the European explorers might have considered when they colonised vast areas of the Earth in the period of the great discoverers. As an exciting 'sci-fi' series, Star Trek is great fun, and really quite amusing when the natives of the exo-planets manage to speak English with an American accent!

How much of this is fact or fiction? Thirty years ago, it must have struck most people as sheer fantasy. We were only just getting to grips with exploring the Moon, never mind about Mars or the other close planets. Now, in the early 21st Century, we have a space station orbiting the Earth, from which spacecraft could be launched out. Space probes, unmanned, have visited almost all the planets in the Solar System, including a comet. What a disappointment that as yet, there is no definite indication of life forms on our near neighbours! But that is the mania of the present age; that of finding 'life' somewhere else. Now that we have become aware of 'exo-planets' associated with other suns (stars), there is excitement that one of them has the right conditions for a life-form of some kind. All of this research costs vast amounts of money, the morality of which is already in question. Whether there would ever be sufficient resources to send a probe to Alpha Centauri, our nearest star, apart from the Sun, to find a few facts about the supposed planet that is orbiting it, is a serious question. But this is all the excitement caused by a certain fictional programme, and others in the same genre. But this all goes to show the fascination and hold that outer space has on our minds, just as it did in the Ancient World; we are dealing with modern Mythology here.

One of the amusing elements in Star Trek is the way that traditional nautical vocabulary is worked into the account. 'Welcome aboard' and 'star fleet' and 'bridge' come round regularly. A ship's wheel is ensconced in Jim Kirk's quarters. When the Admiral comes aboard, he is piped in! One is surprised that Mr.Spock does not wear a tricorn hat! Another amusing incident is when we are taken to see a traditional sailing ship 78 years later (although it is not explained what 'later' means, ie. later than what?). A Klingon, who is friendly with the Confederation, is induced to walk the plank in order to retrieve his hat; they remove the plank and he receives a ducking! Just to confuse us all, inside the ship is a cabin full of technological gadgets; this really raises the question of what time-zone we are in. It is quite comical when Mr. Data sings a snatch from HMS Pinafore!

One intriguing incident is where there is fear that the hump-back whales are about to go extinct. This is clearly a reference to the late 20th century fears that whales were being hunted to extinction, a crisis which appears to have largely been resolved in our own times. The plan is to use the Enterprise to go back 300 years and scoop up two whales from the ocean, take them for a ride in space and then put them back in the ocean '300 years later'! In the event, they stole a Klingon space ship, managed to snatch two whales just as the whaling ship was about to shoot them, carted them off into the skies. The time travel, at colossal speeds, nearly shook the craft to pieces, but they managed both journeys, landed the whales in San Fransico Bay, in sight of the Golden Gate, but managed to crash the spaceship, nearly drowning the crew. Of course, they managed to swim free of the wreckage, because we needed Kirk and his team for the next programme. Crazy as it may seem, the substratum of this episode is that wonderful theory of Einstein's, Relativity. (1) This means that the concept of going backwards and forwards in time ought in theory to be possible if we had a craft capable of such massive velocity. One wonders if such a feat is within the realms of possibility! At one point, there is some discussion of the wisdom of going back in time and altering the course of History. That inevitably raises the question of whether History is actually real or just a figment of everyone's imagination.

One of the main mythological assumptions in Star Trek is the concept of perpetual conflict. We start with the stand-off between the Confederation and the Klingon Empire. It is assumed, quite gratuitously, that the Confederation are the 'goodies' and the Klingons are the 'baddies'. If we were told the story from the Klingon point of view it might all seem somewhat different. The Klingons are characterised as technically very well advanced but morally seriously backward. They seem incapable of being honest and reliable. Almost every episode comes to a climax with the shoot-out between the two empires and of course, the Confederation has to win, usually with Kirk thinking up some cunning scheme.

It is not explained how or when the Klingons were persuaded to play fair and join the Confederation, but later in the series we have Klingons helping to man the Enterprise and join in with the campaign to help poor struggling people on a far away planet. But that does not mean that the war in the skies is over; far from it. A worse enemy, the Borgs are now in the picture. They are some sort of technological masterpiece of robotism, with no mind or conscience. It is some sort of totalitarianism with someone just issuing orders; as it turns out, the dictator is a 'beautiful' woman who is capable of discussing matters. The Borgs can be shot down, but they are clever enough to develop a resistance to laser beams. This means that other more subtle methods have to be used to defeat them, but of course, the Confederation lads always manage to think of a way round it.

It is interesting that this notion of perpetual conflict was (and still is for some people) a basic assumption in the pagan world. There, it took the form of gods and goddesses fighting each other. For those who realised that monotheism was the truth, the conflict concerned battles between angels and devils, sometimes in the skies but sometimes in the soul of mankind. To see the full development of this we only need to look at the Book of Revelation (see my treatment of it in The Theology of Truth, chapter 6). Clearly, it is the human race projecting its problems into the skies; this is a way of saying, 'we can't help fighting; it's the fault of the gods, angels and devils.'

The question of peace is actually raised in Star Trek. The Confederation claims to be in favour of peace, but Kirk does not shrink from a pre-emptive attack. It then emerges that the Klingons cannot afford to go on fighting and there is a peace initiative. Kirk goes to negotiate a deal with the Klingons, but someone fires on them and Kirk gets the blame. He and Dr.McCoy are sentenced to labour in the trilithium(2) mines on one of their planets. In the end, the crafty Kirk manages to escape and the matter is resolved. In one episode Kirk and his crew discover a planet called Nimbus (3), the planet of peace, Paradise City. This is a joke really, since they still have guns and fights. In fact the whole series continues with one gun battle after another. The effort to make warfare obsolete is a worthy project but still beyond anyone to achieve, at least on an inter-galactic level. The truth of the matter is, that if there were universal peace, there would be no interesting story for sensationalists to record. How often does the story descend into scenes reminiscent of the 'shoot-out at the OK corral'! However, Revelation shows us how there can be universal peace and defeat of evil, but that involves talking about God, something that the Sci-fi genre fights shy of, but does not completely exclude (see below).

So often in the stories, there is the tension between pure logic, whatever that might mean, and emotion. Spock is the main focus of this element, and later there is a girl from Vulcan who seems to be a substitute for him. Mr. Data, who is an android, has no emotion, but is tempted to slide in that direction. He is more tempted when he comes across another chap just like himself, whom he realises is his brother. The inference from that is that some sort of brotherly love would emerge. When Data goes berserk and goes on the rampage on a new planet, this indicates that he can fly into a rage of some sort. A little boy offers him the advice 'to enjoy himself a little each day'. That is advice that we could all heed, even if we are encumbered with emotions. As a matching motif, we discover that Spock also has a half-brother and father, and there is clearly some kind of familial attachment there. The general assumption, as a substratum of these scenes, is that logic is superior to emotion, and yet one is not a complete person unless one has a proper childhood and all the experiences of being human. There is one episode where a probe took in so much knowledge that it became a living thing. The machine needs to integrate with a human, and this is shown when Decker and Ilea merge with each other to produce new life which is claimed to be the next step in evolution. This could be a tacit way of saying emotion is necessary in the complete person.

In a way, this ties in with the Freudian-Jungian concept of the human personality. The id and the conscience are the emotions and the ego is the logical element in us. It emerges that long ago, the Vulcans managed to expunge all the animal instincts of 'human' nature, and think themselves as superior for that. If Spock and the other Vulcans only function on logic, then there is something missing in their makeup. It also ties in with what we know of Gnosticism with its emphasis on Gnosis or the Logos, and also that idea that the flesh (human nature) is unworthy. All that acquisition of knowledge is the way to salvation, allegedly.

The question of God is also raised in Star Trek. For those who think God is some sort of giant located somewhere in outer space, here is something to think about. They find the planet Shackeri which is claimed to be the centre of the galaxy, and the place from which creation sprang. Strange flash-backs occur which are supposed to relieve one of the secret pain inside one. So, we see McCoy's father dying, and Spock is seen being born. Every man has a secret pain, it is alleged, and this must be brought out by sharing it with others. This again ties in with Jung's notions about facing up to the id and bringing unpleasant elements to the surface. But Jim Kirk declares that he needs his secret pains and does not wish to part with them.

Then we see a column of fire and a voice coming out of it. It is not unusual to see a column of fire in Star Trek; it is almost certainly a substitute for the world tree, which would have difficulties in fitting in with millions of light years out in space. But there is plenty of fire, even coming out of their fasers, and fire when the space ships blow up. But this column of fire has a voice coming from it, and this reminds us of the pillar of fire and the Burning Bush at the Exodus.(3) The voice is clearly meant to be the voice of God, and when a massive face appears, with a beard and stern voice, McCoy immediately concludes that this is God. How exciting for us all! All too easily this reminds us of the giant Mimir in Norse mythology, and the idea that he has infinite wisdom; his head was chopped off but he continued to speak. However, Kirk keeps his head. When the face starts to demand taking over the Enterprise, Kirk has the presence of mind to ask him why he would want a spaceship. 'What would God want with a spaceship'? he asks impertinently. So this is not God at all really. Then McCoy wants to know why this 'god' is angry; this does not fit in with his idea of God. McCoy also asks 'is God really out there?' But Kirk smiling smugly and proclaiming, as he slaps his chest, that 'God is in here'.

This scene raises a very interesting theological question. It makes various assumptions about what God is or is not, mostly based on people's preconceived ideas. Kirk's view, which has to carry more weight than anyone else's, because he is the 'clever lad' who can answer all the questions, taps into the Humanistic approach to God, which is normally on the lines that God is something inside human nature but not some sort of existence outside it. A more orthodox view of it is to say that God is in and through everything, and yet he is other than his creation; this is a paradox which seems to have eluded the scriptwriters of Star Trek.

Various other elements which are essential to mythology can be seen in Star Trek. In The Wrath of Khan, Spock, and someone else, is actually killed; something that we could hardly imagine. But predictably, someone revives him, and the other one, a girl, and so he is restored to duty. This is not the only case of 'resurrection'; this is a theme seen in so many other mythologies. It tells us that life is indestructible and precious. It goes further than this, since there is a funeral on board the Enterprise; Spock is given a 'burial at sea', but the coffin lands on planet Ruga and can be detected by sensors. The crew become aware that there is a 'life-form' in Spock's old room. When they open Spock's coffin they find that his uniform is neatly folded up but he is gone. They come to realise that Spock's soul has got into McCoy and he is now acting very strangely (that is, more strangely than usual!). In the end, a Vulcan lady revives Spock (and David, Kirk's son), and Kirk rescues them back to the Enterprise just as the planet is destroyed. This means that the concept of living soul and resurrection is endemic in the series. It is a surprise that when Kirk dies, he stays dead; that seems really rather strange. As most of the crew are beamed up, there is one of them, Troy who actually expresses the opinion that he can live for ever. It is all the basic question of how we sidestep death or survive it in some way or other.

Coming nearer to Biblical matters, there was someone on the Voyager 6 sent out from Nasa, 300 years previously, named Vega, who was trying to seek the 'Creator'. It is now coming back to earth, with the threat that it will destroy everything. Vega has achieved a kind of energy completely unknown. They thought that the probe disappeared into a Black Hole, and that must have been the end of that, but that was a wrong assumption. Vega snatches Ilia and turns her into a kind of android. They conclude that Vega is a machine which is lacking something but it does now know what. It also has the mind of a child, emitting tantrums. They discover that Vega is a corruption of the word Voyager. It has taken in so much knowledge in 300 years that it has become a living thing, but it needs to integrate with a human in order to gain completion. Decker, who is in love with Ilia in any case, volunteers to merge with her with glittery accompaniment, and so give Vega what he needs. That solves the problem and the earth is saved. This is dubbed as the next step in evolution, when a machine can take over human emotions! But the other lesson we can learn from this is that LOVE (which is shown between Decker and Ilia) is the completion of knowledge; that in itself is a worthy concept, regardless of how fanciful the story line may be.

Also, there is the episode concerning the Genesis planet. It is a planet analogous to Earth, and has life forms on it. In all appearance it is like the Garden of Eden, and is some sort of experiment to reverse the failures of history and produce a perfect world. Such things as poverty, diseases, warfare, and all manner of unpleasant things will be eliminated. The Klingons have a plan to transplant this world on to the Moon, but we never get that far. The Klingons, who are hostile at this point, are worried that this project will succeed, and plan to destroy Genesis. Kirk is aware of a little boy being on Genesis and that he needs to be rescued. In defiance of orders, Kirk shanghais the Enterprise, goes to Genesis and rescues the boy in the nick of time. It turns out that this little boy is actually Spock, making a fresh start in life. To give us a clue as to what is happening, the 'crabs' that were near Spock's coffin have turned into funny looking snakes. The conclusion is that evolution is happening very rapidly on this planet. What took six days (in the Garden of Eden) is now happening in six minutes! Clearly this experiment is going haywire.

Because of this, it soon becomes clear that Spock is 'growing up' rather rapidly, and that if he is not removed from the Genesis planet quickly, he will arrive at old age again. The fact that we have a boy which is innocent, reminds us of Kaumali in the Huichol mythology.(4) In fact, innocence is an ongoing feature in the series. Also the planet is about to be destroyed. Kirk manages to rescue Spock in the nick of time, but he has still to have his right mind restored. They take him to the planet Vulcan, and in a ceremony strongly reminiscent of a Papal High Mass, McCoy and Spock have their minds transferred and rectified. All this is an admission that there is a soul, even for a Vulcan who only functions on cold logic.

To give the stories some sort of historical grounding, there are many proper names worked in, which are clearly derived from the ancient world. So we have already had Genesis and Eden. There are Latin names too, such as Tiberius (Kirk's middle name), Nimbus, Romulus and Remus, and Vulcan. From Greek there is Alpha, and Praxis. As we have seen, some sort of historical grounding is almost always seen in world mythologies.

Many other mythological features appear in Star Trek. There is a lady who helps Kirk and McCoy to escape when they are stuck in the trilithium mine on Rura Pente; she changes appearance at will, back and forth, just like certain people in Celtic, Norse and Greek stories. Also the Rugans have a dragon beast which is terrifying but is their pet. There is mention of snakes, as we see in the Genesis episode, but this is not a dominant metaphor in the series. Magical weapons are in abundance; the main one is the faser with which one can have a gun battle or just stun people or vaporise them. The space ships have torpedoes and technologically clever weaponry. The Klingon vessels have a cloaking device which makes them invisible.(5) Also there are people who can make themselves invisible,(6) as in the Ramayana, but the 'goodies' do not seem to stoop to such a dirty trick. There is no mention of swords, magic or otherwise; perhaps that was a little old-fashioned for the scriptwriter's taste. The exception to this would be the Klingon chief who has a thing which at first appears to be a sword but turns out to be a bone walking stick. We do have mention of 'shields'; this is something that the Enterprise can pull up to repel enemy attacks. There is even a mention of a new narcotic, not actually named, which reminds us of Soma, Peyote, Kava, mead, or Romulan ale which is turquoise. Other drinks which are supposed to be forbidden, are on offer in the Enterprise. At times there is plenty of smoke or mist, often associated with fire. Occasionally there is an ocean and someone receives a ducking. There are so many metaphoric elements in Star Trek that one wonders if the scriptwriters have studied mythology and deliberately included these matters. At the very least we can say that deliberate or not, these elements appeal to something in human nature; this explains the popularity of the series Star Trek.

It might be remarked that there is no mention of jewels, precious metals or translucent stones. But there are substitutes for this gap; there are plenty of flashing lights on the control panels and in the skies. There are strings of 'pearls' in the sky, as well as what looks like aurora in many scenes. When the Enterprise goes into warp drive, she flashes out rainbow colours in her wake. There is also some kind of electrical static that resembles lightning. Also we have a few giants and dwarfs, although his aspect of mythology is not overdone. Often we have leaders or diplomats who wear silver or gold trimmings, which is suggestive of royalty or authority.

One element which does not figure very often in world mythology, is the matter of music. Star Trek is characterised by a full-blown symphony orchestra with trumpets blasting out across the vast volumes of space. I always thought outer space was a quiet place, except for the occasional super nova explosion! But this can be seen as the great triumphalist exploration of unknown worlds, with fanfares and tubas booming out. It can also be seen as a part of the exaggeratedness of the whole thing with high drama; this is a well-established aspect of mythology. Far more realistic is when we have a string quartet on the Enterprise, playing something from Mozart at a reception. At Troy's wedding, we have a band and Data sings like a crooner.

Another scene which is important theologically, is when the Enterprise crew discover a people called the Ba'ku on a new planet. These people are clearly in a kind of backward age, pre-industrial, non-technological and completely agricultural. They are terrified when Data, who has been assessing the planet, suddenly goes haywire and there are attempts at catching him. He even fires on the Enterprise. Eventually, the Klingon, Work, manages to arrest him, and they discover that Data went off without various chips in his machinery. The point of the story is that these people, the Ba'ku, do not age. They appear primitive, but when Pickard comes to talk to them, he finds that they are anything but primitive; they are fully aware of technology and have rejected it on purpose. They had been living in a solar system that was about to destroy itself with all the clever weapons and gadgets that they had invented. So the Ba'ku had managed to find a new planet and start again. The secret of their 'elixir' was that there was some sort of element in the rings around the planet that was prolonging their lives. This would sound so ideal, except that another alien race has found out about it, and wants to remove the Ba'ku and have the planet to themselves. In the end, Pickard and his crew manage to sort it out so that the Ba'ku can carry on with their ideal way of life.

In this account, there are various comments on us at the present time. How far have we gone in this world, towards producing the means to wreck the whole world and possibly the solar system too? It is a sobering thought that World Peace is an urgent matter; intergalactic peace is never achieved in Star Trek, in spite of various peace initiatives. The truth is that people just do not trust each other. The return to a primitive way of life sounds so ideal, but the reality of it is another thing. Along with so many things in technology that are a danger, there are also the peaceful, helpful matters. This idea of 'going back' to basics has been tried but it has to be admitted that it has not worked. It would seem that Pandora's Box would require a massive effort to close the lid, but that would be a little late in the day. In addition to this, one might find some kind of wonderful life style or ideal situation, but there is always someone who wishes to interfere with it and spoil it. The notion that an entire people can be transplanted into a new territory sounds like an ideal solution, but this too has been tried often enough in human history, and has not worked. Lastly, the idea that a machine can be such a wonderful ruling factor in life, is a complete fallacy. Machines, computers, gadgets, electrical appliances; all of these can go haywire. They need to be kept in their place and not be allowed to rule our lives. Heaven help us if Data and his friends come to control our lives!

In conclusion we can say that Star Trek, apart from putting some wild ideas into people's heads, does have something positive to say to us. There is a strong emphasis on virtues such as loyalty, trust, brotherly love and romantic love. How often do we see that for all their cleverness, these people out in space seem incapable of achieving unity, in spite of the fact that they know it is of vital importance. This is the fundamental lesson that we can learn for our world today.

Who killed Captain Kirk?

This appears in a cartoon book form as opposed to a DVD, but it is interesting in that it depends heavily on traditional Greek mythology, and actually quotes from Dante's Inferno. The importance of this is that the writer is tacitly accepting that The Star Trek motif is actually mythology, or to put it more accurately futuristic mythology.

We have mention of a three-headed dog, but without snakes round his neck; this is Cerberus. On the shore of the River Acheron (some would call it the Styx) is Charon with his boat, the ferryman, waiting to take people across to Hell. There is a neutral zone 'where souls live without praise or blame'. But on the other shore there is dark, mist, fire and frost, and Hell has nine circles, which reminds us of Norse mythology. Spock is found talking to Plato, Euclid and Socrates; these are not exactly mythical people, but since they are found in Hell, they become mythical. While Spock is philosophising with them, Greek soldiers appear and prevent Kirk and his friends from approaching the philosophers on the grounds that no irrational being can come near. There is a sword fight and they defeat the soldiers. It is fortunate that they keep their swords because a dragon with snake-like tentacles attacks them and M'resh, the lion-girl is snatched. They have to chop off the tentacles. They also encounter the Furies, young ladies with a reluctance to wear any knickers but have snakes emanating from their heads, but they too are defeated. Various other monsters appear, clearly derived from Greek thought. All this is being inflicted on them by a crew-member called Castille, but it all comes to an end.

The murder of Jim Kirk is also interesting. It would appear that someone called Bearclaw stuck a dagger in him and nearly managed to kill him. But Dr. McCoy managed to save him. Jim came back on duty, even if weak. Eventually the real murderer made another attempt. He was Garth of Izar, who had cloaked himself as Bearclaw on the first attempt. This explains why Bearclaw claimed he had not done the deed. Spock comes in just at the right moment to save Jim and the true villain is apprehended.

The underlying thought in all this is the same as in the main series, that there is another world waiting for us after death; death is not the end. Life is precious and resurrection is a reality. That essential message is axiomatic to so many myths from round the world.

Star Wars

This is another Sci-Fi series not unlike Star Trek, but with more fantastic and exaggerated ideas to augment the drama. While Star Trek is relatively more thoughtful, personal and philosophical, Star Wars is more aggressive and there is less characterisation in it.

The over-arching theme is the stand-off between The Empire and the Republic. Now we see a strand of American political prejudice coming in. Their basic assumption is that Empires are bad, and find it hard to admit that America itself is an Empire! Republics are assumed to be good because they are supposed to be democratic. The assumption here is that America is democratic (dear me!). Interspliced with this is the element of monarchy in the form of Princess Leia, who joins in the adventures with elaborate hair-dos which never seem to become disturbed. This lady is dubbed as a 'senator' and the fact that she is royalty does not seem to carry much weight, in fact the boys are quite disrespectful at times. This again betrays an American attitude. Also we have the 'champion' element with the Jedi knights and the little boy in training who thinks he will be the most fantastic Jedi ever. That is a very common mythological element; we can compare it with the Shaman, Kauymali of the Huichols,(4) who is an innocent little boy but exceptionally spiritually gifted.

The concept of perpetual conflict in the skies is a very ancient one and with the Sci-fi element, it is now being projected into the future. It is simply the worst of human traits being magnified into something heroic, dramatic and full of virtue for the boys who think they are right. Some of the battles strongly resemble the dog-fights in the Battle of Britain, or the bomber raids over Germany. To complete the historical connection, there are scenes as in the Roman amphitheatre, of extreme violence, with misshapen exaggerated beasts attacking poor defenceless Jedii. Sometimes we have 'cowboy' gunplay, as in the Westerns. There are any number of sword fights, using magical light beams that can slice through anything. The sword is much more prominent in this series.

There are any amount of snakes, in the water or mixed in with grotesque animals. Many of the animals are various kinds of dinosaurs, which again takes us back to pre-history.

The element of resurrection is clearly present, but perhaps not quite so heavily emphasised as in Star Trek. Luke gets frozen up, in a sort of cryotherapy, and later is brought back to life. On a lesser scale, his hand is chopped off but later reinstalled. The 'tin man' who is gold plated, gets broken into pieces and then put back together. His head gets put on the wrong robot, and even manages to speak when bodyless. This reminds us of Mimir the giant in Norse thinking. In the end, the tin man is put back together properly. There are also armies of clones in shining armour, but they seem to be on both sides. One of the most significant remarks made by the trainee Jedi is 'I will learn to know how to stop people dying.'

Strange as it may seem, the Jedi Knights do not wear armour, and yet there is the implication that they are associated with the Knights of King Arthur. One of them, is actually made to look like Jesus, mind you, a suitably American sort of Jesus, which gives us the hint that he is the 'goodie' and the others are the 'baddies'.

There is also the underlying thought that predestination is a reality. Remarks made about destiny, and 'nothing happens by accident' are an indication of the scriptwriter's philosophy. A remark such as 'don't give in to hate, it leads to the dark side,' is worth remembering, and the fact that the little boy Anni has no greed simply emphasises his innocence. When he enters the race (which reminds us of motor racing), it is simply to win a bet to gain freedom from slavery. Sadly, his mother never does get freed, but he does.

All this indicates that Star Wars has a certain moral and philosophical content, but not as sensitively done as in Star Trek. There is romantic love worked in in both series, but then we have to have the romance with the pretty girl to keep people's interest. Otherwise the whole thing is somewhat predictable in its violence and exaggeratedness.

Dr. Who and Time Travel

Another Sci-fi series which started about the same time as Star Trek, has gone through over 813 episodes and is even now going through another reinvention. It is interesting that we have the same idea of some kind of historical grounding, with the London Police Telephone box, but after that the whole thing is completely fantastic. The Doctor, whose part is taken by a whole queue of actors, always has at least one girlfriend to help him, but it does not seem to result in any romance. The main point of interest is the concept of time travel. The Doctor can take his Tardis centuries into the future or the past and land on other planets millions of light years away, sometimes by design and sometimes by some sort of mistake. In fact, the term TARDIS is the initials for Time and Relative Dimension in Space.

What is the reality behind 'time travel'? Is it possible? This is an idea that has resulted from Einstein's Special and General Theory of Relativity. This does not mean that Einstein thought he was able to shoot off into space; the rockets had hardly been envisaged at that time. However, this is an interesting example of how a scientific theory has been captured by the dramatists and turned into what might seem a convincing TV series. This much it has in common with Star Trek, but less so with Star Wars.

There is a chapter in a book called the Scientific Secrets of Dr.Who, by James Swallow, which goes into the feasibility of time travel. It would seem that the physics experts believe that there is a thing called 'time dilation'. I quote the significant passage in full for the reader to assess it for himself;

'... relative velocity and gravity can both alter the rate at which we experience the passage of time compared with observers moving at different speeds or experiencing a different gravitational field from us.' (page 155).

What makes us come to this realisation? It has been noted that in satellites on low Earth orbit, the clocks run slightly slower than on ground level. With satellites further away from the Earth, the clocks run slightly faster. The difference is only ten millionth of a second, but nevertheless it is significant. It means that in a spacecraft going millions of light years out into space, the clocks would go a long way ahead (at least in theory). It would mean that an astronaut using ten years of his time on a journey would use 100 years of earth-time. It would be a 'fast forward into the future.' This is what 'time dilation' means (or is supposed to mean).

This raises the question as to whether the opposite can be achieved, going back into the past. If we can go back into the past, does that mean we could alter the course of 'history'? What about the ethics of interfering with history, for instance, what about shooting Adolf Hitler back in the 1920's?

Here again we have an interesting but speculative answer to that. Some theoretical physicists think that there could be a thing called a 'wormhole', which can take a short cut in space time, so that one can go back and forth in time. All this is highly theoretical and full of wishful thinking, but then, who knows what clever devices may be developed in centuries to come? We notice that in the Dr.Who series, there are all kinds of arguments and confusions over time and timings. An issue that will emerge, if ever this notion becomes a reality, is finding a datum point for a universal date. In this world, we have managed to achieve this. It began with Alexander the Great and went on through the Seleucid kingdom and into the Roman Empire. Before that, all datings had to be related to the regnal years of various kings. Now, we have managed to use the birth of Jesus Christ as the datum point in world history, even if the secularists are not completely content with this idea. Other dating systems are used by the Jews, the Muslims, the Chinese and the Baha'is, but none of them carry complete conviction across the world.

I have to comment that while on the one hand the calendar with its dates has to be a constant flow of days, the sensation of going through life does seem to elasticate or shrink various phases in one's life. So, for instance, one's childhood seems to take much longer than it really is; one's middle age seems to go far too rapidly; one's old age seems also to spin out much longer. It is all emotional, and perhaps in the end we shall find that time itself is far too much a matter of emotion. Even so, the issue of 'time travel' is a matter for consideration.

Footnotes for chapter 20

1. This is discussed at the end of this chapter.
2. Trilithium; This is a synthetic compound, an explosive of great power, and an inhibitor of nuclear reactions.
3. This is clearly based on the experience of Moses at the Exodus, 14:19.
4. Kauymali, the ultimate shaman, seen in chapter 14.
5. Ramayana, a part of Hindu scriptural material, described in The Theology of Truth, chapter 22.
6. Harry Potter has an invisibility cloak which he uses quite and often shares with this friends. See chapter 23. Bilbo Baggins has an invisibility ring. See chapter 8

21

The Myth of Evolution

We have become accustomed, in our own times to think of The Theory of Evolution, as propounded by Charles Darwin, as the truth. Many people take it as proven and do not bother to think about it; others dismiss it as nonsense. Those of a fundamentalist approach will take Genesis chapter one as the final truth and will not allow themselves to think of anything else. However in recent times we have seen not just fundamentalists but various scientists raise difficulties with Evolution; more of that later. I favour the Buddhist approach to Creation; a Buddhist would probably say something to this effect; 'we have no idea how the world began or life that we have now; it is enough to worry about the situation here and now, rather than try to delve into the past.' There is a lot in that view; if it is true that the history of life in this world goes back 500 million years or more, and there was no one there to record these alleged events, how are we ever going to be certain as to what actually did happen? Even if that 500 million years is some sort of mirage, and the world is only 6000 years old (!), as some will continue to insist, it is still the same problem; who was there to see the start of all things? It is all very well to talk of 'evidence', but evidence has to be interpreted, and so far, it has normally been interpreted through 'evolution-tinted spectacles'.

The following remarks are based on Darwin's book The Origin of Species and in addition, Elizabeth Colbert's book The Sixth Extinction and Niles Eldredge's book Evolution and Extinction; also Michael Behe's book, Science and evidence for design in the Universe.

However, Evolution is now more than just a theory concocted by Darwin. It has become an ongoing assumption underlying just about everything in modern life. Even the fundamentalists cannot escape its influence. Whole socio-economic policies and political theories have rested on the assumption that if it is true for biology, then it must be valid for all areas of modern living. We can even see its influence on the Biblical criticism of recent times. There are two assumptions in this; firstly that Darwin was right (was he? Even he had reservations about some aspects of it) and secondly that what is claimed to be 'scientific' must hold good for other matters, including ethics and religious awareness. Strangely, Evolution seemed to strike a chord with the **id** of mankind, and has become the ongoing assumption in just about everything in the modern world. One wonders why; just to say that it is the truth is not enough. The human race has a nasty habit of fastening on to wrong ideas and pretending that they are right. (See my chapter on Mein Kampf in The Theology of Truth). If Evolution were ever to be disproved, whole areas of thinking would have to be thought out afresh. Perhaps that would be a healthy thing!

It is worth remarking that Evolution is not just the bright idea of Mr.Darwin. Traces of this notion can be found in the mythology of Ancient Egypt, in the Egyptian Book of the Dead.(1) Also the Greek philosophers allude to it, Plato, Anaximander (60 BC) and others. They do not go into details as to how it could have worked, but the impression of it was still in some people's minds right into the modern era, but before the publication of Darwin's book, The Origin of Species. It is likely that the Christian dogmatists took Genesis chapter one at face value and smothered any thought of Evolution.

How did Evolution come to be so convincing to people in the late 19th century? For many years, strange bones and fossils had been turning up. They seemed not to relate to any creature seen in the modern world. It was Cuvier, the French collector of such things, that became aware of something called 'extinction'. He rapidly amassed a large collection of fossils that had to relate to large animals no longer found on earth.(2) He could see that there were many other species that had lived a long time ago but had died out. What was the cause? He became aware of a world of giant reptiles belonging to the Mesozoic era; Plesiosaur, ichthyosaur, pterodactyl. Cuvier also was one of the first to apply the principle of 'stratification' as the key to dating such remains. This meant that the deeper one dug, the older the remains. This is something that modern archaeology now takes for granted. Cuvier was opposed to Evolution. Another 'expert', Lamarck(3) was in favour of it and disagreed with Cuvier on the idea of 'extinction'.

Why did Cuvier disagree with Evolution? He had managed to obtain a mummified cat from Egypt. On examination, he could see that it was no different from the cats in saw in Paris. This must indicate that over the period of maybe 3000 years, the creature had not developed at all; in fact it was the same. From that he generalised that creatures do not change with time, and do not develop into something else. The same conclusion could fairly be drawn from comparing Gristhorpe Man, a skeleton preserved in Scarborough; he is reckoned to be 4000 years old, but is virtually identical to us today. In fairness to Cuvier the same could be said of other creatures, such as crocodiles, turtles and horseshoe crabs, and various others, which have remained virtually the same since Ordovician times, 500 million years ago. Recent findings have shown that Trilobites, a kind of shellfish, have continued in virtually the same form and shape from Middle Devonian times for several million years. They are now extinct. So that posed the question, as to why so many creatures, especially the massive ones, had disappeared. This is where the 'disaster' theory comes in; Cuvier was convinced that there had been a cataclysmic disaster which wiped out about 90% of the world's fauna. This was thought to have happened at the end of the Cretaceous period, about 66 million years ago. Then there was a break in the fossil evidence before life began again, except that a few species managed to survive the disaster. About 6 to 7 million years ago, the human race began to appear. Cuvier decided that there had been more than one mass extinction. Colbert thinks there were five extinctions; Eldredge thinks there were seven. Doubtless there are other 'experts' with a different scheme! None of them seem in agreement on the timings. This scheme follows Eldredge's idea: (4)

Extinctions	million years ago	termed as
1	540	end-Cambrian
2	485	end-Ordovican
3	420	end-Devonian
4	300	end-Permian
5	201	end-Triassic
6	66	end-Cretaceous
7	0.01	end-Pleistocene

Many people could not give credit to this kind of idea back in the 19th century. Lyell was one and he asserted that extinction, which was actually a reality, was a gradual process. However, he did not really have an explanation for why the evidence in the fossils showed that certain species came to an abrupt end. Also we now know that some species have an abrupt start.

This issue of an abrupt start and an abrupt end is of some importance. There are many examples of species that just appear in the fossil record without, it appears, any 'parent'. While it is easy to see how a species can come to an abrupt end, in other words, go into extinction very suddenly, because of some kind of drastic alteration in their environment or habitat, it is not so easy to explain the abrupt appearance of species. It has to be admitted that for some species, there appear to be what can be called 'intermediates'. Piltdown Man was supposed to have been an 'intermediate'! This means that the fossil record shows a given species gradually changing into something more 'advanced' adapting itself to changes in its environment. However, Eldredge states 'Virtually all the major groups of animals and plants show the same fossil pattern; rather abrupt first appearances in the fossil record, in a form that is destined not to change too radically throughout tens of millions of years, during the rest of their recorded history.' (page 204). Many 'experts' take this as an indication that the Darwinian model of evolution is wrong; that there has been no gradual change in forms over the millions of years; evolution, if one can call it that, seems to go in fits and starts. It is nothing like as simple and straightforward as was originally thought, and many people still assume. All this has become increasingly obvious as more investigation continues into the fossil record.

Lyell was against evolution. When new species appeared in the fossil record, he had no explanation for it (neither do we now, it would seem). However, by this time, most, if not all palaeontologists were accepting that life on earth was at least 500 million years old, if not more, and that sat uncomfortably with the seven days of Creation as in Genesis, if one must take it completely literally. Nowadays we have notions of the age of the earth being reckoned in billions of years.

So Evolution was 'in the ether' by the middle of the 19th century. It was Darwin who took inspiration from Lyell's books, and propounded his theory of Evolution. He had to hurry up with his publication, because someone called Wallace was on the verge of claiming the same notion. This means that Evolution was not just Darwin's own clever theory. He dismissed disasters and miracles and maintained that extinction was a gradual process, but also that the arrival of new species was a gradual process, so gradual that it cannot be observed. It was all about the struggle for existence, and natural selection. The really shocking implication that Darwin introduced was that the human race was merely a development from more primitive forms. In his first book, he actually only gave a hint of this; he did not actually say that mankind developed from monkeys. That idea was developed later, in his second book,(5) to the bewilderment of many people. To put it crudely, it occurred to people that we might be only moderately civilised monkeys! That is what really caused a storm in the late 19th century.

To his credit, Darwin did actually do a tour of the world and made assessments first hand. One notable case of this was his visit to the Galapagos Islands where he became aware of tortoises with slightly different shaped shells, peculiar to each island. From this he deduced that the tortoises had adapted themselves to the conditions on each different island, albeit over a long period of time. From that he generalised that the same had been happening with all species since the dawn of time. One notable study described in his book was concerning pigeons. His conclusion was that all modern pigeons had a common ancestor, namely the rock pigeon. By selective breeding he found he could produce any variety of pigeon. We have to note that he was unable to produce by selective breeding a sparrow or a hawk, from pigeons. His study was fair enough as far as it went, but to generalise and say that all species must have a common ancestor, is an interesting piece of logic. This is a factor which the objectors fasten on to; that one cannot generalise from the specific to the general; one can generalise from the general to the specific. Unfortunately, scientists often do make this mistake, notably Sigmund Freud. To put it another way, what may have been true for the Galapagos tortoises, does not have to hold true for other creatures all over the world. Also what may be true for the pigeons might not be true for other creatures. We know that different colours and shapes can be produced with creatures such as butterflies, fruit flies, flowers. We now know that that kind of genetic engineering does not work with some other creatures. The classic example is that Hermann Goring wanted to go hunting Aurochs in the forests of Poland. Aurochs have been extinct for a long time, but he persuaded his scientific friends to culture aurochs from bulls, buffaloes and bisons which are thought to have 'descended' from the aurochs. It was true that they managed to produce a beast that looked like an aurochs but it was only in appearance. The beast was essentially still some sort of bull or bison. In other words, the 'common ancestor' idea may be true for some species but not necessarily for all.

With the publication of Darwin's book, The Origin of Species, the idea of Evolution became the prevailing assumption right up to the present day, and many in the scientific world are quite dogmatic about it. What many people fail to realise is that the 'catastrophe' theory, as an alternative idea, has gained much more ground in recent times. It is not the total opposite of evolution, but it does cast a very different light on matters. It would seem that Cuvier 's ideas would hold a lot of water. It was Alvarez (1970's) who came across a gorge called the Gola del Bottaccione, north of Rome, and he came across traces of an asteroid that ended the Cretaceous period; it would seem that three-quarters of species died out. Very telling was the fact that there were two layers of limestone with a thick layer of clay in between. There are such things as 'forams' (in full, foraminifera). They are tiny marine creatures with calcite shells which drift down to the ocean floor when they die. They are what produce the massive strata of limestone in its various types. Under the clay, the forams were of one type, and they come to an end about the same time as the dinosaurs died out, very suddenly. In the clay there are no forams at all. Above the clay, forams appear again, but they are of a totally different type from the ones under the clay. This is highly significant; it means that 'creation' however you see it, had to start all over again. At the same time, certain creatures survived the catastrophe. Another important factor is the iridium aspect. This element is very scarce in the earth's surface, but is very common in meteorites. Testing the three layers gave the results that the limestones of both kinds had the normal iridium content, but the clay had masses of it. The conclusion from this is that there had been a massive meteorite strike about 65 million years ago, when the vast majority of life on earth suddenly died out, then a long period of say several million years before life began to reassert itself. It soon became clear that it was not just central Italy that had been affected, but many sites the world over, from Denmark to New Zealand.

Locating the meteorite strike is also feasible and widely accepted. At a place called Chicxulub in the Yucatan peninsular in Mexico, 'shocked quartz' was found; doubtless Von Daniken would make this out to be the result of a space rocket taking off! But we have already commented on the reality of 'an airburst' (chapter 17) which means that when a meteorite hits the ground, vast heat is produced which vitrifies the rocks. The conclusion has been reached that a massive meteorite, about ten kilometres in diameter, hit the earth at a glancing blow and made a colossal crater. The devastation caused by this would not be so much as the hole in the ground (which incidentally is still there), but the material thrown up into the atmosphere. This would have blotted out the sun for a long time, altered temperatures all over the world and smothered everything in powder. There is much disagreement over the actual workings of this catastrophe; it may have involved an outburst of volcanic activity. This would mean that a few aquatic animals and some birds would have managed to survive, but land animals would not have stood a chance. This would explain the end of the Cretaceous age. It is worth noting that when life did reassert itself, animals would appear to 'shrink', in other words, the massive lumbering beasts of the dinosaur age never reappeared, and all land animals were of a more moderate size. That too is significant, but unfortunately precisely what the significance of it is, is not clear.

In case one were to think that this catastrophe 66 million years ago is somewhat fanciful, there have been recent investigations in the Chicxulub area, involving drillings into the seabed. These have served to confirm this idea. It would be a mistake to say that all the extinctions had been caused in the same way by a meteorite strike. There may have been other causes, possibly rather more gradual. The end-Permian and end-Cretaceous seem to be the most straightforward to evidence. However one sees it, it must cast a different light on the matter of Evolution.

One creature, which is very significant, is the Ammonite, a sea creature like a snail. There are many different varieties of ammonite, and new types are still coming to light. They all belong to the pre-Cretaceous period, and died out completely when this supposed disaster struck. No one knows what the soft parts of this creature looked like, but the shells made excellent fossils. This too is an indication of the abrupt end of the Cretaceous period. Darwin himself knew about the disappearance of the ammonites, but he could not contemplate the 'disaster' theory. With our new knowledge based on recent scientific research, we can contemplate it; it casts a whole new light on the matter of evolution. At the very least, one can conclude that the whole matter is much more complicated than anyone had ever thought before; also it is no longer a matter of imagining a simple straightforward progression, like a tree with its branches.(6) One wonders if we shall ever come to explain the whole thing.

Another factor in all this is the fact that the higher the latitude, the lower the number of species, and vice versa, the lower the latitude, the higher the number of species. This means that in the tropics, the rainforests and associated areas, the faster plants and animals germinate and reproduce. This is because it is warmer and moreover the temperatures are more stable. It has been noted that new species keep coming to light on a regular basis, almost always in the tropics. New Guinea is a notable place for new species to turn up. New plants, new animals and new insects, often in great numbers keep appearing. Is this because the scientists have just been careless and unobservant, or it is that genuinely new things keep appearing? It has recently been commented that a new animal, which seems to be a cross between a rat, a rabbit and a cat, which has not been seen before, has appeared in the forests of New Guinea. At the very least, we can say that as some species go into extinction, others appear to take their place. There are many animals that are on the verge of extinction and are being kept in existence artificially by human intervention. No one seems able to offer an explanation for what seems to be new species appearing. If one believes in the creative genius of God, it is not a problem, but then it is not politically correct to enlist the help of God in explaining these matters, in these modern times of scepticism!

With regard to the appearance of the human race, it is important to see that it is a very 'recent' event in the total picture of life on this planet. There is no way that humans could have been firing arrows at dinosaurs! 'Humanoids' or 'hominins', terms which appear in biological textbooks, are reckoned to have appeared well after the last major catastrophe at the end of the Cretaceous period (65 million years ago), but before the end-Pleistocene disaster which might have been an Ice Age. (4) Again, the picture is nowhere near as clear-cut or straightforward as most people seem to assume. In 1856, the remains of a 'humanoid' turned up in Neandertal, Germany. Admittedly the remains were incomplete, but later a complete one turned up in France. Neandertal man remains have now turned up all over Europe, the Middle East and the Caucasus. Their existence spanned 100,000 years, so it is alleged. The world must have been very cold then, because they wore clothing; it is not proved that they were hairy. Also they had tools such as flint axes. It is even claimed that they did burials and put flowers on the grave! Then 30,000 years ago they disappeared; at least in one sense; in another sense, it is alleged that they had sexual relations with other humanoids which explains why 4% of their DNA is still in humans to this day (allegedly!)

The earliest known hominins so far are evidenced in Chad, the Sahelanthropus Tchadensis of the late Miocene period,(7) and he is claimed to be bipedal. This is going back 6 to 7 million years. There are about 30 examples of humanoids, coming down to about 1.25 million years ago. Many of them are said to be bipedal, and artistic renditions of them give us the impression that they are not noticeably different from modern humans. One difference worth commenting on is their height. It is so easy to have them arrayed, in the picture books, as short (about 4 foot) and building up to 6 foot. What we need to remember is that the same factor applies to us nowadays. There is dwarfism and gigantism in humans now. Also there is the shape of the skull and its volume, both of which vary. But that is true for us also today. Why does it have to be assumed that the size of one's brain has to indicate the level of one's intelligence? In addition we know that bones can be distorted both ante-mortem and post-mortem. It is so easy to generalise from the few remains that we have unearthed. Most of these remains are fragmentary; it is unusual to find a complete skeleton.

We are accustomed to hearing about the first humans coming from the rift valley in Africa, and again there is some substance in this. Darwin predicted this. Modern humans arrived in Europe about 40,000 years ago; they were similar to the Neadertals but not the same, it is alleged. The modern humans drove the Neadertals to extinction, which explains why they no longer exist now. They did not evolve into something more refined, it would seem. There was another kind of 'human' called a 'Hobbit' which has been traced in Indonesia, a smaller version, perhaps like a pigmy. Also yet another called the 'Denisovan' found in Siberia and which is now 6% of the DNA found in the population of New Guinea. It is expected that other strains of humanity may be found as more remains come to light.

It is so easy to generalise, but we must remember that the fossil specimens that we do have are very few, (admittedly a lot more than a century ago) and widely spaced timewise and geographically. The fossil record is very incomplete. It is admitted that we have maybe 1% of the total fossil record, and that many more examples, which may include unknown variants on hominins, are yet to be found. Another complication concerns dating. It is so easy to assume that Carbon 14 dating will tell us which specimens are older or younger. But this will only work on bone material, shell or charcoal, and will only be reliable (!) for times within 5,730 years. All our fossil material goes back from about 12,000 years. There is now something called 'radiometric' dating which gives us an estimate of rock age. But this only works on igneous rock. Most of our fossils are found in conjunction with sedimentary rock, specifically limestone. To gain an estimate of date for a fossil, it would have to be found in a sedimentary rock sandwiched in between two layers of igneous. So easily this sort of thing can become a circular argument. In addition to this, we only have evidence of creatures with some kind of bone structure that will turn into a fossil in the right conditions. Creatures with only soft tissue or with bones that land in an acidic soil (and so decompose) cannot be evidenced. The conclusion from this, as before, is that the whole thing is by no means as simple and straightforward as many people assume. Just assuming that humanity is an easy development from monkeys to 21st century mankind is a gross oversimplification. It is worth remarking that so far, no chimpanzee fossils have been found older than the earliest hominin remains; in other words, the monkey might have descended from the humans, rather than the other way round!(7)

There are people like Pääbo (Swedish) who calculate the DNA of ancient bones and try to work out which strain influenced which. This is not an easy task, as many of the remains have DNA which is fragmentary or deteriorated, so the whole matter is an obstacle course of guesswork and speculation. Carbon 14 dating is nowhere near as conclusive as one might assume it to be. Making up a dating sequence from fossils may appear to be easy, but how much of this is the result of pre-digested thought, ie. assuming a gradual progression from primitive to refined? As one can guess, 'experts' have massive arguments over these matters, and there is no total consensus on accurate dating of fossil material.

Much of the forgoing remarks have been derived from Elizabeth Colbert's book, The Sixth Extinction. This seems to be a very sane, balanced appraisal of prehistoric life, and not inclined to fanciful theories. But here comes the 'eschatological' projection. Since, as it would seem, the world has gone through five (or is it seven?) major extinctions, roughly spaced at about 65 million years apart, we are now about to encounter another major extinction. This one will probably not involve a meteorite strike; it will be induced by the interference of the human race in the workings of nature. It is on much the same lines as James Lovelock, as discussed in chapter 4, but approached in a slightly different way. She is concerned about the level of CO_2 (carbon dioxide) in the oceans. This is where the doomsday element comes in, an assumption that many scientists have. Again, there is the slight admission that the earth's orbit has altered slightly, which could account for global warming, and this might be because of the gravitational pull of Jupiter and Saturn, but Colbert does not develop this line of argument. At no point does she consider that the earth is a self-correcting mechanism. It is interesting, however, that just as she avoids all kinds of mythological possibilities with Creation, nevertheless, it all swings round to eschatology, which is only futuristic mythology.

Various conclusions might be drawn from this appraisal so far. It would seem that some species, for instance, the crocodile, the horseshoe crab and the turtle, have managed to persist from Cambrian times right through five extinctions (or is it seven?) and are still with us today with very little physiological difference. If Evolution is a truism, we have to wonder why these animals have not altered into something else over the millennia. Then we have the impression of the horse family which appears to have developed into various forms and can still interbreed. This might indicate that evolution has played a part in the life of some creatures, but not necessarily all of them.

Then we have the teasing question of species that abruptly disappear or appear. An example of this is the Pterosaur, whose origin is a mystery (so we are told). It suddenly appears in the early Triassic era as a highly developed flying creature. There is no sign of anything that could have evolved into it, no 'missing links' to borrow an important phrase. In addition to that there are creatures that die out, but when they reappear they seem to have no parentage from the previous ones. A good example of this was the forams but there are also the 'graptolites' of the Ordovician era, which did the same thing. This is all very strange and puts a large question mark against evolution, at least in the popularised form that most people take for granted. It looks as though for some creatures, Creation starts all over again with no reference to the past.

Another puzzle is the late Triassic cache of skeletons found on Ghost Ranch, New Mexico in 1947. It would seem that there was a mass death of Coelophysis involving hundreds of them, all on top of each other. Experts are still trying to unravel the implications in this, and needless to say, such a deposit of such magnitude and concentration is seldom found anywhere else, as yet. What the implications of this would be for evolution is still to this day a matter of guesswork.

Something else which no one seems willing to comment on, is the fact that in the Mesozoic age, there were massive creatures. The Diplodochus is reckoned to weigh 20 tons, and the Brachiosaurus 70 tons, and some may have been even bigger. I have to comment that the Brachiosaurus actually resembles a giraffe, with its long neck, but one wonders why such creatures did not collapse under their own weight? Its neck and tail must have been a tremendous weight to cope with. An assessment of the sabre tooth tiger recently admitted that the creature must have been so heavy that it could hardly have pounced on its prey. The issue of weight must have been a problem; it might suggest that the earth's gravity was rather less than now. Another factor which may be of relevance here, is the claim that the earth's atmosphere was more heavily charged with oxygen than it is now, thus giving these creatures more energy.

Another issue which seems not to receive evaluation is the matter of scale. After the end-Cretaceous extinction, all the animals, with a few exceptions, are generally smaller, in other words, scaled down. The question of scale is still with us now. We have the cat family, ranging from lions down to the domestic cat; there is the dog family ranging from the wolf down to the Chihuahua. There are many other such families. From an evolutionary point of view, one might say that the smaller ones grew out of the big ones, or vice versa, or that they had a common ancestor. This might hold true for the horse, since so many variants on it can interbreed.(8) It would be so convenient if the fossil evidence confirmed this, but so far it is nothing like as clear as one would hope it to be. The same applies to the human race. The fossil evidence is not straightforward, so much so that someone thought it helpful to forge 'the Piltdown Man' to help us all feel comfortable about being descended from the apes! That forgery was not the only one, and the lesson from that is that we must be cautious about jumping to conclusions about fossils, their dating, and their implications.

So what is the position over fossils? We have tons of material from the Morrison Formation in the mid-west of the USA, sometimes actually complete skeletons, but usually bits and pieces. Some parts of the world are rich in material and other parts have hardly anything. Many of the conjectures about prehistoric creatures are just that; conjectures, guesswork, and the result of painstaking reconstruction. Arguments rage over almost every aspect of the matter. It is a big mistake to allow oneself to slide into some kind of dogmatism over evolution, but unfortunately many of our leading 'experts' do just that. So far, the only aspect of these matters which I find reasonable to accept, is the extinction argument, as seen in the sedimentary layers. I am not trying to say that evolution is completely wrong, but I am saying that it is only one aspect of the great workings of nature. There are other variables at work. One of these is balance, which modern theorists seem not to take much notice of.

Another factor is the matter of dominant and recessive species. We all know that the rat, which comes in various versions everywhere in the world can be called a dominant species. Its chances of going into extinction are nil! But there are many other creatures that are in the minority and are threatened with extinction. The reason for this threat is usually because humans have interfered with their life-style; if left alone they would probably continue in the minority. If evolution is true, then why have the recessive species managed to survive, when one would expect them to have gone into extinction long ago? But there is always something in the minority along with the majority. The same is true with politics, religion, chemical elements and many other aspects of life; even the letters in the alphabet. Why is this? My conjecture would be that they all fulfil some kind of purpose in the great workings of things. If Evolution were to be the only truth, we would expect to be overrun with rats and swamped with bindweed! But somehow there is some kind of limit put on them which allows other things to have a chance and contribute something to the general picture. Evolution can only go so far but not the whole way. That is my feeling.

The Origin of Species by Charles Darwin

It is now the right moment to review Darwin's landmark book, The Origin of Species. This is a fascinating book, published in 1859, typical of Victorian style. For a serious biological treatise, it is closely argued with the admission that it is only a theory as opposed to a fact. He was uncertain about some matters which might, he thought, cancel out his thesis. It has various bursts of sentimentality. In general, it is hard-going reading and though many a biologist will find it instructive, much of it will be lost on the non-specialist. It is biology and geology before the age of the discovery of genes, chromosomes and DNA; also the concept of continental drift is in its infancy; also the discovery and assessment of early man is not included in his first book.

His main and all-encompassing assumption is that of gradual development of living creatures from basic and primitive forms into what we see today, as highly developed forms. This has been achieved by 'natural selection' or the struggle for existence, which has been going on so gradually over the millennia that it cannot be perceived, but it has been in a simple straight line. This takes no account of what was suspected then and is known now, that life has had at least five or more major extinctions, which have interrupted the (assumed) flow of evolution. Darwin disagrees with that idea. This struggle takes two forms; firstly the survival of the fittest, which means that the weaker creatures die or are killed off; secondly that there is the tussle between the more powerful males to mate with the most attractive females. This aspect of evolution can hardly be denied since we can see it happening now. What we cannot see is creatures gradually turning into stronger or more efficient versions of themselves, and Darwin admits that.

The book is punctuated with examples of biological studies done by himself and others, and on that basis, the book is well researched and can be commended. His work on pigeons which he describes in detail, is noteworthy. His conclusion is that all varieties of pigeon are descended from the rock pigeon, which was their ancestor. It is true that through selective breeding, one can produce pigeons of different colours, shape of beak, display of feathers etc., and that might be held as evidence that creatures can mutate into something else. But he does not manage to turn a pigeon into an eagle or a titmouse! Moreover, just because this selective breeding can work for one species, does not have to mean that it is a general rule for all creatures; this is another case of arguing from the specific to the general. But his idea of 'common ancestor' becomes a prevailing assumption in his book. The other difficulty with this idea is that in the wild, before the interference of mankind, the pigeons would hardly have organised themselves to produce different versions of themselves, unless of course they were really very clever!

We all know that flowers of the same genus can be crossed to produce hybrids. Sheep too can be bred selectively. Butterflies also can be cultured. But no one has yet managed to culture one genus into something different. The sheep is still a sheep, even if it is fatter, woollier and tamer!

One would assume, that if say the horse, the donkey and Shetland pony had a 'common ancestor', going back millions of years, then there would be bone and fossil evidence of this, in a gradual series. Darwin is concerned that there is no such useful series of evidence, not just for the horse but for many other types. He admits there are massive gaps in the fossil evidence which means that there has to be large amounts of supposition. He says in so many words that the fossil evidence is imperfect; that is an understatement. This is still something that is true to this day, even with the discovery of much more fossil and bone material.

Darwin is fascinated by the strange permutations in living forms, in different parts of the world, and especially on remote areas such as islands out in the oceans. This is still something which teases the biologists now; what they omit to mention is that such strange permutations can be found on the mainland, for instance northern Thailand and southern China. Nowadays, we have a much clearer idea of continental drift, a theory which only gradually gained credibility later in the 19th century, but is now more or less accepted doctrine. It is thought that originally there was one land mass where Europe and Africa are now, and other parts like America and Australia drifted away. It is interesting to see how some creatures are not much different from Europe to America, but also some forms are very different. Some of the islands have forms that are not found anywhere else. Darwin does not really have an answer to this, and neither do we now. It is just evidence that the whole matter is incredibly complicated and we do not have the evidence to explain it as yet.

It is rather like having three or four jigsaw puzzles. Someone has removed about 80% of the pieces, not the same from one puzzle to another, and a lot of the edging pieces. We do not know if the three or four are the same picture or different; nor do we know what the picture is going to be. We make assumptions about the finished picture, but assembling the pieces is always guesswork, supposition and confusion, clogged up with dogmatisms. Transferring pieces from one puzzle another is always assuming that they are supposed to be the same picture. The finished size of the puzzles is unknown since many of the edging pieces are missing. If one were to think this analogy is somewhat unfair, it is actually based on one that Darwin gives us in his book! His main 'picture' or preconceived assumption is the 'tree' motif as described on page 121 and expanded on on page 322.(9) It is interesting that world mythologies very commonly have a tree as a central motif; does this mean we are looking at yet another 'scientific' mythology?

Darwin is honest enough to admit that certain features are so complex and highly developed that it is difficult to understand how evolution could have produced them. The example he discusses is the EYE. Could natural selection produce an eye? How would the animal have managed, over thousands of years, with an eye that was half perfected or not functioning properly? Another problem is the electric fish, for example the electric eel.

How would that facility have developed naturally? There are all kinds of anomalies, such as the drone bees, and organs that have no use. There are flightless birds. There are trilobites, nautilus and lingula which are hardly changed from Pre-cambrian times; why did they not evolve into something else? To read his book, we are constantly faced with imponderables. One wonders what he would have thought of the Coelocanth, an example of which was fished up in 1938; a creature that was assumed to be extinct back in Jurassic times; more have been landed recently. His own words are appropriate; 'How little we know of the former inhabitants of the world.' (page 313).

Darwin spends much time discussing animal instincts, and does not really have an answer to some of the most intriguing. How does the bee, in the dark, with thousands of them buzzing around, construct perfect hexagonal cavities for storing the honey? There are many more such puzzles. He is quite happy to talk of animal instinct, though he does not move on to talk of instinct in humans. Freud did. But it would seem that we all have some sort of **id**. Darwin does not attempt to entertain the thought that animals also have some degree of **ego** and of **super ego**. Rationality in animals is not at all out of the question, and we know that some creatures can be unbelievably crafty. Also we suspect that conscience is a factor; it can be seen with domestic pets, but is not completely absent from wild animals. The whole question of animal personality and language is a field only just beginning to be explored, but the evolutionists do not seem able to grapple with it.

Sadly, Evolution has become a first class excuse for those who wish to justify atheism. In fact, the modern outburst of atheism can largely be explained by the appearance of Darwin's book. However, he seems aware of this eventuality and says, 'I see no good reason why the views given in this volume should shock the religious feelings of anyone.' (page 455) I do not think he wanted to wreck anyone's faith. In fact, many times he makes remarks that show he is a believer; '... originally breathed by the Creator into a few forms or into one.' (page 463). He often refers to the 'works of God' or 'the hand of Nature' and other indirect remarks about God. He seems to think that God started everything off but did not intervene during the course of history. Even so, we can consider this remark; 'there is a Power, represented by natural selection or the survival of the fittest, always intent on watching each slight alteration.' (page170); in other words, God is supervising the whole process.

For those who were outraged at the suggestion that mankind is merely the end product of the evolutionary process, in other words, a fairly civilised monkey (!), we notice that Darwin's first book does not include the factor of the human race at all. It is all about animals and plants. The only remark which could cause problems would be; 'Much light will be thrown on the origin of man and his history.'(page 462). Here he is referring to Herbert Spencer, a 19th century philosopher, in the context of humanity acquiring mental power 'by gradation'. But there is no suggestion that we are all shaven monkeys! However, that is one of the big problems that the evolutionists have not yet resolved; if it is true that mankind evolved from monkeys, how do we get from animal consciousness to human consciousness? In fairness, Darwin wrote his book before the discovery of Neandertal man, and also the further discoveries as mentioned above.

The conclusion I reach on these matters is that while there is an element of truth in the theory of evolution, it is by no means the whole truth. There are so many other variables involved, such as animal personality, the balance of nature (something that Darwin mentions in passing but does not develop), long-term survival of certain creatures, changes in environment and habitat, extinctions, the earth as a self-correcting mechanism, and chiefly, the creative genius of God (which we are not allowed to know about these days!)

This is enough to put a big question mark against evolution. I am not trying to say it is totally wrong, but to allow it become the prevailing doctrine of modern times is a big mistake. So many people take it as an established fact to the exclusion of all else. It is fair to say that it has become the myth of the modern world. By this I do not mean 'lie' or 'misapprehension'. I mean that just as at one time humanity thought the world was a system of three shelves, and the whole of their thinking revolved around that, so too everyone's thinking revolves around Evolution. Another example is that just as at one time, everyone thought that the world was stationary and the rest of the Universe was circulating round us, therefore we were the centre of the Universe. Now we know that we are hurtling through space at 67,000 miles per hour, but since this is constant, we have no impression of movement. The ancient world was living with one set of illusions; we are now almost certainly living with another set of delusions. This does not tell us whether Evolution is true or false; it is just the popular assumption. In addition, it has become fuel for a certain type of modern eschatology, namely the future of man, in very optimistic and sentimental terms.

The recent challenge to Evolution

Evolution has never been totally accepted and there have always been those who refused to countenance it. This has mainly been the Fundamentalists, but not entirely. There is now a growing band of scientists who raise cogent reasons for questioning Evolution, not on emotional or mythological grounds, but on solid rationalisation from analysis of complex biological systems.

Michael Behe has raised the question of what he calls an 'irreducibly complex system.' What does he mean by this? To quote; 'a single system which is composed of several well-matched, interacting parts that contribute to the main function, and where the removal of any one of the parts causes the system to effectively cease functioning.' His contention is that any such system could not have occurred gradually by an evolutionary process; it had to have arrived complete if it were to function at all.

The examples he cites can be briefly summarised. There is a thing called a **cilium**, a tiny hairlike organelle on the surface of many cells. It can beat to and fro in synchrony, and its purpose is to move liquid and other particles of foreign objects. The cilia are very complicated molecular machines, and they contain about 200 different kinds of protein parts. If any one element in its structure were missing, the cilium would not work. It has to have arrived in complete working order; just saying it evolved is not realistic.

Another example is like the cilium, but now called the **flagellum,** a long whip-like structure which behaves like a propeller. It requires about 40 different proteins in order to function properly. If any of these proteins are missing, the flagellum will not work properly. In other words, it has to have arrived in complete working order from the start. It is irreducibly complex; something that can hardly have occurred step by step, and certainly not by one 'accident' after another.

In case one were to think that this difficult question has only arisen in recent years, one would be wrong. It was Darwin himself who wondered that if some biological feature could be shown to be 'irreducibly complex' (use Behe's phrase), that would demolish his theory of Evolution. Even in the mid-19th century, there were biologists who knew of a number of biological systems that did not appear to be able to be built in a gradual way, in other words, evolved. Then as now, we know that the EYE, whether human or animal, is a highly complex structure. If one of its many elements were omitted or damaged, that would result in blindness or serious loss of vision.

Darwin himself wondered about this issue, and felt that the eye could not have evolved.

When we consider the general picture, by which I mean, that there are so many structures in the human and animal body which are now seen as highly complex, and additionally, heavily interrelated with other structures, it does put a big question mark against Evolution, in its raw state. This is not to undervalue the work of Darwin; his book has much that is valid in terms of biological research. This in itself must indicate that evolution has played a part in the creation of life on this planet. But to overdo it and say that Evolution is the total explanation for everything, is, in my opinion, wrong. There must have been and still are, other factors involved, many of which we may not be aware of, even now, with our sophisticated scientific methods.

Hominin remains in supposed order of dating

Name	comment	approximate date
Sahelanthropus Tchadensis bipedal	bipedal, late Miocene, Chad	6-7 mys
Lufengpithecus, Lufengensis	China 'Peking Man'	6 mys
Orririn Tugenensis	Kenya 'Millenium Man'	6 mys
Ardipithecus Kaddaba		5.2-5.8mys
Pithecanthropus Erectus	Java 'Java Man'	1 my
Ardipithecus Ramidus	half a skeleton	1 – 4.5 mys
Australopithecus Africanus	'little foot' bipedal	3- 2.5 mys
Australopithecus Anamensis	bipedal	3.9 – 4.2
Paranthropus Boisei	Zinjanthropus 'Nutcracker Man'	3.5 mys
Kenyanthropus Platyops	one skull; bipedal	3.5 mys
Paranthropus Robustus		3.5 mys
Australopithecus Afarensis	'Lucy', Hadar, Ethiopia, tools, fragments	3.5 mys
Paranthropus Aethiopicus		2.5 mys

Australopithecus Sediba		2.5 mys
Australopithecus Garhi		2.5 mys
Homo Habilis	Kenya, S. & E. Africa, stone tools 'Handyman'	1.6 – 2.4 mys
Homo Georgicus	Georgia	1.8 mys
Homo Erectus	Lake Turkana, skeleton like us, came to Europe & Caucasus, stone tools	1.9 mys
Australopithecus	new specimen found, complete skeleton, 4 feet high	1 – 2.2 mys
Homo Rhodesiensis	'Rhodesian Man'	1 mys
Homo Ergaster (Rudolfensis)	(related to Homo Erectus)	800,000 yrs
Homo Antecessor	Spain	800,000 yrs
Homo Heidelbergensis	SE Africa	400,000–100,000 yrs
Homo Neanderthalensis	Europe to Mid. East, bipedal, dense bones	200,000–30,000yrs
Homo Sapiens		200,000 yrs
Homo Sapiens Idaltu	Ethiopia	160,000 yrs
Cro Magnons	old Stone Age SE France	40,000 yrs
Homo Floriensis, Indonesia	'Island Dwarfism', Florensian man, 'Hobbit'	18,000 yrs
Clovis culture	came to America via Bering Strait End Miocene extinction.	12.500 yrs
Cheddar Man		10,000 yrs
Oetzi	ice mummy found in the Alps	5,000 yrs
Gristhorpe man	complete skeleton, bone	4.000 yrs

Most of these remains are fragmentary fossils. The differences between them are often very slight, just as in today's world we have differences in height, skull shape and volume. Fossil evidence is scarce and widely spread. Most of the early material comes from Africa, but then that is a very large area. It is so easy to generalise; the whole picture may turn out to be much more complicated. New material keeps turning up and this may alter all our preconceptions overnight. Arguments rage over almost every aspect of these matters.

Dr. John Sandford. (Cornell University)

Another challenge to the conventional view of Evolution comes from a very experienced biologist. Sandford maintains that there is a something called 'genetic entropy' which means that there is a general degeneration, decay and death at work in the world. All of life is fading, having started at the beginning as something ideal. It is slowly deteriorating. He talks about every person having 100 mutations per generation, and that these mutations are bad. He does not seem to admit that some of them could be good, or at least, the good ones are outnumbered by the bad ones. The result is that physical fitness is declining as well as fertility. Natural selection, far from producing new species, is actually a stabilising force which is slowing down the process of degeneration.

It is not realistic to delve into the intricacies of his argument. One can read the detail in his book, 'Genetic entropy and the mystery of the genome'. It all sounds very ingenious but one wonders if one is being blinded by science. One wonders how he knows that everyone has 100 genetic mistakes in their make up; also if it is true for one person in his research, why does it have to be true for all people? Again, this is arguing from the specific to the general.

In support of his assertions, he shows that the same trend is seen in the early chapters of the Bible. We are confronted with the impression that human life started off as some kind of ideal and then began to degenerate; a symptom of this was the great ages that people lived to, such as Methuselah, and gradually, the lifespan decreased. This view of humanity is not original, nor is it confined to the Bible. Many mythologies from across the world have the impression of a 'golden age' in the remote past, only to find that it all deteriorates in the course of history. The Greek model is the classic one; the age of Gold, then of silver, then of bronze and then of iron. All this is symbolic of the decline of humanity, as opposed to the refinement of it, as the evolutionists would have us believe.

We notice that again, it all swings round to eschatology; what about the future? Sandford believes we are heading for extinction. This does not mean the kind of extinction as described earlier in this chapter. He means the final end of the world. This can only be avoided or modified by the active intervention of God, which is a polite way of saying that the Messiah needs to return. The phrase 'a new heaven and a new earth' is slipped in.

If we compare these thoughts with the philosophisings of Teilhard de Chardin, we see a complete contradiction. De Chardin, whose material I have reviewed in my first book, the Theology of Paradox, was all the rage half a century ago, but is now definitely looking rather jaded and fanciful. He surmised that humanity was going on a steady journey uphill to arrive at an ideal humanity. Fifty years of bitter experience have put a serious question mark against this idea. Clearly he was an evolutionist of the most basic Darwinian assumption, to the point of being crassly sentimental and optimistic about human nature. Sandford has us going in the opposite direction, downhill, which may seem an unnecessarily pessimistic view of the future, but who is to know what the future holds? It is interesting to notice that again, it all swings round to some form of eschatology. Why should one's speculations about human origin form the basis for our expectations about the future? But that is what the human mind does, and the scientists are no exception to it.

I return to my previous thought, that there may be an element of truth in the concept of evolution, but it is by no means the only factor in the process of creation.

Jurassic Park

There appear to be at least two versions of this, but both of them are essentially based on the same idea which is a classic example of modern inventive eschatology. The core idea is that the Americans have taken an isolated island off the coast of Peurto Rico, with the express intention of turning it into a tourist attraction with prehistoric dinosauric animals, like a tropical safari park.

One is intrigued to know how they will obtain animals of the Jurassic age, which are now long extinct. One method mentioned would be to grind up fossil material and obtain the DNA, and from that produce dinosaurs. Another approach would be, assuming that insects had sucked some blood out of a dinosaur, and then been trapped in the amber, then to take the DNA from the insects and produce dinosaurs. Such ideas have actually been tried, but with no success as yet. The creatures in the film are dubbed as 'genetic hybrids' or 'genetically engineered'. They are supposed to be all female and also sterile, which means that they cannot reproduce like rabbits and go out of control.

In the film, the animals appear very realistic, but they are actually the product of 'virtual reality'. It is enough, however , to look very real and frightening for those who do not understand how such a stunt can be arranged. It is somewhat sentimental when we see the young Diplodochus being fed by a keeper as in the zoo. We also see children riding on a Torosaurus. However, this is not to last, as the beasts decide to go on the rampage and also it is suspected that the small ones have managed to escape from the island and are hurting people. A full scale crisis builds up as they escape from their compounds and run riot on the island. It is then realised that just like frogs, which are all female, some can turn into males and this permits reproduction. We are faced with the whole situation getting completely out of control. Also they appear to be very intelligent as well as vicious. The man who claimed to know all about dinosaurs is seen to have a lot to learn rather late in the day.

Obviously, as a science fiction feature film, this is great fun and the excitement is massive. At the same time one wonders if there is any reality in it. It is one thing to accept that there are fossils of creatures going back to the Triassic age but there is no limit in this film on speculating on their behaviour. Could such lumbering creatures have run as fast as that? Were they really as crafty as that? Could they have withstood bullets from an assault rifle? Would it have been realistic to tame them into being children's pets? Here we see the element of exaggeration and fanciful decoration seen so often in mythology.

More noticeable is the way in which mythology has swung round to become eschatology, but using the same motifs. Using genetic engineering, what is to stop the scientists reproducing some terrifying animal from the past and causing mayhem in modern civilisation? This reminds us of Victor Frankenstein with his monster. As with all good disaster movies, we are being told that the future is going to be violent, unforgiving and chaotic. This is a good example of modern eschatology; mythology pointing to the future.

The true value of both versions is firstly (in the film) that two brothers, having managed to escape being mauled to death, and knowing that their parents are getting divorced, decide that they are going to stick together through thick and thin. This is a very positive moral outcome. Secondly, on the tape version, it is clearly hinted that the scientists, with all their clever electronic gadgets, have managed to allow the project to slide into a whole list of problems beyond their control. In other words, they are far too clever for their own good, or anyone else's good. Another lesson.

Jurassic Park; the latest version (2017)

In common with many Sci-fi productions, we have seen another film version of Jurassic Park. It has to be said that this production is no advance on the previous one. The plot is almost non-existent and the whole drama is almost entirely dependent on gunplay, pyrotechnics and destruction. The dinosaurs seem to be even more intelligent than before and also far more aggressive. At the climax of the drama, it is found that the only way to defeat them is to persuade them to fight each other, since bullets and other weapons have no effect on them. But this idea is not original; we recall that at the finale of Dracula the Un-Dead, the same thing happens when Dracula and Bathory have a sword fight and manage to kill each other. What we can say is that this version of Jurassic Park is another example of mythical augmentation.

King Kong

This Sci-fi thriller feature film first appeared in black and white many years ago, but the latest version is a colour remake in the era of 'virtual reality'. The story begins in 1930's New York with a lady called Ann Darrow who does a dance and juggling routine in the theatre. Out of work, she is persuaded to go on a filming expedition to an uncharted island called Skull Island somewhere near Singapore. The island is dubbed as mythical, not on account of its existence, but because all kinds of prehistoric animals inhabit it. It seems that evolution has got stuck on this island as there are all kinds of dinosaurs living as in a past age, and also a massive chimpanzee 26 feet tall. While we can evidence the existence of such things as diplodochus, there has not, so far, been any trace of a monkey as big as that. Here we already see the element of augmentation, so often seen in mythology.

King Kong abducts Ann. While the menfolk with their movie cameras and machine guns are chased by the dinosaurs, Ann seems to strike up a relationship with the massive monkey. He likes to see her dancing, takes her in his hand and protects her from other fierce animals. One wonders if this is love; she certainly calls him 'beautiful' and he seems to appreciate this. What is the implication in this? One basic assumption here is that the human race are in some sort of relationship with the apes, and this is a strong strand in the idea of evolution. Perhaps it goes a little too far; there is any amount of sentimentality, with oozing music wafting out from a symphony orchestra. This is contrasted with the machine gun mentality that the men display towards King Kong. Also they are simply there to capture a sensation for commercial possibilities.

Eventually, with the use of chloroform, they manage to capture King Kong and take him back to New York to display him on the stage at the theatre. Predictably, the great ape breaks free and goes on the rampage, terrorising the human race and climbing up to the top of a skyscraper. His girlfriend Ann follows him up to the top and tries to stop the aeroplanes spraying King Kong with bullets. This is where the terror movie comes to its climax with mayhem let loose in a modern city. We can see the symbolism in it, that the animals resent being humiliated and will fight back. We feel sympathy for King Kong, just as we feel sympathy for Frankenstein's monster. It is the same motif.

Another significant piece of symbolism is the fact that Ann emerges from all those scenes of violence with not a bruise or a scratch on her, her clothing still intact (!), and on the top of the skyscraper she is wearing a clean white dress. Does this indicate innocence, a factor often seen in mythology? While the men are full of violence, greed and hatred for the Ape, she is the one who 'loves' him, thus forming an emotional connection between mankind and the animal kingdom.

While many of the usual features of mythology are missing from this portrayal, the main concern is the 'monster' motif, which is so prominent in many mythologies, notably the Greek culture. There also has to be someone who can defeat the monster. In this case, it is not a man but a woman who does not use violence but attempts to establish some kind of understanding. The menfolk, not just one man this time, in the shape of the US army and airforce are the ones who cripple the monster to such an extent that he falls from the top of the skyscraper and dies.

The whole concept, which is plainly a fantasy, is nevertheless a good of example how a myth can develop. We begin with the assumption of evolution. It is fair to say there were such things as dinosaurs in the remote past, but not fair to claim there were chimpanzees 26 feet tall. However, then comes the big assumptive augmentation, that such creatures still live on a remote island somewhere. Then it is assumed that they can outrun human beings; it is reckoned that such beasts could only move at about 2 MPH! The next assumption is that they would be ferocious and inclined to attack; what if they were docile and inclined to be friendly? Then we have the assumption that the great ape has something approaching human emotions. It is all very imaginative and frightening, and as entertainment great fun. Some people might find it deeply worrying and nightmarish. That would be fair, if we could all see that financial greed overruled caution in introducing a new 'monster' into today's world.

King Kong is another good example of how something historical or legendary can be built up into a complete myth, so that we can all frighten ourselves silly, like the ancients.

The latest twist; two puzzles

A recent TV programme entitled First Humans; the Cave Discovery describes the discovery of the Rising Star cave in South Africa. This has caused great excitement and the admission that all our preconceived ideas may have to be rethought on the subject of the appearance of humanity. In that cave were found 2,000 fragments of human remains and twelve individuals could be pieced together. The fossilised fragments littered the entire cave floor. Since there were no traces of animal remains, the conclusion was that the human remains had been put there deliberately by other humans. This would indicate some form of advanced social behaviour, possibly some sort of burial ritual or possibly a sacrifice. This material is thought to date from about 1.9 million years BC, but no evidence for this was offered on the programme. Two new species were claimed to be found; Australopithecus Sediba and also Homo Naledi. Both of these had traits of both monkeys and of humans. It was easy therefore to start making claims about 'missing links'; however they were still willing to admit that there are massive gaps in the fossil record; the palaeontogists were being a little more cautious this time. One could say that that was very wise!

Apart from the fact that the programme was spoilt by many outbursts of sentimentality and sensationalism, the core of the matter was very instructive. It is so easy to fall into another rut of dogmatism on these matters, but the lesson has to be learnt; what other materials are waiting to be found, which might throw all our theories and preconceived ideas into disarray? The whole programme was saturated with evolutionary assumptions; in this way any conclusions are almost certainly going to be seen as 'proving' the theory of evolution; in other words, it is a circular argument. Would it be possible to view the whole matter from another set of assumptions? That is the challenge that I put to the so-called experts!

Footnotes for chapter 21

1. See chapter 25 in The Theology of Truth, page 467 where 'evolutions' are mentioned.
2. Cuvier, a French palaeontologist in the early 1800's.
3. Lamarck, a French biologist who was an early proponent of Evolution.
4. This is the last known extinction and may equate to the last Ice Age. Humanoids would have experienced this, about 10,000 years ago.
5. The Descent of Man by Charles Darwin.
6. The concept of the 'World Tree' is to be found in most mythologies. It is also found in the popular notion of Evolution, and may be completely misleading. It is interesting to see that the Kabbalah has another version of the World Tree, see chapter 26.
7. This would be long after the late Pleistocene extinction, 65 million years ago.
8. There is a thing called a Zonkey, a cross between a Zebra and a donkey.
9. The tree motif outlined by Darwin has been the model for Evolution, with elaborations, to this day.
10. Oetzi is reckoned by Carbon 14 dating to be about 3,000 BC.
11. This pattern of 'ages' is reflected in Daniel, see chapter 3.

22

Dracula and Frankenstein

I include this tradition because it is a very important aspect of the mythology of the modern world. There are numerous reprints of Bram Stoker's original book of 1897, plus film and tape renditions and a sequel, Dracula; the Undead, written by his great grand nephew, Dacre Stoker. There are museums in America and the castle in Transylvania has become a tourist trap. This in itself indicates the hold that this motif has on the public imagination. Almost certainly it appeals to many of the basic instinctive urges in human nature, what Freud would call the **id.** We all know it is make-believe and yet, the fascination in there. This is modern mythology at its most acute and frightening. Frankenstein with his monster is another example of how a horror story can be augmented into a terrifying movie and integrated with Dracula. It is plainly obvious that the writers have used many of the basic ingredients in mythological symbolism. Whether or not they realised this is beyond us to decide, but the basic appeal to instinctive receptors in the human soul are there. This explains why the books and their derivatives have become so popular.

Dracula

In common with many mythologies, there is some kind of historic-geographical anchorage. The story begins with Jonathan Harker going to Transylvania at the invitation of Count Dracula. The Borgo Pass in the Carpathians is a real place. It then turns to Whitby, then to Hampstead Heath, Purfleet, and back again to Bukovina. We all know the emotion

346

surrounding Hampstead Heath where people mysteriously disappear. In this case, it is very young children who report seeing a 'bloofer lady' who turns out to be Lucy as a vampire. The whole book is done as a collection of diary pages with dates and places. This is a clever literary device to prevent the book from becoming sheer fantasy. There is that bureaucratic atmosphere to the book, which contrasts well with the flights of fancy over the antics of Dracula and the unfortunate people that he manages to recruit into his entourage. Apparently there was a real historical figure called Prince Dracula, who is well known in that part of Europe as one who fought bravely against the invading Turks, but he hardly matches up to the horror story which unfolds! Also we are told that there are such things as Vampire Bats(1) which can suck the blood out of anyone, leaving two little teeth marks. The plot augments this motif by showing that if Dracula manages to suck them too often, he will be able to recruit them into his team. It is not really explained how Dracula came to be a vampire, but somehow he has degenerated into that kind of creature. Here we see the familiar element of exaggeration and augmentation seen so often with mythology.

Blood is an ongoing motif in the story. It starts with Jonathan Harker managing to nick himself with his razor, and Dracula warns him to be careful, not to cut his throat, but for other reasons. The hint comes to fruition almost immediately, as three attractive girls with no shadow try to apply their sharp teeth to his throat. All through the book we find people with tiny pinpricks on their throats, starting with Lucy and working through to Mina and Jonathan himself. The emotion over blood builds up as Lucy requires no less than four blood transfusions in an attempt to save her life. This must have been written at a time when the blood transfusion method was in its infancy, for there is no mention of matching blood types to make a successful transfusion. Symbolically, blood is important as the mainstay of life and in some mythologies it is a cleansing agent. It is pointed out to us that Dracula has to suck blood in order to survive at all. He concentrates on young children and young ladies, with the idea that he can infect them with the same urge and so turn them into vampires too. (2) It is so sad to see how Lucy has been taken over and though supposedly 'dead' is still rising up from her coffin and trying to bite people. She is UN-DEAD and it is horrific! When a stake is driven into her heart, blood spurts all over and froths from her mouth, but then she is at peace. In the final scene, when Dracula is likewise terminated, Quincey Morris is fatally wounded, and as the blood spurts through his fingers, there is the hint of him being a sacrifice.

This brings us to the element of 'innocence' seen in many mythologies. It is particularly so with the Huichols of Mexico, where a boy and a girl who have not had sex, are the focus of rituals and shamanism. How often do we see a child or a young girl, in the Dracula stories, abducted with the intention of sucking their blood? They seem to arrive home safely the next day but showing those tiny pinpricks on their throats. There are two courting couples, blissfully committed to each other; Lucy and Arthur; Jonathan and Mina. The young ladies are paragons of beauty and virtue, and the gentlemen are the pinnacle of gallantry and chivalry. Also, Jonathan himself seems blissfully unaware of the danger he is in in the Castle and back in England. It is the Professor, Van Helsing, who seems to know all about vampires and how to defeat them, who makes Jonathan and others aware of the situation. Van Helsing is dubbed as a 'specialist'; not only is he a medic, but a legalist and well-versed in matters of the occult. He comes over as the senior guru who almost represents the priesthood; more obviously he represents Jesus Christ. Not only does he hand out crucifixes, but bits of communion wafer and (strangely) garlic. It is not explained how garlic will repel a vampire.

This brings us to the element of snobbery in the book, but this is done in a slightly different way. We start with a fantastic Gothic castle on a massive precipice a thousand feet high, with a magnificent view. This is the same appeal as places like Neuschwanstein,(3) the Kehlstein,(4) and Masada,(5) and resonates with that feeling of megalomania in many people. The fact that we have a professor is another appeal to snobbery; he is some sort of expert in many aspects of life. He hands out little silver crucifixes which jar on Jonathan's Protestant susceptibilities. But the precious metal element is there nevertheless. There seems to be various mentions of gold, or jewels, which is not overdone. Van Helsing has a gold crucifix. There are piles of gold coins in the castle, and golden tableware and jewels, and when Dracula is attacked in the house in Picadilly, gold coins and bank notes fall out of his clothing. There is a blue flame which indicates where a treasure is hidden (rather like the end of the rainbow in Ireland). The fact that Dracula is some sort of aristocracy and royalty augments the snobbery element. The team of young champions includes Arthur, Lord Godalming, and Jonathan Harker himself is a young solicitor. The whole setting, as a Gothic masterpiece published in the late 19th century, is a clear appeal to the sentimentality of the Victorian

Age, with its romantic notions about the Middle Ages. This kind of appeal is somewhat diminished nowadays.

There is the fascination over the **boxes** which arrive at Whitby, and have to be transported down to London, to Carfax, the house that Dracula has obtained. We suspect that Dracula is inside one of them; the others contain soil from his castle. It is not clear what the soil is intended for, but Van Helsing sees it as important to 'sterilise' the contents by putting a fragment of wafer in each one. The box containing Dracula reminds us of Pandora's box.(6) The difference here is that the heroes manage to catch him in his box just before sunset and stick their knives into him, thus ending the curse. We are told that Dracula can appear as different things and in various sizes, sometimes becoming invisible. He can only do this in the night; in daylight he has to return to normal human form, even if he looks ghastly. This is a very common element in mythologies, though not normally tied in with daytime or night. He is very strong, and is almost certainly the monstrous dog that jumped off the ship at Whitby. He can disappear through closed doors and leave a mist behind him. He leaves no shadow and no reflection in a mirror.

On the subject of magic weapons, which is a strong feature in mythology, this idea is somewhat restrained. We do not have massive gun battles or flashing swords. There are guns in the story when it comes to the climax at the end, but not a shot is fired. When they behead Lucy in her coffin, a knife is used but it is not dubbed as magic. A stake is driven through her heart, using a mallet. But that is not some kind of spectacular weapon. What is 'magical' is the holy communion wafer that Van Helsing produces. It is not explained from which church it has been obtained, but we might infer that it is from Roman Catholic sources somewhere in the Netherlands. When it touches Mina's head, it sears a mark on her brow. This mark disappears the minute Dracula is terminated. The wafers do have a marked effect on the vampires, as do the crucifixes. Van Helsing describes a circle in the snow, using the wafers, in order to protect Mina. The 'weaponry' is nearly always used as a defensive measure rather than for aggression. We do not seem to have the fantastic gadgetry as seen in other horror stories. This is probably because the book was written when the age of electricity was in its infancy.

The whole book revolves around the concept of being 'un-dead'. When they open Lucy's coffin, sometimes she is in there and sometimes she is not. She appears as a dim white figure hovering around the church yard, blood splattered on her mouth and clothing. She runs back into the tomb via a closed door, leaving a child unharmed. Obviously she has died but paradoxically she is in some way alive and behaving as a vampire. There is clearly some kind of state in between life and death, not exactly being a ghost because she is a menace to all innocent people. It requires the men to drive in the stake and decapitate her; this releases her to go to heaven and be at rest with the angels. In this we see the usual fascination of life, death, and resurrection. This, as ever, raises the question of what life actually consists of and what is death. This is a basic substratum in every mythology the world over. The only thing missing here is the heavy emphasis on the motif of the three-tiered universe. It receives a few passing mentions but is not a thoroughgoing theme. We can understand that since in late Victorian times, everyone would have known about the earth being spherical.

One unusual element included is the factor of hypnotism, which locates the story in the era of modern psychotherapy in its infancy. There is the sad case of Mr.Renfield who is clearly a schizophrenic and is attended by Dr.Seward who is some kind of 'ur-psychiatrist'. Dracula has clearly infiltrated the asylum and harassed Renfield to death. Mina asks to be hypnotised and under the trance is able to give a hint as to where the box is, namely on board a ship. This happens repeatedly, and this is how they work out that Dracula is returning to his castle. This in fact means that she is not unlike Kauymali (7)and the Cargo Cult prophets.(8) She is in fact the shaman in the whole story.

The most obvious strand in the story of Dracula is the ongoing battle between good and evil. Clearly Dracula is the evil element, occasionally dubbed as the Devil, or Satan, and the way the vampires react to the crucifix tells us that they are the opposite of Christ. Professor Van Helsing is clearly the good element, though he is never dubbed as God, or Jesus or a saint. All the others are the innocents who have to be warned and protected against evil. With the 'death' of Dracula, we are left wondering how long this will last and there is the hint that Dracula will somehow reconstitute himself and again return to plague humanity. After all, if the villain is dead, there will be no more interesting story! Ominously we are told that Dracula is eternal. Clearly the symbolism in this is that evil is not just a human problem which can be stamped out by killing someone. Evil is an eternal problem which is in an ongoing battle with good. The book does not go on to include any eschatology; the Biblical answer to this is that there will be a final battle in the skies and God will defeat evil permanently.

The book can be admired for its build-up of fear. This starts with the peasants in Roumania crossing themselves copiously because they are in terror of Castle Dracula. This builds up as Jonathan comes to realise that he is being held against his will, in the castle, as a prison. We have people shrieking with horror at times, not just the young ladies but anybody. This is all augmented by the howling of wolves, which is calculated to strike fear into anyone's soul. This sound recurs quite often in the book, along with the howling of dogs and the teeming of rats. This incidentally is a feature of many mythologies, that of certain animals being associated with certain gods. The element of fear is very often there. The storm at Whitby is another fear-motif, as the fishing boats scramble back into the harbour just in time. The schooner, with all its sails set, miraculously slides into the harbour and collides with the shore. Everyone is amazed to find the steersman lashed to the wheel, but he has been dead for at least two days. It is the same dread-fascination which surrounds the Marie Celeste incident. We all realise that that monstrous dog is actually Dracula as he jumps off the ship.

To strengthen our understanding of Dracula as some kind of mythology, there are the occasional indirect references to ancient mythology. A good example of that comes when Lucy is near to death, Van Helsing mentions the 'waters of Lethe'. This is a factor in Greek mythology, in which the underworld has two rivers; Lethe and Mnemosyne. If one drinks the latter, one will recall details of one's previous life; if one drinks of Lethe, one will forget. That would be very helpful for Lucy if she could forget the horror surrounding the end of her life. There are various other passing remarks which recall ancient mythologies.

There is no mistaking the basically Christian tenor of the whole book. Van Helsing is deeply religious, and we suspect that he is a Roman Catholic, though this is never actually stated. Jonathan and the others we take to be Anglicans. They are always making remarks about God protecting them or saving them. They often pray together. One could infer from this that one of the implications of this book is that Christians of all kinds ought to minimise their differences of opinion, and concentrate on working together to defeat evil. That could be the main agenda of the book. The other agenda, a cautionary thought, is that anyone, however innocent and well meaning, can become enmeshed in evil quite inadvertently, and turn violent and have a tortured soul. This in its turn will imply that we need to take our Christian religion seriously and not regard it as something trivial and irrelevant in today's world.

Dracula the Un-Dead; by Dacre Stoker and Ian Holt

We all know that Dracula has gone through various permutations and remakes since the original book appeared. Sadly, Bram Stoker never lived to see the popularity and fascination his idea came to exert on the public. It was in 1912 that the idea of extending Dracula into another volume was mooted. Bram's great grandnephew, Dacre with Ian Holt, hatched the idea of such a development. The previous volume left us with the impression that Dracula had been 'kllled' by the champion team of five just outside his castle in Transylvania. However, there was the hovering thought that Dracula was eternal and could hardly be terminated completely. The fear comes to realisation when, twenty five years later, there comes the suspicion that Dracula is far from dead and is looking for vengeance. The term 'un-dead' is the key to the whole thing. There is this life, and the life of heaven (to which Lucy has gone, we hope), but also something in between, not exactly limbo but the state of being 'un-dead'. This means that during the daytime, Dracula can materialise as a human being but at night he can prowl around, not exactly a ghost but as some kind of horror monster that can suck blood out of people.

One by one, the five heroes are hunted down and disposed of. Dr.Seward, now a morphine addict, observes a vampire woman, Elizabeth Bathory carve up an innocent maiden and bathe in her blood. He is horrified and flies to Paris to warn an actor called Basarab of what to expect. Seward is run over in the street outside the theatre by a driver-less coach. Jonathan Harker, having an encounter in a London alleyway, is found impaled at Piccadilly Circus, much to Mina's horror. Arthur Holmwood, Lord Godalming, at first tries not to become involved in the matter, but cannot allow young Quincey to drift into trouble and comes to London with Mina to try to establish good. He falls out of a hotel window and dies in the street. Van Helsing, now old and feeble is drawn to London in an attempt to help, but he too falls from the same hotel window to his death. That leaves us with Mina Harker and her son Quincey. In the closing scenes, Mina in despair throws herself off the cliff at Whitby. Quincey manages to escape, only to trick his way on board the Titanic on its maiden voyage; we all know what that will mean!

Once again we have the ironic contrast between those in the know and the pathetically innocent. Quincey Harker has deliberately been kept in the dark by his parents. The wisdom of this is highly questionable. He does not really know what he is up against. The irony builds as he becomes mesmerised by the acting brilliance of Basarab; he tries to obtain information from Basarab on how to deal with vampires. The irony is completed when only later do we come to realise that Basarab is none other than Dracula in disguise. When Quincey realises that it is Dracula that has killed his father, he is consumed with the urge to wreak revenge, but he has no idea of what trouble he is asking for. The other innocent parties are the London police, as typified by Cotford. He has taken it into his head that Van Helsing murdered Lucy and was in fact Jack the Ripper. Again, Cotford has no idea what he is up against; he ends up with his head rolling down the stairs of the Underground, to the consternation of Mina.

This brings us to the clever way in which historical realities are worked in as the background to the story. Cotford is still obsessed with trying to solve the Jack the Ripper crimes going back to 1888. His colleagues think he is crazy and it is damaging his career. Ironically, he is not far off the mark. It transpires that Elizabeth Bathory, Dracula's wife, who goes round with a surgical lancet, is the real culprit. As a demonstration of her callousness, the driver-less coach picks up a prostitute from the street, and a few minutes later she is dumped in the Thames along with her fee, a golden coin. It now transpires that Dracula came to London all those years ago to try to restrain Bathory. The way that the Lyceum Theatre, Henry Irving, Waterloo Bridge and the Titanic are worked in is rather clever. This time, we do not have a system of diary entries, but there is enough of historical background to ensure that the story is not just purely and simply a fantasy. Even that tiny detail of the seaman Coffey, who decided he had a superstition about going on the Titanic, ties in with a historical reality. As in the other book, we have much detail about Vlad the Impaler and how Prince Dracula championed the cause of Christianity against the Turks.

The element of snobbery surrounding gold is again in evidence, though not quite so heavily emphasised. The black driver-less coach is lined out in gold. The appearance of those golden crucifixes is included, but not as prevalent as before. Bathory actually stamps on Mina's cross; this is symbolically saying that evil will overpower good. The little gold crosses do not seem to have the same effect on the Vampires this time.

The mythological importance of Blood is much more heavily emphasised in this book. There is gore everywhere and the Vampires seem to manage to suck blood from many more people. It is heavily stressed how they desperately need to suck human blood to keep themselves alive. Animal blood is a poor substitute. It is heartrending to realise that Mina and Jonathan have been infected with Dracula's blood, and so in turn Quincey. It means that they begin to grow forked teeth. Ironically, they also begin to develop enormous strength, and because they have not grown into full-scale vampires, they are able to stand up to people like Bathory. At first they do not know their own strength; later it becomes increasingly apparent.

In general terms, the mythological elements are very largely augmented in this book. There is even more thunder and lightning with wolves howling. There is an enormous fire as the Lyceum Theatre goes up in flames. A dragon belching fire emerges from the Underground Station. The whole story is far more dramatic and exaggerated than before, which builds up the excitement and the feeling of horror.

This brings us to one of the most tortuous elements in the story; the difference between good and evil. This is nowhere near as clear-cut as before, and in a way this is much closer to real life. Van Helsing is a case in point; in the previous book he is the pillar of goodness who knows exactly how to combat evil. Now, he has become infected with vampirism and is not exactly on the side of evil but somewhere in between. But the vampires are intent on destroying him in any case. Mina, who loves her son Quincey to distraction, has a love-hate relationship with Dracula, and hovers between rejecting him and accepting him. Quincey, who is bent on revenge, finds himself in a dilemma when Dracula tells him that he is actually his son, and Jonathan is not his real father at all. The final confusion comes when it seems that Dracula, after all his misbehaviour, is actually on the side of God! We are left wondering where good and evil are to be found, but the reality is that as the sun comes up in the morning, symbolising God, we assume, the Vampires of all kinds deteriorate into ashes.

The worry is, that if the Vampires are so strong and overpowering, how is anyone going to defeat them? Even if Mina and Quincey have extra strength, they still cannot overpower someone like Bathory. There is a glimmer of hope as Mina manages to attach Bathory to an electric cable and toss her out on to the live rails in the underground tunnel; this injures the vampire greatly but we soon learn that she is still alive and regaining her strength. There seems to be no answer to this until it becomes clear that the Vampires hate each other and are set on killing each other. There is a bloodthirsty sword fight by Whitby Abbey and as the climax of the book, Dracula and Bathory manage to kill each other. At least, that is what it appears to be; will they re-emerge for another attempt at causing mayhem?

All this may seem a crazy story, and in terms of the literal truth, it is. But the substratum of it is just as important as before. Evil is not just a nasty trait in human nature. It is an ongoing eternal problem. In the book, Bathory actually refers to the fallen angel that disagreed with God, before the world was ever created. This means that the stand-off between good and evil is an eternal matter as opposed to a socio-human problem. The difference here with this book is that good and evil have a subtle intertwining so that we are left wondering who is a 'goodie' and who is a 'baddie'.

As these two books progress, we see the augmentation and exaggeration building up to greater and greater heights. All the time, it is becoming less and less realistic, but the drama is gripping and irresistible. Everyone knows the fascination which appeals to our deepest instincts of fear, cruelty, hate and love. This is why the Dracula motif has an enduring hold on the public imagination.

Frankenstein

The popular assumption is that Dracula came first, followed by Frankenstein. However, the book, by Mary Shelley hails from 1818 but there are many elements in it which suggest a later age, and the full development of Frankenstein really belongs to the 20th century. One could say it is a book before its time. As with Dracula, Frankenstein continues to have a wide readership to this day, and that is understandable as it appeals to the same instinctive fears as Dracula does. Both of them can fairly be called part of the myth of the modern age. As Paul Cantor puts it, 'Frankenstein has as much claim to mythic status as any story ever invented by a single author'.(9)

So how is Frankenstein different from Dracula? We can begin by saying that the same literary technique is used, namely, that letters sent between

Robert Walton and his sister frame the whole story. The centre of the account forsakes the 'letter' method, but even so, the effect is that the account is somehow brought down to earth. Frankenstein is not just pure fright-fantasy. This is reinforced by the journeys of Victor Frankenstein as he goes to Ingoldstadt University, Geneva, England, Scotland, Ireland and back to Geneva to get married. There is that element of the mundane in it which balances with the fantasy aspect. Robert Walton in effect has no part in the story and only incidentally frames the whole picture; he is a very ordinary person who has really no idea of what is going on. In general terms, the way it is done is much more restrained than in Dracula. The style of prose is typical of middle to late Victorian melodrama and sentimentality, and the characterisation is not particularly strong. They all talk in the same flowery, affected way, and that includes the monster himself. That element is really quite strange, if not amusing. We do not have the overtones of the occult, indications of the next life, and certainly nothing about being 'un-dead'. There are a few references to God, but in general, the religious tone seen in Dracula is much toned down.

What is going on? Victor Frankenstein, a young student is sent off to university to study science. He manages to discover a way of artificially producing 'life', and in theory at least, to manufacture a human being. He is thrilled with the idea that he can conquer death! That is the first mythological strand to emerge, but not very original. After months of work he manages to produce something roughly in human shape, but much bigger and uglier; but also much stronger and we suspect more intelligent. It does not occur to Victor that this will spell trouble.

Trouble is soon to be encountered. Victor's little brother, William is found dead at Geneva, and his sister, Justine, is accused and found guilty. Viktor knows full well that the monster has done this, and later comes to realise that he has planted a jewel on Justine in order to incriminate her. We notice the inclusion of another mythical factor here. Viktor is rent with guilt; not just about William but also about Justine being unfairly hung. But he can do nothing about it. Who would believe it if he tried to explain it in full? This is a recurring theme in the book; no one will take him seriously even when he does try to render an explanation. Moreover, he is at pains to keep the monster as secret. In this we see the heart-rending emotion often experienced, when we know the true answer to some kind of problem, and feel guilt which cannot be assuaged.

The monster too is at pains to avoid advertising himself to the public, at least until the closing phases of the account. He would dearly like to befriend people, and does various kindly acts, including saving a little girl from drowning. But he is rewarded with bullets and panic when people actually do see him. With this he turns nasty and is bent on revenge, especially for his 'creator'. How true of life; the bright ideas we have do have a nasty habit of rebounding on us in some kind of backlash. In a way, Frankenstein is only portraying, in mythical terms, the human condition.

This becomes more obvious when Victor gets into conversation with his monster. Now we hear the monster's side of the story. Apart from the fact that everyone is terrified of him and hates him, he is also desperately lonely. He has no wife or companion. To compound this, he has picked up a copy of Paradise Lost and finds out about Adam, of all the creatures in the Garden, he is the one with no mate. He also finds Victor's laboratory notes on how he fabricated him. So that sets him on to thinking, who am I, what am I, what am I supposed to be doing? This is a very human line of questioning and is the basis of virtually every myth the world over. Because he realises he is loathsome, not wanted and unable to relate to human society, he is consumed with remorse, hate and hell in his soul. He persuades Victor to fabricate another monster so that he can have a mate. Victor at first agrees to this, but then begins to have reservations.

When Victor, on his grand tour, sets up his laboratory in Northern Scotland, the monster makes another attempt at arranging for a mate to be produced. One cannot help feeling a modicum of pity for him, since he has some kind of human soul which cannot find solace. Victor gets so far in the manufacturing process but then decides it will cause mayhem for everyone else, so he dumps the materials in the sea. It is uncanny how the monster knows what has happened, and then murders Henry Cerval, Victor's best friend, on the Irish coast. Victor, on landing near the spot, is instantly accused of the murder. How ironic! In literal terms, he never murdered Henry at all, but in another, indirect sense, he did. It was his fault that the monster turned nasty and killed his best friend. Victor is in torments over this, as also with the subject of William and Justine. This is compounded by the fact that when Victor and Elizabeth go on their honeymoon, the monster fulfils his promise to 'be with him on his first night'. She is found dead in the bedroom. This is augmented by Victor's father, already aged, dying of a broken heart over the incident.

It would seem that Victor is without help from anyone. When he goes to the judge and explains everything in great detail, the judge just smiles beneficently and passes the buck. He clearly sees Victor as completely crazy. The result is that Victor has to set out by himself to track down the monster and kill him, before he can cause any more trouble. One might say, why did he not do that at the start; but then there would have been no horror story! Victor tracks him to the Arctic, across the ice and encounters Robert Walton in his ship. By now, Victor is so enfeebled that he cannot chase the monster any more. As he lies dying, the monster appears in his cabin and proclaims that he is satisfied now that his creator is dead. So he jumps out of the window on to an ice floe and that is the end of that; or is it?

There is so much of theological truth in this. How often do people have a grudge against their maker, ie. God? It is the age-old problem of theodicy, and accounts for so much of atheism and failures of faith. Is the story in a way saying that God is in effect a very clever but ill-advised student experimenting with life and has no idea of the problems he is making for humanity? One could say that with some certainty about the Theory of Evolution, that all of life is one gigantic experiment to see which creatures survive and which die out.

However, there is an object lesson included in this account, that all scientists could take note of, and have failed to do so in the past. What will be the long-term effects of the clever ideas one might have? Are we going to create some kind of 'monster' that goes out of control and wreaks havoc to our own destruction? This is a particularly relevant point at this time when scientists are probing the very building blocks of life and there is so much potential for creating problems for ourselves in the future. Only recently we hear that someone is trying to reproduce a mammoth by taking the DNA from ancient remains and merging it with a living elephant. What will be the result, if indeed it can be achieved? Many people may not know that in the early years of Soviet Russia, Stalin had the idea of producing a cross between a human and an ape. This was based on the notion that since genes and chromosomes of a human and a monkey were very similar, it would be possible to produce a cross between the two. After all, this had been achieved with a donkey and zebra, by a scientist called Ivanov. The experiment with a human and an ape failed and the Communists lost interest in this project. This is probably providential, as the results of it, if it had been successful, might have been disastrous for us all.

One of the salient features of Frankenstein is the love between Victor and his intended bride Elizabeth. Even if it is a sort of 'arranged' match, they are genuinely in love with each other, having been childhood sweethearts. Victor is also massively fond of his friend Henry Cerval, but there is nothing untoward in that. It does not clash with his love for Elizabeth. This intense love is in contrast to the hate that the monster generates, and how Victor hates himself for engendering such a problem.

What the story lacks in violence and hyped-up drama is made up for in internal conflict and torment. In a way, this is far nearer to basic realities than Dracula. Looking at it from a Freudian angle, Victor has far too much super-ego in relation to other dimensions such as id and ego. He is crashingly overburdened with guilt and fear and sometimes indecision. The monster is in a way his overpowering conscience. That of course is true for us all; the guilt that we carry is almost always a burden that we have made for ourselves through some careless or silly behaviour in our youth. Ridding ourselves of it is not easy, and the 'monster' has unbelievably clever ways of catching up on us and in a way holding a mirror up to ourselves in accusation. The monster himself, strange as it may seem, has more than his fair share of human mental traits. His id is very strong, so that he is given to bursts of temper, hate, revenge, and even kindly feeling, laced with self-pity. Also his super ego is overpowering to the extent that he feels crashing guilt and fear about his loneliness. One wonders if Stalin's ape-men would have had such emotions? In this way, the conflict is internalised but is every bit as searching and nail-biting as the externalised battle seen in Dracula.

Cleverly, the account ends with a sort of 'cliff-hanger' in that the monster is not actually seen to die. This leaves it open for other writers and film-makers to develop the theme, and indeed they have. In these we see the augmentation of the basic theme, a factor seen in so many myths. It all builds up to frightening proportions, with the tension between life and death and resurrection portrayed in massive terms. It leaves us with the question, what is life all about and what is the destiny of the human race? In this we can see the role of myth, as a way of expressing basic instinctive fears and yearnings in symbolic terms, as opposed to purely literal terms.

The Film; Van Helsing

As one would expect, the theme of Dracula and Frankenstein's monster is wide open for further development and this is seen in the film of 2004, Van Helsing, directed by Stephen Sommers. The two strands are worked in together so that we see Victor Frankenstein being terrorised by his monster, who is just the thing to be used by Dracula for his purposes. We see the monster being augmented to extremes of violence in scenes which remind us of King Kong who balanced on the top of a skyscraper.

Van Helsing, who is supposed to have died in the book Dracula the Undead, now reappears as a young man who is charged, by the Vatican, with the task of killing Dracula. Van Helsing is dressed like a cowboy, with a Stetson and leather clothing, and a pseudo American accent to complete the illusion. He has a reluctant helper called Carl, a timid monk from Rome. Carl has all the appearance of being naive and innocent, which is an important element is mythological sagas. This also betrays a common misapprehension about monks, so he fits a sort of stereotype. However, he is anything but naive. He is Van Helsing's armourer and in a scene reminiscent of M supplying James Bond with all kinds of clever weapons, Carl is the one with the know-how. Later in the drama, Carl comes across as the one with a generous degree of sanity and non-violence. To complete the impression that Van Helsing is a cowboy, he, and Carl, ride off into the sunset, as indeed all good westerns come to completion, with heroic music to complete the illusion.

Many of the usual mythological elements are seen in the film. Jewels and precious metals seem to be understated, except to say that Van Helsing's gun needs to fire silver bullets.(10) A sword goes right through Dracula but he just smiles and says that he is already dead, so it makes no difference. There is any amount of fire in the film, augmented by flashes of lightning and vast amounts of static electricity, almost to the extent that it becomes tedious. The most interesting 'magical' weapon is Van Helsing's elaborate crossbow which can fire bolts in rapid succession, just like a machine gun. It is of very little effect on the vampires and the Harpies, but Carl advises him to dip it in Holy Water, and that does make it effective! There do not seem to be any snakes in the film, but this is compensated for by people swinging to and fro on ropes or lianas, like monkeys in the jungle. There is no rainbow, but there is a perilous kind of bridge leading into Castle Frankenstein, which seems even more forbidding than Castle Dracula.

The romantic element can not be omitted from such a film. Firstly we have the love of Anna for her brother Volken, and she fails to cope with the idea that he has turned into a werewolf and must be killed. Later, Anna turns her attentions on to Van Helsing, in a brief moment of passion. But Van Helsing is not the marrying type, we assume. Dracula tries to recruit Anna into his coterie of wives, to replace the one that Van Helsing shot, but she is not impressed. Dracula has found a method of breeding vampire bats which are virtually indestructible. At one point Van Helsing himself turns into a monster as well as Dracula and they fight, trying to rip each other's throats. Van Helsing prevails over him and Dracula collapses, dying, whereupon all those vampires also collapse and the horror is over. This is ironic, since at the start, Dracula claims that he will live for ever and wreak havoc in what he calls the 'final battle'. Here we see a touch of eschatology, but it never materialises.

Much of the original sensitivity is lost in this film, with its incessant augmented and senseless violence. Only a few short scenes of relative calm seem to make a contrast, but most of it is hyped up death and destruction, to the point that it becomes tedious. It would be true that the basic tension between life and death is present in the film. The transition between monster and human, which happens rather often, is quite confusing and there seems to be no logic to it. It is, of course, a feature of traditional mythology, but there, it is not overplayed and tends to follow some kind of rationale. As an example of modern exaggerated and augmented mythology, this film is not exactly a masterpiece but is typical of the late twentieth century horror movie with virtual reality which makes it all the more frightening, that is, unless one sits back and roars with laughter!

Footnotes for chapter 22

1. Vampire Bat. A small creature that bites its prey to suck the blood, normally of animals but can be humans. The wound can become infected. The tradition about Vampires, in Europe and Asia goes back to about 1720, and it usually concerns criminals, suicides whose soul is not at rest. This explains the term 'un-dead.'

2. See the chapter on the Huichols; also I John 1:7.

3. Neuschwanstein Castle, built by Ludwig 2nd, in Bavaria.

4. The Kehlstein, the Eagle's Nest at Berchtesgaden, built for Hitler.

5. Masada, a palace by the Dead Sea used by Herod the Great.

6. It was actually an urn with a lid on it, and Pandora, the Greek equivalent of Eve, could not resist lifting the lid. Out flew all the evils of the world.

7. Kauymali, the ultimate child shaman, as in Huichol mythology.

8. The Cargo Cult prophets of Oceania, chapter 13, were convinced that ships would arrive bearing all kinds of consumer goods, armaments and the spirits of dead ancestors.

9. A quotation from the preface of Mary Shelley's book.

10. Silver bullets; the Lone Ranger, a western of the 1950's, had the hero firing silver bullets.

23

Harry Potter

Many people have been delighted and indeed obsessed by the latest twist in modern mythology; it is the phenomenon of Harry Potter. Since 1997, a whole series of books, following Harry's school career, has delighted millions. Films have been made and railway engines have been painted red. Many teachers and parents have been pleased, not so much for the content of the books, but for the fact that young people are actually reading something as opposed to just fiddling with electronic gadgets.

One wonders why this series has captured the imagination of so many. After all, the name itself, Harry Potter, is nothing out of the ordinary, and in fact is deliberately so, so that the boy is initially seen as a very ordinary lad who is completely unaware of his special background and potential. But this is the first great irony; his parents, who were killed when he was a baby, were both witches with magical powers, and he has inherited their abilities. It is all part of the irony. His uncle and aunt, the Dursleys, are desperately keen to prevent Harry from going that way. But the truth will out when he reaches the age of eleven and is ripe for secondary school. In a way, this reminds us of the way that Rama, in that great mythology, the Ramayana (see my treatment of it in The Theology of Truth, chapter 23), does not realise he is an avatar of Vishnu until almost the end of the drama.(1)

In this way, the mythological elements of the Harry Potter saga begin to surface. I understand that J.K.Rowling realised this and included such elements on purpose. The books include so many elements of mythology, that it is obvious that that explains the success of the whole portrayal. Those important elements, which have been seen before, keep appearing. They appeal to something instinctive in the human soul, what Freud would have called the **id,** and Jung would have called 'archetypes'. In the first book, the Philosopher's stone, we have the appeal to that magical gadget which is supposed to turn base metal into gold and also provide the elixir of life. Harry actually manages to purloin it, but it is some kind of illusion, and it does not actually work, and this gives us a kind of anti-climax to the book.

But there are plenty of other mythological elements in the first book. We have giants and pixies, elves and leprechauns. There are tunnels with vaults containing jewels and hoards of golden coins. Snakes appear in many places, and snaky tendrils appear and someone with a snake's face. At one point, Harry Potter has the illusion that he is a snake himself, and gets the urge to bite people. This is because Voldemort has a method of getting into Harry's mind; vice versa, Harry has a way into Voldemort's mind.(2) Voldemort's familiar is a massive snake which in the final battle, is decapitated. Plenty of people fly through the air and some lucky people have an invisibility cloak. Ghosts ooze out of the walls and the faces in the pictures and in photographs and newspapers speak and pull funny faces and make cheeky comments. Mirrors are not forgotten. All of these elements are related to life, its meaning, the question of eternal life and what does death mean, if indeed there is any 'death'.

Many of these elements are clearly taken from Norse, Greek and Celtic mythology. From Greek mythology, the most notable instance is the appearance of Cerberus, the three-headed dog who is guarding the magical stone. Also there is the maze which has four contestants trying to find the prize; this reminds us of the Labyrinth at Knossos, but this time there are three monsters to contend with. One of them is a sphinx with not just one tricky question but three, but when Harry solves them, the Sphinx does not have to kill herself. In the Forbidden Forest there are Centaurs, one of which actually is recruited to teach lessons in the school. In the final battle against evil, the centaurs, as well as other ferocious creatures, join in on Harry's side. Also there are unicorns in the forest. Dumbledore has a Phoenix which is his special postman, behaving like the owls which carry messages. This Phoenix does actually get burnt but not killed, but the original motif of the Phoenix involved him being burnt to death and then resurrected. This explains why, in the early years of the church, the Phoenix became a symbol of the Resurrection. The stadium with the Quidditch matches reminds us of the Olympic and other Games from Greek tradition. One of the subjects on the curriculum is star-gazing, which again relates to the calculations with the Zodiac and foretelling the future. The Greek influence is probably the most prominent. This indicates the strong appeal to instincts in human nature which goes a long way to explaining the popularity of Harry Potter.

From Norse tradition, we have the dwarfs in their vaults guarding the savings bank, and that is a clever piece of adaptation to the modern concept of banking. There are giants and trolls, elves and all kinds of strange creatures. Each home has its own 'house elves'. Some of them at the bank are noted for their craftwork, such as the Sword of Grippendor with its jewels. Hagrid, the half-giant, reminds us of Thor. Hermione prides herself on specialising in the interpretation of magical runes, a feature of Norse culture. There is mention of Fenrir, the wolf, who was associated with Tyr the god of war.

From Celtic traditions we have dragons belching fire. They are ferocious, as in western thinking as opposed to the Chinese dragons which are gentle and very good luck. There is the faint allusion to the Knights of the Round Table as Sir Cadogan appears in a picture. There is no mention of King Arthur, but there are suits of armour on show all around Hogwarts, and when it comes to the final battle, they all clank off to play their part in destroying evil. The wizard Merlin is often mentioned in the context of swearing. Cadogan, which is a Welsh name, is portrayed as completely crazy, as he changes the password two or three times a day. The main theme of the book is about wizardry and that, in this part of the world, at least, is descended from the Druidic traditions which go back to Celtic times. It is no accident that Cho Chang and Harry kiss under the mistletoe at Christmas time.

The author is also clever in that she takes many of the motifs of mythology and gives them some kind of adaptation or augmentation. A good example of this is when Harry stands in front of the mirror he can see all his dead relatives, including his parents, but when he turns round, there is no one there. When Ron Weasley tries it, he cannot see his past but he can see his future, as he expects to become head boy. (This is a prophecy which does not actually happen). This is a very clever way of indicating predestination or fate, a motif which very often surfaces in the novel. The chief element from just about any mythology is the 'champion' factor. Clearly, Harry is the champion who is going to defeat evil, even if the odds are increasingly stacked against him. This reminds us of people like Theseus and other great heroes, and perhaps even more of that innocent shamanistic boy Kauymali (see chapter 14).

One might assume that this book is a resurgence of paganism, and in a way it is. However, Christian motifs keep surfacing. We have Christmas advancing, and Christmas Day is celebrated with great stress laid upon it. Easter receives a passing mention, but is not a prominent feature. Hallowe'en also is mentioned in passing but seems not to be emphasised. There is mention of Harry's parents getting married and appointing him with a godfather. Two couples actually get married in the sagas; Tonks and Lupin, and Bill Weasley and Fleur. Also there is a very solemn funeral and entombment when Dumbledore is killed. An insignificant little old wizard appears to conduct the ceremonies, but there is no explanation as to his status; is he a priest, a registrar or what? This might seem a little strange if they are all pagans. Also Friday is seen as a special day as also is Sunday. I would say that the book is completely clean and fit for children's reading. The only exception to this would be that there are certain passages that are quite sadistic and frightening. An example of that would be when Umbridge forces Harry to write lines and the words are carved on the back of his hand very painfully. However, there is never any salacious material, still less perverted sexual content, as far as I can see. There is love indicated between Harry and Hermione, but it is not sexually orientated, since he regards her more as a sister than as a potential wife. Harry and Cho Chang are attracted to each other, but nothing seems to come of it; they fall out regularly, which is typical of teenage flirtations. Later in the sagas, Harry falls in love with Ginny Weasley, but he has the decency to shelve the matter with her, until he has completed his mission, to defeat Voldemort. Valentine's Day is celebrated, but the sexual element in it is a matter of embarrassment. Harry does not wish to receive a card from Ginny! Percy Weasley does not wish to admit to having a girlfriend. This is no surprise as they must be something like sixteen or seventeen, being in the sixth form. Telling lies is quite a common feature in the book, but it does take a certain amount of effort, and the headmaster, Dumbledore, stresses that he will not tell Harry a lie. One important undercurrent is the righting of wrongs; Harry having been deprived of his parents, stands in line to receive some kind of advantageous favours, and is seen to be heading for even more fame than he already has of right.

In common with many other Sci-fi productions, there is a certain amount of realistic grounding which acts as a foil to the fanciful ideas going on at

Hogwarts Castle. We have the Ministry of Magic, and quotations of rules and regulations, which seems rather comical when compared with the antics of the witches. There is the Department of Magical Catastrophes, and the Magical Law Enforcement Squad. There is an horrific prison called Azkaban, which reminds us of Alcatraz, from which one is not supposed to escape. They do escape sometimes and occasionally there is a mass breakout. Indeed, Hogwarts itself is a mass of petty regulations, school rules many of which seem to have no particular logic. The bureaucratic element is somewhat comical and yet it has the effect of balancing the crazy antics of the witches. The other factor is the use of King's Cross Station, with its platform nine and three-quarters! There is a train with a red locomotive, bound for Scotland; if it had been the LNER, the locomotive would have been green, but never mind! Places in London are cited, such as Tottenham Court Road, and we come down to mundane realities when the pupils go home for their holidays. Harry's regular return to the Dursleys has the effect of balancing up the crazy activities of the witches.

Some of the author's ideas are clearly not particularly original. We have the flying Ford Anglia, but this idea goes back to Chitty, Chitty Bang-Bang,(3) and even to Bessie the Black Taxi with David Kossoff.(4) Even so, the idea is augmented in a novel way when we find that the entire Weasley family plus Harry are able to sit comfortably in it, plus ample space in the boot for all their luggage. When this car lands at Hogwarts, because Harry is late for school, it goes crazy (minus a driver) and rampages all over the Forbidden Forest. Providentially, it appears just at the right moment to rescue Harry from one of the monsters. The idea of automatic relocation is not missing either. Just as Scotty could beam people up and down, so the Weasleys have something called 'Floo powder', which when tossed into a fireplace can transport one to another place, albeit rather painfully. There is a magical bus which collects up stranded witches and takes them back to London. There is a method called the 'Portkey' which involves clinging to a certain object charged with magic, and this will transport one to a chosen destination. There is something called Apparition which can only be done by fully qualified witches. For the trainees there is the broomstick method, but that can only be used at Hogwarts. Changing appearance to look like someone else or perhaps an animal is certainly not a new idea, neither is the invisibility cloak that Harry shares with his friends. That idea comes in the Ramayana and the Iliad.(5) What appears to be something of a rare idea is that Harry can hold a conversation with snakes; not that he realises this at first, but his friends are amazed to point it out to him. It is termed 'Parcelmouth', and takes us back to Eve in the Garden of Eden; this facility seems to hold a lot of significance for the trainee witches, but this is not explained. As we know, the motif of the snake is an important symbol in world mythology; it symbolises life and paradoxically death. If Harry is on conversational terms with that, it implies that he is some sort of undying, eternal factor, as opposed to just an ordinary schoolboy. That would be a fair deduction from later developments in the sagas; Harry is in some sort of negative collusion with Voldemort. It is a painful experience because that lightning scar on his forehead gives him much discomfort. It indicates that Voldemort is near, or is planning something. The good guy and the bad guy turn out to have the same wand each, which cancel each other out. So there is some kind of balancing situation, rather like what we see in the Ramayana (see Theology of Truth, chapter 22).

There are some ingenious new ideas in the Potter sagas. There is an escalator that goes up a spiral staircase to the Headmaster's study. Also there is a chess game in which the men move themselves and comment on the wisdom of the moves; that is quite a novelty. Another case of augmentation is the game called Quidditch. The way it is described reminds one of American football, but it is all elevated on broomsticks and pupils moving at colossal speeds to control not just one ball but several. Also, plates of food just to one's taste appear in the Great Hall but also other places; the schoolboys' wildest dream! Really quite ingenious is the way that Tom Riddle's diary, which appears to be blank on every page, gives Harry a lead into the mystery of the monster. He finds June 13th and concentrates on the little picture of a TV screen; he goes through it and finds himself in the Headmaster's study with the previous headmaster and so gains information about what happened fifty years ago when the monster struck before. This is a subtle way of integrating modern technology with time travel, but the way it is done is really quite convincing and original. Thus we can see that the author draws on existing motifs but is also inventive in a quite convincing way. We can say it is sometimes quite ingenious.

The other quite convincing element is the way that Harry, and Ron, as boys are realistically portrayed. One might almost conclude that J.K.Rowling is of the male gender, since she tells it all from a boy's point of view and seems to understand a boy's thinking. The three of them form a team, Harry, Ron and Hermione, but they are portrayed very differently, which means that the characterisation is good. Harry is the little innocent who is almost completely unaware of his true potential; how true that is of many a youngster! Then gradually, he finds it out by coming into contact with Hagrid and then his friends at school; always there is the element of innocence and a touch of laziness about his studies. This is in contrast to Hermione. She begins by being somewhat stand-offish and superior but this develops into something more respectful when Harry and Ron save her from a troll. Hermione comes over as the typical 'blue-stocking' swat, a prissy little madam who gets in excess of top marks every time. In the final crisis, it is Hermione who sticks by Harry when all else have deserted him. This is an excellent example of loyalty, but there is no romance between them. Ron, who has been brought up with witches as his parents, has a lot of information to give to Harry. It is a relief to us all to find that Harry is welcome in Ron's family; this is in contrast to how the Dursley's treated him. We also have the contrast between the decent, generous, conscientious pupils like Harry and the nasty, loutish element like Malfoy and his cronies. (6) These boys from Slytherin House are in collusion with Snape and Voldemort. In the great crisis at the end, Malfoy realises the mistake he has made and is glad to be saved from death by Harry. This brings in the basic rift between good and evil on a pupil level. This is a substratum which pervades the whole saga; how is lurking evil to be defeated, as it should.

The characterisation of the teachers is also well thought-out. We have McGonagall who is extremely stern and threatening and yet there is a slight touch of humanity about her, a slight tear in her eye, and with just a suggestion of humour. There is Snape who is always trying to victimise Harry but favours people like Malfoy; how many of us in school have had that experience? We find out later that Snape has a grudge against Harry because of a bad relationship with his father years ago. Snape does not like to be reminded that Mr.Potter saved his life on one occasion, and later we discover that Harry's mother, Lily, was the object of Snape's romantic intentions. There is Lockhart who is constantly trying to advertise his supposed successes in life and ingratiate himself with the pupils, but no one takes him very seriously. The new teacher, Lupin, makes a very good impression on the pupils and is prepared to give extra help on the side when it is realised that Harry is terrified of the Dementors. Lupin comes across as one of the sanest teachers with a lot of decency about him, and in the big crisis, it is Lupin that supports

Harry with great enthusiasm. The Headmaster, Dumbledore, is stern but when one comes to speak with him in private, he is remarkably sympathetic and sensitive, and even supportive. His big mistake is to trust people rather too much, especially Snape. He also gives Harry private support in ways to defeat Voldemort. All of these are traits which we may have noticed in our teachers in our schooldays!

The mystery and snobbery of a Gothic castle in Scotland is the scene for all these antics. We have turrets and dungeons and suits of armour that move, with ghosts emanating from the walls. The drama is augmented by the secrecy element. We have a secret room with a troll walled up, which Hermione discovers. Then there is the trapdoor guarded by the three-headed dog, under which the Philosopher's stone is hidden (another mystery), and also another room with some kind of murderous monster which seems to escape and cause consternation in the school. The Order of the Phoenix, organised by Harry, meets in another secret room. There are secret tunnels all over the castle and tapestries that hide entrances. The secrecy element serves to augment the drama and bring each book to a crisis.

There may be those of a tender disposition who would find much of this frightening. The way round this is to put in plenty of humour and poking fun. There are all kinds of funny names like Hufflepuff, Winky and Dumbledore which are intended to make us laugh. There are comical situations, the most appropriate being when Vernon Dursley and his son find they have grown piggy curly tails; highly appropriate since they are both pigs of the first quality! Vernon Dursley's sister, who can only be termed a nasty piece of work, takes great pleasure in saying hypercritical things about Harry and his parents. Harry has great difficulties in controlling his temper, and eventually, he snaps. That is Harry's chief failing, that of having a nasty temper when aroused. Can we really blame him? Aunt Marge, who is already grossly overweight, swells up like a balloon and sails up to the ceiling. That is the final straw as far as Vernon is concerned, and Harry is unceremoniously excluded from the house. He feels terrible as he is not supposed to do magic outside of school, and the Ministry of Magic is bound to find out. The other witches manage to redeem the situation by deflating Aunt Marge and erasing her memory of the incident. There are so many comical situations worked in that one has to laugh; clearly the author is poking fun at the witches! Perhaps the funniest is when Hermione brews up a special potion which works well on the boys, but when she takes it, it turns her into a cat with furry face and whiskers, and it will not wear off for several weeks. All the spells are enacted with pseudo-Latin phrases, most of them clearly intended to be comical. 'Reddikulus' is a good example and 'Mobiliarbus'. How they remember all these funny words is a mystery, but then Hermione is deeply engrossed in it all.

All the time, there is the fraught relationship with the 'Muggles' which are the non-witches, in other words, ordinary humans. This is accentuated by the attitude of the Dursleys who cannot cope with the thought that Petunia's sister and brother in law were witches, and place Harry under great stress to prevent him going that way; or so they think. All the time there is the tension between the humans finding out or suspecting that there is magic going on, and the witches doing what they can to conceal it. The humans seem to be unaware that there are Death Eaters mysteriously appearing, intent on killing people, not just witches but humans, for no particular reason. All this helps to build up the suspense as creeping evil looms up in the sagas.

The age-old question of free will as opposed to predestination often surfaces in these sagas. The fact that the newspaper is called 'The Daily Prophet' is an indication that the witches all assume that they are predestined in some way or other. This is emphasised by the batty old Professor Sybill Trelawney who is a recluse but forecasts the future. This reminds us of the system of prophecy in the Graeco-Roman world, where almost every large town had its own Sybil, issuing prophesies of doom. She comes down to join the Christmas lunch, saying, 'Who am I to refuse the promptings of fate?' but when she realises that there are thirteen at the table, she is terrified that the first one to get up will die. Strangely, Dumbledore and McGonagall pass this off as trivial scaremongering. 'Come on, the turkey's getting cold'! It is Dumbledore that provides the balance between fate and choice, when discussing Harry's acceptance into Gryffindor as opposed to Slytherin. 'It is our choices, Harry, that make us what we truly are, far more than our abilities.' This is a roundabout way of saying that he refused to go in for an evil gang and preferred good company . The tension between free will and predestination is a substratum of the book. Harry is supposed to be the 'goodie', but he is cornered into being downright sly, telling fibs and disobeying his teachers.

One of the main features of the sagas is the ongoing terror of creeping evil and hate. We have monsters hiding the basement. There are Boggarts, Manticores, Hinkypunks (note the humour), Grindylows, massive man-eating spiders, Unicorns, Crups, Nifflers, Porlocks, Murtlaps, Knarls, Hippogriffs, and a full giant called Gawp; all strange mythological beasts that are best avoided. Harry is constantly under threat and has not to be left on his own, even in the school. There is an evil witch called Sirius Black, who was his father's friend, but turned nasty and betrayed him. He was the one who allegedly murdered Harry's parents and is now, having escaped from Azkaban, assumed to be bent on killing Harry himself. It turns out, however, that Sirius Black is Harry's godfather and guardian, and although he has to remain in hiding, promises to help Harry if anything untoward threatens him. In fact, Harry's life is blighted by the awareness of his parents' murder and their death- screams haunt him every time he sees a Dementor. Beneath it all is the terror element of Voldemort. No one dare even say his name, except that Harry, quite innocently blurts it out sometimes. This serves to show us that the witches are not all of one opinion. Some are good witches and others are evil; they have gone over to the Dark Side. There is constant fear going on. This is accentuated by the fact that one of the houses in the school, Slytherin, is composed of nasty-minded pupils, Malfoy being the chief genius behind it. He is quite confident of his influence because he is in favour with Snape, the nastiest teacher in the school, and also his father is influential on the board of governors. Very little of this relates to Dracula or Frankenstein's monster, except to say that the Dementors, who seldom show their faces, strike terror in Harry (and others). They have the ability to suck one's soul out of one's body, leaving one as an empty shell; this is a permutation on vampirism.

Another amusing feature is the way in which Sir Cadogan, a mediaeval knight comes to be the 'gateguard' at Gryffindor tower. He has a crazy habit of changing the password two or three times a day, which means that pupils with a bad memory (like Neville Longbottom) find themselves stranded until someone else turns up with a good memory! The name, Sir Cadogan , is clearly a reminder of the Knights of the Round Table of Arthurian legend. This is reinforced by the lines of suits of armour that clank and jangle in the corridors. They light up at Christmas time, and sing Christmas carols; not that they manage to recall all the words, but the poltergeist, Peeves, fills in with naughty versions of them.

There is a curious sort of stand-off between Muggle technology and that of the witches. In many ways, the witches are living in a past age and have no ambition to move into the modern world. Hogwarts Castle is not wired for electricity. All the lighting is done by torches and magical candles floating in the air. There are no televisions or computers or anything electrical. When Mr. Weasley visits the Dursleys he is intrigued by these modern gadgets. Hogwarts has no telephones either; communication is done entirely by sending off owls which behave like two-way homing pigeons, with little messages written on parchment attached to their legs. There is no modern paper; parchment is used with quill pens and bottles of ink. A simple thing like a matchbox is a puzzle to the Weasleys; the witches simply flick their wands to produce fire. Paper money is also a puzzle to them; they are still on the gold standard, and their basic currency is in gold Galleons. If one's bed is cold, warming pans are used. The witches are puzzled by the 'please-men' who keep order in the Muggle world. There seems to be no need for the Police in this other world.

Paradoxically, the witches are well ahead of Muggle technology in some respects. Miss Skeeter has a quill that can write automatically on parchment, rather like a ticker-tape machine. When one goes to a Quidditch match, one can purchase an 'omnocular', not unlike binoculars, except that this gadget will replay parts of the match in slow motion, or speed up again; this reminds us of the action replay facility at snooker matches. Strangely, the wizards have their own Wireless Network, which might seem a little strange if they have a newspaper which manages to reach everyone in the wizard world. Also there is a golden aerial which behaves as a secrecy sensor. When people tell lies, it begins to vibrate. This, however, is not much use at Hogwarts, since they are all fibbing away all the time, especially Harry Potter. When he does try to tell the truth he gets into even more drastic trouble.

To reinforce the idea of them living in the past, there is the element of slavery going on behind the scenes. All that food and other amenities at Hogwarts is provided by house elves who are not paid, never get a holiday, or sick leave, or a pension and are not properly clothed. Hermione is up in arms about this when she comes to realise the plight of people like Dobby, Kreacher and Winky, but there is not much she can do about it; it is endemic in the system. Occasionally a house elf gets the sack and that causes much distress because it is difficult to gain another posting, and as Dobby finds out, even more difficult to find paid employment. We have much sympathy for the elves that show amazing loyalty to their masters in spite of being exploited. In the final crisis, Dobby's actions are decisive in helping Harry.

With this we see a thinly disguised polemic about liberation and support for downtrodden peoples.

Unfortunately, Voldemort has the idea that he must commit murder in order to support his assumed immortality. The issue of blood, in a literal sense, is a constant theme in the sagas. People like Malfoy have it in their heads that one needs to be a pure bred witch in order to be a proper witch. The term 'Mudblood' keeps emerging, as a sort of insult.(7) Harry Potter is sneered at for being a half-blood, and yet he has capabilities that many witches do not have. It turns out that he is the only one who can stand a chance of defeating Voldemort. Hermione, who has no witch blood in her at all, outdoes all the rest of them in their studies and gets more than full marks in the exams. Ron, who is a thoroughbred, has trouble with his academic work and only just manages to scrape through. This just goes to show that racial background and parentage can be irrelevant to becoming a witch, or indeed to achieving any other skill. In this we see a thinly veiled polemic against Nazism (see chapter 4 in Theology of Truth).

It is not possible to side-step the relationship between good and evil in this mythological system. We have noticed that in many myths, there is a distinct chasm between good and evil and there seems to be no grey area in between. It is like the Trenches in the First World War; one is either on one side or the other and there is a 'no-man's-land' in between. But with Harry Potter mythology, this is not so, or at least, the difference between good and bad witches is nowhere near as clear-cut. Sirius Black is a case in point; everyone regards him as the worst kind of murderous criminal, and they continue to do so, even when Harry discovers that Black is his godfather and claims that he is innocent. He then incriminates Wormtail, alias Peter Pettigrew, who appears early in the series as a nice person. Professor Lupin, who is noted for being easy-going with the pupils, turns out to be a werewolf. We are left in suspense about Snape, who has all the hallmarks of being thoroughly evil, but there are hints that he is a 'goodie' in spite of appearances. At the very least he is some sort of double agent; in the end he kills Dumbledore. That in itself is not decisive since Dumbldore's death is predestined. This is all part of the suspense; we do not really know who in the Ministry of Magic is on the Dark Side or not. Only Dumbledore, we assume, is thoroughly committed to destroying Voldemort. At times the plot becomes so entangled and complicated that it sounds like an Agatha Christie thriller. But this is more true to life in its own way. We have to go through life not knowing for certain where evil or good really lie; they are often enmeshed and interwoven and we have to rely on our basic instincts and impulses to know which way to turn. For this reason, the Harry Potter myth is not only a truly modern system of thought, but it is also highly realistic, in spite of all the extraordinary high jinxes that go on.

One of the important elements in this stand-off between good and evil, is the fact that people are unwilling to face up to the reality of evil. To quote Dumbledore again; 'It's hard to convince people he's (Voldemort) back, especially as they don't want to believe it in the first place.' Page 89 in The Order of the Phoenix. How true of life, especially in these days! The modern Humanist mentality cannot cope with the idea of evil as a spiritual force. Talk about devils and Satan is subjected to ridicule. But the truth is that evil may appear to have been defeated, but just reasserts itself on finding an opportunity. The main opportunity presents itself when people imagine that there is no evil.

It is interesting how the author slips in contemporary issues in such a way as to leave a question mark, rather than a dogmatic statement. The issue of corporal punishment runs past us. Harry was expecting to receive the cane on being sent to Professor McGonagall, but nothing happened. He received an excess of detentions. One series of detentions with Professor Umbridge involved him being carved on the back of his hand, which produced more pain and disfigurement than any of us could justify. We are all delighted when Umbridge gets her comeuppance! More importantly, the whole issue of government interference in education surfaces. The Ministry, or at least some of the 'experts', are coming to the conclusion that Dumbledore is getting past it and ought to be sidelined. That is part of the ironic tension, since he is one of the few that can face the truth about Voldemort's resurgence. The ministry sends in this new teacher called Professor Umbridge who will not admit to Voldemort's reappearance. She clearly has her eye on becoming the headteacher; in this she is briefly successful. We are left wondering whether she is just trying to throw sand in the eyes of the pupils or whether she really believes what she says. The point is that influential people in the ministry and on the governors are trying to cancel out the good influence of Dumbledore. He has the experience in education, the good intentions and the necessary power to protect his pupils, but there are those who seek to undermine this. How like today this is, with so-called experts from the Ministry of Education interfering with the well-intentioned efforts of the teachers!

The stunts done by the witches become increasingly fantastic as the trainees at the school move up to be instructed in ever more complicated spells. That magic wand that they all carry is used as a cross between a ray-gun, a firelighter, a mend-all, a flame-thrower and a stun-gun. Fortunately, the students are not allowed to use their wands outside of school, during the holidays. They are supposed to pose as Muggles; but that is rather difficult when people like the Dursleys taunt them. A broken wand is a serious matter; Ron has to stick his together with selotape! There are different qualities of broomsticks. It depends on what one can afford. Harry, being rich, can afford the top quality broomstick which means he can fly faster than anyone else. This all adds to the humour of the sagas.

The stand off between good and evil develops into a rising tension as Harry and Dumbledore manage to probe into the mind of Voldemort. There is a kind of strange logic going on over Voldemort's idea of becoming immortal. It is no use acquiring the elixir of life since that only fades off and one has to take it repeatedly. The clever scheme devised by Voldemort is to divide his soul into seven parts and imbue certain artefacts each with a portion. Harry's task, on realising this, is to find these artefacts, for instance a golden locket and the Sword of Gryffindor, and cancel them off one by one. This, it is hoped, will bring about Voldemort's demise. The final scenes are taken up with Harry frantically locating these 'Horcruxes' and destroying them. The final irony is that the last Horcrux is Harry himself. The final battle, which reminds us of Armageddon, ends with a truce, as Voldemort, quite cynically, offers the fighters in Hogwarts a reprieve if Harry hands himself over.

Harry decides to comply with this, knowing that he has to die in order that Voldemort too will die. He walks into the Forbidden Forest and allows Voldemort to kill him. But is that really the end? Harry finds himself in King's Cross Station conversing with Dumbledore, who raises the question as to whether he would like to go back. Harry does, and as Hagrid carries the inert body of Harry up to the school, the final phase of the battle breaks out and Voldemort and his minions are defeated. Harry is alive again.

This is a motif seen in so many myths, that of resurrection. It raises the question of what is life and what is death? But it is a new life for him, as the scar on his forehead does not hurt anymore, which indicates that Death is defeated on a permanent basis. Voldemort has gone for good.

On the face of it, this is a story all about witchcraft and another world of magic that normal people are incapable of coping with. There is the humorous side to it which is a strong indication that we must not take it too seriously or literally. If we look at the symbolic aspect of it, then many good things can be seen.

Dumbledore, the wise and kindly Headmaster who is thought to be out of date and irrelevant to today's needs, appears to be dead, but is he? His influence still carries on. Is this God the Father, who, for many people, is assumed to be a thing of the past and irrelevant? He certainly acts as a father figure to Harry who is an orphan and is constantly troubled by images of his parents being murdered. So is Harry the Son of God, symbolic of Jesus, who realised that he would have to die in order to defeat Death? We notice that Harry's innocence is emphasised, his generosity, his willingness to rescue even an enemy from death. We feel bad about all those that have had to die in the final battle, fighting on his side. We notice that he never actually kills anyone himself. At the final climax, he comes alive again and inspires everyone, even the wild creatures in the forest, to end Voldemort's tyranny.

Voldemort, who began life as another orphan boy, Tom Riddle, epitomises evil and manages to enlist, blackmail and terrorise so many people into his campaign. But Harry can work out what he is doing and the reality of his return when so many people refuse to accept it. The way it is described reminds us strongly of the Third Reich, with its racial discrimination and persecution of racial minorities. The final truth is, as was with Nazism, that the fountain head itself has to be cut off. In other words, it is no use just chopping bits off the snake's tail; one has to cut its head off. This was true with Hitler and can be evidenced with any totalitarian regime.

So the basic polemic with the Harry Potter saga is about freedom; freedom of speech, religion, politics and artistic expression. Unfair discrimination is also shown up in a bad light. In a positive light the author shows that international understanding and co-operation is to be desired. So Bill Weasley marries Fleur Delacourt and Hermione takes a fancy to Victor Krum, albeit briefly.

This brings us to the reality of witchcraft in the modern age. It is foolish to treat the whole matter simply as a joke, even if Harry Potter is depicted in a humorous way. Since 1950, when the Witchcraft Laws were repealed in this country, we have seen the reappearance of witchcraft, to the dismay of many people. Even if the witches remain secretive and out of sight for now, there is still concern over the re-emergence of Satanism and what may be its long term effects and influence. As a postscript to the chapter, we shall briefly consider Arthur Miller's important play, The Crucible, as an example of how hysteria over witchcraft can destroy a complete community. It is no use trying to say that that is long in the past; the same sort of 'witchhunt' hysteria still surfaces today, and is a favourite football for the media. It does not, at the moment concern witches; it centres on things like 'child abuse' and police clearance, on the assumption that a piece of paper from the police station will stop people misbehaving themselves. The Shetland Child Abuse scandal is a case in point; it became a mania with the press some years ago, but turned out to be a complete paper chase.

More seriously and importantly, it is claimed with a lot of foundation, that the occult had a significant effect on the course of the Second World War. This is described in Michael Fitzgerald's book, Hitler's Occult War. It would seem that Hitler and various leading Nazis were steeped in the occult, though not making any public pronouncements about it. Many, if not all, of the major tactical decisions made by the Germans were governed by occult or zodiacal methods, and this was known about in Britain before war started. The British invited various occultists to direct their efforts into defeating the Nazis. As the war progressed, the Americans and the Russians did the same. Just how this worked is described by Fitzgerald. But it just goes to demonstrate that witchcraft, although it appears to be stupid, must not be underestimated. It can have its effect, and if someone with malevolent intent, for instance, a Satanist, is working some sort of agenda behind the scenes, this can have genuine results in the world of reality.

The misleading element in the Harry Potter sagas, (at least one hopes), is that there appear to be hordes of trainee witches at a special school of magic. The truth is more likely to be that there are a certain number of occultists in various countries, and they are in collusion with one another, but they are not an overwhelming number. It is true that occasionally a child is born with unusual gifts, and that gift may be some kind of spiritual power which is not always appreciated by his parents. The other truth is that the Christian faith is opposed to occultism in its various forms. Any responsible Christian minister will warn one of the dangers of becoming involved with spiritual forces that can wreck one's mind. It is very much to the point that the Bible tells us not to get involved in such things. One of the main contradictions in the sagas is the heavy emphasis laid on Christmas. Is this a confusion of thought, or is it a hint that Harry is symbolic of Jesus? We have two very apposite quotations from the Bible. One is from Jesus but spoken by Dumbldore; 'Where your treasure is, there will your heart be also.'(8) Another is from St.Paul, again from Dumbledore; 'the last enemy that shall be destroyed is death.'(9) And indeed it was, as Voldemort is defeated.

So is there any substance in 'magic'? We are not talking about conjuring tricks which are great fun on the stage. We are talking about ways and means of putting ideas into people's minds, and there are those with the spiritual power to manage this quite successfully. That was one of the methods that the witches used to disrupt Hitler's war effort, such as putting a mistaken idea into his head. It is not good enough to say this is all imagination and nonsense. What people think and imagine conditions their actions. Maybe one of the wisest and most pertinent remarks that Dumbledore made with regard to what Harry thought was happening to him, goes like this; 'Of course it's happening in your head, Harry, but why on earth should that mean it's not real?'

This brings us back to the basic question of what is reality, what is life and death and the next world.

The Crucible, by Arthur Miller

One of the most remarkable factors which is absent from the Harry Potter sagas, is any mention of God, the Devil or of Jesus Christ. We have already considered that the whole depiction is some kind of parable concerning the cosmic battle between good and evil, and that Jesus Christ had to die in order to defeat Satan finally. But there is another literary production, stemming from 1953, which approaches the matter in a far more obviously theological way than the Potter sagas.

Arthur Miller takes us back to the early years of European settlement in the American continent, to Salem Massachussetts, in 1692. This is a setting in which this new province is dominated by a theocratic regime, deeply Protestant and what appears to be Congregationalism. It is a time when a strongly fundamentalist approach to the Bible is accepted as the norm; Heaven and Hell are a reality, Satan is also a reality and witchcraft is genuinely feared. It is not clear, from the play, how seriously the young girls are dabbling in the occult, if at all, but the inescapable reality is the hysteria that this engenders. It is unnecessary to give a blow by blow account of the plot as it develops, but there is no doubt that it is based upon real events, with a certain latitude that Miller has given himself for the sake of drama.

Mr. Parris, the minister of Salem, has become aware of strange goings-on in the woods at night, with young girls dancing, possibly naked, and boiling up some sort of soup. He immediately finds this suspicious. Also the fact that several babies have died for no apparent reason, and his daughter, Betty, has some strange illness that baffles the doctor. He invites in Mr. Hale of Beverly, a minister who is supposed to be an expert at diagnosing witchcraft. From there the whole thing escalates into a hysterical toxic swamp in which no one can really assess the truth. Masses of people are accused and put into goal, awaiting trial and hanging.

It would seem that there is a coterie of silly teenage girls who are happy to hand out accusations, without any substance. The judges who are called in to sift truth from lies, are easily taken in by the girls. Mary Warren, who was the first to instigate accusations, tries to withdraw her testimony, but then finds herself condemned for contempt of court. In other words, she is between the Devil and the deep blue sea. When the other girls are pressed to tell the truth, they go into a hysterical session, clearly intended to throw sand in the eyes of the judges. Ironically, they are the ones who receive no punishment.

Mr. Hale, who is probably the sanest in the play, can see what is happening and tries to bring in a little common sense. He can see that the girls are simply putting on an act. He is ignored by the judges, who feel that once they have hung a few people for witchcraft, it would be unfair to reprieve all the rest. The end result is a farming community completely desolated for many decades; cattle straying about with no owner and orphans left to wander around begging.

The final irony is that the one farmer with the most integrity who is cajoled into signing a confession which is not the truth, is hanged anyway. So the most godfearing, honest and devoted Christians are accused on the slightest of evidence and the judges will not listen to anything to the contrary.

The Salem witch hunt was not the only one in those days, but it was the one that must have finally convinced people that theocracy was a difficult matter. When the Church and the judiciary are coterminous, we can expect problems to arise. It is far safer to allow the church to deal with spiritual matters and let the judiciary apply normal canons of common sense over evidence. The problem was, in Salem, that any slight thing could be held up as evidence of witchcraft; reading a book, making a doll, mumbling, dancing, going cold. It just goes to show how a superstitious ethos can result in all kinds of crazy accusations, and tear a community apart.

How is this of any relevance to Harry Potter? Firstly, there is the fiction that there are masses of witches. While it is true that there are a few people involved in the occult, and they are very secretive, it is a wild exaggeration to say that there are hundreds of them. But Salem and Harry Potter do give that impression. It is also highly misleading to allow the whole matter to be seen as some sort of joke. We notice that Harry spends a lot of his schooldays injured, bleeding and close to death, with evil looming over him. This aspect of it is not funny; neither is the death toll at Salem. This is not a comfortable thought, even if it forms some kind of fascination for people.

The other factor is that the hysteria at Salem easily took root and the vast majority of the population took it seriously. This is evidence that the whole matter of the occult appeals to something instinctive in human nature. The same can be said about Harry Potter, and this helps to explain his popularity. I am not trying to say that the vast majority of people take it seriously, although one suspects that some may do so. But the whole concept, in spite of the jocularity worked into the stories, does resonate with something in the human **id** (as Freud might put it). One further element, which tends to be missing from Miller's play, but is strongly represented in Harry Potter, is the symbolic element. This is a factor that is inescapable when dealing with mythology and confirms, in my mind, that Harry Potter is a very good example of modern mythology.

Whether one could go a little further and see it as modernistic eschatology would be an interesting question. There is nothing in Harry Potter to indicate the future, except to say that in the final pages, Harry and his family and friends appear on King's Cross Station a decade or so later, as they send off their children to be educated at Hogwarts. Perhaps this is a way of saying that life never ends, or that history repeats itself, or even that the sins of the fathers are visited on the children to the third and fourth generation. But there is hope, for Harry touches his scar on his forehead and there is now no pain; does this mean that evil has finally been defeated?

The Harry Potter series of films, culminating in the Deathly Hallows

All of the Harry Potter books have been turned into feature films and there has been a strong inclination to make the film versions faithful to the books.

This portrayal, in particular, is very largely faithful to the book, and this, we understand, is because Joanna Rowling attended the filming and would not allow the film scriptwriters to alter things unnecessarily. But there are exceptions to this. We notice that there are quite a few augmentations to the drama. One example of this is the way in which the Dementors terrorise people walking across the footbridge over the Thames and the bridge collapses like the Tacoma Bridge; all very dramatic but not in the book. A plus in the adaptation would be the way in which the international element is giving slightly more emphasis. A minus would be that Dumbledore's two quotations from the Bible are missing, thus reducing the Christian influence in the theme.

With regard to the later films, especially the last one, the main shortcomings are as follows. There is a lot of darkness and indistinct photography in it which never seems to receive a contrast with light and colour. Many of the scenes are obscure with faces slightly out of focus so that it is difficult to identify people. Many of the teenagers look so alike that one is left guessing as to their identities. One would guess that the audience is expected to have read the books and possibly seen the previous films in order to divine who is whom. Generally speaking the characterization is nowhere near as strong or clear as in the books. Much more could have been made of Ginny Weasley who was actually Harry's girlfriend, but this never really surfaces. Professor McGonagall could have been given much more prominence, but we have difficulty in guessing who she is. Hagrid, the amiable half-giant appears but is not properly identified. Neville Longbottom, who is not very bright, and a bit younger than Harry, could have been given a much clearer characterization.

Much of the speech is indistinct and slurred which makes the progression of the drama difficult to follow. The film is far too reliant on the spectacular stunts with magic wands being waved around and destruction on all sides. The strange logic of the wizarding world is very largely not clear. One can be forgiven for losing track of the plot completely. However, one does have some knowledge of the basic ideas, if one has followed the sequence through from the start.

Perhaps the biggest mistake is the omission of the scar on Harry's forehead, which gives him pain every time Voldemort is making some kind of move. The scar is highly significant as it relates him to the tragedy of his parents being murdered when he was a baby.

We are expected to know the logic behind the Horcuxes. These are the artefacts which Voldemort has imparted his soul to, with the intention of becoming immortal. This is never really explained clearly in the last film. This means that we are left guessing as to why Harry has to find the Sword of Gryffindor, the pendant and the Tiara in order to destroy them. It is a strange sort of logic, but then the logic of wizardry is on a different level to that of normal people. With that we may recall that the Muggles hardly ever become involved in this last saga, which means that the contrast between normality and craziness is lost. As the Dursleys are being moved out of their house, there is no explanation given for that; one has to have read the books in order to understand the logic of it.

As a horror movie typical of the modern era, this film is quite exciting but loses out on much of the potential for irony, characterization, climax and anticlimax, which is latent in the books. .

Footnotes for chapter 23.

1. An avatar is an earthly appearance of the Hindu god Vishnu (or other gods).
2. Voldemort, literally, 'flight of death' (French).
3. A major feature of Chitty, Chitty Bang Bang is the way the antique car sails through the air and brings them to Neuschwanstein Castle. Based on the novel by Ian Fleming.
4. Bessie the Black Taxi was children's programme in the 1950's, done by David Kossoff. When he got stuck in a traffic jam in London, he would say, 'Bessie, Fly!', and she did.
5. The Iliad, included in my chapter on the Ramayana, in The Theology of Truth.
6. Malfoy, literally, 'bad faith', (French).
7. One of the main tenets of Nazism was on the matter of purity of blood, which is how they decided that the Jews and other elements were not fit to breed with so-called pure Germans.
8. Matthew 6:21.
9. I Corinthians 15:26.

24

Rudolph Bultmann; Demythologising

The twentieth century has seen a new approach to the Theology of the Bible. There are those, such as Rudolph Bultmann who cannot cope with mythology and feel it is essential to leave it out. This process has been going on in recent times, in an attempt to make the Christian message not so heavily dependent on traditional metaphors. As one would expect, this has not met with total support from the Christian community, in fact many object to it strongly. But the existentialist movement in Theology is a strong one; it is an attempt to rephrase the Christian message in the philosophical, sociological and psychological jargon of modern times.

One interesting fact about Bultmann's thoughts is that he does not seem to attempt any evaluation of the Old Testament with its mythology. Still less is there any attempt at dealing with other mythologies from around the world. We have found, so far, that there is much richness of ideas coming from the traditions of different cultures, and these ideas almost certainly stand as symbolic for something important in the way these peoples think.

One has the impression that Bultmann cannot cope with mythology and has a totally negative view of it. That may be so, but what he fails to realise is that mythology is endemic in the human psyche. It is not something that we can just isolate and cancel off. It is an instinctive element in the **id**, as Freud and Jung would tell us. It is helpful to come to realise this and face up to it. But eradicating it from our mental make-up is not realistic. To put it very bluntly, we all need to have some kind of mental framework, some kind of basic assumption about life, otherwise we would just drift along with no purpose.

As Bultmann says, it is true that the traditional myth about the world being a three tiered structure; heaven, earth and hell, has had to be abandoned. Geographically, this is now impossible. However, people still continue to carry this motif in their minds, and pattern their lives accordingly. To put it really crudely, **up** means good, well done, winning, nearer to God; **down** means bad, failed, corrupt, loss, nearer to the devil. That kind of motif is instinctive in us all and is the basic assumption in every myth we have described, even if there are slight variations on it.

Bultmann points out that the New Testament is based on the assumption of the three tiered world. That would be a fair comment, but a fairly obvious one. Everyone at that time thought like that; it would hardly have been possible to think anything else. The few people who did think the world was spherical were almost certainly regarded as crazy.(1) With regard to Jesus himself, if he was genuinely human (and that is one of the essential points in the Christian faith), then he would have been thinking the same as everyone else. Even if he did have an awareness of what we now know, would it have been any use trying to tell people that the world was spherical and that there were such things as 'light years' and quasars and red giants, and that the earth circulated round the Sun?

We can, of course, see it the other way. That the Old Testament, with its mythical assumptions, which were filled out by Zoroastrian ideas,(2) provided a mental basis for the coming of God's Messiah. That mental basis included the Creation accounts in Genesis, plus various additives from the Psalms, and then eschatological material which is largely not included in the Old Testament, but which nevertheless had a strong bearing on the thinking of people in first century Israel. We have already seen that the book of Enoch had a considerable influence on the New Testament writers, and Jesus himself. Jesus himself could hardly have escaped these influences, and indeed why should he have? We can see it in this light; that God provided the mental basis for the coming of the Messiah just as much as he provided the historical and geographical basis. By that I mean that the land of Israel was enjoying a relatively peaceful period under the Pax Romana, with Herod the Great keeping the hooligan element under control. That was really quite unusual for that part of the world; it has always been turbulent and still is to this day. If the Messiah had arrived literally anywhere without any kind of groundwork or preparation, how many people would have realised who or what he was? The establishment of the people of Israel, in their homeland

and with their distinctive beliefs and laws clearly provided the appropriate setting for the Messiah to come. That groundwork clearly included all kinds of mythological material as well as laws, customs and a framework of historical development.

One of the basic problems with any treatment of the Bible, is the extent to which it can be taken literally, or alternatively, as figuratively. There is one kind of fundamentalist who takes every word of the scriptures completely at face value, and will not admit that there are certain contradictions. But there is another kind of fundamentalist, who takes everything in the scriptures on the same level of validity or truth without recognising that some material is mythical, some poetic, some historical, some legalistic and many more types of literature. If everything is taken on the same level of spiritual authority, then one clearly misses out on the intention of the different authors. Their intentions may be doctrinal, or devotional, or ethical, or even quasi philosophical. One has to use a certain amount of discernment as to what is the nature of any given passage of scripture. Then there is a third kind of fundamentalist who takes the whole Bible literally, decides that so much of it is impossible, rejects it all, and refuses to consider that the truth might be conveyed in various metaphors or symbolisms. There may be many an atheist who feels like this but even so, it is difficult to avoid being influenced by the Bible.

This brings us back to the original question when we dealt with Greek mythology. How literally did these ancient peoples take their myths? Admittedly there were certain aspects of their myths which must have been seen in a literal light, but did they really take all of those fantastic stories at face value? There were certain people such as Caligula and Commodus who did take it literally, but that might in itself have been a political ploy to assert authority. For most people, those stories might have been for them like our modern soap opera combined with science fiction; they may have laughed about it as much as we do. It has to be admitted that there are comical scenes in the myths; at least we see them as amusing. It is far more instructive to consider the symbolisms in these ancient myths. It is foolish to regard them as nonsense; they clearly stem from something in human instinct and in a way, the myths are describing ourselves in lurid terms. The figurative language, the metaphors, the exaggerations, all point to the same thing; it is life, in its various situations and permutations, writ large, making it easier for us to moralise and philosophise. To give strength to this claim, we can see that the same motifs seen in the ancient myths keep reappearing in the modern and futuristic myths of our own times. Human nature still feels it necessary to ponder the great issues of life, death, divinity and eternity. Even the same metaphors and figurative language are used. Clearly, Bultmann does not understand the true nature of myth and the fact that it cannot be eradicated from the human psyche.

How does this work with regard to the New Testament and the life and death of Jesus? We have seen that every mythical system, ancient or modern, lays a very heavy emphasis on the value of life. Everybody knows that instinctively we wish to preserve our lives; suicide takes an enormous amount of effort. The question of death hangs over us all; on the one hand we are all in denial of it and paradoxically we are fascinated by it. No one really knows for certain, what happens to us, but there is the assumption that there is another life after this earthly life is over. Most people assume that the next life will be an improvement on this life, but that is only a hope; it might turn out to be a lot worse, but the fear of Hell is now politically wrong!

How does the Bible approach this question? On the mythical level, in the Garden of Eden, death is introduced, but the implication is that it will one day be defeated. We have the 'assumption' of various people, such as Moses and Elijah, which tells us that the end of one's earthly life is not the end really, but coming into the presence of God. At the end of Matthew's gospel, we have a brief insertion of myth, when Jesus, having died on the cross, the rocks were split, the tombs opened, and the bodies of the saints rose again and were seen in the holy city. What this is saying is that there is resurrection, not just for Jesus, but for all those faithful people who have died. This is a sample of the mythical approach; now for the literal approach. Elijah and Elisha both rescue a child from death. Both these accounts are clearly meant to be taken literally, but they are figurative in the sense that they tell us that the human soul lives on even if the body dies. The gospel writers record several instances in which Jesus raised people from the dead, the most dramatic of which was the raising of Lazarus. Again, this is intended to be taken literally, but the implications in it are that death, as we know it, is not the end; there is another life waiting for us.

The most graphic case of this motif comes with the death and resurrection of Jesus himself. There is nothing mythical about the four accounts of the crucifixion. It is described in detail with all the horror that went with it, and St.John makes a point of showing us that Jesus really did die. It was no pretence, not a fable, a parable or a philosophical theory. The only mythical element in it is that Jesus was fastened to a 'tree' which reminds us of the 'world tree'. Even so, this tree, the cross, is a real piece of wood as opposed to an imaginary 'yggdrassil'.(3) The spear that pierced him, has mythical overtones. The spear, like the sword, symbolises truth and the righting of wrongs. How true; Jesus' wound gave us the water and the blood which were for the cleansing of the whole world.

Even more heavily emphasised is the reality of the resurrection. The gospel writers are at pains to show us that Jesus was really alive again, not as some kind of ghost or chimera. Each writer does it in his own way. Matthew emphasises it by recording how the Sadducees and the Pharisees tried to secure the tomb so that Jesus could not be stolen away. But the resurrection could not be smothered. He burst out of the tomb and defied all their attempts at denying it. Admittedly, there are mythological elements in the accounts of the resurrection, but not overdone. These accounts are intended to be taken literally. They do, of course, defy the rationality of modern scientific minds, but then we are not dealing with the logic of mankind, but the logic of God, which is a different matter. No one has managed to rationalise the resurrection, nor will they ever manage to.

What the New Testament is saying through mythical elements and through literal accounts, is that all those factors in human myth which relate to life, death and resurrection, are brought to completion in real terms. God is essentially saying, 'you are right to value life, and you need not fear death; there is a better world waiting for you after this one.' God speaks to us through symbols such as precious metals, jewels, mirrors, the snake, and also through the reality of the life of Jesus. God speaks to us not just in our own languages but also through our own instincts and thought forms.

When we come to compare the four gospels with the mythological material we have seen earlier in this book, we are left with the distinct impression that the writers are very economical with mythological symbolism. There is nothing mentioned on the subject of jewels, mercury, translucent stones, or mirrors, all of which are symbolic of eternity and the avoidance of death. Gold is mentioned seldom. We have one of the three gifts of the magi; traditionally this has been taken to symbolise royalty. Another gift was the incense, the smoke of which symbolises deity. But these are not heavily stressed as mythological matters in their context. The only other mention of gold comes in that strange passage in Matthew, in which Jesus tells Peter to catch a fish that has a coin in its mouth. This, however, is in the context of the need to pay one's taxes, and has nothing really to do with mythology.(4) There are no snakes mentioned in the gospels, except for that situation in St.John 3:14, in which Jesus refers to the situation in Numbers 21:9 when snakes had bitten some of the people and Moses made a bronze effigy of a snake and held it up, thus bringing the people back to life. There is that mythological element here, in that the snake symbolises life and death, but the passage in St.John is not dependent on the story in Numbers. Jesus is only using it as an illustration; the basic truth here is that Jesus has to be crucified in order that life may be given to us all.

One might maintain that the Star of Bethlehem is an example of mythological thought. We have noticed that the stars and planets do not seem to be an important element in most world mythologies. It is only with the Greeks, Persians and possibly the Incas that this subject held much fascination. However, recent research has now pointed out that the Star was almost certainly not mythic, but a real conjunction of planets which would have occurred in 6 BC, and indeed only recently another such a conjunction was noted. The Star does not have to be mythology at all; it was almost certainly a historical fact.(5)

Bultmann would say that the miracles described in the gospels are mythological. But that is his opinion, and possibly of many an atheist. What they do not discuss is the emergence, in recent times, of the healing ministry of the church. Such names as Harry Edwards, Christopher Woodward and Russell Parker are now well known. I have not yet found a doubter who could explain away the healing ability of Linda Martel.(6) That spiritual healing is a reality, cannot be underestimated. What we are seeing in Jesus is someone who had massive numinous energy that could cure all manner of health problems. On the other hand, when people had no faith in him, it did not work. If he could cure blindness, deafness, leprosy and many other problems, why could he not control the elements? Why are such things regarded as impossible? It is impossible if we subject it to the logic of mankind; but we are dealing here with the logic of God, as already touched on over the resurrection. One can admit that there are mythical aspects to such scenes as the stilling of the storm on Lake Galilee. The motif of the boat carrying a significant person is a minority idea but the assumption that the great deeps symbolise evil and primeval chaos is a strong motif. However, the main thrust of that story is that the disciples should not be afraid, but trust in God, and that Jesus cares for his embryonic church. The mythological elements in it are incidental but form powerful images.

The Ascension, which is recorded in the Acts 1:6-12, does have mythological aspects; they were up a mountain, and a cloud came down and Jesus was taken from their sight. Also two men in white (who are not stated to be angels) appear and tell the disciples that Jesus will return. We might guess that the two men are Moses and Elijah, two who were 'assumed' into heaven, or at any rate, never had a tomb. We notice that those two appeared at the Transfiguration and at the Resurrection. What is this saying in picture language? It is saying that those two great prophets were watching over Jesus, and that Jesus was a prophet of the same standing as they were. The whole point about 'assumption' is that someone, or certain people, are with God in a special way, which means they can intercede for humanity. The same applies to the tradition about St.Mary being 'assumed'. Again, this factor is beyond human rationalisation.

It is interesting to note that there is another account of the Ascension, at the end of St. Luke's gospel (24:50-51). This account, which comes from the same writer, is much abbreviated, stating that they were at Bethany, and 'he parted from them'; other texts say that he was carried up into heaven. It looks very much as though Luke, on reflection, found that that verse was insufficient for an explanation for how Jesus just physically disappeared. He began with the Acts of the Apostles having a fuller account, which is even so, just as mysterious.

In general terms, the Gospels are quite economical with the mythological element. The parables are very down to earth, and in fact there is a lot of literal language included, especially in St.John, in those long discourses. It is when we come to Revelation that we see the full development of mythological expression. The whole of Christ's ministry is portrayed in exaggerated, magnificent and overpowering expression with almost every aspect of mythological motifs. For a full discussion of Revelation, see my book on The Theology of Truth. The way it is expressed is so massive that many people find it difficult to cope with, probably like Bultmann. However, we have to take on board the element of exaggeration and also of symbolism. Bearing these two matters in mind, it is possible to see Revelation in not just a positive light, but as the grand finale to a wonderful symphony, the work of saving mankind from its own stupidities.

We can also consider the matter of dualism, which means God with a band of good angels and the Devil with a band of bad angels, or evil spirits. This was very much the assumption in the world Jesus was born into. He could hardly have thought any other way. If we look at the two versions of the Temptations, Luke (4:12) we see that the devil is mentioned, and although Jesus overcomes the temptations, the devil is waiting for another opportunity to trap him. If we compare this with Matthew (4:1-11), the devil is again stated as being present, but is partially demythologised, being called 'the tempter' at one point. At the end, it says that 'angels came and ministered to him,' thus bringing in another element of mythology. It is worth noting that there is no mention of the serpent, as in the Garden of Eden, but the temptations of Jesus are clearly intended to be the counterpart of Adam and Eve's big mistake. Elsewhere in the Gospels, Satan is mentioned chiefly as the instigator of Judas Iscariot's treachery. The most dramatic and frightening scene concerns the Gerasene Demoniac, in Mark 5:1-20. Clearly, evil spirits are understood to be a reality, and Jesus is seen as the supreme exorcist. This is mythology at its closest to medical fact. Most people may not be aware that exorcism is practised nowadays by specialist priests; the term used for it is 'deliverance ministry'. This again is an attempt at demythologisation. Very often they have to deal with people who have been foolish enough to dabble in spiritualism or the occult, and it has wrecked their minds. However one tries to explain this, it is a matter of fact that exorcism is a part of the Church's ministry and it has a certain degree of success. This kind of miracle that Jesus performed may be expressed in mythological terms, because that is how people would have understood it in those days. In our times we talk of schizophrenia and other mental disorders, but does this really explain what happens when someone is seriously mentally disordered? Is it enough just to tamp them down with drugs? That is a matter for discussion.

The whole question of dualism is worthy of serious thought. It is not enough just to say that the Devil and Satan are just superstitious matters best left out of our theological horizons. If Jesus thought like that, ought we not to give the matter a lot more consideration? The Christian tradition down to very recent times, has accepted this thinking. That does not have to mean we have to go into hysterics over evil spirits, as they did at Salem, Massachussetts.(7) The problem is, that if we try to pretend there is no evil, whether spirits or however one sees it, that is when evil can work its way into our lives. Dumbledore was right in what he said! It is interesting that as the Devil has become politically wrong (and we must not frighten ourselves with such things!), nevertheless the way in which Harry Potter has gained credibility, with Dementors and frightening monsters and Voldemort, just goes to show that this element is still there in the human psyche. Dualism is not just a silly theological theory; it is somehow instinctive in human nature, and cannot be underestimated. In a strange way, the modern expression of horror sci-fi, such as Dracula, Frankenstein's monster, King Kong and the Harry Potter sagas, are simply replacing what the churches and the philosophers are trying to ignore or rationalise. Mythology will not go away; indeed, why should it? If we can accept that God speaks to us in our own language, why can he not speak to us in our own thought forms, our own instincts and our own cultural assumptions?

Demythologising tendencies in BC period

If Bultmann and others think that demythologising is a feature of the modern world, then they are mistaken. We have already seen the tendency within the New Testament itself, but it goes much further back than that. If we look at the Analects of Confucius,(8) a treatment of which I have done in The Theology of Truth, we find that the great thinker has no interest in gods, devils or anything that might be termed 'mythology'. His religion is almost all a this-worldly system of thought. Where mythological ideas are worked in, it is entirely coincidental and does not impinge on his essential message, which is about 'benevolence'. The same can be said, in general terms about the Tao Teh Ching,(9) the Taoist scriptures. Even if the basics of Taoism concentrate on every day conduct, Lao Tzu does not set out a mythological scheme, nor does he assume it. There is nothing on the subject of the Jade Emperor and other elements of Chinese mythology. These are described also in The Theology of Truth. What Lao Tzu does do, is to talk about the Tao, and how this basic concept is worked out in a physico-philosophical system of thought. Clearly, this is an intriguing gnostical system. It has nothing to do with gods, devils, angels or anything that some would regard as mythical.

However, the most notable attempt at demythologising comes with the Buddhist system of thought.(10) Clearly Siddhartha had grown tired of the countless gods in Hinduism, plus all those strange spiritual creatures like asuras, raksasas and siddhas. These can be read about in that epic, the Ramayana, which I have reviewed in The Theology of Truth. Siddhartha's message is that Nirvana can be achieved by anyone who follows the correct discipline. Nirvana is not heaven; it can be seen as a demythologised heaven, a state of permanent peace and escape from the pain of this life. All those aspects of life, whether actual or mythological, are bundled up into the Wheel of Becoming, and we can circulate round this wheel from one incarnation to another, endlessly, unless we put our minds to escaping from it to Nirvana. How much of this concept stemmed from Siddhartha himself, or was a later development, is not clear. But that, in essence is what Buddhism is about. One finds that instead of the Eternal Creator, we have philosophical principles in the skies. One could actually be an atheist and still be a Buddhist. It is possible to see Buddhism as a demythologised version of Hinduism. Not that this works absolutely and completely. We have such things as Yama, the god who holds up the Wheel of Becoming, like a mirror, so that we see what we really are. There is a mythical king called Amida (11)who accrued so much merit that it is available for those who cannot manage to gain merit. There are also many strange mythical ideas in Tibetan Buddhism, which I have described in The Theology of Paradox. But as an attempt at demythologising, Buddhism stands out as quite successful, and continues to be so now.

This brings us to the time of Jesus. It is clear that certain ideas from Buddhism had worked their way into the thinking of Greek and Roman philosophers. This explains why Gnosticism appeared, a collection of ideas which I have touched on in this book, chapter 3. This development in philosophy used much of the vocabulary from Buddhism, though whether they meant it in quite the same way is debatable. Like Siddhartha, the Gnostics had grown tired of the hundreds of Greek gods with their crude and lewd behaviour. They turned the whole thing into philosophical ideas. So the sky was no longer populated by hooligans like Zeus and Athena; it was one basic principle, which equated to some sort of monotheism, and then all kinds of aeons or demiurges emanating from it. This was clearly another attempt at demythologising. The influence of it is seen on the New Testament in a few places, not least in St.John's gospel in which Jesus is termed 'the Logos' (the word of God). That, by the way, does not mean that John was a Gnostic, but he does not shrink from borrowing their vocabulary. The Gnostic influence did however pose a considerable threat to the later thinkers in the Patristic period. The early church was at pains to insist that Jesus was not just some kind of spiritual principle that had managed to find a way round the bad influences of the demiurges. The fathers were insistent that

Jesus was completely and genuinely human, but at the same time absolutely divine. The Christian theologians never allowed themselves to indulge in imaginary heavenly principles, that might have supplanted the angels. They did, however, manage to respect the New Testament in its mention of angels having an influence on the life of Jesus.

How does Humanism relate to these matters? To begin with, Humanism is not one consistent unified system of thought, any more than Gnosticism was. However, the strand in Humanism which claims that one can have ethics and an awareness of morality without having to involve religion, could also be seen as a form of demythologisation, or at least, an attempt at it. The theists would almost certainly assert that if one removes the rationale or theological basis for ethics and morality, how long will it be before it all fades out? Putting it in real terms, assuming that God gave us the Ten Commandments, and the Humanist says we can have the commandments without believing in God, how long will it be before people lose the motivation to keep the commandments?

Is it fair to subject the Judaeo-Christian system of thought to demythologing? The main thrust of both Testaments, is exactly this; Covenant. God making an agreement with certain persons, and thereby showing his love for his creation. In this we see God , not as some kind of distant, neutral, philosophical principle, but as personal. God has a personality which is characterised by love. It is a personal relationship with Abraham and with King David. The essence of the New Testament is that each and every one of us can have a personal relationship with the Almighty. This is a long way from some kind of abstruse philosophical theory. Covenant can be termed as a sort of metaphor but it is certainly not myth. In all the myths we have described in this book, there is nothing equivalent to the God of Abraham or of Moses. It is religion on a historical and a day-to-day basis, and also a futuristic basis. Admittedly mythical language is included in the description of these covenants, but that simply serves to augment and emphasise the importance of these encounters with God.

Mediaeval attempts at proving the existence of God

Christian philosophers have always worked under the influence of the Bible, but other influences from ancient Greece have worked their way in. So,

Platonic and Aristotelian ideas have given added flavouring to basic Christian tenets. One of the most notable aspects of this has been the way that scholars have tried to prove the existence of God. This is a trait seen in the Hermetic literature, stemming from ancient Egypt (see The Theology of Truth). The Bible itself never embarks on this line of argument. But people like Anselm and Aquinas did feel it necessary, but their arguments are not original; they can be traced back to the Greek philosophers. Needless to say, if any one of their reasonings had provided a proof in the sense that we mean it now, there would be no such thing as atheism. All their 'proofs' only work for those who are inclined to believe in God in the first place.

For a more detailed discussion of this theme, see my chapter (12) in The Theology of Paradox. To summarise briefly, there is the argument from design. The world and indeed the universe is so intricately fashioned that to talk of it being one coincidence after another is ludicrous. This is the teleological argument. Then there is the cosmological argument which means that there has to have been something to start everything off. A thing as vast, complicated and interrelated as the Creation can hardly just kick-start itself. Then there is the aesthetic argument which means that in this world there is beauty, but never do we see actual perfection which we strive for. We assume then that absolute perfection must exist somewhere; that perfection is God. The moral argument is on similar lines, but takes note of the fact that we all have some kind of moral sense, but fail to implement it fully. The perfect ethics are with God himself. Finally there is the ontological argument which is rather difficult. It includes the phrase 'God is that than which nothing greater can be thought.' If you can conceive of something, then it cannot be God. This one is hard to digest, and yet it keeps recurring in scientific circles when they talk about the Big Bang, and then what happened before that, and before that and ad infinitum. This situation has emerged in many mythologies so far.

What this means is that all those instincts in us that demand an explanation about how the world came about, how mankind arrived and where we are heading have been turned into philosophical reasonings as opposed to picture language and metaphors, or even scientific speculations. This does not mean these arguments are worthless; far from it, but unfortunately they involve rather a lot of circular argument, or begging the question. Personally, I feel that the argument from design carries a lot of conviction, especially as scientific investigation is now showing us how intricate, subtle, clever, purposeful and amazing the workings of nature are. I find it very strange when 'experts' tell us that creation is the result of a concatenation of coincidences or accidents. However one sees the 'proofs' for the existence of God, they do not seem to go away, and weigh on people's minds in spite of all the Atheism that is thrown at us. This is because these arguments are located in the same place as mythology; namely in the **id.**

Another matter that arose in the Middle Ages was the nature of the elements in the Eucharist. It was Aquinas who formulated the doctrine of transubstantiation. This was a development of Aristotle's idea that everything has its substance and accidents. The net result was, for Aquinas, that the bread and wine may appear to be still bread and wine, after the priest has consecrated them, but they actually become the body and blood of Jesus, in spite of their unaltered appearance. This doctrine is still with us in the Roman Church, but it is a good example how something symbolic can be remythologised, or given a greater spiritual power. It is instinctive in people of faith to understand the Eucharistic elements as spiritually potent after they have been blessed by a priest. All that Aquinas did was to give that instinct some kind of rationale. This became one of the issues at the Reformation, but Luther refused to allow the words 'this is my body' to be rephrased. His word for it was 'consubstantiation.' Although the Aristotelian rationale was left out, Protestants still regarded the bread and wine to be seen as something spiritually different. Demythologising it altogether was left to the extremist Protestant splinter groups. They could only see the Eucharist as symbolic and nothing more. Some, who were terrified over the sacrificial implications of the Eucharist, went the whole way and had no sacraments at all.

One chapter in this book is on the subject of Emmanuel Swedenborg, a Swedish Protestant who had visions of angels. Analysing this work is most instructive and of much relevance to mythology. It would seem to be a first class example of demythologisation. This does not mean that he explains away angels and devils, but he does show them in a rather different light. It would be interesting to discover how much of Swedenborg's ideas stimulated the so-called Age of Reason which pervaded the 17th century. One of the characteristics of this new approach was the attempt to discard all of the old mythological metaphors and motifs on the basis that it was a lot of superstitious nonsense. This had profound implications for the theories on the subject of the Atonement. See The Theology of Paradox for a discussion of these matters. The net result was to give the Moral Theory central ground and sideline anything that sounded bloodthirsty and lurid. As the Age of Reason ran its course, it resulted in some kind of demythologised religion which the French Revolution was based on. Temples to 'rationality' were erected. Much of the reasoning behind it was the notion that there had been a Golden Age when people were equal, sharing and peaceful. Strangely, it seemed not to occur to them that that idea was just as much a piece of mythology as any of the other traditional myths. In other words, the impression of The Golden Age is to be found in many mythological systems the world over. Even so, that idea continued to be the substratum behind the modern Socialist and Communist outburst, and is still a basic assumption with many people in spite of various bits of evidence to the contrary.

The need for Myth

We have seen how mythology has been an important aspect in the mentality of the human race from very early times. Many of the old myths are now seen to be obsolete and characteristic of a paganism that is largely, though not completely, superseded by Christianity and Islam. The idea that mythology has no place in the modern world, is, however, a lot of nonsense. In our own times, we have seen fresh outbursts of mythology, almost always somehow related to the original myths. Gnosticism, which was originally an attempt at sanitisation of Greek and Egyptian thought, keeps reappearing under different labels; Swedenborgianism, Christian Science, Scientology and many others. Evolution, which is emphatically not a new idea, holds a fascination for many people, but not everyone. It is the myth of the modern world. Then we have the magico-fanciful material which is simply a rehash of ancient superstitious ideas; Star Trek, Star Wars, The Water Babies, Harry Potter and countless others. It is one thing to laugh at such productions but we have to explain how and why such material catches people's attention and is taken seriously. This is because it appeals to something in the human instinct, the **id.** The question arises, can we ever get away from myth? Would it be wise to do so if it were possible?

My conclusion is that we have to have myth in some shape or form, otherwise we are not really human. One of the positive messages from Star Trek was that it sounds very clever to be completely logical, but is such a person a complete person? There has to be emotion in our lives; it cannot be excluded, at least, if one tries to exclude it, one damages oneself unnecessarily. To be a complete and well balanced person, one needs to have instinct, rationality and conscience in a delicate balance, otherwise one becomes maladjusted. In this, Freud was right, even if he was mistaken on other matters. I maintain that the myths, whether ancient or modern, are there for a purpose, and to try to eliminate them is a fool's errand.

The completion of Myth in the Christian Faith

In a mysterious way, the Bible has a habit of raising and answering its own questions. In the Old Testament we see myth being given to us. It starts with the Creation and the Garden of Eden. How literally one takes this is a matter of personal choice, but it is inescapable that mythical elements are used in the accounts; examples of which are the snake, the flaming sword and the world tree. The symbolism in these is essential, and connects with something deep in the human soul. Mythological expression does not stop there; it is worked in in so many ways all through the historical and prophetic areas of the Old Testament. It is a very important way of emphasising essential theological ideas. This goes on right into the apocrypha with the history of the Maccabees. At the same time, we can see the drive to produce something which is not quite philosophical as seen in ancient Greece, but is a few steps towards demythologisation. So, for instance, the Wisdom literature, particularly Job, tries to get to grips with the mechanics of Creation by personification of Wisdom. We notice, however, that figurative language is still used and in fact cannot be eliminated. This is still true for us today; we can only express the deep matters of God and humanity with the use of metaphors. One could say that there is some kind of stand-off in the Old Testament between the anthropomorphists and the transcendentalists; this could amount to a paradox. The Jahwistic source in the Pentateuch represents what might be termed the 'crude' way of describing God, but nowhere near as crude and lewd as the Greeks did. The Priestly source deals with God in a far more spiritual way. The Elohistic source is somewhere in between. All of these appeal to human nature in different ways, but essentially, it is to the instincts, for we all know deep down in ourselves that God is a reality, in spite of some of us being in denial of him.

With the four Gospels, we see mythology in a special relationship to the ministry of Jesus Christ. It is quite clear that the gospel writers are at pains to show that Jesus was a real historical person, and not some kind of fiction or flight of imagination. This comes out particularly in St.Luke, who goes to some lengths to relate the life of Jesus to real historical criteria, especially the Herods and the Caesars. But this element is not absent from the other gospels. Clearly they do not attempt to relate every detail of Christ's life, for as St.John admits, the world would not contain the books that could be written about him.(12) That does not prevent each gospel writer from presenting Jesus in a slightly different interpretation; each writer has his own slant. But the way in which they agree far outweighs the slight differences of opinion that occur.

Nowadays we take St.Mark as the first gospel to be written, and he is very down to earth. The mythology in his gospel is done in a special way. The Baptism, the Transfiguration and the Passion; these three great events tie the whole gospel together in a sort of arching method. At the Baptism in chapter one, the heavens open and the Spirit descends on Jesus like a dove.(13) Jesus is identified as the Son of God. Bultmann would, we expect, baulk at such a mythological scene, but what is the symbolism in it? The dove is the bird that Noah sent out and it returned with a sprig of olive.(14) The implication in this is that the cleansing of the world is completed and the olive branch implies peace and reconciliation. The dove clearly came to symbolise the Holy Spirit. The whole episode is clearly telling us that the Eternal God is fully supportive, in agreement with, and in a paternal relationship with Jesus. How literally one takes this episode is a matter for personal faith, but the mythological symbolism in it is of great value to all believers. I personally cannot see why this episode cannot be taken at face value, but there will be others who cannot cope with that.

The next significant incident, the Transfiguration in chapter 9, is another confirmation of Jesus being the Son of the Almighty God. The mythical elements in it are stronger this time. The three disciples are given a glimpse of Jesus' heavenly glory. 'His garments became glistening, intensely white, as no fuller on earth could bleach them.' Again, the symbolism in this is important. White is the colour indicative of purity, or innocence, which is a common feature in mythology. Moses and Elijah are seen with Jesus. These are the two notable ones who were 'assumed' into heaven, in other words, they did not have an earthly grave. They are seen in harmony with Jesus, which indicates what we know from elsewhere (St.Matthew) that Jesus had come to fulfil the Law (of Moses) and the prophets (as typified by Elijah). In a way, it is saying that Jesus did not come to introduce a new religion; he came to fulfil, simplify and bring to completion the faith of Israel. When Peter, somewhat confused, blurts out, 'shall we make three booths?' he is probably thinking of the Feast of the Tabernacles, but clearly he had no idea of what to say, or at least anything logical. Again, I cannot see why this episode cannot be taken as non-mythological. If we compare this with the remarks about the angels and heaven from Swedenborg, this account makes perfect sense. That does not prevent it having much mythological symbolism worked in.

The Crucifixion scene in Mark can be noted for its realisms; mythological elements are minimal but present. On the way to Golgotha Jesus is offered wine mixed with myrrh. This was the normal procedure at a crucifixion. The potion would have dulled the pain, since myrrh is a strong drug not unlike opium, a painkiller. Jesus refuses it; he does not want to take the easy way out. The division of his clothing was the normal way for the crucifixion party. The various times in the day are given, which adds to the realism of the scene. They may also be intended as symbolic. The third hour would be nine o'clock, the sixth hour, midday and the ninth hour 3 pm. So Jesus was on the cross for six hours; does this mirror the six days of creation, and also the fact that Friday was the sixth day of the week? The seventh day, the Sabbath was coming at 6 pm that afternoon. Then we have the mockery and the taunts to induce him to come down from the cross. For some, this might have been a genuine request; some might have wanted Jesus to prove himself as the Messiah, the King of Israel.

It is strange how the darkness from midday to three in the afternoon seems to have no effect on the bystanders. One could say this was an eclipse of the sun, but then, a very prolonged one. Is it meant to be symbolic, in that evil was having its last throw at destroying Jesus' ministry? Or is it saying that the act of creation is coming to completion as Jesus dies on the cross; he is in effect creating a new relationship between God and humanity? This is confirmed when Jesus dies and the veil of the Temple is rent in two; this implies that we can all now see into God's presence and have that personal relationship with him, as such people like Moses and Elijah did. Enigmatically, Elijah is involved in this scene. Some of the bystanders misunderstand what Jesus says, 'Eloi, eloi...' and think he is appealing to Elijah for rescue. It is rather strange that they put vinegar on a sponge and push it up against his mouth. It seems to be an abbreviated version of what we see in John 18:28 in which Jesus says that he is thirsty. This may be an allusion to Psalm 69:21; 'and for my thirst they gave me vinegar to drink.' That must have been a sadistic move, as the vinegar would have made him desperately thirsty. But it implies that since Elijah was known to have been assumed into heaven and was with God in a special way, he would be able to come to the rescue. There was a tradition at that time that 'The prophet', someone of the stature of Elijah or Moses, would appear to solve all their problems. We see this alluded to in John 1:21, where it says, 'are you the prophet?' The basis for this came in Malachi 4:5 where it says 'Behold, I will send you Elijah the prophet...' The final 'arching' remark comes from the centurion who, on seeing that Jesus has died, says, 'Truly this man was the Son of God', or 'a son of God'. With this, the structure of this gospel is complete.

We notice that essentially the crucifixion is based on realities. However, there are mythological and symbolic elements worked into it. This is important as St.Mark is at pains to emphasise the significance of the scene. It was not a normal routine crucifixion scene, of which there were so many at that time. This one was earth-shattering and bringing all of God's works to a massive conclusion; God giving of his very self to bring about a new world.

If we compare Mark's account with Matthew's we see substantially the same arching method, which ties the whole gospel together. Matthew begins in chapter 1 by saying that Jesus is the son of David, the son of Abraham. This is significant as providing a balance between Jesus as the Son of God, which emphasises his divinity, but relating him to important figures in Israelite history places him firmly in the human orbit. Matthew's version of the Transfiguration is virtually the same as Mark's except that he adds the fear element. The disciples were terrified at what they saw, but Jesus touches them and tells them not to be afraid. The fact that he touches them shows that he is not some sort of apparition but solid human flesh. In this we see the counterbalance between that mythological experience and the down-to-earth contact with Jesus. Matthew quite faithfully follows Mark's version of the crucifixion, but adds a remark claiming that Jesus had said he was the Son of God (27:43) and that he trusted in God. This is counterbalanced by Jesus crying out in despair, 'Why have you forsaken me', which is a very human feeling; something that we all sense at some time in our lives. We notice that in both accounts, the Jews are 'wagging their heads'.(15) This may seem strange to us in today's world; unfortunately it does not specify whether they were wagging their heads sideways or forwards and backwards. In several contexts in the Old Testament, wagging one's head was a sign of derision or insult. But there is another possibility here; we can see Jewish people wagging their heads (forwards and backwards) at the Western Wall to this day; it is their approach to worship. This implies that they were worshipping Jesus as the Son of God, but with an element of hypocritical mockery. The irony in that is that Jesus really was the Son of God. In general terms, Matthew quite faithfully retains Mark's framework concerning the identity of Jesus, but with a few small embellishments. One of them is the augmentation after the veil of the Temple is rent; there was an earthquake, and the rocks were split and the tombs were opened. Once more there is the allusion to the life of Elijah at Mount Horeb, as the rocks were split. But this additive tells us in effect that the death of Jesus was an earth-shattering event; also it shows that the salvation brought about by it applied to those who had gone before as well as everyone else. Again this mythological additive serves to emphasise the importance of Jesus' death.

How does Luke address the matter? He retains the same basic arching method from the Baptism to the Transfiguration to the Crucifixion. But there are significant differences. Straight after the Baptism, Luke places his version of Jesus' genealogy, going back not just to Abraham but back to Adam. This in effect points out that he was clearly a member of the human race and not just Jewish. This must be balanced with the claim at the Baptism that Jesus was God's beloved Son. The Transfiguration is also faithfully related, though perhaps slightly less spectacularly. The chief difference is that Moses and Elijah outlined the end of Jesus' ministry in Jerusalem; this is a clever way of linking the Transfiguration with the Crucifixion. The Crucifixion too is related faithfully with a few additions. There is the penitent thief who is promised to arrive in Paradise. There is a strong emphasis on forgiveness, as indeed there is much emphasis laid on the innocence of Jesus, and for the Roman centurion to exclaim that this man was innocent, simply tells us of how faulted the Roman legal system was. There is no mention of the Jews wagging their heads; Luke might have felt that his (assumedly) Gentile readership would not have understood that approach to worship. The application of vinegar is done in such a way as to avoid any mention of Elijah coming to the rescue; again, Luke's Gentile readers might not have understood that element. We only have mention of the sixth and the ninth hour, thus losing the symbolism of six hours on the cross. Also he does not mention Jesus as being the Son of God; we have 'the Christ of God, his Chosen One' instead. In general terms, Luke's version is slightly less mythological and symbolic than the others.

With St.John we have a very different approach; the arching method is not present. The Transfiguration in the centre of Jesus' ministry, is never mentioned. However, the identity of Jesus receives much attention, as seen in the prologue, where Jesus is identified with the LOGOS. This is where Gnostical mythological language almost becomes literal language. Jesus is the Word of God, but also 'the only Son' (1:18). This means that John does not disagree with the other gospel writers; he just enlists more metaphors from a partially demythologised source, namely the Gnostics. John introduces the metaphor of 'light' and 'glory' here, reminding us of the Transfiguration, but not actually recounting the incident. At the Baptism, John the Baptist gives us the metaphor of Jesus being 'the Lamb of God' and this receives more emphasis than the title 'Son of God'. At the Crucifixion, there is a very heavy emphasis on the Kingship of Jesus, but not as being an earthly, political kingship but an eternal one. The fact that the title board on the cross was in three languages (the other gospel writers do not mention this) is highly appropriate; it shows that Jesus is not just the King of the Jews, but the king of the Gentiles as well. Also the allusions to him being the Passover Lamb, the ultimate sacrifice is interwoven. The Sonship of Jesus is not mentioned at this point.

John does not mention the times of the day or the three hours of darkness, but his awareness of the fact that this is Friday is given a different thrust of emphasis. It is the day of Preparation, with the Passover landing on a Sabbath day, which means that crucifixion victims should be removed to avoid offence. This is John's way of showing that Creation comes to a conclusion as Jesus is entombed just before twilight on the Friday evening. Mythology is down to a minimum with John, and symbolism is present but stated to be a reality at the same time. A very significant remark, 'Jesus, knowing that all was now finished...' (John 19:28) tells us that the work of creation and salvation has come to a conclusion and completion, as he dies.

It is important to remember that at that time when Jesus was conducting his ministry, there was the backdrop of the pagan world with its ideas about gods and their offspring. We can refer back to the chapter on Greek mythology, where the idea of gods producing sons and daughters was not at all an outlandish idea, in fact it was just a commonplace. No one minded too much if an upstart decided to claim to be a god or produced by a god. Now we can understand why, in the gospels, the writers deal with the sonship of Jesus in a very careful manner. It is not overdone. The title 'Son of Man' is much more widely used. They were trying to avoid people gaining the wrong impression about the nature of Jesus. They did not want people to gain the idea that Jesus was just another elaborate idea stemming from Greek mythology. In fact, he was not a part of mythology; he was a part of historical, physical reality. It would have been so easy to picture Jesus as some sort of divinity begotten in the skies but by the same physical procedures as humans are; husband and wife and human reproduction. Calling Jesus a 'Son' has to be a metaphor, just as much as 'Lamb', 'glory', 'light' and many other metaphors which are found in the New Testament. It has to be done in metaphoric language; it is not possible to describe God in any other way. Many of these metaphors are derived from mythical ideas; but that does not mean that the One True God is a myth, still less Jesus Christ. This is where the tension between mythology and historical reality comes to breaking point; over this crucial factor of the identity of Jesus of Nazareth.

This is where the importance of symbolism comes in to help. It is easy to see how the concept the 'Lamb' is symbolic. Jesus is weak, vulnerable and the ultimate sacrificial victim. 'Glory' and 'light' are reasonably straightforward. In Genesis 1:3 light is provided by God, not the sun and moon, which appear in verse 14ff, but the light of God. St.John is equating Jesus with that light. The 'Glory' is the glorious overwhelming light which Moses encountered on the mountain, which explains why mortal man cannot stare straight at God. What does the metaphor of sonship convey?

In an ideal world, the relationship between father and son is pictured as something really special. A son was expected to continue his father's profession and perpetuate the family name. In the modern world, this does not always work out quite so neatly, which means that this metaphor is not quite as apt for us now as it used to be. Essentially, what the ancients were trying to say when they talked of gods producing next generation gods, was that their work of creation would continue into the future. Also their standard of craftsmanship would be maintained. But the filial relationship, not just physical but spiritual was and still is essential. The old saying 'blood is thicker than water' sums it up. There is some kind of unbreakable bond between father and son. When Jesus said 'I and the Father are one,' this sums up all of the implications in these remarks.

With this we can see how the relationship between mythology and reality is a close one and also not easy to distinguish. Clearly the concept of 'Son of God' is a borrowed one, but that is not saying very much. Many of the attempts at describing God in the Old Testament use borrowed metaphors or motifs. One might safely ask, whether it could have been done in any other way. However, what we can see in all this, is that Jesus brings all these mythological concepts to a fulfilment that no one could ever have imagined. He fulfilled not just the faith of the Israelite traditions but also of the pagans too. It was not just a matter of fulfilling their beliefs but also of correcting them, especially on the subject of violence and forceful domination in the skies. He came to show us that God is essentially loving and giving. That is the relevance of the metaphor of the Lamb. This is where the Suffering Servant as described in Isaiah is of such importance. It shows us a God who is prepared to give his very self to bring about the salvation of a broken world. This is what Jesus came to bring into reality as a correction to all the wrong ideas going on in world mythologies. This explains why the Romans reacted with such hostility to nascent Christianity; it went against everything in their value system about force, empire-building, cruelty, greed, power; it still stands as a warning against any ruler or nation that embarks on this kind of policy. 'Your rationale for your empire, your mythology is leading you astray; learn from the humble Messiah of God.'

It is with the resurrection that the issue of literal fact and mythology comes closest to breaking point. Bultmann thinks that modern man cannot take on board the Resurrection. That would be true, but then it has always been true right from the start. It has always been the biggest challenge to faith, but also the essential ingredient in the Christian Faith. One would expect something as crucial as that to attract mythological expression, and indeed it does. Again, if we compare the four accounts, we see something interesting happening.

This time we begin with St.John's account, chapter 20. This is because it is almost certainly an eye-witness account by John himself; it has so many realisms in it. This can lead one to believe that John's gospel is closer to the real Jesus than the others, but that is a matter of contention. The story from verses one to nine is very basic and betrays the dismay and panic as the disciples realise that the body of Jesus has disappeared, and his previous promise of rising again has clearly not penetrated their heads. Then comes the only part that could be termed 'mythological', as Mary Magdalene sees two angels in white. One wonders why Peter and (presumably) John did not see the angels. This makes perfect sense, since some people are spiritually sensitive while others are not. One immediately thinks of Moses and Elijah who appeared at the Transfiguration and at the Ascension. Then Mary sees Jesus but does not recognise him at first, until he speaks. He tells her not to touch him; the Greek of this actually means 'do not cling on to me',(16) which implies that he was solid and not some kind of apparition, and she was trying to hold on to him. This account keeps the mythological element to a minimum, and is very down to earth and literal, but also deeply sentimental, if indeed Jesus had a special affection for Mary. If one accepts that there are such things as angels, there is no mythology in it at all.

St.Mark's account is much shorter and again, unspectacular. This time there is one young man dressed in white, seen by not just Mary but three ladies. Jesus is not seen, but they are told he has gone back to Galilee. The whole account is characterised by amazement and fear. The postscript to Mark's gospel, verses 9 to 19, is clearly an addition by another writer, but adds little to the basic account. It looks as though the postscript simply summarises parts from the other gospels. This account is probably the least mythological of the them all; even the young man is not dubbed as an angel.

St.Luke adds little to our knowledge of the Resurrection. The mythological element is the two men in dazzling apparel. They are not dubbed as angels, and we assume that they might be Moses and Elijah again (though this is not stated). The account is characterised by the unbelief of the disciples, as the ladies tell them what has happened. Again, the mythological element is kept to a minimum and the account is unspectacular.

St.Matthew has by far the most spectacular resurrection. There is a great earthquake, an angel of the Lord rolled the stone back and sat on it. Then he tells the ladies not to be afraid, but go and tell the other disciples about Jesus going back to Galilee. The account is cleverly given more tension and perhaps a little humour, as a seal and a guard had been placed on the tomb to prevent the body being snatched away. But this was all to no avail, and the guards had to be bribed to keep their mouths shut. What it implies is that the authorities knew it was the truth but could not admit to it. Matthew has the most mythological account and yet this is balanced by the skulduggery and machinations of the authorities. The mythological element is not overdone, but it does serve to emphasise the earth-shattering importance of the resurrection.

We can see the element of augmentation running through these accounts, a feature that we see with many myths. It begins with some kind of historical reality or legend and is built up, exaggerated and augmented; the purpose of it is to underline its importance and glorify the event. This is all assuming that Matthew was the last account to be written, but that is a fair assessment, since his gospel is more inclined to mythological expression than the others.

There are hardly any of the normal features of mythology in the resurrection accounts. The motif of resurrection itself is the basic reality, as seen in virtually every world mythology. But what is happening here, is that Jesus is bringing all those hopes about resurrection into real terms. It is not just the faith of the Christians; it is the faith of everyone, that death is not the end and that life is eternal, and not just a matter of survival, but something wonderful and glorious.

In Conclusion about Demythologising

It would be fair to say that certain aspects of ancient mythology have to be reconsidered in the light of modern scientific and geographical knowledge. The ancient idea of the universe as three shelves has got to be modified, even if it cannot be eradicated from our thinking. But the dividing line between mythology and historical reality is a very thin one. As we have seen with several mythological systems, creation myth slides gently into historical facts without a jolt. The same kind of thing is seen in the four resurrection accounts; mythological factors are worked into the story quite seamlessly, and it is remarkable how restrained the writers are when depicting the greatest triumph the world has ever seen. It is quite likely that the ancients never even tried to separate the two; this must be a particularly 'nit-picking' feature of the modern mentality. It is clear that myth is an essential element in human instinct and it would be unwise as well as impossible to attempt to remove it. If perchance we ever did eliminate myth we would be left with a faith which was not a faith at all, but a list of banal ethical statements.(17) There would be no challenge to belief and no mystery left in the relationship between God and humanity. Myth is an inevitable response in us all when we view the wonders of creation and find ourselves asking, 'what is it all for; how did it begin; where do we fit in, in relation to the rest of it?' This leads us on to the inevitable nagging question, 'what is it all leading to; what will be our latter end?' Eschatology is an unavoidable factor springing out of mythology, and faith is the vital ingredient in making it all credible.

Footnotes for chapter 24

1. It appears that some of the Greek philosophers suspected that the world was round as opposed to flat. The Mithraians depicted the world as a sphere.

2. Zoroasterian ideas appear to have infiltrated the thinking of later Old Testament writers and apocryphal ones.

3. Yggdrassil is the Norse version of the World Tree; see chapter 8.

4. Matthew 17:27. It is not stated that the shekel was of gold, but it might be a fair assumption.

5. See Molnar, The Star of Bethlehem.

6. The Legend of Linda Martel, by Charles Graves, describes an infant who did faith healing.

7. See The Crucible, by Arthur Miller, discussed in chapter 23.

8. The Analects of Confucius, discussed in chapter 7, The Theology of Truth.

9. The Tao Teh Ching, the scriptures of the Taoists, chapter 10, The Theology of Truth.

10. Buddhist philosophy is described in The Theology of Paradox, chapter 11.

11. Amida or Amidabha is the Buddhist mythical king who gained merit; Asoka is the Hindu king who did the same thing.

12. John 21:25.

13. Mark 1:10.

14. Genesis 8:9ff.

15. 'wagging their heads' . In Psalm 22:7 and other places, it is clearly meant to be insulting. But the Hebrew verb NUAH literally means 'to wobble, shake, totter', and the intensive form used here indicates violently wagging one's head, but it does not specify whether it is sideways or forwards and backwards. The Greek verb used to translate this is Kineo, but this does not specify either.

16. The traditional rendering 'do not touch me' is misleading; 'do not keep clinging on to me' is much nearer the meaning of the Greek in John 20:17 'me mou haptou', 'don't keeping hanging on to me.' This implies that Jesus was not a ghost but solid flesh.

17. This could describe the Baha'i system of thought, which does not rely on miracles or anything mysterious. Strangely though, the two founders are described in terms of great glory. See chapter 16, in The Theology of Truth.

25

Swedenborg; Heaven and Hell

Emanuel Swedenborg, who was born in 1688 and died in 1722, was a Swedish scientist and gained the post of inspector of mines in Sweden. As a man of science, it is interesting to find that he experienced visions of angels and had conversations with people in the world of the spirit. He was a prolific writer and this assessment is based on his book, Heaven and Hell. It was written in Latin but has been ably translated into English by George Dole in 2002. To read his book, it sounds very modern with vocabulary and phrasing which seems to be derived from psychology and sociology. One wonders what the Latin of these would have been! Occasionally, the scientific mind breaks into the description.

What do we make of his claims to have had contact with the other world? Clearly, those who deny the reality of another world which we move on to at death, will find this book very strange. They may reject it altogether; indeed Swedenborg discusses such people in various places. For those who have some awareness of the next world, much of this will make sense. Swedenborg assures us that there is heaven and hell. For some people nowadays, this may find a certain degree of acceptance, but of course, hell is regarded as 'politically wrong', even if the tabloid press sometimes demand that certain persons ought to be consigned to it. A lot depends on how much credence one allows for Swedenborg, and additionally, how literally we need to take all this. Was he just inventing all that about angels and visions, or was it the truth?

It is important to notice that he does not appear to try to induce these 'visions'. He talks about his 'out of the body' experiences. This kind of experience has recently come to the fore and is not to be discounted as nonsense. On page 255ff the process is described in some detail but still leaves us with many unanswered questions. It begins with his physical senses becoming inoperative, almost like dying. However his deeper life and thoughts remain intact. His physical breathing almost stops but his heartbeat becomes synchronised with the heavenly kingdom. He is completely conscious and stays like that for several hours, and can converse with angels and spirits of the 'dead'. We notice that there are no drugs involved, nor any spiritualistic sceance. It is a gift from the other world.

It is interesting to note that a lot of what he says ties in with things that Jesus said, and in some ways casts a slightly different light on his teachings. It would be wrong to say that he actually contradicts Jesus. What he does do is expand on the Gospel teachings.

If we compare Swedenborg's material with that of Joseph Smith, someone else who claimed to be inspired by angelic visitations, the difference is quite noticeable. Smith was clearly setting out to produce an additional 'bible' so that Mormonism could develop in America. But there are so many anachronisms in it that the work is, in my opinion, clearly a forgery. For a detailed explanation of this, see my chapter on this in The Theology of Truth.(1) However, Swedenborg's work is vastly different in intention and quality. There is no historical material that would admit anachronisms. There are no claims concerning brass plates inscribed with a strange language. There is no attempt at producing an alternative Bible; very much the contrary, his material complements the Bible. There is sensitivity and positive spiritual insight, even if it is somewhat repetitious. My personal impression is that Swedenborg's work is not fraudulent, but genuine. If one is inclined to discount his works, I would suggest that one should read his works first before arriving at a judgement.

If we are to take Swedenborg's assertions about angels, heaven and hell, as being real, as opposed to pure imagination, this must cast a wholly different light on the matter of mythology. So far, our understanding of mythology has been in terms of a three-tiered universe as in the ancient world, but modified under the influence of recent space explorations. But the mental framework of heaven, earth and hell is still there in people's minds in spite of recent developments. Indeed, Swedenborg himself must have known about the earth being spherical as opposed to three flat platforms. What it means is that mythology is the truth, but on a different level of truth to that of geography and astrophysics.(2) At the very least we can say that mythology is the truth

410

about the instinctive responses in the human soul, what the psychologists would call the **id.**

That would leave us with the question of why there are so many different mythologies in different parts of the world. It would be fair to say that many of the details, metaphors and motifs often differ, but the main outlines or framework are largely the same regardless of race or religion.

Swedenborg is quite insistent on his experiences with the angels. To quote him;

'As for angels being human in form, this I have seen thousands of times. I have talked with them face to face, sometimes with just one, sometimes with several in a group, and as far as their form is concerned, I have seen in them nothing different from that of a human being... and to prevent it being said that this was some illusion or hallucination, I have been allowed to see them while I was fully awake, or when I was in full possession of my physical senses and in a state of clear perception' . Page 39; 74.

'On grounds of all my experience, which has lasted several years now, I can say with full confidence that in their form, angels are completely human. They have faces, eyes, ears, chests, arms, legs, and feet. They see each other, hear each other, and talk to each other. In short they lack nothing that belongs to humans except that they are not clothed with a material body. I have seen them in their own light which is far, far greater than noonday on our earth...' Page 40;75.

He also claims to have been allowed to talk to people who lived more then seventeen centuries ago, people who are known from the literature of their times. One such he thought was Cicero, who was aware of the Supreme Deity. Also he knew about Jesus Christ as coming into this world. He admitted that there was no other way in which the human race could have been saved. Swedenborg mentions others that he conversed with, but is somewhat vague about their identities and their remarks.

One of the difficulties with these claims, is that Swedenborg does not mention anyone else sharing these visions at the same time. We have only his word for it that this sort of thing actually occurred. However, the way in which it is related and described seems to ring true, at least, to me personally. Others will doubtless find it difficult to accept. Others will ask the question, 'Why can't I have such angelic visitations? Is Swedenborg anyone special?' Firstly, he does not claim to be anyone special. Secondly, the way it is described it is possible that many more people have had this kind of experience but did not realise what was happening. If it is true that some angels look just like a normal human person, one might not realise that anyone talking to them was actually an angel as opposed to someone earthbound.

At all events, this kind of experience can help us to understand some of the parts of the Bible that some people find 'difficult'. Daniel, Ezekiel, Revelation, and above all the pseudepigraphal book of Enoch which specifically describes heaven and hell. Revelation and Enoch have been reviewed in my book The Theology of Truth, and Daniel is treated in chapter 3 in this book.

Heaven

Heaven is not just one location, although its location is not described. It works on an eternal dimension which has nothing to do with geography, or history or even time itself. There are three levels in heaven. There is the central or third heaven, in which the angels are completely naked, which indicates their innocence, and this reminds us of the Garden of Eden. There is an intermediate or a second heaven and a third or outer heaven. The angels in each heaven are graded according to their level of perfection. This threefold arrangement corresponds to the shape of the human body; the head, the torso and the feet. In a way, heaven is not something outside of us; it is within us. It is not a matter of searching for it; it is a matter of realising it is within us. Page 20.

In heaven there are communities, and houses which are like those on earth but much more beautiful, their heavenly dwellings.(3) There are palaces of pure gold with jewels and rainbows. There are beautiful gardens, flowers, lawns and trees. The angels wear clothes, except the ones in stage three. As people come to heaven, they are graded according to their level of love, wisdom and conduct, and placed in their appropriate heaven. Little children that have died are all accepted, no matter what the attitude of their parents had been, but there are angels appointed to care for them and educate them. There is language rather like Hebrew, and writing and worship, and in fact most of the features of everyday life. One is inclined to think that heaven is a mirror image of this world, except that one could rather say it is the other way round.

At one's departure from this world, one arrives in a kind of antechamber, an intermediate stage. It is called the world of the spirits, in which the Lord sorts people out. Now we see the relevance of calling Jesus the Eternal Judge. It is so like this world that many of the arrivals do not even realise that they are 'dead'. They express amazement when someone tells them that their funeral is actually taking place. They have brought with them every aspect of their earthly life, memory, emotions, attitude to life, except that they have left their earthly body behind. They can talk to each other, friends, relatives, as if in the physical world. Then comes the sorting procedure. This can take a few hours, or days or even months. For those who have led an exemplary life of love and adherence to God's truth, they are taken straight off to heaven; the opposite happens to those who have opposed God and are determined to be evil. For those who are some kind of mixture of good and bad, there are three states or stages. There are doorways into hell, which the blessed cannot see, and vice versa, there are doorways into heaven which the evil ones cannot see.

The first stage, which can last several days or even months, is where one can carry on as 'normal', chatting to friends and family in a life that can hardly be distinguished from earthly life. What is happening is that the good and evil spirits are being discerned. All forms of pretence are being unmasked; hypocrisy is being stripped away in a process of purification. All the public face or 'respectability' of earthly life falls away and we are seen for what we really are. Is it deep down love for others or is it love for oneself? One might be shown some of the communities to see where one might fit in; that would be with people of the same spiritual inclination.

The second stage, where outer interests become dormant, concentrates on the inward, deeper concerns. All the secrets of the heart are brought out and one has to face up to one's bad deeds. Evil is punished. Swedenborg does not go into details about what punishments are administered, but it is for the positive motive of removing the evil from one's inner soul. The good ones do not need to have punishment.

The third stage is instruction for heaven. The good ones are taken by the Lord himself to various teaching sites. It can be a shattering experience to have one's wrong ideas smashed. Each one has his own angelic teacher. This is where the non-Christians are put right. The Muslims come to recognise Christ as the essential prophet, and the pagans who led a good life are guided aright. It is essentially knowledge leading to a useful life in heaven that is taught. When they are ready, they are dressed in white and led up one of eight paths upwards into heaven by guardian angels. The Lord himself introduces each one to his community.

One's wealth is not the essential criterion for entering heaven. The rich and the poor are found in there, and there is nothing intrinsically wrong with being rich. The important thing is one's attitude to wealth or poverty. Envy or coveting is a minus, but a wealthy person who is eager to show love with his wealth is a plus. Wealth can seduce one away from heaven and so too can poverty. When wealth becomes an end in itself or is used purely for one's own self-importance, that becomes a problem.

However, no one gets older. The old people that do arrive, steadily get younger as time goes on. The children get older but everyone seems to stabilise at their youth and stay like that eternally. There is no government except to say that everyone observes mutual love and caring. The angels do go in for marriage, for there are male and female angels, but when they marry, it is two minds merging into one. The mere thought of adultery is upsetting for them and polygamy is non-existent. If one were to think that the angels have no interest in the things of this world, one would be wrong. They are active in this world and guide and inspire people, and also defeat evil people.

It would be a mistake to think that non-Christians would be excluded from heaven. The Lord is eager to save everyone, even if they have tried to ignore him in earthly life. The non-Christians will find the truth in the next life. The angels will give them instruction in the truth. The essential quality in one is whether one has love regardless of which religion one comes from, and we know that there are many religions that do foster love, as well as Christianity. A telling remark is 'we are all saved by knowing heaven within ourselves,' and also 'heaven is within us, and people who have heaven within them come into heaven.' Page 175.

It is interesting that some of these ideas tie in with other religions. The Taoist doctrine says that there are up to 18 heavens and also 18 hells. The Egyptian mythology was firmly convinced that the next world was just another version of this world, which explains why their tombs were furnished with all kinds of grave goods, including food.(4) See my chapter on The Egyptian Book of the Dead, in The Theology of Truth, chapter 26. In Chinese mythology, the royal palace in Peking is a mirror image of the Jade Emperor's palace in heaven. Also, Jesus tells us that 'in my Father's house there are many mansions', which means dwelling places or compartments. Swedenborg takes this a little further by saying 'communities'. However, he never mentions the need for people in heaven to eat and drink.

The whole thing is characterised by heavenly peace, love and wisdom. The eternal God is their Sun; this is not the created sun which lights up our solar system. It is the uncreated light that inspires all those who belong to heaven.(5) In a way this is the corrective to Egyptian mythology. So there is a sense in which heaven is in people's hearts in this world, as well as something waiting for those who qualify for it after 'death'. There is a strong sense in which one consigns oneself for heaven or hell. God does not damn people out of hand. It is all a matter of one's own attitude; is one completely self-orientated or is one lovingly orientated to caring for others. Many who arrive in heaven become angels and are given some kind of task. Sometimes it is in heaven itself but otherwise it might be some kind of influence in the physical world. With this we see the concept of the 'guardian angel' which Jesus mentioned and also St.John in the Revelation.(6)

Other worlds

Swedenborg has a strong awareness of there being other worlds populated by people like us. Obviously at that time, there was no idea of 'exo-planaets' as we now believe to exist. But he does believe that just as there are millions of stars, so too there must be millions of planets with their own populations just like us. These people too are aware of God and Christ and accepted into heaven. Disappointingly for Swedenborg and the modern astrophysicists, no such populations have yet been found in our solar system and as yet there has been no firm evidence of any further out in space. This might, in time, put a question mark against his ideas, at least if one takes his writings completely literally. This might be a case of him talking figuratively in some way. Should such populations ever be found, heaven is so vast that it can accommodate all of us, as long as we have the right attitude in our souls. The way it is treated sounds all very modern.

Hell

It is important to realise that God is in control of all areas of life, and that includes not just heaven but hell as well. The two entities are in balance with each other; the false versus the true; evil versus good. The Lord himself keeps the equilibrium. If the balance is lost, then so is our freedom. Nothing exists without a relationship to its opposite. This sounds like the scientist that Swedenborg was. If he were here today, he would probably relate it to plus and minus, positive and negative in electricity. Plus (heaven) has the power but minus (hell) does not. Even so, the one cannot function without the other.

There are the same number of communities in hell as there are in heaven. There are three levels of hell just as in heaven, and people are sorted, or rather they sort themselves, according to how evil they are. People wear rags, their houses are hovels and stink, there are 'control freaks' and domineering people and this results in violence. Some are megalomaniacs. Some of them try to break up marriages. Sometimes the angels are sent into hell to calm things down. The evil spirits have to be governed by fear, and have limits put on them. Often the evil spirits inflict punishments on each other. It is all characterised by falsehood and evil, which basically comes from love of oneself. They are recognisable as nasty by their ugly and lifeless faces(7) which means there is no room for a facade of respectability, as there was in earthly life. Hell is mostly caverns in the ground, gloomy, with glowing coals and sulphur. There is a monstrous creature on guard; is this his version of Cerberus?

We have read about hellfire in the Bible and elsewhere. This is where Swedenborg admits to a little on the question of how literally we take all this. He says that it is not literally fiery; it is meant in the sense that that love for the world and oneself becomes a great pain for oneself. It all depends on how one receives heaven's warmth which comes directly from God. For the devils it is a kind of torture. We notice that Swedenborg does not mention the idea that fire is metaphoric for cleansing. The gnashing of teeth,(8) which Jesus mentions, is not to be taken literally. It means the constant clash and strife of false ideas and convictions which are claimed to be true. This goes further when he says that the Devil himself is not to be taken literally. He disagrees with Enoch about there being a fallen angel. Everyone in hell is some kind of devil; all those who in their earthly life have practised evil, have now cast themselves in hell. This is in spite of the angels trying to guide us and encourage us to head towards heaven. There are those who are 'hell-bent' and refuse to face up to God. 'The Devil' is symbolic of the lowest level of hell, and 'Satan' is symbolic of the upper levels. 'Lucifer' stands for Babylon or Babel.

One thought missing from all this is the question of whether one has to remain in hell permanently. We notice that in many mythologies, there is the possibility of being redeemed from hell. In the New Testament, more than once, it appears that being consigned to hell is not for eternity. But Swedenborg does not venture to give us an answer to this. Another significant omission is the matter of repentance, whether in this world or the next. I cannot find one reference to this, but it is an essential element in the New Testament and the teachings of Jesus. One can come to one's senses, renounce the mistakes one has made and ask for mercy from God. But Swedenborg seems to think there is a point where God's mercy comes to an end, assumedly at the moment of death. Admittedly, he claims that the evil in us will be stripped away in the world of the spirit, in preparation for heaven, but he does not explain why really wicked people cannot be cleansed and saved, since Jesus is always eager to rescue anyone from going to hell.

Another interesting element in Swedenborg's thinking is the dilemma between good works and faith, as being essential for salvation.(9) He seems to say that just having faith is not enough. He talks about the person who has led an evil life on the assumption that he can repent at the last gasp with a deathbed repentance, and so be saved; Swedenborg does not accept that. He says that one's earthly life should be characterised by good conduct as well as faith and acceptance of the truth in order to be accepted for heaven. Some who have been exemplary do not need to be 'stripped ', and can go straight up. Others who are more like normal people with minor faults and failures have to be 'stripped' before they can be instructed and allowed into heaven. This is the only admission that almost all of us are a mixture of good and bad, since that is unavoidable in human nature. Then comes the dividing point, which he pictures as a path with a big stone blocking the way. The good go on one path to heaven and the bad on another path to hell. This is the chasmic separation which we see in so many other mythologies around the world, and also in the Parables of Jesus.

In a way, this concept ties in with the Roman Catholic doctrine of Purgatory, which means a preliminary state in the next life where one's imperfections are removed as a preparation for heaven. Not that Swedenborg has any time for Roman Catholicism; he is quite damning about the Pope and Catholics, and seems to think they will be going downhill as opposed to uphill.

It is an engaging assessment of heaven and hell and if we take it literally, it is quite frightening. A lot depends on how much we can take at face value, or as some kind of figurative expression. After all, he admits that some of this is figurative. It is interesting that some of his Protestant Lutheran assumptions break through at times, though not always. Is this another case of someone projecting his preconceived ideas into the skies? This factor was plain enough with Greek and Norse mythology, how the story-tellers in their descriptions of the gods, were really only describing the worse attributes of human nature. Is this sort of thing happening with Swedenborg?

Worthwhile elements in Swedenborg's work

I would say that Swedenborg's work comes across as a semi-demythologised system of thought. It has much scientific and philosophical content which cuts out the sentimental, approximate thinking of many theological thinkers. The concept of balance, or equilibrium is very important. It would seem that there is a balance between good and evil, just as there is the balance of nature, with God in control of the whole thing. This means that we have the freedom to make moral choices. We can turn to God and allow Jesus Christ to encourage us heavenwards. But since we have freedom, there is the scope for people to reject this and head in the other direction. This is what might be seen as a very 'modern' approach to the problem of Theodicy, the problem of evil. There is evil in the world because some people love themselves as opposed to loving God and their neighbour. That in itself is a worthwhile concept, and the fact that we have freedom to make a choice. If we did not have that freedom, it would become meaningless; we would become like robots. That freedom, he claims is dependent on the balance between good and evil. If the equilibrium were to be disturbed, everything would fall apart. Quite how the logic of that works out is not clear, at least, not to me, but it seems to be a worthy concept. It is interesting that Swedenborg lived three centuries before the modern concept of atomic theory was devised. This, probably more than anything, exemplifies the need for balance between tiny electrical impulses which produce atoms, molecules and larger structures. From the point of view of physics, if plus and minus did go wrong, literally everything would fall apart.

One missing ingredient in Swedenborg's scheme, is that of eschatology. There is no mention of the end of time or the consummation of all things. We could assume from his book that the eternal juxtaposition of good and evil will indeed continue forever, with no resolution. Basic Biblical and Christian thinking involves a time, in the future, in which God, in the form of the Messiah, will intervene in human history (as he did once before) and bring everything to a conclusion. That will mean the final defeat of evil, in whatever concept one likes to have it, and everything will be heaven. Christian thinkers have pondered the possibility of the Devil being redeemed. Others have said that the defeat of evil has already been achieved in the ministry of Jesus Christ, but that leaves us with evil put under a certain limit. Those who are foolish enough to involve themselves in evil, obviously will have trouble in this world and the next, but they do not have to go that way. Swedenborg only partially embarks on this line of argument. It is safe to say that he does not embark on eschatology, which is an important futuristic aspect of mythology, nor does he give it much credence.

The most worthwhile aspect of his theology is his emphasis on love and truth. These factors emanate from God himself. If one loves oneself, one becomes greedy, tyrannical, dishonest, scheming, suspicious, and everything one does is with the basic motive of serving one's own interests. This is the way to perdition. For those who are heading in the right direction, their love is aimed at God and at helping other people; those who are completely selfless are on the fast track to heaven. The emphasis on love is the most worthwhile element in the whole scheme, regardless of what religious label one applies to oneself. Swedenborg in effect equates love and truth, saying that heavenly knowledge is essentially about love and truth. There is nothing about violence, hate, or divisiveness in the whole book. One could call him a universalist, since he can see people of all religions being prepared for heaven if their heart is in the right place. This is really quite amazing coming from someone at a time when there was so much religious extremism and violence. We can say that his ideas are of great value, regardless of the veracity of his claims over the visions.

As mythology

We need to assess Swedenborg's visions on the basis of mythology, since this is the theme of this book. After all, dreams and Theophanous encounters are an important element in the Bible, so why can we not take Swedenborg's visions at face value? We notice that many of the features of mythological expression are missing or understated. It would be true that the snake appears once, jewels, crystal and precious metals are worked in, but they are not dominant metaphors in this scheme. The world tree is not to be found at all; we do not hear about blood. In fact cruelty and violence are hardly ever involved, except to say that that is what the devils do to each other in hell. We do not have giants, elves, strange variants on the human or animal forms. There is only one monster, and that is a passing remark. Swords, spears and arrows are missing and there is no mention of magic as applied to weaponry or anything else. Fire is understated and 'demythologised' while water hardly receives a mention. Cleansing is imparted by 'stripping' and the angels imparting knowledge. The chief element relating to traditional mythology is the cosmic battle between good and evil, but with a difference. Although the devils try to invade heaven and the angels go into hell to calm things down, there is no all-out battle in the skies. It is all very non-violent. The great champion hero, as so often seen in the Greek mythology is transmuted into Jesus Christ, but he is never portrayed as someone like 'Desperate Dan'. He is gentle and persuading as opposed to aggressive.

For these reasons, it can be seen that Swedenborg's scheme is a partial demythologising approach which anticipates Bultmann by about three centuries. One could go further and say that Swedenborg is yet another outbreak of Gnosticism (see chapter 4 for my assessment of Gnosticism) as a philosophical version of mythology. Indeed there are various elements in common with Gnosticism, for although he does not embark on all those strange names for the heavenly principles which are supposed to emanate from God, he does have some sort of ranking of all those compartments in heaven, and different qualities of angels. The new element would be to say that hell is a mirror image of heaven, only nasty as opposed to lovely. That was something that the Gnostics did not seem to embark on. We notice that 'knowledge' is heavily emphasised; this was an important factor in Gnosticism, as a vital ingredient in salvation, and reminds us of the LOGOS.

It makes very little difference whether one accepts Swedenborg's visions as genuine or not. The whole thing can be seen as a form of mythology with some valuable theological ideas included. Whether or not there are such things as angels and devils is a matter for discussion, but essentially the Christian believer only needs to know what it says in the Creeds. Firstly that Almighty God created everything whether physical or spirit; secondly that the Messiah Jesus came into the world to save us all; thirdly that the Holy

Spirit is active in the world inspiring, guiding and warning, as the course of history moves along. Beyond that there is no requirement to believe all kinds of complicated and speculatory ideas. One example of this would be the question of 'multi-life'. Is there such a thing as reincarnation as the Hindus and Buddhists maintain? It is interesting that Swedenborg never makes mention of this.(10) He seems to confirm the western view that we live once and then face judgement.

It may seem strange to some people to talk of angels and devils, and an awareness of the next world, but so much of Swedenborg's work ties in with recent awareness of these matters. Out of the body experiences are one such, and many people will attest that they have had some kind of paranormal experience. I have to say that I personally can understand a lot of what he says. That does not have to mean that I have to believe every detail of his claims, and in fact it is not necessary to do so. What is necessary is to accept that God is love;(11) we have love which should be directed in the right direction, and that there is such a thing as evil. Perhaps that is enough for most people to take on board.

There are many publications on the subject of the afterlife. One such is Ian Wilson's The After Death Experience. It would seem that in recent years, the whole matter of 'the next world' is being taken far more seriously than it has been. Many of the accounts of near 'death' or apparent 'death' tie in to some extent with Swedenborg's descriptions. There is no need to quote a whole list of such experiences, but there having been so many reported, the matter cannot be brushed off as fanciful. What it amounts to is that there is another world waiting for us at death; that death is not really death but a transition to another state. The implication in this is that this life is some kind of preparation or testing ground for the next one.

Wilson notes that many people have been unwilling to admit to an out of the body experience. The reason for this is that they are afraid of being regarded as deranged, and possibly even victimised. One wonders why this is, that the majority of people see this sort of thing as unacceptable. Again, this must go back to the instinctive reaction, namely that we are all in denial of death. We never like to have to admit that it is going to happen. When someone starts maintaining that they have been there and come back, it sets up a negative reaction in many people. Others are totally fascinated by it; that is because in spite of being in denial of death, we are also fixated on it. If we were all inclined to give credit to someone like Swedenborg, we would probably all shoot ourselves in order to get to heaven more quickly. But God wants us to value life in this world as well as the next, so we are held back from suicide by deeply entrenched instincts concerning the importance of survival.

If it is true that there is a next world waiting for us, then that strand concerning life, death and resurrection is not to be regarded as 'myth'. It is a reality. That does not prevent religious belief from making exaggeration and augmentation so that the whole matter does become mythological. This is an interesting case of where the boundary between mythology and actual reality is a difficult one to determine. One wonders how many other mythological strands are actually literal realities.

Footnotes for chapter 25

1. The Book of Mormon, see chapter 11 in The Theology of Truth.

2. For a discussion on the subject of different levels of truth, see chapter 1 in The Theology of Truth.

3. This ties in with what Jesus says in John 14:2, 'in my Father's house are many mansions', something that also occurs in Enoch.

4. The Egyptians thought that one would work, eat and carry on as normal in the next world. See The Egyptian Book of the Dead in The Theology of Truth, chapter 25.

5. In Genesis chapter 1 the light of God comes before the light of the sun and the moon.

6. The concept of the Guardian Angel comes in Matthew 18:10, and also each church has its guardian angel, in Revelation.

7. The faces of Dracula and Voldemort are appropriately displayed in the films as lifeless, ugly and blank.

8. Gnashing of teeth comes in Matthew 8:12 and several other locations.

9. St.Paul in Romans, and other epistles, discussed the issue of faith in relation to good works.

10. Karma, the belief in reincarnation, is essential to the Hindu and Buddhist systems of thought. This is discussed in chapter 11 in The Theology of Paradox.

11. This an essential strand in I John 4:8 and other New Testament locations.

26

Symbolism

Up to this point, this book has concentrated largely on legend and mythology. Symbolism has mostly been mentioned as a concomitant of mythology. It is impossible to separate symbolism from mythology, just as it is impossible to draw a distinct line between historical material, legend and myth. This chapter will give symbolism first consideration. It is an important aspect of everyday life. It is an economical and sometimes poetic way of stating facts quickly and strikingly, in such a way as to surmount language barriers.

To take a few examples, our traffic light system is accepted all over the world. Red means 'stop' (danger), green means 'you can go' (safe), amber means 'caution'. A circular sign is mandatory; a triangular sign means caution; a rectangular sign is purely for information. A black thing looking like a propeller is the warning for radio-activity. Black is associated with funerals and white with weddings, although it is a bit different in the far East. A skull and crossbones means death or piracy. We could make an endless list, but all it will indicate will be the importance of symbolism in our modern world.

The most obvious and commonplace system of symbols is over the letters of the alphabet. Going back to Ancient Egypt, with its hieroglyphs, this developed into an alphabetic system. The Mesopotamians with their cuneiform writing impressed on clay tablets, approached the matter in a different way, with coded marks which stood for spoken sounds. The Chinese had their own method using pictograms. It is possible that the Hebrew alphabet was one of the first to be a system of letters as we know it now. The original script can be seen on the walls of the Siloam Tunnel in Jerusalem. Under the influence of Aramaic, Hebrew lettering came to be what we now see on the signs outside synagogues and in copies of the Hebrew scriptures.

It is thought that Greek and eventually Roman lettering were parented by the Hebrew, although Crump(1) thinks it is the other way round. It is not often realised, that every letter of the Hebrew alphabet was also a numeral;(2) there were no separate figures as in nought to nine as we know it. The same was true with the Greek alphabet. So Alpha was one, Beta was two and so on. With the Romans we see selected alphabetical letters used for numerals, such as X for ten, M for a thousand, and L for fifty. This prevailed into the Mediaeval period when people became aware of Arabic numerals which were quickly seen to be a far more convenient way of doing arithmetic.

Numerology

At this point it is worth spending some time on the subject of Numerology. This is a system of thought which runs parallel to the astrological-Zodiacal mentality. It is not quite as well known as the Zodiac, neither is it anything like unified. Again, people's attitudes vary greatly on this matter. Some take its prognostications very seriously and others regard it as nonsense. But the importance for this book lies in its use of number symbolism and also its reliance on mythological ideas about the heavenly bodies. It is easy to write this sort of thing off as crazy, but there is truth in it, in so far as it tells us something about human nature, every bit as much as mythology does.

The origins of Numerology go back to the ancient Chaldeans and it is almost certain that the Magi of that area were conversant with this kind of thinking. It is also likely that Abraham and his forebears would have known about this kind of thinking. To strengthen this idea, it can be noted that the name Methushael, which means 'man of God' is a Babylonian variant on Methusaleh; this indicates that the genealogies in Genesis 4 and 5, with their enormous ages, have some relationship to ancient Chaldea (Babylon). But the 'Father of Numerology' as such is regarded as Pythagoras, a philosopher, mathematician and astrologer, who was convinced that numbers had mystical properties and contained the secrets of the universe. His basic ideas are still used by numerologists to this day. The other major source of inspiration for numerology is the Kabbalah. This seems to have appeared well after Biblical times, even well into the Mediaeval era. It is a fascinating area of thought; what a shame its pundits seem to disagree on so many points!

A useful starting point is the following fact about the nine-times table.

1 x 9 = 9

2 x 9 = 18

3 x 9 = 27

4 x 9 = 36

5 x 9 = 45

6 x 9 = 54

7 x 9 = 63

8 x 9 = 72

9 x 9 = 81

10 x 9 = 90

11 x 9 = 99

12 x 9 = 108

If we add 1 and 8 we get 9; if we add 3 and 6 we get 9;
If we add 1 and 0 and 8 we get nine again; it works for all of them.
If we turn 18 upside down we get 81; if we invert 36 we get 63.
If we take any multiple of 9 and add its numbers together we get
back to nine; eg. 378 which is 9 x 42.
Add 3 + 7 + 8 this equals 10 + 8 which equals 18; 1 + 8 = 9.
Is this magic; no, but 9 must have some special significance.
Some of the Hebrews thought that 9 was symbolic of God; others
thought it represented the Devil. We have noticed that number 9
has appeared in various world myths, including the Norse and various African ones.

When this number nine is seen in relation to human personality, we arrive at a diagram like this;

	Thought; Air; Individualists	Activity; Earth; Organisers(things)	Power; Water; Influencers
Sunlight; Head; Independents	3	6	9
Produce; Heart; Organisers (people)	2	5	8
Soil; Stomach; Reformers	1	4	7

All this will seem very strange to anyone not familiar with this kind of mentality. But all these numbers are seen as symbolic of something, and the whole system is a method of analysing one's personality and making predictions about them. We notice that this system functions on the assumption that NOUGHT is non-existent. Templeton (a very up-to-date pundit) insists that 10 is in the frame. Coates, whose ideas are a little dated, stops at nine.

There are three important numbers in everyone's life; the birth date, one's name and the 'balancer'. Once we calculate a figure from these, it is possible to assess one's personality and potential. It is likely that this method goes back to very ancient times, but in today's world, different numerologists apply these methods in slightly different ways. One wonders how they know what variations can legitimately be made!

Firstly, one's birth date. My date is 26:11:1943. Add all these digits up and we obtain a single digit in the range 1 to 9. So; $2 + 6 + 1 + 1 + 1 + 9 + 4 + 3 = 27$; then $2 + 7 = 9$. This is my 'directional sense' (whatever that means), according to Templeton, my 'ruling number'. Then there is a 'personal day number' which is based on the days of the month. So, for instance, I am on 26, which added together gives 8. According to Templeton, that means I am very loving but do not like to be ordered around. There is also a 'personal year number' (PYN) which is calculated in my case by adding 26:11 and 2017 (but not my birth year), so obtaining 11 which will not be reduced. 11 says that I am extra sensitive and nervy; I must be considerate, friendly and patient.

Secondly, one's name in letters. Mine is William Andrew Sumner. Some analysts will accept a nickname or a shortened version, such as Bill, but to do it properly, it should be the name as on the Birth Certificate. To obtain a number from this, we need another diagram, as follows;

1	2	3	4	5	6	7	8	9
A	B	C	D	E	F	G	H	I
J	K	L	M	N	O	P	Q	R
S	T	U	V	W	X	Y	Z	

Transferring my name into numbers works like this; W = 5, I = 9 and so on. To save space we arrive at;

$5 + 9 + 3 + 3 + 9 + 1 + 4$ (William) = 34; so $3 + 4 = 7$

$1 + 5 + 4 + 9 + 5 + 5 =$ (Andrew) = 29; so $2 + 9 = 11$; $1 + 1 = 2$

$1 + 3 + 4 + 5 + 5 + 9 =$ (Sumner) = 27; so $2 + 7 = 9$

Now add $7 + 2 + 9 = 18$; thence $1 + 8 = 9$. This is my personality number, or 'the soul' or 'inner urge' number, which happens to be the same as my directional sense. If we add the two together, $9 + 9 =$ that gives 18; then add again $1 + 8 =$ we arrive back at NINE once more. So 9 is also my 'balancer'.

According to this, I should be a mass of energy, very independent, multitasking, polymathic, forgiving, rebellious and a few other interesting traits. My comment is that there is an element of truth in all this, but how many other people with the same number would be the same? If I had been born a woman, it would not be the same. A woman would be a career person, interested in science, a good motorist and a good sportsperson. Quite how one arrives at this would be an interesting question. But the truth of the matter is that a numerologist will see all kinds of significance in these numbers, especially if one adds up to ELEVEN or TWENTY-TWO. 33:6 (obtained by adding the two threes to get six) has come to be auspicious in recent years. All the double numbers up to 99 are included in this idea, and each has a separate bearing on one's personality, They are called the 'master numbers', and each have special significance.

Going on from here, the details of one's personality can be found by using the grid again. We take each of the letters in my name and put a ring round each number for each one;

I have got no 2s, 6s, 8s, or 7s. But 1 scores three; 3 scores 3; 4 scores three; 5 scores six; and 9 scores five. From this we derive a 'stress line' from 1 through 5 and into 9. This is supposed to be the commonest line of worldly success. According to Coates, this is someone who begins with a humble start and rises to power, money or fame. Templeton thinks that $1 - 5 - 9$ shows a spirit of determination. At this point, the birth number may have some influence on the result, which in my case was 9, precisely what effect it has is not clear.

Templeton thinks that this method can be worked with one's birth date. So, 26:11:1943 comes out as the following;

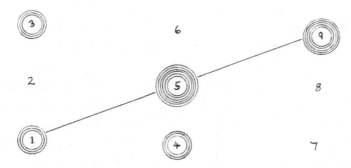

If I have three ones, this means I am a chatterbox!Christie thinks that 9 indicates one is associated with Neptune; one's 'Sun sign' is Pisces (the Fishes), and one's lucky days of the month are 9, 18, and 27. One is associated with divine love, completion, talent, spirituality and karma; one is a giving sort of person. One can be religious, possibly too much so! But all analysts will agree that 9 indicates power. On that basis, Coates thinks one ought to be involved with atomic science, radiation and hydraulics, engineering and large scale construction; also investment and speculation. It is the number of all or nothing.

This is all very fascinating and one wonders how the pundits arrive at these conclusions. They will admit that if one's name is expressed in a different language, such as Chinese or Sanskrit, it will have to be transliterated into Latin letters. Christie goes even further and says that one's home address or one's car registration number can be used to prognosticate on one's potential! One's telephone number can be enlisted to help in the analysis. No comment is made in the eventuality of one's telephone number being changed by the GPO, or of one's car being changed! It even goes so far as to give one hints on the right sort of person to marry, and the name given to one's child!

We notice that numerology has some relationship to astrology, though this too is not explained properly. So for instance number one indicates energy, the planet is the sun, the sign is Leo and the keyword is 'positive'. Each number up to nine has a planet and a constellation tied in with it. We notice that some of the planets would not have been known to Pythagoras, such as Pluto, Neptune and Uranus, which means that they must have been worked in in recent times. Another aspect is that each number is assigned a colour, so for instance 1 is light green, 5 is yellow and nine, my number is white, indicating a higher spirit. This is according to Christie; Templeton has a different colour scheme! Perhaps I should wear white all the time? Another aspect, which goes back to Pythagoras, is that the odd numbers are termed masculine and the even numbers as feminine. This reminds us of something from Taoist (Chinese) philosophy with the yin-yang understanding of numbers. (3)

How is all this of relevance to mythology as discussed so far? It has been pointed out that so many mythological schemes have a key number which dominates the culture of that area. So, China and Japan have 8, the Norsemen have 9, the Huichols have 5, and Judaeo-Christians have 7. We have already seen that the numbers one to nine each have some kind of significance or dynamic force. It would be interesting to see if any of this links up with the theorisings of numerology.

One is the number of literature, theory and new ideas.

Two is the number of the mask; duality and duplicity.

Three is the number of the liberal arts and sciences, music and history.

Four is the number of pure mathematics, physics and chemistry.

Five is the number of military professions and industry.

Six is the number of law and law-making, also of exploration and discovery.

Seven is the number of agriculture and also of defence.

Eight is the number of banking and insurance; also medicine.

Nine is the number of power.

There are some differences of opinion over what these numbers stand for, in fact the Kabbalah has its own system which bears hardly any relationship to what we assume to be Pythagoras' ideas. The same is true of Templeton; she goes on to take 10 as the creative force, 11 as idealism, spirituality and faith, and genius. 22 (a master 'builder'number) , the conjuction of spirit and matter. 33 is the number of Creation, doubled. Doubtless all the other master numbers would have even more exciting meanings attached to them.

Templeton goes one further and outlines a method using pyramids (not the ones in Egypt!). I have devised my personal pyramid based on procedures described on page 198 in her book. My birthdate is 26:11:1943, ruling number 9.

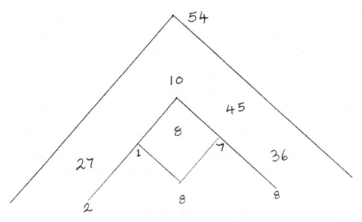

All these numbers in their positions are supposed to hold some significance. Taking my birth date; 26:11:1943; eleven is contracted to 2 and goes at the bottom left. The day, 26 becomes 8 and goes bottom centre, and the year, 1943 contracted goes as 8 in the bottom right. Then we add the month and the day number, 2 plus 8, giving 10 which gives 1, and this goes on the first peak. Then we add the day number to the year number, 8 plus 8, which becomes 16, which becomes 7 and this goes on the second peak. We now add 1 and 7, giving 8, which goes on the third peak. Now we add the month number to the year number, 2 plus 8, which gives 10 (this is not reduced) and this goes on the fourth peak. Now I must subtract my ruling number, which is 9 from 36 (which is from ancient times known as the 'number of man'). That gives us 27. Now we add 9 to 27 and get 36. Then we add 9 to 36 and get 45. Then we add 9 to 45 and get 54. All very ingenious!

All kinds of interesting prognostications are drawn out of this sort of pyramid, and Templeton does not go into much detail about it. Doubtless I should be classed as an idiot for not seeing all kinds of mysterious symbolisms in this diagram! It all seems rather arbitrary and different experts have varying ideas on how to interpret these patterns, but this kind of mentality has been going on for centuries, right back to Ancient Mesopotamia, and shows no sign of fading out. Much to the contrary, in modern times we see more developments and possibilities which on the face of it, are really rather strange!

The Kabbalah system

It would be misleading to call this a system; it is a multi-layered body of knowledge with all manner of opinions at work. It is an element in Judaism, the mystical element, which does justice to the core of the faith of Israel, monotheism. It helps to have a working knowledge of Hebrew, but not essential. It is claimed that the first elements of Kabbalah were given to Abraham and then on through the Ten Commandments, but there is no clear evidence of this in the Hebrew Bible. The central written corpus of the Kabbalah is the ZOHAR, or the Book of Radiance, which is considered sacred. Some claim it was written about 200 AD and others that it was produced in 13th century Europe by Moses de Leon.(4) It is a very long, complicated and abstruse; it would take a lifetime of study to come to grips with it. For our purposes, just a general idea of Kabbalah is necessary, as an indication of how post-Biblical Judaism has developed an entire tradition, which in many ways reminds us of a kind of Gnosticism which is completely different from that seen in the mid-Roman Empire. The following outline is taken from the book Kabbalah Made Easy by Barrie Dolnick.

The chief advance on earlier numerology is the admission that nought does exist. So we have number analyses worked out on one to ten. This is done by the use of the Tree of Life which is the Kabbalistic version of the World Tree, however it is depicted rather differently. It is not a tree with branches coming up from the ground; it is the Creator at the top emanating power through three channels down to the Creation. The tree has ten power centres called Sefiroth (which means 'numbers').(5) Each Sefirah has a Hebrew name and a number, one of the alphabet, and they interrelate with each other to produce different aspects of Creation and also each human soul. Paradoxically, the whole tree can be turned upside down so that number one comes at the bottom and becomes the roots instead of the crown of the tree.

Looking at the diagram shown below, the circles are the Sefiroth, going from one to ten. Each circle has a number going along with the relevant letter of the Hebrew alphabet; it starts with aleph(6) and goes through to yodh.(7) The whole Hebrew alphabet has a number apportioned to each letter, but this diagram does not take them all in. The other diagram, called Jacob's Ladder, shown below, does take in the whole Hebrew alphabet.

Each Sefirah has a Hebrew word given to it, such as Hochmah, meaning Wisdom. I have only given one word for each, but there are various ideas on more words, and they are not necessarily in total agreement. However, Keter (crown) represents God,(one) the Creator, and Malkuth (ten) is the earth. The meaning of it is that God's creative power comes through to the physical level through various interrelating channels. These interconnecting lines indicate all the different permutations on Creation. There is an 11ᵗʰ Sefirah, not included in every diagram of the World Tree, called Da'at, or Knowledge, and is not interconnected with all the other Sefiroth. It can transmit knowledge between different levels, or drain away ideas when they are too strong.

We notice that all these Sefiroth are colour coded, except to say that there is no total agreement on which colour ought to go where. Hodh (eight) could be orange or yellow. We notice that each Sefirah has been associated with a planet. One wonders how this was done before the discovery of Pluto and Uranus! Also the signs of the Zodiac are apportioned but sadly two have to be missed out and Da'at does not appear to have one. All this is supposed to be deeply symbolic.

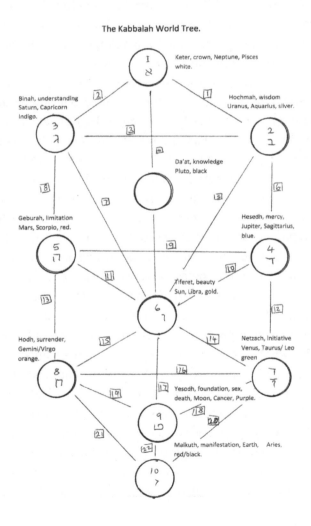

The Kabbalah World Tree.

A few further comments on the Kabbalah World Tree

In addition, all the Sefiroth are related, with their colours to the main features of the Menorah, the seven-branched candlestick. So for instance, Keter (one) comes on the middle candle and Malkuth (ten) comes on the base of the candlestick.

We also find that the triangles formed by the interconnecting lines can be coloured in so that various aspects of one's personality can be assessed. So for instance, the triangle formed by numbers 2, 3 and 6 is light blue, indicates the throat of Chakra,(8) the level of communication and psychic awareness (whatever that might mean!)

Another aspect of this is that all the lines of communication have numbers in squares. These are not the same as the numbers in the circles. The purpose here is to relate the lines of communication to the Tarot cards. Each number (in a square) is a letter of the Hebrew alphabet, this time 22 in number, so none are left out. Each Tarot card(9) is placed against a number. So for instance, Aleph (one) equals Tarot Card, the Fool, and it means 'potential'. Kaph, (eleven) equals Wheel of Fortune and indicates Destiny. Quite what the logic of all this is, is an interesting question, but this method is thought to go back to ancient times. There is the use of 'archetypes' which reminds us of Jung; maybe he would have found all this fascinating, and probably have given us an explanation for it in terms of basic instincts.

Something that could not be included in the diagram is the Evil side of the Tree of Life. All those Sefiroth also have a negative label as well as a positive one. So for instance, Hochmah, Wisdom receives the opposite, confusion, ignorance. Tiferet (six) Beauty turns into Narcissism, and Hodh (eight) becomes lying, deceit. But Keter (one) holds both good and evil, but that is the exception. All these emanations have a darker side and there is a balance between these properties.

Another permutation with the Tree of Life is the way in which the Ten Commandments are worked in to good effect. Predictably, Keter (one) which represents God, is tied to the first Commandment, 'Thou shalt have no other gods before me.' After that the relevance of the Sefiroth to each Commandment is somewhat difficult to see. 'Do not commit adultery' is placed on Netzach, 'initiative', and 'do not commit murder' is aligned with Tifereth, beauty. Da'at, Knowledge has no commandment associated with it at all. However, the number ten does become a significant number in Hebrew and Kabbalistic thought.

Yet another permutation is on the subject of prosperity and one's attitude to money. Keter (one) becomes 'acknowledge a higher source' which is quite appropriate. Hesedh, (four) becomes 'giving' which is also in line with mercy and love. Binah (three) is still 'understanding' which is a good arrangement. However, why should Tifereth (six),' beauty' be associated with 'gratitude'? Da'at is not given a new label. In general terms, this analysis of Prosperity fits in quite well with the basic idea of the Tree.

One can even relate each Sefirah to a position of the body and also one of the stages in life from infancy to death. With this idea, we start at the bottom with (ten) Malkuth as a baby and work up to puberty and marriage with Netzach (seven) and arrive at Keter as we die and go back to God (one). Clearly this Tree has so many permutations and applications that it could be used to prognosticate on just about anything and everything.

Perhaps the most interesting element in the use of the World Tree is the way in which the spiritual powers are allotted to each of the Sefirah. So, we see that the angels are the closest to earth and are placed on Malkuth (ten). Above them are the archangels of which there are four (nine). Then going up come Principalities and Powers, Thrones and Dominions, and on two and three come the Cherubim and Seraphim. These are so bright that they cannot be seen by mankind any more than the Metratron which represents God as number one. We notice that Da'at does not have any apportionment. We notice that St.Paul makes mention of some of these factors but does not make it an essential aspect of Christian teaching; he says that Jesus Christ is superior to all these things. If one were to wonder how one can ever know anything for certain about these spiritual entities, one might be right. However, it goes further than this, because the Kabbalah is quite comfortable with the idea of 'earth spirits', fairies (!), goblins and devas. This is where we see a certain influence from Hinduism and the Kami of Shintoism.

Having studied the Kabbalah Tree of Life, we now need to think about another 'tree' which appears in Kabbalistic thinking; it is called Jacob's Ladder. It is hardly likely that Jacob's Dream included a curious structure like this; it almost certainly is a post-Biblical development based on Jacob's Theophanous experience. This Tree has 28 Sefiroth (29 if we count Da'at) and again it is in three columns with connecting lines which form various triangles. These can be coloured in to give various permutations. The top ten Sefiroth symbolise the divine which is out of sight of mankind. The next nine symbolise the spirit; the next nine give us formation; the last nine lead us into the physical, again with Malkuth at the bottom. It is an extended version of the World Tree, and in terms of mythology, it appears to be a very good example of augmentation. By this I mean that a basic idea is extended and magnified to open up more possibilities. There are so many more emanations and speculative ideas in it. This strengthens my view that Kabbalism is yet another version of Gnosticism.

The whole thing is fascinating but also pure speculation. I personally could not feel obliged to persuade anyone to believe all this. However, what it does indicate is a certain element in human nature. We live in a world which is (at the moment) dominated by raw scientific facts, or alleged facts in some cases, but this is not enough to satisfy the human soul. There is the need to assess oneself and find a relationship with the unseen world. We need to interpret the world in terms other than purely scientific or mathematical realities. This applies to both systems of numerology as described above, the Pythagorean or the Kabbalistic one. It is the same urge, to calculate on some kind of logical framework, one's own worth, potential and even destiny. This also raises the ongoing question of the dilemma between predestination and free will. The pundits all seem to insist on free will, but even so, there is still the implication that just as one's future is governed by the stars, so too, one's destiny is somehow conditioned by the interaction of elements in the spiritual power of numbers. This would apply to both systems of thought, whether Pythagorean or Kabbalistic. No one seems to have any idea of reconciling these two systems. It looks very much as though one can pick and choose which system to take seriously, assuming that one is tempted to take any of this seriously. But it does tell of something of human nature, in that there is the urge to attempt to anticipate the future and take steps to offset its most upsetting aspects. Seeing it that way, it is clearly some kind of mythological system, but using symbolism in a most elaborate and fanciful fashion.

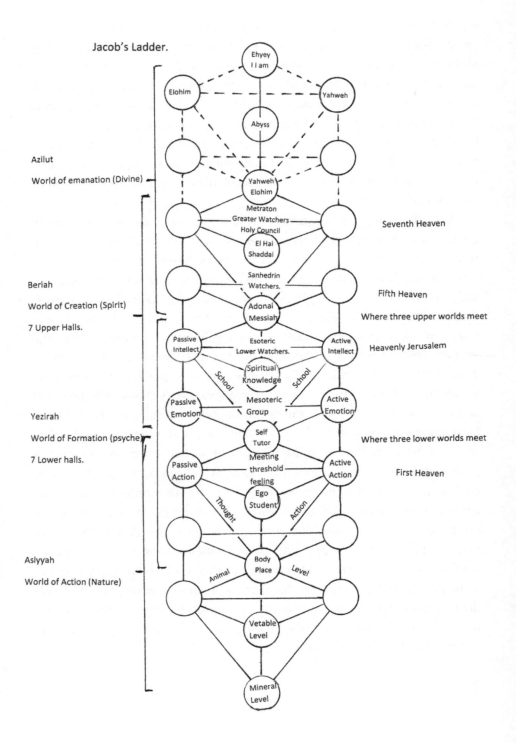

Jacob's Ladder.

Azilut

World of emanation (Divine)

Beriah

World of Creation (Spirit)

7 Upper Halls.

Yezirah

World of Formation (psyche)

7 Lower halls.

Asiyyah

World of Action (Nature)

Ehyey I I am

Elohim

Yahweh

Abyss

Yahweh Elohim

Metraton
Greater Watchers
Holy Council

El Hai Shaddai

Seventh Heaven

Sanhedrin
Watchers.

Adonai Messiah

Fifth Heaven

Where three upper worlds meet

Passive Intellect

Esoteric
Lower Watchers.

Active Intellect

Heavenly Jerusalem

School

Spiritual Knowledge

School

Passive Emotion

Mesoteric Group

Active Emotion

Self Tutor

Where three lower worlds meet

Meeting
threshold
feeling

Passive Action

Active Action

First Heaven

Thought

Ego Student

Action

Body Place

Animal

Level

Vetable Level

Mineral Level

Numerological methods applied to the Bible

If it is true that Numerology started in Ancient Sumeria, and also that most of our mythical material in Genesis originated in that area, then it would stand to reason that the esoteric understanding of numbers would appear in these accounts. We cannot expect the Kabbalists to have had any influence here, since that system of thought only really took shape after the Bible was completed. Nevertheless the Kabbalists almost certainly derived their ideas from a pre-existent Numerological system of thought. We notice the numbers are very often quoted as if there is some special significance in them, even though this is never clarified. The significance of them was probably obvious to the people of those times, but is now lost on us. All we can do is make informed guesses.

The Bible has all kinds of number symbolisms at work, and there appear to be various different systems at work. This is understandable since the literature of the Bible spans many centuries and that gives plenty of room for ideas about numbers to develop. We are still seeing this nowadays with the modern pundits. The book of Revelation, reviewed in The Theology of Truth, has been given a thorough treatment, but it has to be admitted that the full significance of everything in that book has not been analysed. One of the most intriguing passages in the Bible comes in Genesis chapter 5 in which ten generations of ancestors have massive ages, going up to 900. It is also pointed out how old each ancestor is when his son is born. This seems to have some importance, since it is well emphasised, but the precise significance of this is not explained. The passage is mirrored in Genesis 11:10ff, where another scheme of ten forebears lead us from Shem, one of the sons of Noah down to Abram. Again, the age of each man at the birth of his son is pointed out. This factor must have held much importance for them in those days, as it appears again when Isaac's sons were born (Esau and Jacob), but this aspect seems to fade out by the end of Genesis. Clearly we are seeing some kind of cultural feature which is lost on us now. Possibly it is to some extent symbolic. It is possible that the passages are trying to show the continuity of the family of faith from Adam down to Noah and then on down to Abraham. The use of ten generations, twice over, may be a hint that these were the people who were exhibiting correct moral conduct before God (as stated clearly in the Ten Commandments later on in Exodus) while the rest of humanity were going astray.(11)

Massive ages in Genesis chapter 5

It has always been a puzzle as to how people managed to live to such great ages; Methusaleh is symbolic of a very old man, as he is recorded as living to 969 years! There are various possible ways of coping with these claims, none of which are completely convincing. One way is to take it completely literally, that people did live to such great ages at one time. I think most people will find that a problem especially as it is claimed that they fathered children at the age of 187 or 130! Another remote possibility is that we are seeing some kind of mummification practice which entailed the dead ancestor being preserved (as was done in Egypt) and kept about the home for a long time as if still alive. We know that this practice did happen in other parts of the world. It is a telling remark made by Abraham on the death of his wife, Sarah, '..that I may bury my dead out of my sight.' This could imply that often, or even usually, the dead were not buried out of one's sight, but kept on sight in the house for some considerable time. The passage gives this element a certain amount of emphasis. Clearly they had an idea of when a corpse ought to be properly interred in a tomb.

Another remote possibility is to say that they were using a different method of calculating years, though to be fair, there is no evidence of this coming from ancient Sumerian archaeological findings. What we do know is that the Mesopotamian city states all had different ways of calendar calculation and there was much fascination about the manipulation of numbers. Also we know that in Biblical times the terms 'day', 'year', 'week' are very often interchangeable; this is a strong element in the book of Daniel. We can also remark that in Mesopotamia, they all worked on a lunar calendar, which would entail 13 months in a year. Supposing they were assuming that these massive ages were not years but months in our literal sense. That would mean that Methusaleh's 969 years can be divided by 13, which gives us just over 74 years in our reckoning. That would be quite plausible. The youngest one, Enoch, at 300 years would turn out to be about 23 years, which again is plausible. I offer this as just a remote possibility; in no way is it a proven fact! At the very least, we are seeing into a completely different culture with what we would regard as 'strange' burial customs, or methods of calculation.

Another approach, which may contain more convincing ideas is to take the symbolic route combined with elements from numerology. We already suspect that numerology originated in ancient Sumeria, and this is where Abraham and his forebears originated. It would be strange if there were no trace of numerology included in these early Genesis accounts. We have already seen that certain parts of the Bible are riddled with number symbolisms; the book of Revelation is a case in point, as so many ideas are presented in number code form. This is an indication of how people's minds worked in those days. In the case of Abraham, it is stated that he and Sarah were 99 years old when Isaac was conceived, and when he was born that would make his parents 100. What is the significance of this? In the book of Enoch, it is stated that the number of God is 100, although the reasoning behind this is not clarified. Is the birth of Isaac presented in a way which shows that Abraham's life was coming to a completion in the eyes of God, as Isaac was born with God's own number? Do we have to take this passage completely literally, or can we see it as carrying a symbolic message?

Now we come to consider those massive claims in Genesis chapter 5. Whoever these people were, they must have been associated with the ancient Sumerians, culturally and theologically, and if numerology might be missing from their ideas, it would be a surprise. To read these massive numbers, such as 930, is it fair to assume they were using our methods of decimal calculation? By this I mean we use base ten for everything except computers, simply because it is easy to count up to ten on our fingers and then start again with eleven. What happens if we say 900, whatever that implies, then 30, whatever that symbolises?

We have found that in numerology, 9 is a very significant figure, symbolising power and also God. Such a person is likely to be spiritual, creative and compassionate. 900 is 9 times 100, the number for God. Nine is augmented which means that these people were very well related to God, with great spiritual power. That would make sense because these were the ancestors coming down from Adam to Noah. Who knows what their real, literal ages were? Clearly there is some kind of code being used here, though not quite the same as what we see in Revelation. One could point out that not all of these worthies score 900. Mahalalel gets 800, Lamech gets 700 and Enoch 300. Is there some kind of reasoning behind this? We know that 7 is a very important symbolic number in Judaeo-Christian thinking. It implies the four corners of the earth and the three layers. To say that Lamech has 777 years could be saying that he was very much the completion of God's plan. We recall that Jesus used 777 times for how often we should forgive people their offences; is this saying that Lamech was a very forgiving sort of person? Mahalalel has 800. We know that 8 is the code number for healing. 8 times 100 suggests God's healing power in this person. As for Enoch, with 300, that seems to be something of an anticlimax, and it elicits an explanation from the writer. Enoch 'walked with God, and he was not...'(12) This was taken to mean he was 'assumed' like Moses and Elijah and this gave rise to the book of Enoch which elaborates everything that he saw in heaven and hell, and was allowed to return to earth to warn people of what was waiting for them. But 300 in itself is significant, as 3 tells us of the three layers, heaven, earth and hell. Multiplied by 100 implies that the whole structure is given and controlled by God. The fact that Enoch is calculated to have lived for about a third of the others, is an indication that the passage cannot be taken literally.

This brings us to the other figures such as Adam having 30, Noah with 50 and various others. It can hardly be their actual, literal ages as Enosh would then be a little boy of five and Kenan aged ten! But the numbers again may be symbolic. Unfortunately our knowledge of ancient numerology may be rather sketchy, moreover the figure nought did not play any part in their thinking until the Kabbalists managed to work it in somehow. We suspect that nought was not really conceived of until well after Biblical times.

A possible way into this system of thought, if it is indeed some kind of 'system', is to note that Noah was 600 years old when the Flood came. 6 we can see as symbolic of evil, things going wrong; the number of the beast in Revelation is 666, ie, an augmentation of 6. 6 multiplied by 100 implies that it was God who was behind it all, which is what it says in the passage; God decided to cause the Flood. It is also emphasised that Noah was 601 when the Flood subsided and dried out. Moreover, it is stressed that it was the first of the first month, presumably Nisan.(13) This implies a new year with a fresh start to everything. What is the significance of one? If we refer back to the first verse in Genesis, day one was the first day of Creation. This implies that as Noah was emerging from the Flood, Creation was starting all over again. We notice also that in Exodus 40:1 Moses is commanded to erect the Tabernacle on the first day of the first month, so that the Ark of the Covenant can be properly housed. From one Ark to another! If we try to take this passage literally at this point, Noah would have to have had enough supplies on board the Ark to feed himself, his family and all the animals for a year; a little unlikely! It goes a little further; according to Leviticus

23:4ff the Passover is ordered for 14th Nisan, the first month and the Feast of Unleavened Bread lasts for 7 days, starting on the 15th Nisan. (Deuteronomy 16:1ff has the month of Abib as the Passover month).(14)

The Genesis passage goes on to state that the earth was dry by the 27th day of the second month. This seems to be an alternative version of Genesis 8:13, but there may be some kind of reasoning in citing two dates. We notice that on the second day of Creation, (Genesis 1:6) God separated the waters below, the oceans, and above, the firmament which was assumed to be an ocean in the sky. In other words, God prevents the Flood from happening again. This number 2 implies duality in numerology, namely, the two oceans and it was the work of God, as is emphasised by the use of 27 which is 3 cubed.

Returning to the passage in Genesis 5 we note that there are several interesting features about it. The passage is clearly schematised and there is some sort of significance in the repetitive statement that the father was of such and such an age when his son appeared. For instance, 'When Enosh had lived ninety years, he became the father of Kenan.' (verse 9) and then lived 815 years. It is almost like an ostinato, perhaps mirroring 'the evening and the morning were the first day.'

If we compare this passage with an alternative version in Genesis 4:17ff, this is not schematised at all. It is only eight generations from Adam to Jabal and Jubal and does not mention Noah. Some of the names are the same, or nearly the same, and also in a different order. Nothing special is mentioned about Enoch. Irad and Jabal do not appear in Genesis 5. What we do notice is that some of these people have special skills. Jabal is the original cattle-drover. Jubal is the original musician and Tubal-Cain is a metal forger (just on the cusp of the Bronze and Iron Age). Could this be the key to understanding the rest of the figures in the other list of names?

This suspicion is strengthened when we see that in Genesis 4:24 'Cain is avenged sevenfold and Lamech seventy-sevenfold.' In Genesis 5:31 we hear that Lamech lived 777 years! So it is fair to say that these enormous life-spans are some kind of coding or symbolism, though how it works for the others is not at all clear, on the face of it.

Another aspect of this list of names is the fact that each name has a meaning in itself, and this does not appear to coincide with the numbers cited. So for instance, Jared means 'to go down, descend' (with all the theophanous implications involved). Mahalalel means 'the praise of God' and Enoch means 'trained, dedicated and consecrated'. Most significant is Methusaleh which means 'send, direct and extend', and the other variant on it, Methushael, in Babylonian, 'means man of God'. It looks as though this passage is saying, in symbolic terms, that the family leading up to Noah were the people of God who were not inclined to go astray; they were the ones who kept to God's standards; the ten generations adhered to the ten precepts of God.

Similar things can be said of the list in Genesis 11:10ff, going from Shem down to Abram. Shem lives for 600 years, Arpachshad lives 438 years, Shelah lives 403 years, Eber lives 464 years, Peleg lives 239 years, Reu lives 239 years, Serug lives 230 years, Nahor lives 148 years, and Terah lives 205 years. We notice also that each father produces his firstborn son in his early thirties, give or take a few years. What significance could that hold? We notice that at the death of Moses, there were 30 days of mourning; does this mirror the thirty years of waiting for a firstborn son? Also we can note that these names in Genesis 11 do not have such clear meanings in the Hebrew. Reu is actually a pagan god; however, Abram means 'exalted father.' Also the life-spans of these people are much shorter; could this mean that they are using a different method of calculation as compared with Genesis 5; this could be explained by the fact that the family had moved from Ur, northwards to Haran and then into the land of Canaan, where different methods of calendar calculation were in operation? This passage is clearly schematised as was the passage in Genesis 5. If we look at Genesis 10:21-32 we see a similar list but not so clearly schematised. Many of the names are the same, it is not patterned into ten generations, and many different names are included. This passage is trying to show how the family of Noah proliferated and divided off into different territories, rather than showing how Abram is directly connected to Noah. At the very least we are looking into a culture which was very different from ours, especially on the matter of calculation and burial customs. We have to admit that we do not know enough about Mesopotamian culture to arrive at any neat answers.

The temptation is to overdo this approach and try to force a numerological or entitling significance to every detail. Clearly we are seeing into a culture in which numbers and names held great importance, but we now cannot see all of the implications in their method. Genesis 5 and 11 are two very good examples of symbolism which is now lost on us in the 21st century. Even so, we can glimpse some of the aspects of it and guess at what the writer(s) are portraying. The chief impression given is that there was the continuity of the family of God from Adam to Noah and then down to Abraham, and these were the people who were faithful to God's precepts, even if the Ten Commandments had not been issued formally.

The Da Vinci Code by Dan Brown

'The phenomenal international bestseller' is how this novel is dubbed. Published in 2003, it has made an enormous impact on people's imagination. There is so much in it of mythology and symbolism and this goes a long way to explaining its popularity. In common with most mythologies, it has a certain amount of historical and geographical anchorage. The Louvre in Paris, The Temple church in London, Rosslyn Chapel in Scotland and many famous old masters all add to the fascination. The story is of course total fiction but is kept within the bounds of realism. The most real element is the strand of snobbery which never fails to stir people's imagination. There is Sir Keith Teabing who has more money than is good for him, Professor Richard Langdon from Harvard University, Agent Sophie Neveu who turns out to be distantly related to St. Mary Magdalene, the Roman Catholic Bishop Aringarosa who is in contention with the Vatican but obtains a suitcase containing 30 million Euros, and Silas the albino muscular ascetic monk who does not hesitate to commit murder. All of these, contrasted cleverly, help to build up the drama and fascination. There is also a certain degree of restraint which is unusual for modern mythological productions. One expects Sophie and Richard to slide into a romance, but this element is kept right to the very end when they arrange to meet up in Florence.

The whole plot pivots on one major assumption, namely that if it were evidenced that Jesus Christ had been married, or at least, had a girlfriend (allegedly Mary Magdalene), and possibly had children, then this would blow the Christian religion to smithereens! One wonders why. It rests on the assumption that Jesus had to have been celibate and so 'pure' as far as sexual relations are concerned. While it is true that certain people see this as an important issue, it is also true that many people would see it as irrelevant. I personally can see no reason why Jesus should not have been married; after all, it was the normal thing for Jewish boys at the age of puberty to be found a wife. Strangely, the New Testament says nothing on this subject, one way or the other. The reason being that the writers had much more important matters to include in their accounts. It is quite clear that the first disciples were married. If Jesus had been married or at least in love with someone, that would have the positive element of evidencing his humanity, a factor which is all to carefully emphasised in the Gospels already. However, the Opus Dei people, the diehard traditionalists like the bishop are terrified that evidence could emerge that Jesus was married.

The whole novel is spent in attempting to decipher one code or cryptic message after another. It is all supposed to lead Richard and Sophie to the Holy Grail. It works like a treasure trail until they arrive at Rosslyn Chapel only to find that the Grail is not there; however to their amazement something is there that they never expected; Sophie's grandmother and brother. This, in effect, was the true Holy Grail, the reuniting of the family after years of Sophie being isolated and unable to trust her grandfather. Perhaps the true lesson in the book is that one's real focus in life should not be some ancient artefact that may or may not still exist, but rather on family cohesion and love.

One is amazed at the ferocious fanaticism involved with people trying to trace the Grail. This is an obsession which has been going on for centuries, and reminds us of the Arthurian Knights who attempted to find it, but failed. It never seems to occur to people that the Grail might be symbolic rather than literally true. We can see it as the ancient Celtic Church asserting that it was the true version of Christianity by contrast with what came from Rome. This became the basis of the Church of England at the Reformation. Neither does it occur to Richard, Sophie and the others that the Mary Magdalene motif might also be symbolic. This was a woman who had been a schizophrenic prostitute, but Jesus had healed her and reformed her. She became the first person to witness the Resurrection. What does this tell us? It tells us that no matter how far we can go wrong or out of one's mind, there is always a way back with God's help, and that Jesus loves every one of us however far wrong we have gone. To love Mary does not have to mean that he had a romance with her or married her. Love does not have to be erotic love. As a balancing motif, Jesus clearly loved all kinds of people and cared deeply for them, especially his mother.

It is very strange that a book which alludes to all kinds of symbolisms and codes, never mentions numerology or the Kabbalah system of symbolism. It seems as though Dan Brown has never heard of them. However, we do have one interesting instance of Hebrew cryptology which appears on page 420. The word SHESHACH which appears in Jeremiah 25:26 and 51:41 is actually an encodement for BABEL, meaning Babylon. It is done by the 'reverse alphabet' method which(15) involves taking the first 11 letters going from Aleph to Kaph and then putting the next 11 letters underneath, going from Lamedh to Tau, so that Tau comes under Aleph. Then one substitutes the letters so that SH – SH – CH comes out as B – B – L. It is called the Atbash Cipher. The false impression given here is that this discovery is a fairly modern one; but the equation between Sheshakh and Babylon has been known to Hebraists at least since 1907. So this idea is not such a stunning new discovery after all.

The importance of The Da Vinci Code for the purposes of this book is this; it is strong evidence of the fascination that symbolism and encoding has for people. Some of them become completely immersed in it to the exclusion of all else. A telling comment which contains a lot of truth comes on page 231. 'A career hazard of symbologists was a tendency to extract hidden meaning from situations that had none.' This could well apply to Rosslyn Chapel, which appears to be full of symbolism, but is it? Is it just the artistic expression of the people of that age? Like everything else in human affairs, there is the tendency to overdo it. That could well be said of our assessment of Genesis 5! It could also be said of the Da Vinci Code novel itself. To take one example, on page 342, it is alleged that the descendants of Jesus (in the literal sense) became the first kings of France. The Merovingian king Dagobert being the first one. Is this a piece of hyper-mythology? The history of the Merovingian kings is known to us now, but there is no suggestion that they were literally descended from Jesus Christ. It could, however, if taken seriously by certain elements, become a time bomb waiting to destroy the present day French constitution.

In general terms, The Da Vinci Code is a notable example of modern mythology. It is nowhere near as frightening as such things as Star Wars and Dracula. One of the strangest aspects of it is its polemic against the Roman Catholic church. Are we really supposed to believe that monks go round murdering people, or that the Vatican pays out vast sums of money to silence what it may perceive as a threat to its basic teachings? Is there such a person as bishop Aringarosa with a fanatical reactionary group that is bent on using any extreme method to silence what it sees as an attack on the 'Truth'? The reality is, as we all know, that the Roman Church has come under a lot of pressure over alleged child abuse matters, especially in Ireland. One can speculate that Dan Brown is a disaffected Roman Catholic who is trying to discredit his church. It is strange that he never mentions the Protestant and the Orthodox elements in Christendom; they would be perfectly capable of continuing their work regardless of what happens in the Vatican.

Rosslyn Chapel

The Da Vinci Code has stirred up a lot of controversy. One book which is the result of careful research and historical evaluation, is **Rosslyn and the Grail** by Oxbrow and Robertson. In it, we find a detailed account of the history of Rosslyn Chapel and Castle, which are found a few miles south of Edinburgh. It would seem that Rosslyn, or the family of the St.Clairs, had nothing to do with the Templar Knights, or the Holy Grail, but may have been connected to Freemasonry in its early stages. It may be true that King Arthur and his knights were active in that area, as they were all over the British Isles. As far as Merlin's prophecy is concerned, this is quoted in full in this book, on pages 278ff. The interesting matter for us and for Arthurology, is how Merlin, as a young boy, prognosticated that beneath a hill called Dinas Emrys in Wales, there were two dragons, one red and one white, fighting each other. In the end, the red one prevailed, and this is the one portrayed on the Welsh flag nowadays. The red one symbolises the Celts and the white one symbolises the Saxons. However, this has absolutely nothing to do with The Da Vinci Code or the Holy Grail.

The importance of Rosslyn Chapel for this book, is the rich symbolism found in the stone masonry in this church. This is a church which was expected to be much larger, possibly a cathedral, but never got beyond being a small chapel associated with the castle. However, the interior is covered with elaborate carvings, especially the apprentice pillar. All kinds of fanciful interpretations have been offered for the symbolisms in the stonework. The same can be said of many mediaeval churches and cathedrals in this country and in Western Europe. This is because that was their mentality in those times. Unfortunately we do not have the key to explaining all of these symbolisms; we can only guess at some of them. On the face of it, they have nothing to do with Dan Brown's 'pseudo-history' which has caught the imagination of so many people. A few good examples would be; the two battling dragons as described above; the green men who 'age' as one moves around the church; the angels with open books which remind us of Revelation. Richard Langdon's words are very appropriate here; there is so much scope for imaginative interpretation at Rosslyn Chapel, that one could make almost anything mean something interesting or symbolic, ideas which the original builders like the 'Apprentice' may never have thought of.

What Dan Brown did not think of was that he was not the first person to imagine that Jesus could have been married. In 1969, someone called Henry Lincoln found a book in France. It was about the Templars and the Holy Grail and also about Jesus being married and having children by Mary Magdalene. How far this tradition goes back is hard to say, but it was not Dan Brown who originally thought of it.

The net effect of The Da Vinci Code has been to publicise Rosslyn Castle. It still goes on as a worshipping community to this day, but they are inundated with visitors demanding to dig up the floors to find hidden treasures and imagine all manner of hiding places for the Holy Grail. What this indicates for the purposes of this book, is how people will take a mythical tale or a piece of symbolism and turn it into historical reality and allow it to become a mania. The tendency to literalism is found in so many aspects of life. When we tell a joke, there are some people who will take it literally. When we write a poem, there are those who will take it at face value. When we pass over a five pound note, there are those (possibly everyone!) who will take it at face value as money, and never stop to see it as a token, a symbol or a piece of pretence. It is a fact about human nature; we have to have imagination, interpretation and self-deception in order to make life have any kind of meaning.

The Lion, the Witch and the Wardrobe, by C.S.Lewis

I include a few comments about this very famous book stemming from 1950, because it seems to me to be symbolism done on a reasonable basis. It is not overdone, but it also leaves much scope for the reader's imagination to work out all kinds of possibilities. As the children step though the wardrobe they find themselves in another world, of the spirit or eternity. As they step back into this world, no time is lost; this must be an interesting insight into 'time travel' which has been discussed in chapter 20. This world of eternity is overshadowed by the permanent winter which the White Witch is imposing on them all. Anyone who opposes the White Witch is turned into a stone statue, but everyone is waiting in hope for the defeat of this evil. If we are looking for a 'world tree' this could be the forest, but more likely it is that lamppost which appears strangely at the start and at the end.

The story comes to its most symbolic with the coming of Aslan, the lion, who is the only one who can defeat the White Witch. The only way he can do it is by allowing himself to be put to death in order to save all the other people and creatures of the forest. He gives himself up to be killed on a stone platform, like an altar, but then, miraculously, he comes back to life and joins in with the apocalyptic battle which finally defeats evil. The symbolism in this is profound and is clearly alluding to the sacrifice of Christ in defeating evil. It also reminds us of how the Harry Potter sagas come to a conclusion; it is possible that J.K.Rowling took this motif and expanded it.

Eventually the four children come to occupy the four thrones in the castle, and rule wisely in a wonderful kingdom. Even Edmund, who mistakenly sided with the White Witch at one point, is redeemed and forgiven. There are so many major and minor factors in this story which are symbolic of the Christian life and the triumph of good over evil. However, the symbolism is not forced or too elaborate. Some of it may escape the reader, but then it leaves the matter open for one to meditate on and enrich one's spiritual horizons.

This is the true importance of symbolism.

Concluding thoughts on symbolism

Just as mythology is an inevitable aspect of human expression, so too is symbolism. The two elements are inextricably linked. Mythology is so often symbolic of what is going on in our deepest instincts; symbolism is often a simplified and possibly secularised version of mythology. Virtually every religion in the world has a mythology as its starting point. There are very few exceptions to this. One example would be the Baha'is, but then they have something else as a substitute, namely two elaborate Messiahs. In the same way, most religions have some kind of ritual which springs from its basic mythology. It is important not to underestimate the importance of ritual; we all have it regardless of whether we have some kind of religious practice or whether we think we are totally secularised. It is fascinating to watch a popular TV programme, Strictly Come Dancing, and realise that it is far more heavily ritualised than most church services! We can deduce from that that ritual is another important element in our instincts. It has been going on from time immemorial, ceremonies of one kind or another; still we have them chiefly connected with birth, marriage and funerals. These are the 'rites de passage' in the Christian orbit, but most religions have some kind of 'rites de passage' which is some kind of expression of how their mythologies relate to each person's stages in life. It is beyond the scope of this book to delve into details about ritual; that is an entire subject in itself. What we can say in general terms, is that rituals are almost certainly symbolic of deeply held beliefs which in turn spring from basic mythological assumptions.

I have kept alluding to symbolism when discussing the various mythologies. I have not gone into too much detail about it, because the interpretation of symbolism can be a very personal thing. The reader is left free to see all kinds of implications in the mythologies as described.

Footnotes for chapter 26

1. Crump; a writer on numerology, book now out of print.
2. The values of the Hebrew alphabet are now listed Aleph 1, Beth 2, Gimel 3, Daleth 4, He 5, Waw 6, Zayin 7, Heth 8, Teth 9, Yodh 10, Caph 20, Lamedh 30, Mem 40, Nun 50, Samekh 60, 'Ayin 70, Pe 80, Sadhe 90, Qoph 100, Resh 200, Sin 300, Taw 400.
3. Odd numbers are regarded as 'yang' which is male, and even numbers as 'yin' which is female.
4. Moses de Leon; A Spanish Jew from Leon who wrote in a strange artificial Aramaic, mostly a commentary on the books of Moses.
5. Sefirah, plural Sefiroth; the root is SPHR from which the word Sepher 'book' is derived.
6. The first letter of the Hebrew alphabet.
7. Yodh is the tenth letter of the Hebrew alphabet.
8. Chakra; a Sanskrit word meaning 'energy centre in the body', relevant to meditation and healing.
9. Tarot, a card game with three suits devised in the Middle Ages.
10. Ephesians 1:21.
11. The Ten Commandments are found in Exodus 20:1ff and also Deuteronomy 5:6ff.

12. Enoch is mentioned in Genesis 5:21.

13. Nisan, the first month in the religious calendar but the seventh in the civil calendar. Jewish months were derived from the Babylonian calendar, which they adopted in or after the Exile. We do not know much about pre-exilic Jewish months.

14. Abib; this is equivalent to Nisan.

15. The Atbash Cipher works like this;

Aleph	beth	gimel	daleth	he	waw	zayin	heth	teth	yodh	caph
Taw	sin	resh	qoph	sadheh	pe	'ayin	samekh	nun	mem	lamedh

To work the code, we substitute the letter either above or below, so Sh-sh-ch becomes b-b-l

27

Concluding thoughts on Mythology

Every year, as December approaches, we have the biggest outburst of mythology in modern times. Even Evolution has to take a back seat! It is the hysterical session known as 'Christmas'! I think we all must know that the real Christmas, 2000 years ago, was a much more modest affair, involving a baby born in a stable and visited by shepherds who would have had BO! Like all mythologies, it starts with some kind of historical or legendary anchorage and is then augmented into something fantastic. Our Christmas turns out to be expensive parties, drinking bouts, pantomimes, decorations, sprigs of holly, mistletoe, old men dressed up in red, guzzling, lavish amounts of gifts which are often a complete waste of money, and the final 'tummy ache' DEBTS which can take months to clear.

At the heart of it, however, is a major truism. We have the Christmas tree, a custom which is alleged to have come over with Prince Albert, but the symbolism in it goes much further back to ancient times. It is the world tree, which is seen in so many mythologies under different names, but the meaning of it is the same. The tree is the connection between heaven, earth and the underworld. This is something that humanity needs to know about; how the three regions of existence are connected and interact. We are of course talking figuratively here, but at one time it was taken far too literally by just about everyone. If we have just a plain tree, we feel that that is not enough. It has to be decorated, and the more elaborate and glittering it is the better. But what about the top? If we leave that bare, everyone thinks there is something missing. It needs a star, or a fairy, or Santa, or even the baby Jesus. The top of the tree has to have something special, indicative of the other world, symbolic of God.

The same is true in so many aspects of life. The top of the government has to have someone living in a lavish palace; a monarch, a president, a prime minister, a dictator or whatever. Someone has to be at the top of the pyramid. This does not mean I have to be a monarchist or a republican, but we all know that someone has to be at the top of the pyramid, as a substitute for God. The board of directors has to have a chairman. The town council has to have a mayor, or chairman. The ship has to have a captain.

In the ancient world, they were wise enough to see that just having human guidance from the top was not enough. Nowadays many countries try to ignore this, but it is being seen not to work, at least not for very long. One way round it was to have no 'king' but allow the prophets to relay God's guidance to the populace. That was the faith of Israel, and is still seen in the Mormon system, at least faintly reflected. The other way was to promote one's king to divinity; in other words, regard one's ruler as one of the gods, or possibly the chief god. To put it in picture language, the top of the tree had to have some kind of divine representation, if government or rulership were to have any stabilising or unifying influence on a country.

This, I suggest, could be the nub of mythology. It all starts with the question of who we are, what about our origins, what is life all about, what is our destiny? Our earthly and heavenly rulers are the ones who supply so many of the answers to these imponderable questions. So many of the metaphors or symbols used in mythology have some kind of relationship to life and death. Precious metals, jewels, glass, crystal, all indicate eternity. The snake is symbolic of life but paradoxically also of death. The sword or spear, especially in the hands of a heroic super-man is symbolic of justice, fair play and the righting of all wrongs. The relationship between humanity and the animal kingdom is also important. There are various versions of humanity and humans blended with animals. The question of Theodicy is almost always a substratum of the motifs in mythology. Why is there evil and unfair punishment in the world? Are there good and evil spirits that interfere with our lives? All these are interrelated and are to do with our origins and also our future. Eschatology is the mirror image of Creation.

This must raise the question of whether God is actually no more than a part of mythology. Just because almost all mythologies involve an original god of some kind, does not have to mean that God is a myth. It is like saying that the Garden of Eden is a myth, therefore the God who provided it is also a myth. This is faulty logic. The question concerning the existence of God has been discussed earlier and also in my book, The Theology of Paradox. Some of these 'proofs' go back to earliest times; others are very modern. What it shows is that people have a need to render in terms of logic what they intuitively know in the first place. For those who have had some kind of encounter with the divine, some sort of Theophanous experience, proof is irrelevant. No amount of 'disproof' will alter their conviction. God may be some kind of myth for the atheist, but then such a person may be in denial of the whole thing anyway.

It would be fair to say that many of the expressions about God in the Bible are mythological. Phrases like 'the Lord of Hosts' which means 'armies' do not have to be taken literally. It does not mean that God is a Field Marshal like Montgomery or Rommel. It is metaphoric, and symbolic of God's power to defend his people. It does not mean that God is a myth.

Then there is the issue of angels and devils. Many people assume that this is an element of mythology. But is it? We have the testimony of Swedenborg that such entities do exist in the next world. For those who have had this kind of encounter, there is no discussion. Such things as angels and Satan appear in the Bible; why do we need to doubt it? Why can we not give credit to Bernardette Soubiroux and many others who have had a vision of the Virgin Mary? What about Linda Martel who made remarks about seeing Jesus and Mary? That does not mean we have to live in fear and trembling over demons who might drag us off to hell; that is where the augmentation comes in. This is what happened in the Middle Ages, as we see in the stained glass window in Fairford Church. We can take Swedenborg's advice and turn towards God with love in our hearts, and stop worrying about evil.

Mythology in relation to History

We have seen that with so many mythologies from different parts of the world, that there is usually some kind of anchorage in historical realities. The best example is the 'folk recollection' of the World Flood, a disaster which is mentioned directly or indirectly in so many parts of the world, and is now being taken seriously as a genuine disaster in remote prehistory. From this we see all kinds of mythological permutations, the best known of which is Noah's Flood. It is interesting how this motif matches up with the current scientific view of 'disaster theories' in which all but a remnant of life survived to begin all over again. This anchorage in historical realities is not always 'history'; it can also be some kind of discovery. A good example of this would be Darwin's discovery with regard to pigeons and other creatures that can be cultured. From this comes an entire theory of evolution, a grandiose augmentation and gratuitous generalisation, and a dogmatism that has come to dominate virtually every aspect of life through the 20th century.

Somewhere there is a fine line to be drawn between myth and historical reality. That line can be very indistinct and indefinite. A case in point comes in the early chapters of Genesis, where the mythology of Creation and the Garden of Eden gradually merge into historical realities, so that by chapter 14 we find Abraham being involved with battles between various kings of Mesopotamia and the Jordan Valley. There is no reason to doubt the historicity of these recorded events, even if there is no corroboration from archaeology. By this stage in Genesis we are firmly into the history of the Hebrew people. That does not mean that mythological elements no longer appear; we have the incident of Jacob's Ladder, a Theophanous encounter with important mythological features. But that does not prevent it from being a real encounter with the divine.

So often we see the same pattern in world mythologies, where we start with the awareness of the gods or the world of the spirit, or the mystery of Creation, and then it gently slides into worldly realities. The Japanese pattern, which I have reviewed in The Theology of Truth, follows the same motif, as it comes down to the identity of the Mikado and of other lesser rulers in that Empire.

That fine line, which we think we can draw nowadays, probably never existed for the ancients. History and mythology were almost certainly coterminous for them. It is only our so-called logical climate of today, parented by scientific investigation, that has produced this fussy approach to information from the past. It is Star Trek, chiefly, that in effect warns us of the dangers of trying to be absolutely logical. Mr. Spock and Mr.Data even more so, present us with two beings which are capable of considering any problem purely from the point of view of logic. Heaven help us if we slide into a world like that: but it is happening. Even Mr. Spock could not avoid a tinge of emotion, and Mr. Data, the robot-machine had an inkling of emotion, even if he could switch it off. The programme is clearly telling us that to be genuinely human, we need to have emotions. Falling in love is just one aspect of it. Instincts and intuitions must also be allowed to play their part in life. This is where the importance of mythology in relation to modern life must be admitted. Essentially, our awareness of the wonders of Creation and the loving, guiding hand of God, are a product of our emotions. This is a natural feeling in any normal person who asks himself what the world is all about. It is one thing to talk about 'proofs for the existence of God', but these are basically circular arguments. The real proof, if that is the right word, is in our instincts, what Freud would call our **id.** We have seen in our own times, what appears to be an upsurge in atheism, and this is understood by many to be a result of Darwin's theory, Evolution. But this is a classic example of a major illogicality in 20th century thinking. Darwin never intended to destroy anyone's religious faith, and there is no reason for Evolution, if it happens to be true, to be seen as a motive for Atheism. On the contrary, Evolution, whichever version of it one regards as convincing, can be seen as an amazing pattern of life in the making, every bit as mysterious and wonderful as any other mythology.

I call Evolution a 'mythology', not because I want anyone to feel that it is untrue; mind you, it may yet turn out to be largely wrong, but never mind. It is a 'mythology' in the sense that it has become the prevailing world view in modern times. Just as the ancients believed there was an ocean up there in the sky and the world consisted of three shelves, with God up on top, a view which has had to be modified since our recent space explorations, so now we picture Creation as evolutionary. It is really quite fascinating and amusing to see how the astro-physicists are busily engaged in engendering new mythological ideas, which are even more fanciful than ever. There is the mania for inventing colonies of living creatures analogous to the human race on faraway planets. For an example of how ridiculous this can become, see my chapter on Von Daniken and the UFO's mania.

I conclude from this that there has to be emotion, along with rationality in human life, also conscience. Mythology, in whatever form it takes, has to be an important element in our make-up. Trying to pretend that it is nonsense, only engenders more mythology, much of which has an eschatological colouring.

Eschatology

It is not just my own idea that eschatology is the mirror image, or counterpart of mythology, but I realise that this claim may seem rather new for many people. We have just lived through a period in Christian history in which eschatology has been down played or understated. It was a product of the liberalistic mentality stemming from the Age of (so-called) Enlightenment. However, it was a gift for splinter group churches with a doomsday mentality. The Jehovah's Witnesses are a case in point, but there are any amount of others. In more recent times, the mainstream churches have begun to take eschatology rather more seriously. No longer do we downplay the apocalyptic passages in the teachings of Jesus; even so, many Christians find Revelation difficult to take on board. Before devaluing Revelation, I would suggest that one should read my treatment of it in The Theology of Truth.

We have noticed that eschatology employs most, if not all, of the motifs, metaphors and imagery of mythology. This is being done deliberately; it serves to show that the beginning is glorious and God-given, and so too is the End. The whole of human history is framed with the glory of God's inventive genius. It is like an elaborate picture frame which serves to enhance the contents of the picture itself. Obviously, some pictures are given an inappropriate frame, and we all know that that simply detracts from the impression intended by the picture. But the picture of human history, with all its failures and stupidities, is framed by something glorious, which serves to correct and justify us all. It is like the situation over Judas Iscariot. He embarked on a venture that he almost certainly thought was very clever, to force a confrontation between the authorities and Jesus, but in fact it all turned sour and resulted in Jesus being condemned to death. But in the wisdom of God, this betrayal became the starting point for the salvation of the world; if Jesus had not died, there would have been no Resurrection. This means that God used the failure of mankind to bring about the triumph of divine love. The same thing happens to us all when we think we are doing something so marvellous and it all goes wrong; how often does that happen? But God is able to justify our actions and bring out of them a greater good. The interplay between divine wisdom and human logic is a subtle and convoluted thing. Now we see the importance of mythology and eschatology; God is in effect showing us that all our deeds, good, bad or indifferent, can be turned into something glorious and fulfilling. The course of human history is seen to make sense, even if it is punctuated by human follies.

We have noticed that it is not just the religious community that thinks in terms of eschatology nowadays. We see that Lovelock and Colbert have their own versions of eschatology. There is the awareness of another 'extinction' which may be due any time. There are also those who confidently predict that the sun will turn into a Red Giant and engulf us all, thus bringing the end of the world. We notice the evolutionary assumption in this; that since other stars appear to go through the process of red giantism, so will ours. How do they know that every star, including ours, will go this way? There are others, of a doomsday mentality, who expect that we shall blow ourselves to smithereens with all those atomic weapons that are stored away, waiting for some lunatic to unleash them. And of course, the climate change fanatics are full of warnings about how this world could turn out to be like Venus with some kind of 'greenhouse' effect. It would seem that we have to have a panic mode coming from somewhere. At the moment it is not coming from the churches; it is coming from the scientists! What a paradox!

The shape of modern mythology

We began by looking at the three major mythological influences on modern life in the Western world; the Greek, the Norse and the Welsh. They are deeply rooted in our minds, as deeply rooted as Santa Claus and King Arthur. The focus of this is mainly Britain today, but by extension, the English speaking peoples all over the world have the same mindset. Some elements of these are so deeply ensconced in people's minds and command such a fascination that much time and money is being spent on research which is intended to substantiate these ancient traditions. It may never be possible to come to a firm conclusion on such matters as the Atlantis myth or King Arthur's empire. However, it is interesting to say that so many myths seem to have some kind of historical or factual starting point in the remote past. Also, the important aspect of it is the way the myths are used as the justification for some kind of political regime or religious settlement. It would seem that a 'new' idea is not enough in itself to carry conviction for the public; there has to be some kind of historical sanctification for it.

Once we come to recognise the modern myths for what they are, it is easy to see how they borrow ideas, metaphors and motifs. Although they are varied, there is a sense in which they all follow the same patterns of thought. We can see the contrast between material such as Star Trek and Freemasonry; the Economics of money and Dracula; Harry Potter and Evolution. It is true that modern mythology is exceedingly varied and in some cases just as fantastic as the ancient material. But the modern world has introduced, sadly, a banal element which all but disguises its distinctive mythology. How many people would have guessed that Evolution, Psychology, and Economics are essentially mythical? But they are and there is one more that has not been discussed so far.

Just as it is highly likely that the ancient myths were circulated like some kind of soap opera in ancient communities, so nowadays we have any number of soap operas on the media. What are the values that they assume? One important value is the tension between the 'goodies' and the 'baddies' and that in the end the good will prevail and bad will be unmasked and abashed. It would be so pleasing if life were as simple as that! Unfortunately, in real life, the 'baddies' do prevail. It is the same with all those 'who-dunnit' detective tales, starting with Sherlock Holmes and on through Agatha Christie and on into Dixon of Dock Green and the plethora of detection brain-teasers on the television nowadays. How wonderful that the villains are always caught! The reality is that sometimes criminals succeed in evading justice, at least, in this world. Here is mythology at its most banal and 'kitchen-sink-worthy'. But the assumption of everlasting justice is still the substratum of it all. It was seen with all those cowboy western films we used to see; now they are politically incorrect, because the 'injuns' must not be regarded as the villains.

That brings us to another element in modern mythology, that of equality and fair play. In these times of supposed democracy, we all feel the need to have equality of opportunity and fair play in all areas of life. This is one of the offspins of the Reformation, that we are all equal in the sight of God. Two violent revolutions, one in France and one in Russia have brought it home to us the importance of social and legal equality. But have we really achieved that? In our own country we have very largely achieved that, but only because we have swept the problem under the carpet by removing the poverty problem out of sight into the so-called third world. Equality and fair play remain some kind of wishful thinking in most people's minds, but this is no different from how people thought in the days of ancient myth. How often do we see in the ancient myths that if some kind of wrong or unfairness is perpetrated, it is rectified by some sort of poetic justice? It is the same need in human nature; the difference in the way it is expressed now is almost always horribly banal.

Symptomatic of this banality is the tendency to leave God out of the picture, or at least, the world of spirits or the divine element. It used to be the gods having an altercation in the skies; now it is human experts and sometimes scientists having a wrangle. In many ways the scientists have managed to fill the space left by God being omitted from the picture, or at least, this was the case going back half a century. Today, people have become far more critical and wary of scientific dogmatisms; sometimes they turn out to be complete nonsense or some kind of illusion. Even then, God just occasionally manages to infiltrate the myth! What about Von Daniken, who thinks 'gods' arrived in chariots to inform the cavemen of all kinds of wonderful ideas? What about that episode in Star Trek, in which they nearly found themselves confronted by God!! As for Harry Potter, the configuration of loving, protecting Father (Dumbledore) and innocent, vulnerable Son (Harry) is clearly there, even if the Almighty and Jesus Christ are not actually mentioned in so many words. Something similar can be said of E.T. who is dubbed as a god of some kind. The implication in this is that any kind of myth in some way or other reverts to an understanding of the divine and by contrast, human nature; it is inescapable.

Literary techniques used in mythology and eschatology

It has to be admitted that exaggeration, or hyperbole, is the most prominent of literary techniques used in mythology. Many will find this difficult to accept today, in a world where we deal in exactitudes and precision, and imagine that this is very clever. But exaggeration is not confined to mythology by any means. We only need to consider the teachings of Jesus to see that he is a master of exaggeration. If we try to take Jesus completely literally, as some have done, it can become very difficult. This was not purely and simply his own idea. Many of the prophets indulged in exaggeration, especially Ezekiel. The Psalms are full of them. Some of the passages that are clearly intended to be historical use the technique of exaggeration. This could certainly apply to the account of the Exodus, just as an example.

Why is exaggeration used so freely without feeling that it is untruthful? We have to remember that written material in those days did not have the facility of upper and lower case letters. The New Testament was originally all in uncials (Greek capital letters) with no spacing in between words. Hebrew still is presented like this, all in letters of one height. There was no idea of underlining. (Queen Victoria would have been somewhat stuck!) The only exception to this was the cartouche idea seen in the Egyptian royal tombs. That was a method for 'underlining' that important name of the Pharaoh. Hebrew and Greek never indulged in that kind of technique. So how were they to emphasise matters that to them seemed of great importance? The answer is that they went in for exaggeration (and also repetition). If one were to think that the opposite was never to be seen, one would be wrong, because understatement, or litotes, is also found in the Hebrew and Greek material, but nowhere near as extensively.

One can only see it as appropriate that the ministry of Jesus Christ, which was so significant for the whole of the world and the destiny of humanity, should be portrayed in such magnificent terms in the book of Revelation. The work of the humble carpenter from Nazareth is portrayed against a massive cosmic background. How could the Bible come to a conclusion with something banal or understated? The same is true for the beginning as well as the end. Creation is portrayed in glorious terms; how could it be expressed otherwise? Is a banal piece of scientific guesswork enough to understand the wonders of the physical world? The beginning and the end are expressed in massive expression of exaggeration and beauty, and they frame the tortuous course of human history. The same is true for the tension between life and death and also the state of being 'undead'. This explains why such mythical material as Dracula and Harry Potter are portrayed in such massive terms, using so many mythological motifs and metaphors.

Another important literary technique used in mythology is that of paradox. This element has been discussed in my first book, The Theology of Paradox. How can we understand the great and mind-teasing matters of the divine in relation to humanity, unless we see it as a massive paradox? The same is true of the Incarnation of Jesus; this paradox comes only second to the first overwhelming paradox of Creation out of nothing. If these matters are discussed in terms of mythological metaphors, then the paradoxical side of it is hardly noticeable. But we have seen that attempts at demythologising, for instance with the Gnostics, the Taoists, and the Buddhists, have resulted in the element of paradox coming to the fore. We can see this as some kind of substitute for myth, but it still does not explain away those deep matters of life; the divine, humanity, theodicy and the next world. We have to face the fact that essentially, life and death are a mystery, and that any religion worth having, will not attempt to bypass this problem, but will embrace it and allow the mystery to enrich our lives and hopes for the future.

Another important literary technique used in the scriptures is that of parable or allegory. Jesus is a master of parabolic expression, and many of his parables include paradoxical elements. Why does he do this? It is because it is not possible to see God face to face, or describe him or deal with him in literal terms. It always has to be done in parabolic terms. With Jesus, he is talking about God's intervention in this world, and one of the essential paradoxes in this is a main theme in his parables. The master, or king sets the men to work, leaves them to toil away and then suddenly returns in the hopes of finding some worthwhile results. But he is often (though not always) disappointed. This was primarily aimed at the people of God in those days, but there is the futuristic aspect to this motif. It may be that God has gone quiet in these days, with so much disbelief and cynicism about religion. But is this his way of leaving us to get on with things and then suddenly reappear to find out who has been faithful and who has not? The essential message of so many of the parables is that we should always be ready, alert and aware of his coming.

The use of parables is not confined to Jesus and the New Testament. There are some good examples in the Old Testament and the Apocrypha. Jesus simply augments the method.

This brings us to another literary technique which is not normally described by experts in literature. Augmentation is, however, a common feature in musical composition. It often comes at the end of a piece of music and is characterised partly by exaggeration, but also, slowing up, increase in volume, decoration of the basic theme and brings us to the final two chords which are normally a perfect cadence. Augmentation in mythological expression works slightly differently, but has a similar effect. The best example is from the Bible, where we start with evil symbolised by a snake and at the end, the snake becomes a dragon, again symbolising evil, but much more aggressive and less subtle. The whole motif becomes much more dramatised and tensed.

A similar process can be seen with Harry Potter. Many of the normal motifs and metaphors belonging to mythology are worked into the stories, but as the books progress, there is augmentation which racks up the drama. This all culminates in the final battle between Harry and Voldemort. We are faced with the anticlimax of Harry having to die, but the climax is resumed as he comes back to life and Voldemort is defeated. We can see the same process in the Dracula novels. The original one uses the normal mythological modes of expression and is not overdone. In the second novel, Dracula the Un-dead, the violence, the bloodshed and the cruelty build up almost to the level of self-cancellation. By the time we see the film, in which Dracula is combined with Frankenstein, the augmentation reaches the level of the ridiculous and laughable; in other words, it is overdone and becomes senseless. In other words, it is just one long exhibition of the traditional 'shoot-out' with very little subtlety to relieve it.

In a strange way, the myth of Evolution exhibits the same tendency. As a scientific theory which still falls short of certainty or proof, it becomes the prevailing mindset of the twentieth century. Going on from that it stimulates Sci-fi speculatory material like Jurassic Park and King Kong. This is sent in a slightly different direction by material like Star Trek and Star Wars which makes all kinds of assumptions about Evolution progressing in other worlds. The whole motif has gone right out of control and simply confuses people about the true state of matters in relation to Evolution. One might be tempted like Bultmann, to say that these matters ought to be demythologised, but that is not being realistic.

The use and abuse of myth

Like every other feature in this world, myth can be used for positive and helpful purposes, but also abused. It is like a hammer; it can be used to drive in nails and pull them out, but it can also be used to injure or kill people. With regard to religion, myth can be a very positive factor in coming to understand any given religion. There are not many religions that are not based on some kind of myth. Most religions begin on some kind of non-rational basis which taps into the mystery of faith. This applies regardless of whether one's religion is based on Western thinking with its historical anchorage or based on Eastern thinking which is largely (but not entirely) based on subjective ideas. We have seen how a legend, with almost certainly an element of historical truth, can be built up into a complete mythology, and then be used to substantiate a religious or political settlement. King Arthur is a case in point, but not the only one. That is the positive and worthwhile use of myth.

However, the most important and the classic case of myth in relation to a religious faith comes with the Biblical pattern. We start with the early chapters of Genesis which are largely though not entirely mythical.

(Those who wish to take it completely literally can do so, if they wish). These chapters form the basis for the Israelite people and then on to the coming of the Messiah. In this way, the ministry of Jesus is given meaning, explanation and relevance. Jesus comes in to complete not just the Law and the Prophets, but also those important myths which foreshadow his coming. In this way the Christian religion is given a firm basis, justification and explanation. One element in that is how the First Adam is brought to completion in the Second Adam, but there are other elements in it too. This is the positive and constructive use of myth, and long may it persist.

On the other hand, myth can be used to cause a lot of harm, misinformation and violence. The classic case of this is how the Atlantis myth, which may have a certain degree of legendary grounding has been augmented and elaborated into the Nazi mythical material which turns into a nasty racist policy. Something similar can be said about the application of myth in Japan, which entailed the Mikado and various local rulers seeing themselves as descended from the gods, and the Japanese people as a whole regarding themselves as the epitome of humanity. This allowed them to justify their behaviour in the Pacific War. Other examples could be found.

We can conclude therefore that mythology, like religion, is only as good or bad as the people who concoct it and apply it. Whichever way it goes, it is usually the root cause of one mania or another. Some manias are good; others are bad.

Myth as inevitable

With all its faults, inconsistencies and silliness, we have to admit that myth will not go away. Clearly, it is rooted in the instinct of mankind, what Freud and Jung would call the **id.** It is only natural to ponder the beginning and the end, and that inevitably draws in some attempt at understanding the world of the spirit and deity. Life has to have some kind of meaning or interpretation or purpose; trying to do without that renders us down to a very banal level. The problem arises when that idea of what life is all about becomes a complete mania.

What are the manias of the modern world? The pursuit of money is one of them. Not that this is anything new, but because we have all kinds of substitutes for real money (ie. lumps of gold), it is all the easier to allow bigger and bigger sums to become a self-augmenting obsession. One could make a list of modern manias. One that comes to mind is the mentality of fame. Again this is nothing new, but has been augmented by the antics of Hollywood and other media sources. People find it a fascination to try to achieve fame in one shape or another. What they fail to realise is the pressure and lack of privacy that fame imposes on those trapped in it. Another mania is the allure of perfect sex. It is easily forgotten that many people find it difficult; others are impotent or incapable of deriving any enjoyment out of it. But the film-makers love to foist the great romance on us as something fantastic and ideal for everyone. That is very hard on those who cannot attain to such wonderful flights of self-delusion.

We can conclude with one mania which dominates modern life, namely the motor car. Again, this is nothing completely new. There used to be chariot racing, and tournaments on chargers. However, since someone invented the internal combustion engine, this has meant that many more people are able to take to the roads and indulge in that feeling of power as one accelerates down a motorway. In a way, this mania, perhaps more than the others, brings us back to mythology. We all become little gods as we power along, the fancier and more expensive the car, the better. That is, if one is foolish enough to allow this instinct to take over!

In a way, this brings us back to our first image in chapter one, The Wind in the Willows. Here we have a character who is typical of so much in human nature. Mr. Toad is the one who goes in for one mania after another. Conceit and self-importance are the substratum of it. It is a lesson to us all to keep our manias, our self-delusions, our wishful thinking firmly under control. As the story comes to its conclusion, Toad in spite of all the lessons he has had to learn the hard way, is still making funny noises under his breath; 'tick-tick-tick' and 'Poop-poop! Poop-poop!' His friends give him a serious talking-to on the subject of motor cars, and we see him in appearance taking the matter to heart. No longer will he drive like a lunatic, smashing up expensive cars, never again will he pinch someone else's car, the thought of honking at people to clear a way for himself will not return. He will be a serious, sober, responsible Toad! Or so it would seem.

However, what about a bit of augmentation to conclude the saga? Can we imagine him in his Hall, arranging the chairs into the shape of a car, making 'brem-brem' noises and under his breath intoning, 'Poop-poop! Poop-poop!' To which I say, human nature may change a little, but not completely!!

Index

Bibliography

Behe, M. Science and Evidence for Design in the Universe (Ignatius).

Belcher, S. African Myths of Origin.

Bernstein, S. The Power of Gold.

Bertholet, A. King Arthur.

Brown, D. The Da Vinci Code.

Buchanan, M. The Numerology Guidebook (2013).

Bultmann, R. Kerygma and Myth.

Christie, A. Numerology (2005) also Simply Numerology.

Coates, A. Numerology. (1974).

Colbert, E. The Sixth Extinction.

Coogan, M. Ancient Near Eastern Texts.

Daniken, E. Von. The Chariots of the Gods.

Darwin, C. The Origin of Species.

Dougherty, M. Norse Myths.

Ducie, S. What is Numerology? (2016).

Eldridge, N. Evolution and Extinction.

Erasthenes and Hyginus, Constellation Myths.

Fitzgerald, M. Hitler's Occult War.

Fleming, I. Goldfinger.

Ganeri, A. Chinese Myths and Legends.

Garner, A. The Weirdstone of Brisingamen.

Grahame, K. Wind in the Willows.

Graves, C. The Legend of Linda Martel.

Hall, C. A Primer of Freudian Psychology.

Jacobs, A. The Gnostic Gospels.

Jung, C. Jungian Psychology made easy.

Kingsley, C. The Water Babies.

Kotzwinkle, E.T.

Lao Tzu, Tao Teh Ching, Hua Hu Ching.

Lewis, C.S. The Dawn Treader. Also, The Lion, the Witch and the Wardrobe.

Lovelock, J, The Revenge of Gaia.

The Mabinogion.

Matyszak, P. The Greek and Roman Myths.

Miller, A. The Crucible.

Milton, J. Paradise Lost.

Molnar, The Star of Bethlehem.

Mooney, T. Understand Chinese Mythology. Also, The Numerology Bible.

Morgan, G. The Holy Grail.

Plato, Timaeus and Critias; Selected Myths.

Pritchard, D. Play and win Mah-Jong.

Rowling, J.K. Harry Potter series.

Shelley, M. Frankenstein (1818).

Spenser, E. The Fairie Queen (Douglas Brooks-Davies).

Stoker, B. Dracula (1897).

Stoker, D. and Holt, I. Dracula The Un-Dead.

Swedenborg, E. Heaven and Hell.

Templeton, R. Numerology.

Tolkien, J.R.R. The Hobbit.

Tomas, A. The Atlantis Legend.

Wagner, R. Siegfried, Tristan und Isolde, Parsifal.

Worsley, P. The Trumpet shall sound.

Zingg, R.M. Huichol mythology.